GOD MOCKS

God Mocks

A History of
RELIGIOUS SATIRE
from the
HEBREW PROPHETS
to
STEPHEN COLBERT

Terry Lindvall

NEW YORK UNIVERSITY PRESS
New York and London

NEW YORK UNIVERSITY PRESS
New York and London
www.nyupress.org

References to Internet websites (URLs) were accurate at the time of writing. Neither the author nor New York University Press is responsible for URLs that may have expired or changed since the manuscript was prepared.

Library of Congress Cataloging-in-Publication Data
Lindvall, Terry.
God mocks : a history of religious satire from the Hebrew Prophets to Stephen Colbert / Terry Lindvall.
pages cm Includes bibliographical references and index.
ISBN 978-1-4798-8673-9 (cl : alk. paper)
1. Satire—History and criticism. 2. Religious satire—History and criticism. 3. Arts and religion. I. Title.
PN6149.S2L54 2015
809.7'9382—dc23 2015019581

New York University Press books are printed on acid-free paper, and their binding materials are chosen for strength and durability. We strive to use environmentally responsible suppliers and materials to the greatest extent possible in publishing our books.

Manufactured in the United States of America

10 9 8 7 6 5 4 3 2 1

Also available as an ebook

To my blessed wife,

Karen,

who holds up

the mirror of folly

for me

Mock on, mock on, Voltaire, Rousseau:
Mock on, mock on: 'tis all in vain!
You throw the sand against the wind,
And the wind blows it back again.
—William Blake

CONTENTS

ACKNOWLEDGMENTS

If a good editor functions as a satirist, cutting and slicing an author's vain words, then Jennifer Hammer reigns as the best artist this work could know. Whatever is clear or compelling in this book is due to her incisive skills. I thank Constance Grady as well for keeping me on target, or at least shooting toward the target, for Dorothea Stillman Halliday for managing such an unruly imp, and for the anonymous "tmh" for turning confusion into coherence. My deepest debt of gratitude goes to Gabrielle Linnell, essentially my coauthor, whose research and editing enhanced everything good in this work. Special thanks must be extended to fellow fools, to those mocking men with whom I meet every week amidst laughter and some wisdom, and to laughing critics Cary Sawyer, Ben Fraser, John Morreall, Craig Wansink, John Lawing, Gil Elvgren, Andrew Quicke, Bill Brown, Dennis Bounds, Robert Darden, Fred Weiss, Ben Haller, Steven Emmanuel, Russ Spittler, James Edwards, Kellie Holzer, Josh Weinstein, Joyce Howell, Jeffrey Timmons, Adam Tobey, Gaby Alexander, the Stroyeck sisters (Morgan and Lauren), Patty Clark, Ariane Avery, Kelly Jackson, Jenny Erdmann, Matt Hatcher, Joe Martin, and Joe and Kathy Merlock-Jackson. To graphic artist Sharon Swift, some squiggly gratitude. Jolly thanks to Jim and Joy Bolander for spurring me on with wine on the dock and to Father Andy Buchanan for sermons that sparked confessions and imagination. To my favorite ladies of Connecticut, Barbara, Babsy, and Dolly, I smile like the Cheshire cat. And to my family who makes me laugh loudly, Karen, Chris, and Caroline, I owe deep and abiding love and joyous thanksgiving. Gratitude finally goes to Virginia Wesleyan College, a place that gave me sanctuary, and its gracious former president Billy (and Fann) Greer, and its academic dean Tim O'Rourke, and to Frank and Aimee Batten Jr. who made my laughing place possible. *Soli Deo gloria.*

Introduction

In 1494, just before the onslaught of the Reformation, Sebastian Brandt, a conservative Roman Catholic scholar living in Basel, looked at the reeking vice and folly of the church of his day and wrote *Das Narrenschiff*, a *Ship of Fools*. As the prologue tells us, "One vessel would be far too small / To carry all the fools I know."[1] Brandt's veritable floating tub of dolts and sinners heads for an unknown destination, a land of Fools, and functions as a harbinger of an imminent schism. Eulogized as *divina satira*, divine satire, *Ship of Fools* catapulted Brandt into the ranks of Dante, at least among the Germans.

While not particularly original, Brandt shrewdly painted a hundred vices of his contemporaries in a sparkling mosaic, sketching bad parents, misers, gluttons, ostentatious church-goers, and even those who are noisy in church. In an English prologue, readers are warned that when one ignores the Bybyll (Bible), then "Banysshed is doctryne, we wander in derknes Throughe all the worlde: our selfe we wyll not knowe." We know not God, nor virtue, nor even ourselves. A faithful Roman Catholic, Brandt skewered those causing the decay of his beloved church, but he did it with humility, knowing himself to be a shipmate.

Brandt's floating community of fools personifies the compelling place of laughter and satire in religious life. If satire is to be defined as the ridiculing of human vanity, folly, and hypocrisy, one finds no better metaphor than a boatload of stupid people obliviously drifting toward the edge of the world. To recognize the church as a similar tub of rogues and village idiots is to recognize a fundamental truth about human nature, within or without the Christian community—namely, that none are righteous or wise, but all have fallen into the folly of sin.

Brandt dipped into the prophetic Hebrew tradition of religious satire to showcase the discrepancies between what God's people were supposed to be and how they actually acted. Using a free and easy style, he translated folly into the vernacular. Brandt published the first "printed book that treated of contemporaneous events and living persons, instead of old German battles and friend knights."[2] It is a product of his own era, even as he lashed out at his own religious tradition, striking at the "dreaded Hydra of popery and monasticism." His religious satire appealed to people who wanted to read "the history of their own times."[3]

This book chronicles the evolution of religious satirical discourse from the biblical satire of the Hebrew prophets through the mediated entertainments of modern wits such as Stephen Colbert. It traces the place of such sharp comic discourse in the checkered history of the Christian church, where laughter resides both in the pulpit and in the pews. Mapping the historical cockeyed caravan of eccentric characters and their mocking performances is to find an overarching pattern to the calling of sacred satirist. There are methods to the madness of mockers whose motley garb is often clerical vestments. One finds wild comedy in the carnival festivals of sinners and in the fellowship of saints.

Yet in outlining satiric laughter through history, one also finds remarkable differences. Each age presents its own corruptions, and each age summons forth particular gifts from its religious satirists. The earthy coarse language of Martin Luther and Sir Thomas More during the freewheeling spirit of the Reformation period contrasts with the enlightened wit of the diminutive Augustan poet Alexander Pope. The religious satirist does not need to be part of the community of faith, as Voltaire and Ambrose Bierce can attest. All they need is an eye and ear for the folly of religious poseurs.

The satirist is a slippery creature. He (usually a he) plays the role of trickster, but with a purpose. When the Apostle Paul listed various gifts of the Spirit to the church at Ephesus, this particular vocation was seemingly absent among the teachers, apostles, evangelists, and even administrators ordained by God for the building up of the church. One category in Paul's list of gifts and offices did admit the satirist, however, in the figure of the prophet. The prophet's is an office that tears down in order to build up. Hebrew prophets once assumed the mantle of holy mocking to uproot the brambles in God's vineyard so that grapes might grow. Within the religious world, the satirist as prophet tries to assume a place among those with more decorous callings. The prophet/satirist points to the second psalm, where the poet notes that "God mocks."

The Hebrew prophets comprise one root of satire within the Christian community. French sociologist Jacques Ellul wrote that humor was a peculiar way in which ancient Israel adjusted to life in foreign cultures. They "take a word and change a letter to give it a totally new sense. They play on words in such a manner as to ridicule the text or person or to achieve a very different effect."[4] They subverted their own culture, turning the world upside down and finding comedy on the bottom. The playful juxtaposition of words opened up oft-inelegant humor: the prophet Amos compared the elite sophisticated women of the Northern Kingdom of Israel to the "cows of Bashan," that, no matter how sleek and well-fed, were about to be slaughtered (Amos 4:1). His wit exposed the limits of their complacency.[5]

The reputation of Jewish humorists was so renowned that the *Qur'an* even denounced them for their puns (or words of ambiguous import)—for "twisting their tongues" and thereby mocking their religion (Surah 2:104, 4:46).[6] Jewish suffering gave birth to such wry Yiddish proverbs as "If the rich could hire other people to die for them, the poor could make a wonderful living." Job would be their poster boy. But their prophets would polish their arts so that their humor pierced like an arrow or stung like a bee.

The prophet does not predict events as much as he speaks forth the judgments of God. He attacks idolatry and adultery with mockery, even with rhetorical raillery, called *diasyrmic* in Latin, which means tearing or cutting a man apart. As if to remove a social cancer, satire must cut to heal. At times, sarcastic railing may delight only in the brutal sport of slicing and dicing one's target.[7] Hebrew prophets, however, attacked their targets with this incisive wit *and* an overpowering sense of spiritual vocation. Literary critic Northrop Frye argued in his *Anatomy of Criticism* that the one essential element of satire is an attack on an object of criticism.[8] And prophets practiced this razor-sharp chastisement.

However, the biblical satirist shares in the blame and shame of his defendants. He may be God's prosecutor, but he is also entwined with the people he ridicules. A true satirist sits in the dock with those who are guilty and identifies as an integral member of the satirized community. The identification of satirist and his target occurs in the trope of a mirror. The mirror offers a comic frame in which to look at and to look through the heart; the satirist finds that none are righteous, including himself. But he also knows that he is witty, and he takes Shakespeare's words from *King Lear* that "jesters do often prove prophets" and turns them into a mental palindrome, that prophets do often become jesters.

In his classic study of *Rabelais and His World*, Mikhail Bakhtin begins with a call for a history of laughter.[9] The mysteries of laughter hold deep philosophical meaning for existence, pose challenges to the question of power and being, and offer clues to universal issues of what it means to be human. The sixteenth-century court poet Pierre de Ronsard affirmed that

> God who subjected the world to man,
> To man alone permitted laughter
> To be merry, not to the beast
> Who has neither reason nor spirit.[10]

When this divinely bestowed gift of human laughter is connected to religion, it opens up new and risky realms for investigation.

The Hebrew psalter stands as the gateway for the religious satirist—first as a warning, then as a model. How blessed is the man, wrote the poet, who does not walk in the way of the wicked, stand in the path of sinners, or *sit in the seat of scoffers*?[11] In a nomadic society, to settle into evil and set up one's tent among mockers is the final stage of a reprobate pilgrimage. To have only the laughter of cynicism is to pull up one's chair, sit with the unblessed men (and women), and settle into sarcasm. Against this downward tendency of satire—creating jaded hearts and crooked eyes—there is another seat, that grand and easy chair of Rabelais, where one can sit down with friends and laugh in the good presence of God.[12] One can laugh at oneself.[13]

The scriptures declare that God disciplines those whom he loves. The question arises as to what might be the means and modes of that discipline. The verbal counterpart to sackcloth, ashes, and a hair shirt might appear in the rhetorical art of satire. The satiric word can lash as brutally as a cat-o'-nine-tails. We find a catalogue of incisive metaphors used in describing satire as a weapon, from lances, thorns, axes, knives, darts, rods, hammers, razors, quills, fangs, venom, and poison, to ordinary stings and slashes. For Protestant reformers, satires were sacred weapons, militantly seen as "scrap metal that the printing press, like a cannon, spews forth."[14] Scholars Edward and Lillian Bloom put forth another pungent image of satire as a punitive deterrent, describing "a sea gull impaled upon a pier to warn off the other gulls."[15] The warning of satire should awaken a sense of danger.[16] It should whip one into shape. The satiric weapon of the Spirit as a two-edged sword pierces the human heart. In afflicting the sinner, satire works as a scourge of God, purifying the soul through a kind of comic mortification.

While the first psalm warns against those who cynically jest, the second psalm sets up the example of God as a satirist, who mocks from heaven. He not only scoffs at the fools that are his creations, but he provides a model for the satirist. Many satirists write out of a sense of moral calling, a vocation to correct what is ill and foolish in their worlds. A biblical satirist like Isaiah uses the same tropes, tools, and tactics to attack his target as the secular social satirist, such as the acidic Roman satirist Juvenal. What differs between them is the object of their wit. Secular satirists take on the corrupt state and the mores of the people. Religious satirists focus upon the people of God, their own community of faith, and its hypocritical leaders. Such satirists have existed since the Hebrew prophets and have evolved throughout history, altering their strategies and emphases as the times have changed themselves. But their message remains the same: my fellow people of God, get right or be obliterated.

Laughter, as sociologist Peter Berger unveils it, is a comic dimension of human experience. But operating in the immoral world of a fallen human nature, satiric laughter dwells on that reality, and secondarily on the hope of redemption. In *Rumor of Angels*, Berger even marks laughter as a sign of transcendence. Yet, as numerous scholars from Berger to Frye have observed, the origins of satiric laughter is militant, aggressive, and a weapon of attack.[17] Laughter must purge before it can redeem.

A study of comic satire necessitates recognition of its heterogeneous evolution; as a multifaceted form, it oscillates or mutates throughout various historical eras. However, the umbrella definition of satire employed in this book distills two recurring characteristics. First, as satire is used to attack, it aims not just to slice and dice, but to correct and reform. I argue that the heart of true satire is recognition of a moral discrepancy between what is proclaimed and what is practiced, often with an attempt to remedy it. It ranges from moral outrage to mischievous exposing of the Emperor's new clothes. It demonstrates the core of orthodox Christian thinking that all people know they should live in certain ways—and that no one does. Second, satire employs wit and humor; it entertains. It is not always funny, but it appeals to a recognition of the ridiculous. In this way satire can often be misconstrued or misused. It can dwindle down into sounding like mere mocking and scoffing. But wedding wit to moral concern makes for the most blessed, fertile state of satire.

The changing costumes of religious satirists have fit their times. What might be appropriate attire for the early church fathers would not wear well with Chaucer's pilgrims. The saucy laughter of the eighteenth-century national poet of Scotland Robert Burns does not translate well into the ironic voices of nineteenth-century Danish author Søren Kierkegaard, but then his sly indirect and ironic communication would not convert easily into the Scottish taverns. Sometimes the religious satirist acts as prophet; sometimes a rooster; sometimes merely an onion lurking in the salads of life. Thus, to follow the paths of the satirist is to encounter the odd and peculiar treasures who are God's mouthpieces. To retell their tales, parables, and witticisms in the cause of moral and spiritual reform is to look back into universal mirrors that confront us with our own stupid and selfish ways.

The Christian Satirist

The calling to be a Christian satirist still sounds oxymoronic; however, it is rooted in the nature of a God who mocks, exemplified in the practice of Hebrew prophets, and certified in St. Augustine's concept of Egyptian gold. In defending the Christian's use of the pagan art of rhetoric, the Bishop of Hippo declared that when the Israelites left Egypt, God gave to them all the gold, silver, cattle, and possessions of their slave masters, primarily because the Egyptians had not used them properly. By extension, while the pagans misused rhetoric, they also discovered some useful precepts "dug up from certain mines of divine Providence, which is everywhere infused, and perversely and injuriously abused in the worship of demons." These items should not be feared, but "taken from them as from unjust possessors and converted to our use."[18]

As Augustine commandeered rhetoric from the pagan Greek and Romans, so their principles and practices of wit would contribute to an evolving art of Christian satire. Satirists would employ techniques of humor and attempt various ploys to tweak the consciences of their targets. Christian satire would flash throughout history with unbridled wit and moral indignation, aiming to correct the corruption and folly of the saints. Its function was to provide a redemptive art that cleansed the infection of the ailing religious body.

The fundamentals of satire, from pagan to Christian, remain the same. From biblical prophets and Roman professionals, to the entertaining celebrities of modern media, these two key elements endure.[19] At its best, Christian satire combines laughter and a vision of reform, in what scholar Ralph Wood once called a comedy of redemption.[20] However, either can exist without the other. Satirical laughter without the hope of correction can devolve into mere sneering and scoffing. A passion to reform without wit can be sheer zealotry or cranky meddling. Traditional satire, from the gentle Roman satirist Horace, his sardonic counterpart Juvenal and the Hebrew prophets, to the mediated satire of Monty Python, is marked by this double pronged presentation: it makes us reconsider our lives stained with hypocrisy and folly, and it makes us laugh.

The Historical Turn

Presenting a historical overview of religious satire is daunting, with all the various literary artifacts, graphic antiques, and archival bits of Western culture involved. A bumpy tour through Rome, Jerusalem, and Lilliput ends up in Comedy Central and, along the way, showcases the various hues of one thread connecting old prophets and new satirists. Each era offers a particular and peculiar contribution to a general portrait of Christian satire. Some characteristics are gained or lost as one traverses history, but such time travel allows one the vantage point of standing on a steeple to inspect the broad countryside and traditions of satire. Yet one should also step down into the pews to experience the juicy moments of satirists showing people their depravity and folly.

The primary aim of this book in exploring the history of satire in religious contexts is to build a model, the Quad of Satire, which identifies four key elements on two axes: moral purpose versus ridicule and humor versus rage. The utility of the Quad is to first help discern true satire with an intention to reform from merely entertaining satire. Second, it separates satire from mere derision or ranting. One continuum assesses the moral or religious purpose of the satire, from a positive site of moral reform to the negative extreme of ridicule, which uses sheer scoffing for no redemptive purpose. The second continuum measures the range of the affective nature of the discourse, from anger and rage to a sanguine use of humor.

Renaissance humanist and cleric François Rabelais, practicing a true satire by jesting with moral purpose in his gargantuan novels, finds his place in the upper right (UR) quadrant, where he could poke religious authority with lively, vulgar humor. Hebrew prophet Isaiah, employing the rhetorical art of moral confrontation with less humor and more righteous wit, would reign in the lower right (LR). A mocking Continental like Voltaire would fit smugly in the upper left (UL) section, teetering between redemptive satire and taunting, with a motive more inclined to insult than to reprove and improve (although, I concede, others may interpret him differently). The dark soul of American poet Stephen Crane would inhabit the lower left (LL) realm of rage and ridicule with more of a howling satiric diatribe. Likewise, the far upper left quadrant would include those comedians who simply want to tease and make fun of their subjects. Without a motive for moral or spiritual repair, they fall under the category of an unripe satire, no matter how funny they are. The far lower left quadrant provides an equivalent site for venting and vituperation, joining in our category of unripe satire, no matter how moralistic their screeds are.

A graph of satiric laughter may be laughable, but it helps us to put some variables into focus. Others have set forth a measuring scale or hierarchy of laughter itself. In his diabolical *Screwtape Letters*, C. S. Lewis provided four categories, ranging from the heavenly laughter of Joy through the earthly laughter of Fun/Play and continuing through the Joke Proper to the scum-dwelling Flippancy. Satire sits uneasily between the Joke Proper and Flippancy. Another scholar of laughter, James Feibleman, listed an ascending valorized series, from Scorn, Wit, Sarcasm, Satire, Irony, and Humor, to Divine Comedy (which "criticized with love") and at the apex, Joy. Noticeably, satire fit right in the middle of the pack.[21] This grid recognizes the twin features of satire, namely wit/humor and morality, with the ideal or true satire occurring in the upper right quadrant.

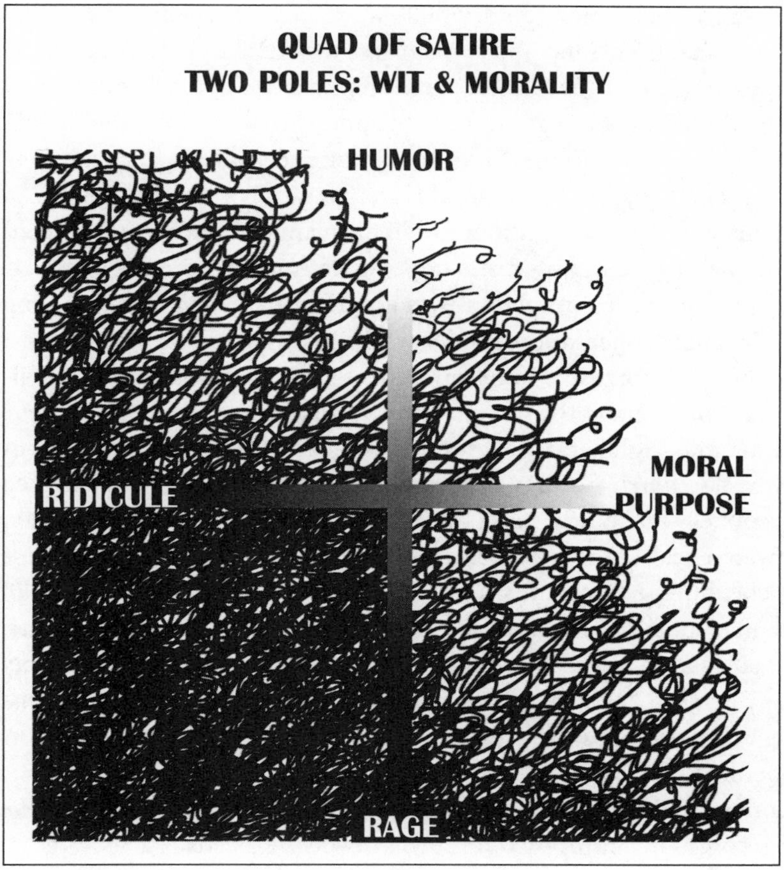

Quad of Satire. Two poles: wit and morality.

The origins of satire hearken back to both the early Hebrew and Roman eras, when satire was practiced both by those with direct callings as prophets and by those professionals who found that they could not *not* write satire. Either ordained directly by God or provoked by the corruption of their age, they wrote with parables and scathing wit. While both scribbled satire, the Romans claimed the art as their invention. In spite of the Greek comedies of Aristophanes against birds, gods, war, and old, hen-pecked Socrates, that old Roman rhetorician Quintilian made the jingoistic claim, "satura . . . tota nostra est," alleging that satire was quintessentially Roman. Comic countryman Horace, the leading lyrical satirist of the first century BCE, wrote personal, gentle satires and odes on wine, friendship and *carpe diem*, celebrating poetry during the golden age of Augustus Caesar. A century later, his cynical counterpart Juvenal argued that it was "impossible not to write satire" when decadence had despoiled Rome. Each Roman subscribed to a particular tone of satire, be it the nimble humor of Horatian satire or the scalding wit of Juvenalian. Across this continuum ran the gamut of witty words uttered in ridicule, rage, and optimistic hope for reform. Horace fits comfortably in the upper right quadrant as his humor was lively and teasing while Juvenal slipped to the border where his angry wit against the lost Republic grew corrosive in his attempts to call attention to moral failings. Yet both inhabit the UR quadrant of ideal satire.

In the mid-eighteenth century, when the Enlightenment had all but won the day, when German philosopher Georg Hegel's dialectic helped philosophers make tidy sense of contradictory quandaries, and when the Evangelical Lutheran Church of Denmark celebrated christenings with cocktails, a gawky misfit and satiric genius walked the streets of Copenhagen. Søren Kierkegaard took on the ecclesiastical pomposity, bourgeois fatness, and spiritual lethargy of his day. He served not only as a spy for God, but as a moral assassin. He shot his darts at smug, complacent churchgoers as fat geese that had forgotten how to fly. In contrast to a public that wanted no disturbance to their lives, his pseudonymous Johannes Climacus suggested, writing "pen in cheek," that what "the world, confused simply by too much knowledge, needs is a Socrates."[22] Irony may lead to true edification; religious satire to genuine reform.

To grasp that religious satire need not always be so ironic, intense, or acerbic, one has only to encounter that great Cockney humorist, G. K. Chesterton. A rotund convert to Roman Catholicism, Chesterton would counteract prevailing trends and jolly the world with paradoxical laughter to make it change.

Both Chesterton and Kierkegaard managed to find spots in the UR quad, where wit weds moral purpose. Each practiced his distinctive brand of true satire. While Chesterton lacked the varied voices of Kierkegaard, he possessed a wardrobe of capes and fool's caps to champion orthodoxy. He could marry serious Christian doctrines with buffoonery, in the same way that the "miracle plays of the Middle Ages would deal with a sacred subject such as the nativity of Christ, yet would combine it with a farce," as C. S. Lewis observed.[23] In Chesterton's playful defense of orthodoxy, he allowed that "if there is one element of farce in what follows, the farce is at my own expense. . . . No reader can accuse me here of trying to make a fool of him; I am the fool of the story, and no rebel shall hurl me from my throne."[24] If his arguments were a joke, they were a joke against himself. The weapon of the satirist, argued Chesterton, is the "sword of the spirit," but it is a sword that should be used "with ease; the weapon should be light if the blow be heavy."[25]

Religious satiric laughter is in need of a history, a story of its odd and quirky practitioners fulfilling a peculiar vocation. For satirists become their own parables. Saints mock and are mocked. At best, they are mirrors exposing our folly. But in order to see the self in a mirror, it is first necessary to get a clear understanding of what such a mirror is and is capable of doing. While the shape and the contours of the looking glass have changed over time, the face that looks back, as artist Hans Holbein's illustration in Erasmus's *In Praise of Folly* shows too clearly, remains the same.

Philosopher of comedy John Morreall argues convincingly for a comic understanding of the human spiritual journey. He observes that humor not only fosters virtues, but "is best seen as itself a virtue."[26] The various threads of religious humor stretch some three thousand years with hues as variegated, vulgar, and brilliant as their times. The single thread that is satire weaves its way whenever folly reveals tears in the cloth of humanity. And the satirists, whether prophetic or entertaining, whether in the Church or not, would find that the Church needed them, suggesting that they did have a divine and virtuous calling to mock. They sought to imitate a God who mocks.

1

Circumcised Satirists

Blessed is the man who does not sit in the seat of mockers.
—Psalm 1:1

The task of chronicling a history of the intertwining of Christianity and satire seems Herculean, like cleaning the Augean stables, and with much the same material being collected. Satire within the biblical texts exposes the follies of God's people with both sexual and scatological imagery, such as the Hebrew prophet Ezekiel lying naked, writing about the large-membered mules that Israel runs after, and baking nauseous barley cakes with human dung. Such images unleash a shocking satiric judgment upon the unfaithfulness of God's people.[1] While the moral and spiritual outrage far outweighs the humor, prophets did practice holy wit.

Within the sacred texts lie traces of holy taunting. The books that chronicle the wanderings of God's children include the satiric words of the prophets. They call attention to a disparity between how the Israelites were called to live and how they actually behaved. In this gap, the stage was set for satire.[2]

The rivers of satire flowed from two springs in the ancient world. The Roman aqueducts of Horace and Juvenal are well known. Less well known are the wells of wit and reform marked throughout deserts and in the Promised Land itself by Hebrew prophets. These seers were commanded to speak the word of the Lord, for whom the words "rain" and "teaching" were synonymous.[3] Their words were not mere symbolic forms of expression, but dynamic acts in the service of God.

The Hebrew *dabar* translates primarily as "word," but includes the idea of action.[4] When the word signifies either a blessing or a curse, it becomes as powerful as if one gave a neighbor a couple of expensive camels or threw daggers into an enemy's gut. In the ancient Middle East, it was allegedly believed that Arabian poets could kill with their words of satire (*hija'*).[5] One could insert curses in verses. As a weapon of the spirit, words could magically enter the soul and demoralize and demolish an enemy. So satirical poets might lead troops into battle, hurling satirical curses the way the warriors hurled spears.[6] In fact, one of the most pervasive themes in the books of Psalms and Proverbs is the damage that is done by the tongue in its boasting, gloating, mocking, and folly.

When one looks at the familiar story of shepherd boy David going up against Goliath, the preliminaries to the battle are verbal spats, or an early form of "flyting," a spoken duel in which two contestants insult one other until one gives up. The giant Philistine champion mocks the puny, almost naked Hebrew boy: "Come here runt, and I'll give your flesh to the birds of the air and the beasts of the fields" (1 Samuel 17:44). The battle of words is the beginning of the "dozens," in which verbal combatants joust with personal slurs, employing them as a military strategy. "Your momma . . ."[7]

Humor in the Hebrew Bible expresses itself primarily in the malicious scoffing, gloating, finger-pointing sort, the kind that comedian Lenny Bruce would later practice. And that is just the output of the good guys.[8] For the prophets, humor is secondary to proclaiming the word of the Lord. They want to shame their audiences into repentance. In the Satire Quad, such satiric prophets set their camp in the lower right, full of righteous rage, warning their audiences of a day of judgment. But they are not without wit.

Scholar Peter Berger categorizes such satire as a weapon that strikes the flesh and bleeds the target. It pierces more sharply than a two-edged sword, even "dividing soul and spirit, joints and marrow; it judges the thoughts and attitudes of the heart" (Hebrews 4:12). The words of the prophet are written sharply.

The Hebrew Bible follows the vicissitudes of God's chosen people like an early Punch and Judy comedy, with Israelites being continually knocked down, clobbered, and dragged out, only to have to learn the same lessons over again. A dominant characteristic of the laughter directed at this wayward people is sarcastic—harsh, railing, combining ridicule and put-downs. It is useful when attacking true enemies of holiness. Several psalms repeat the refrain that "He that sits in the Heavens shall laugh; the Lord shall have them in derision." God's laughter asserts his authority over the enemies of Israel and serves as a warning to his own people about iniquity and injustice.

God frequently laughs at the wicked. Striving to do evil, they are caught in their own snares. God laughs when calamity comes as a tornado upon them (Proverbs 1:26–28). While it is mostly the heathen who receive the mocking of God, Job points out that in this life, it feels like even the "upright man is laughed to scorn" (22:19). Job does earn kudos for one of the most biting ironic lines in the Bible, when he turns to his "comforters" and blasts the windbags with "surely, you are the people, and wisdom will die with you!" (Job 12:2, 16:3). Yet Job feels that he himself has become the object of God's mocking. He has become a "laughingstock" to his friends; he is a cousin to jackals and hyenas.

At its best, the satiric word of the Lord, delivered by God's chosen prophets, penetrates into the heart of God's chosen people. Their razor-like wit seeks to cut out the idolatry of Israel. Isaiah warns that the Lord made his "mouth like a sharpened sword," and Jeremiah foresees the effect of the Lord's word to be like that of fire and of "a hammer that breaks a rock in pieces" (Isaiah 49:2, Jeremiah 23:29). But as the *Revelation* of St. John alludes, the double-edged sword that comes out of the mouth of the Son of Man can both condemn and save (Revelation 1:16). Satire wounds to heal. It mocks to remake and reconcile.

Smart Ass

A curious zoomorphic trope for the period of the prophets is the psalmist's portrayal of God's people as a mule. During the Solomonic monarchy, the mule was considered a royal animal; it was imported by Solomon as the Hebrews were forbidden to breed them (Leviticus 19:19). But the stubbornness and waywardness of this beast of burden provided some fodder for comparison with hard-headed fools. Psalm 32:9 warns, "Don't be like the horse or mule, which have no understanding." Ezekiel also likened Israel's running after foreign gods to a pornographic obsession with the large members of donkeys and the emissions of mules. However it was the rebuke by a dumb donkey speaking with the voice of a man that would satirically confront an obtuse and wayward prophet (2 Peter 2:16).

The story of Balaam, the prophet from Pethor near the Euphrates, who is hired to curse the Israelite people with his word, illustrates the nature of the prophetic *dabar*. When King Balak of Moab recognizes how God had delivered the Israelites from the Amorites, he quivers in great fear about being licked by these hicks on their way to the Promised Land. So Balak sends for Balaam, trying to hire him to curse the Israelites and noting: "he whom you bless is blessed, and he whom you curse is cursed."

When Balaam finally sets out, God is not pleased. An angel stands in Balaam's path with a drawn sword to stop him from exploiting his gift. His donkey sees the danger and turns off into a field. Balaam, oblivious to God's messenger, strikes the poor donkey. At another narrow junction in a vineyard, the angel stands before them again. The donkey stops again and crushes Balaam's foot. Then, the angel stands in front of them a third time. Now, the wise but oppressed creature lies down and refuses to budge. Balaam beats him.

The grand joke occurs when the donkey opens its mouth and complains in fluent Hebrew: "What have I done to you that you have struck me these three times?" Balaam replies, "Because you made a mockery of me. If I had a sword, I would have killed you."

"Hey, I have been with you a long, long time; have I ever done this before?"

"No," says Balaam. Then, when the Lord opens Balaam's eyes, he sees the angel of the Lord with his sword, and the prophet bows to the ground to receive his scolding and repent. When he arrives at the city of Moab, Balaam is taken to the high places of Baal and recounts his story of how Balak had called him to curse Israel, but now Balaam says, "How shall I curse whom God has not cursed?" Then Balak sees that Balaam has not cursed his enemies, but blessed them. Over and over again, Balak's enraged commands to curse do nothing to sway Balaam from uttering blessings (Numbers 22–24).[9]

One moral of the story is that mules can be satirists. Balaam is blind to the angel standing before him, holding a sword that could cut his words or sever his tongue altogether. Thus, the prophet himself is resisted by an ass that is divinely inspired. Reproved by the ass, the prophet realizes the power of God's word. Hired to curse, Balaam discovers he can bless with his words—the satiric *dabar* can be employed to do good.[10] Whether *dabar* is used to bring blessing or curses, however, its efficacy is recognized by Balak: "For I know that those you bless are blessed, and those you curse are cursed" (Numbers 22:6). He sees that Balaam's prophetic words possess the power for weal or woe.[11]

A Baal and a Ho

The prophetic moment that stands as the exemplar of all biblical satire erupts out of the curmudgeon prophet Elijah's confrontation with the Canaanite prophets of the god Baal. As they compete to bring down fire upon a sacrifice, the worshippers of Baal rant, rave, and lacerate themselves to attract the attention of their god. "What's wrong," sneers Elijah, "is he on vacation? Is he taking a nap or out relieving himself?" His coarse latrine mockery savagely strips away the falsity of the Baal cult. When God hears Elijah's prayer and pours fire on a site drenched with water, the power of *dabar* reappears, in that God's actions match his words.[12]

While Elijah's own exaggerated words and actions are more akin to ridicule than reproof, he is never the clown. His satire tends to deteriorate into sarcasm, that diasyrmic railing, reviving the image of ripping a man's flesh to shreds. With the heathen prophets of Baal whipping and flailing themselves into a frenzy, Elijah's choice words tear away muscle and sinew of the soul. So, too, with the ill-fated young men who mocked Elijah's heir, the generally gentle prophet Elisha, by calling him "baldy"; they are slashed apart and chewed up by she-bears. *Dabar* has rarely been so literal.

The connection between the satiric word and its slicing impact shows that sticks and stones may break bones, but words also hurt. Slanderers who assault the psalmist David with mocking speech are described as ravenous beasts, "whose teeth are spears and arrows, whose tongues are sharp swords" (Psalm 57:4).[13] They, too, would tear their victim with words. In fact, when the psalmist calls down God's judgment upon venomous snakes, he implores God to "break the teeth in their mouths" and to tear out their fangs. (Psalm 58:6). Sarcastic mocking is never gentle.

Elijah's satire makes wayward saints into laughingstocks. Numerous one-liners that ridicule their subjects appear throughout the Hebrew scriptures: the knees of marching men in Ezekiel 7:17, for example, will "run with water." The righteousness of God's people in Isaiah 30:16–22 is compared to an unclean menstrual rag. The problem is that most of the irony and satire falls on deaf ears, or hardened hearts. Yet as Edward and Lillian Bloom suggest in *Satire's Persuasive Voice*, while it may be "folly to expect reformation to burst forth," satire does raise consciousness.[14]

They argue convincingly for what they call a moral satire of *humanitas*, versus a negative, amoral *antihumanitas*.[15] This restorative art of exposing folly and sin and summoning one's audience to be corrected and cleansed begins with the Hebrew prophets. The primary purpose is not to get the audience to get the laugh; it is to help and heal one's neighbors and one's enemies (who often turn out to be the same people). Yet David's second psalm recognizes that God, who sits in the heavens, does not hold back His displeasure. The Lord himself holds the wicked in derision. His actions match his words. For the psalmist, the mocking component of satire possesses a divine origin, one that Christians also find in Jesus's encounters with religious leaders and lawyers. In both cases, before satire can be fully *humanitas*, it must destroy the idolatry and pride of its targets.

The *dabar* given to the Hebrew prophets placed them in precarious positions, handling the sword of God before a stubborn and rebellious people. They were not executioners, but individuals called to restore the people's hearts to God. Perhaps no other prophet incarnates the doubled-edged, word/action paradigm as much as Hosea.

Hosea mocks the construction of a wooden phallic idol worshipped by a high priest of Israel as one who makes "inquiry of his Wood, and his Staff reports to him" (Hosea 4:12). The sexual metaphor of one's "wood" is not subtle. The ridiculing of false gods, particularly the nature of sex gods and Israel's proclivity to worship them, is meant to shame the people back to the righteous worship of the one God. But Hosea's calling carries its own ironic fulfillment of *dabar*. Called to marry the unfaithful Gomer, mirroring the way God betrothed himself to unfaithful Israel, he becomes the father of three children with odd names: Jezreel is "God will sow judgment"; Lo-ruhamah, "I will no longer have compassion;" and Lo-ammi, "You are not my people." God mocks the idolatry and adultery of his own people by naming the fruit of their sin with his rejection. She who has rebelled against God will fall by the sword. Yet, the end of this warning and mocking promises restoration: if Israel returns to the Lord, the names will be changed and the people redeemed.

Curiously, Hosea's incarnate satire illuminates the potential efficacy of *dabar*. The words become flesh that connects the satirist with his audience. When the Hebrew satirist tries to whip God's people into shape, he does so by becoming identified with his own words. By sharing in the prophecy, he also shares in its judgments.

The satiric words of prophets do penetrate deeply, but that power may originate in their divine purpose. The great twentieth-century Jewish theologian Abraham Heschel characterized the prophet as poet, preacher, patriot, social critic, moralist, and iconoclast.[16] Even when they were laughingstocks, they stood against the idolatry of might and power, because they had been in the presence of a holy God who revealed himself to them. Later satirists would respond to the exigency of rhetorical situations as if it were only an itch or urge, or merely an opportunity for play or spite, but for the Hebrew satirists, "the Word of the Lord" came to them. It was a word they could not contain and a calling they could not refuse.

2

Caesar Salad Satirists

In risu veritas.
—James Joyce

If a Hebrew prophet found his satiric authority rooted in vocation, in a calling by God, the Roman satirists followed careers of publicly attacking the stupidity of their times for pleasure. These professional satirists developed a grammar and rhetoric of mocking. Following Aristotle's art of seeking all the available means of persuasion in any given situation, the Romans mastered the craft and practiced it with aplomb, setting the foundation for centuries of future satire.

In his cultural history of *Greek Laughter*, Stephen Halliwell suggests that as ancient Greeks laughed, they were both obeying animal instincts and sharing a unique characteristic with both satyrs and gods. Even biblical humans shared the animal nature of the earth with the divine nature of the breath of God: satyrs were part goat and part human. Aristotle observed that man is that unique incongruity, a laughing animal, just as C. S. Lewis observed the human as stuck between two worlds, a natural one and a supernatural one. It was God's great enterprise, said Lewis, "to make an organism which is also a spirit; to make that terrible oxymoron a 'spiritual animal.'"[1] This discrepancy, this tension between flesh and spirit (or the human and the universe), provides raw material for the joke. The discrepancy is that the two things do not fit together. The laughing human animal is related to both the gods and satyrs.[2]

The rhetorician Quintilian (35–100 CE), who had set up a school for public oratory and defined the model Roman citizen as "the good man speaking well," claimed satire as the Roman's literary gift to the world. His use of the Latin term *satura*, from which we derive such words as "saturated" (complete, replete, full), denotes a literary genre that is full to overflowing. *Satura* offers a ritual "full dish" containing various fruit and foodstuffs for the delight of the consumer. The designation of *lanx satura* thus means a "full" salad of elements, a comic medley of styles and subjects. It serves as a poetic sort of tart fruit salad offered to the gods for all the disrespect shown them (often for good reasons). This full dish is composed of humorous verse or prose that deals with human follies while sharing similarities with sermons. It employs liberal doses of ridicule, irony and burlesque to make a moral point. Thus, from the Romans, we inherit the formal term, *lanx satura*, that medley of fruit, a mixed salad of beans, onions, and perhaps a jalapeno lurking among the lettuce that feeds both body and soul.

In ancient Athens, the Greeks originated the Attic comedies, broad plays of buffoonery, in which they lampooned individuals. Aristophanes spoofed Socrates in *The Clouds*, maliciously denounced Cleon in *The Knights*, and mocked horny, bellicose men held captive by beguiling women in *Lysistrata*. The Greeks also celebrated the god Dionysus in bawdy comic entertainments known as satyr plays, in which wanton and insolent half-man/half-goat masked creatures performed with sight gags, phalluses, mock drunkenness, and burlesques. Medieval and Renaissance poets connected these satyr plays to their understanding of satire. Satyr plays were marked by hyperbole, grotesqueness, bawdiness, lasciviousness, obscenity, and crude forms of ridicule, akin to what you would find in a typical sketch from the British comic Monty Python troupe. One must remember that the adjective "satyric" evolves from those rascals with goat-hoofed feet and profligate appetites. On the stage, actors were masked as leering creatures, lusting about the countryside, scampering after Dionysus, the great god of fertility.

Satire evolved into a literary form that seeks to censure and correct human vice and folly wherever it might be found, hoping to bring about improvement. Indirectly, it seeks to define the good person and recommend ways she or he should *not* behave. Its modes of expression range from ridicule, double-entendre, sarcasm, parody, whimsy, exaggeration, passionate invective, and persiflage to all means of drollery, wit, and humor. It also appears in a variety of forms: verse, narrative, fable, parable, anecdote, epigram, dialogue, or even graphic and visual media. Roman satire primarily dressed in one of two literary costumes, the dactylic hexameter (the rhythmic meter of six feet practiced by Horace and Juvenal), and the Menippean, a cynical blend of prose and verse that skewered mental attitudes of braggarts, bigots, and incompetents

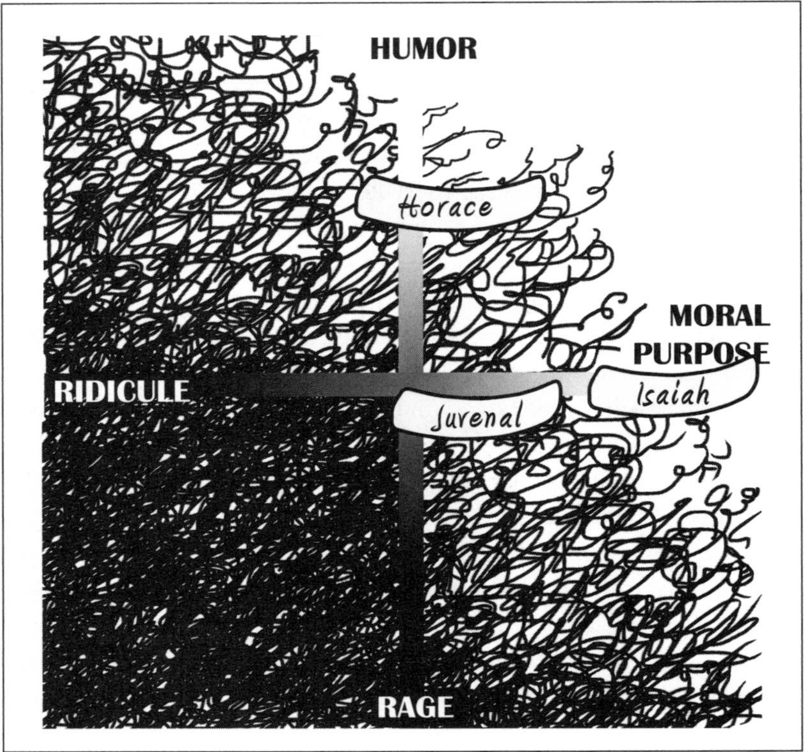

Horace, Juvenal, and Isaiah on the Quad of Satire.

practiced by the dissolute Roman satirist of the debauched age of Nero, Petronius, in his wild story *Satyricon*.

As a persona could be a mask, so the masks of Roman satire had multiple faces, from the genial and colloquial chatting (*sermo*) of Horace to the bitter commentary of Juvenal. As the Quad illustrates, these two Roman satirists form a continuum from the genial, urbane tone of the earlier poet to the caustic attitude of the latter. Both sought to be funny and both sought to alter the world around them. They drew from different Greek sources—Horace, from the "laughing philosopher" Democritus, and Juvenal, from the tragic Heraclitus. Jesse Bier has contrasted the morning waking of optimist and pessimist through a mere change in syntax. The optimist greets the day with "Good morning, God!" In contrast, his counterpart groans, "Good God! Morning."[3] The Horatian hopes and prays that satire will reform. The Juvenalian falls into the abyss of cynical satire. The optimist teases and prods with feathers while the pessimist boils over, licking his lips with *Schadenfreude* when something bad happens to his or her target. Each is tempted to extremes.

The good-humored Horace, Quintus Horatius Flaccus (65–8 BCE), worked as a government clerk, but his pay was so low that he that had to moonlight as a poet. Through charming self-deprecation, Horace offered indirect, good-humored criticisms that did not alienate his targets. He confessed to being only a freedman's son with a laughable record of military service; he was so servile, even his own slave mocked him. He explored what happens if the prayers of the people are granted, warning them to be careful what you pray for—you may get it. Horace's amused voice points to deluded desires that frustrate everyone, inviting all human fools to smile at their own folly.

In Horace's hands, *satura* became didactic; his motto, *ludentem dicere verum*, telling the truth laughingly, was one that later saints would adopt. The classical satire of this friendly and fallible fellow calls for conformity to standards of right and wrong, of wisdom and good common sense over folly. Avoiding what he viewed as excess, Horace strove for a poke in the ribs. Juvenal, however, offered a poke in the eye. Where Horace gently made fun of his targets, Juvenal (50–128 CE) lived in a decadent age of Rome and thus depicted such emperors as Domitian as cruel and corrupt. Juvenal's verse seethes with righteous anger at the status quo.[4] Even though he hoped his satire would persuade, his exercise of it tended to be misanthropic and even malicious. The nadir of Roman decadence summoned forth the zenith of Roman invective in his bitter and angry *Satires*.

For Juvenal, the crop of vices was never richer than during his time, yet his satire bore little fruit in reformed behavior. Juvenal hit small targets and larger monsters. He drew blood on many topics, from the blatant sexual perversions of Claudius's wife to a whole catalogue of social deviance of hypocrisy and homosexuality, all the while wrapping his hostility in iambic pentameter. Where Horace would whisper, Juvenal would rant and rave, spitting out his spite at everything that vexed him. The "mixed mash" of his verse encompasses all human endeavors, from human joys and pleasures to their angers, fears, and even prayers. Satirists sometimes mock "irrelevant" or trivial targets, but such random shootings fit with the basic features of *satura*, with a diversity of targets fitting in the mixed dish. One can eat the salad and suddenly note a leek or onion demanding one's attention.

Juvenal painted pictures in blood: a bulging fat man riding a sedan chair, gigolos vying for an old lady's money, a coarse and insulting waiter at a banquet. Worst, however, and suggesting Juvenal's own misogyny, is his indictment of spoiled, wealthy women. Married men, he averred, must endure the intolerable inflictions of libertine and depraved housewives. Where chastity was once the reigning virtue, now women such as Messalina were as horny and decadent as Roman men, but more disgusting to Juvenal because they came from distinguished households.

Juvenal's attack upon the adulteress is scathing. When her lover summons her, all is well, and she will wantonly roam the deck of a ship flirting with the crew with brazen delight; however, if her husband calls her, "oh how changed the case! 'Sick, sick,' she cries and vomits in his face." In his acidic tone, Juvenal catalogues all manner of degenerate women, from female gladiators to pretentious intellectuals. A special target is those stupid women who practiced cultic orgies or those litigious women who took each other to court. He castigates those who are addicted to fashion and flog their hairdressers for failing to achieve the style of the day. In contrast, the Apostle Paul's appeal to women to dress modestly sounds downright liberating.

These Roman professionals shared much with their early Hebrew counterparts. For those prophets, satire *usually* denoted some comic form of ridicule with a corrective purpose. They hoped that ridicule and castigation would result in spiritual and moral reform, seeing their satiric responsibility as "that of a watchdog; no one expects a watchdog to do the double-duty of alarming others that the barn is on fire and of putting out the blaze. Satirists try to rouse us to put out the fire. They encourage our need for the stability of truth by unmasking imposture, exposing fraudulence, shattering deceptive illusion, and shaking us from our complacency and indifference."[5] The prophet warns of the fire to come, sounding the alarm.

In spite of the seven hundred years separating them, there is a remarkable similarity between the Hebrew prophets and the later Roman professionals. Again, both adhere to the two basic criteria that underlie satire. The first, and most necessary, is that it acknowledges some standard, a reasonable norm against which audiences or readers can measure what is good and right. Thus, it must address some folly, vice, or hypocrisy in individuals or institutions that begs to be corrected, or at least addressed. It thus works, as Chesterton was wont to point out, as a standard against which to contrast actual behavior. One must be able to compare a golden mean against which the target is merely dross. True satire edges to the side of the continuum for reform, rather than declining into ridicule.

Pholly of the Phallic

Several fascinating parallels exist between a Hebrew prophet like Isaiah of around 700 BCE and a Roman satirist like Horace in the first century CE. Neither had protection for free speech, and both were prepared to suffer the consequences of their communication. Neither suffered fools or folly, idols or idolatry. Both mocked those false idols men made out of wood, using the tactic of shame to shake up their subjects. Although Horace seemed fine with the traditional apparatus of Roman religion as a magical superstition, he did appear to enjoy satirizing divine interventions in human affairs. He believed in satire's "missionary art," in that it was not enough to "make your hearer grin with laughter"; one had also to do well with the world.[6] As both Isaiah and Horace used their wit to awaken their audiences to alter their behaviors, they dwelt in the upper right heavens of our satire grid—although the Roman got better laughs.

In his first *Satire*, Horace takes on two hags trying vainly to invoke magical power through their wild incantations. However, they stumble upon the phallic god Priapus, a deity of fertility and sort of sexual totem made of fig-wood who mocks his own origin: "once I was a fig tree, good-for-nothing wood, when the craftsman after hesitating a while trying to figure whether to make me a stool or a Priapus, decided for the god."[7] Priapus stands erect as a symbol of raucous festivity. His sacrament is the orgy, and Horace mocks the two hags who try with their magical incantations to control the spirit world through this wooden stick. However, Priapus, the unredeemed and unruly male symbol, disperses these two crones in fear with an enormous clap of thunder from his hinder parts: he farts. Pagan religion is dismissed with merry vulgarity.

Obscene language and behavior has been historically connected to the arousal of laughter. The cult of the phallus, used like a scarecrow to protect crops from crows and thieves and like a Viagra charm to invigorate fertility, was one that promoted extravagant laughter. While not as crude as his Roman counterpart, the hoary Isaiah centuries earlier deconstructed the same god-making process, particularly against those who would make such gods for their pleasure and prosperity. In a call to recognize the only true God, Isaiah outlined the origin of false gods:

> All those who make no-god idols don't amount to a thing, and what they work so hard at making is nothing. Their little puppet-gods see nothing and know nothing—they're total embarrassments! Who would bother making gods that can't do anything, that can't "god"?
>
> . . . The woodworker draws up plans for his no-god, traces it on a block of wood. He shapes it with chisels and planes into human shape—a beautiful woman, a handsome man, ready to be placed in a chapel. He first cuts down a cedar, or maybe picks out a pine or oak. Then it can serve a double purpose: part he uses as firewood for keeping warm and baking bread; from the other part he makes a god that he worships—carves it into a god shape and prays before it. With half he makes a fire to warm himself and barbecue his supper. He eats his fill and sits back satisfied with his stomach full and his feet warmed by the fire: "Ah, this is the life." And he still has half left for a god, made to his personal design—a handy, convenient no-god worship whenever so inclined. Whenever the need strikes him he prays to it, "Save me. You're my god." (Isaiah 44:9–20, NIV)

Isaiah mocked the stupidity of praying to a stick of wood. Witnessing one of the most turbulent times in Israel's history, Isaiah prophesied that the people of Zion who defiled themselves with their silver idols and gold images would one day throw them away like a filthy menstrual rag, shouting "away with you!" (30:22). Isaiah's confession to having unclean lips suggests that he knew of his tendencies to use the vulgar to shock and shame his adversaries. These same foul lips remain the professional tool of the satirist, one that always needs forgiveness for such untimely spoken trespasses. Yet the prophet believes that God made his mouth "like a sharp sword" from his mother's womb.

Isaiah saw God laughing at his own children, both men and women, as they blamed their misdeeds on their ersatz gods: "my idols did it; my wooden image and metal god ordained those things" (48:5). The wicked were like mute dogs with mighty appetites (remember the Jews thanked God that he did not make them as Gentiles, women, or dogs), which never have enough. They call each to drink more wine, believing that tomorrow will be even better than today. Their sexual lust was out of control. "Whom are you mocking?" asked Isaiah. "At whom do you sneer and stick out your tongue? You are so stupid that you burn with lust among the oaks, and under every spreading chestnut tree sacrifice your children to Molech. Look what you're doing: pouring out drink portions to stone idols, making beds on high and lofty hills." Isaiah derided those who provoked God to his very face by eating the flesh of pigs and rats; such people "are smoke in my nostrils" (65:5, 66:17).

For Isaiah, the consequences of satire included being mocked in return (66:3–4). Isaiah suffered the scorn of the callous-hearted people who flippantly pointed fingers at him. Yet Isaiah didn't hide his face from those who pulled out his beard, but offered his cheeks to their spite and spit. No shame, no gain, for the Lord would help and restore the poor prophet and comfort Zion with gladness. He would not be disgraced, for the sovereign Lord would vindicate him. "Don't fear the reproach of men or be terrified by their insults," Isaiah preached, "for the moth will eat them up like a garment; the worm will devour them like wool" (51:7–8). Every tongue that accused the righteous will be refuted. While the ending passages of his prophetic satire offer the people of God a blessing rather than a curse, including the promise of being called by a new name, Isaiah's last word pummels those who are rebellious and obstinate. For them, "the worm will not die, nor will their fire be quenched, and they will be loathsome to all mankind" (66:24). Not a pretty ending.

Horace and Juvenal maintained a rhetorical distance as professional satirists, careful not to expose their own vulnerabilities to the authorities lest their jabs disturb a hornet's nest. Isaiah and the Hebrew prophets, however, engaged personally with their targets. They were called to speak forth to them of blessings and curses; yet they knew they shared the same fate with the family of God.

3

Satire Made Flesh

Do not look dismal.
—Matthew 6:16

Hebraic satire continued into the New Testament. In the Gospels, Jesus took on legalistic Pharisees, politically compromised Sadducees, and others, with vim and vigor and no slight bit of satire. With playful exaggeration, Jesus pulled the rug out from under the religious leaders.[1] He unveiled a Gospel ethic of satire that Molière adopted for his own times centuries later; for Jesus and those who follow his satirical school, vanity does not accord well with piety. Hypocrisy does not harmonize with true religion.

In the Gospels, satire works as a refining fire that often punishes, but also seeks to purify. Satire finds an unexpected theme song in the *Magnificat*, as Mary sings the words, "He has put down the mighty from their seat and has exalted the humble and the meek." God removes the haughty and uplifts the humble. Curiously, this is the liturgy used to inaugurate the celebration of Twelfth Night and the medieval Feast of Fools, when young clergy drive the bishops from the cathedrals and celebrate a topsy-turvy world where the fool, or Lord of Disrule, mounts the throne and altar.[2]

Early Christian satire grappled with balancing the moral purpose of satire against the admonition of the Apostle Paul to avoid foolish talk (*morologia*) and coarse jesting (*eutrapelia*). The latter term, *eutrapelia*, however, contrasts with the translation given by Aristotle (and subsequently Thomas Aquinas) as a "good turn," rather than a "bad twisting." In contrast to lewd, scurrilous, and depraved jesting, Aristotle and Aquinas interpret *eutrapelia* as a virtue, a good turn of speech. Aquinas associates it with jocundity and sprightliness, an enjoyment in which the mind is relieved and recreated. He labels the person who exhibits its moderate balance of humor and play *eutrapelos*, a pleasant person with

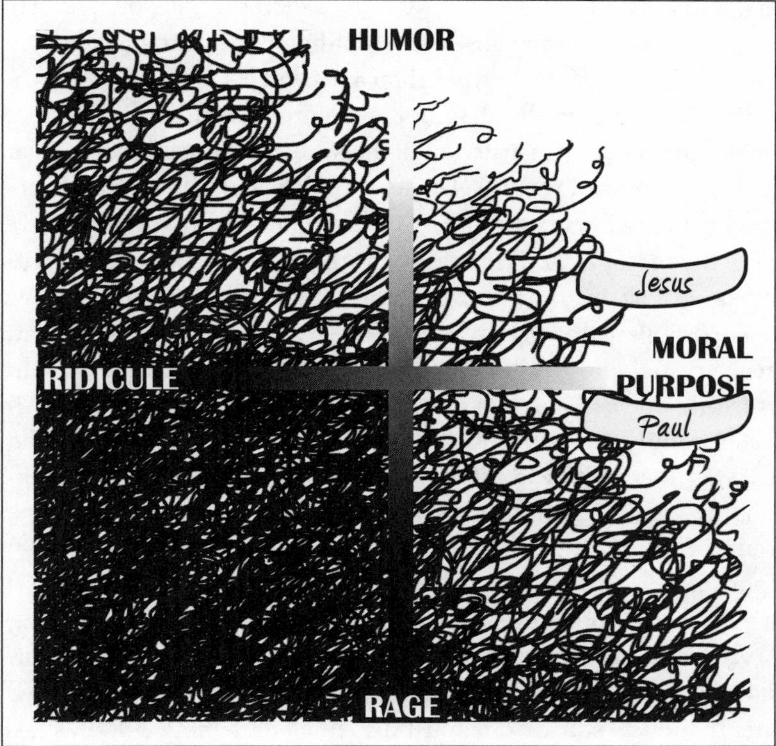

Jesus and Paul on the Quad of Satire.

a happy cast of mind who gives his words and deeds a cheerful turn."[3] He admonishes, like Aristotle, those who practice the vice of humorlessness, those who laugh too little as much as those who laugh too much.

Satire within the Gospels carries a prophetic Jewish flavor, with shrewd irony and hyperbole practiced by Jesus and his disciples. Jesus had warned his followers, "do not look dismal," and one suspects that he didn't.[4] His extravagant bantering includes bits on letting the dead bury the dead and recommending that people pluck out their eyes. Elton Trueblood, in his insightful—but, alas, unfunny—book *The Humor of Christ*, notes that a "misguided piety has made us fear that acceptance of His obvious wit and humor would somehow be mildly blasphemous or sacrilegious."[5] Trueblood identifies the witty language of Jesus in confronting the leaders of his day and sharing bread with drunkards, sinners, and tax collectors rather than the sanctimonious people.[6] His humorous rejoinders at the obstinate stupidity of his hearers (Mark 3:5) contains profound points, sharper than a two-edged sword.

Dudley Zuver argues that "Humor is the propaedeutics to the cross." It provides preparatory instruction on how humor "degrades all human pretensions with one arm and elevates humility with the other."[7] In the Apostle Paul's discourse on death, "O death where is thy sting? O grave, where is thy victory?" Zuver sees a grand joke being displayed, with death exposed as an imposter; in a comic stage play Satan's shadowy masks are dropped. Against this deceit, Paul exulted and laughed. Death has been tricked and can be mocked. For church fathers like St. John Chrysostom, one can laugh at death as one laughs at comic villains. In an Easter homily, Chrysostom thundered, "Hell was in an uproar because it was done away with. It was in an uproar because it is mocked."[8] So, too, the great French satirist François Rabelais laughed as his own final curtain was being drawn, echoing the festive laughter of Easter, *risus paschalis*.[9]

The Gospel, as good news, presupposes bad news. As inevitable tragedy precedes unexpected comedy, so the fallen and foolish state of humanity sets up the coming of biblical satire. In discerning the place of laughter in biblical stories, one must dispel "all darkening clouds, shake the book free of all dusty religious notions, and be prepared to smile, snicker, or even laugh out loud."[10] One must read with comic eyes; a hermeneutic of suspicion must be replaced with a hermeneutic of humorous recognition. Like the Hebrew prophets, Jesus confronted religious and political authorities with sly wit, trying to nudge them into consciousness of their ridiculous plight.

The most public example of diasyrmic outbursts happens at the crucifixion of Christ.[11] The violence of execution is matched by the violence of the language. The biblical nadir of scoffing for the Christian occurs with laughter at the foot of the cross by the Roman guards. Throughout his ministry, Jesus had been mocked by various categories of adversaries. Many wagged their heads and "taunted him about rebuilding the Temple in three days."[12]

This mocking had no moral focus; it degenerated into sarcasm. During the trial of Jesus, ridicule exacerbated the physical scourging and spitting. Soldiers sat in the seat of scoffers and crowned him "King of the

Jews" and made a bogus crown of thorns that ripped his flesh. As Jesus hung on the cross, they jeered, "He saved others; let him save himself if he is truly the Christ, the Chosen One of God."

Art history is replete with numerous painters illustrating the humiliating moment of the derision of Christ. In Fra Angelica's *Mocking of Christ* (1445), a detail of a bodiless person spits at the Savior and unattached hands slap him. *The Mocking of Christ* (attributed to Lucas Cranach the Elder, c. 1550) showcases a fat scoffer wagging his tongue. In Francesco Trevisani's *Christ Crowned with Thorns* (c. 1700), a brute faces the spectator with a smirk and a pointing finger. In Hieronymous Bosch's *Christ Carrying the Cross* (1515), Jesus is held up to ridicule with obscene gestures, grotesque faces, and vulgar expressions of sneering mirth. One almost hears the impious scoffing of "King of the Jews" and "He saved others, but cannot save himself" in these embalmed moments of art.[13]

Pagans relished the monotheistic faith as a ripe target for their jibes, reserving "special scorn for the awe-inspiring moment of the crucifixion," as Paul Scholten observes.[14] The death of a God was ludicrous to them. The Apostle Paul argued that the Crucifixion was the restoration of a broken covenant, a necessary sacrifice for the breach between God and his creatures. As such, this foolish and scandalous act of dying was an extension of the covenantal act of circumcision. Both crucifixion and circumcision offered a literal and figurative diasyrm, a cutting off of life and skin, to affirm the covenant of God to his people. But both are vulnerable topics for pagan satire.

Mocking exists as the sewer of satire. It substitutes sarcasm and rage for wit and humor and has no conscience for reform. Most of the twenty-nine references to laughter in the Hebrew Bible are connected to mocking. Renaissance scholar M. A. Screech identifies four types of this tormenting laughter directed at Jesus in the Gospels.[15] The Latin Vulgate translation of *illudo*, derived from *ludo*, meaning to play or sport, denotes ill play, or mocking. The Greek term *epaizo* suggests trifling and scoffing like a child, with pitiless and heartless cruelty. When the thieves taunt Jesus on the cross, the word used is *oneidizo*, to treat one as an object of ridicule. Erasmus translates the Greek *convicia dicere* as the act of hurling insults. The terms *derideo* and *ekmusterizo*, conveying contempt of the haughty, are manifested by the heathen rage found in psalter (2:1–4). These terms connote nonverbal behaviors such as baring one's teeth, laughing down one's nose, snorting, and wagging one's head (Psalm 22:7, 35:16, 58:6, 64:8). This *blasphemeo* culminates at the cross in reviling, calumny, and slander, as religious leaders and soldiers cut up Jesus for mere sport.

Yet another laugh appears—a last laugh—and one that lasts. An added meaning emerged out of the medieval Easter laughter (*risus paschalis*). After the mockery of the cross, the Resurrection of Christ now mocks death. Theologian Karl-Josef Kuschel suggests that "by being mocked himself, Christ grants the ridiculed and the mocked their dignity and rights."[16] Taking on the sin and sufferings of the world, he also took on the scoffing.

One almost flippant question arises from this mocking of Jesus: at what would God laugh? He allowed the raucous scoffing of his own Son, but to what extent does he condone such laughter? Does laughter have a place in the holy of holies or must it remain in an outer court of the temple? Does he wait for his final judgment to have what poet Robert Frost saw as his final joke on humanity? Or was there something in the Incarnation, in the emptying of all divinity, that welcomed the scourging and scoffing of his beloved creatures so that they might get the point of his grace?

The question of whether God jokes provides such an almost imponderable difficulty that it raises basic Christological issues.[17] As we have seen, God's laughter in the Hebrew Bible is mostly derisive; he laughs from the heavens at human pretensions. He is more of a satirist at this point in human history. But then when Jesus ascends the cross, where human mocking is bitter and mean, where all the suffering and pain of the world reach a crux, the humor becomes dark, gallows humor. If, as Hans Geybels claims, the "secret of Jewish humor lies in self-depreciation," for Jesus, a Jew, this ultimate denial of the self for the world would stand as consummate Jewish humor.[18] Here a song from Monty Python's *Life of Brian* (1979), "Always look on the bright side of life," is just right for this darkest of hours, almost as an opening number of a divine comedy.[19]

Dying Laughing

For many church fathers, laughter connoted irrational tendencies. They held dim and frowning views of it.[20] The key verb they reacted against was *skoptein*, meaning to deride or mock, but also to joke or jest non-maliciously.[21] The Greek verbs divide laughter a bit more clearly and conveniently, with *gelan* and *katagelan* meaning, respectively, to laugh and to laugh at or against. The former has a kinder, more humane sense to it.

During the years of persecution of the saints, one discovers the presence of *gaudium spirituale*, the spiritual joy of saints during suffering. Gregory the Great echoed this shout of joy of saints throughout martyrdom, celebrating that notion that the church "will laugh in the time to come."[22] The aged Polycarp, Bishop of Smyrna, stood in the amphitheater as the first great martyr of the early church. When told by the emperor to dismiss the atheists (Christians who believed in only one God), Polycarp would wave his hand at the mob in the coliseum and utter ironically, "Away with these atheists." In the third century, the nursing mother Perpetua and the pregnant Felicity became Christian martyrs in Carthage. In an account of her arrest and imprisonment, Perpetua's catechist shared the young woman's vision of heaven, in which she proclaimed, "Thanks be to God that, as I was merry in the flesh, now I am even merrier here."

The early church suffered the verbal arrows of stinging satire, both in the satires of Lucian, who scoffed that Christians would worship a mere man, and of the second-century Celsus, who accused Christians of being "worthless and contemptible people." In response, great Christian satirists arose to strike, rather than to turn, the other cheek. Latin patriarch Tertullian wrote in his *Apology*, "If the Tiber floods the city, or if the Nile refuses to rise, or if the sky withholds its rain, if there is an earthquake, a famine, a pestilence, at once the cry is raised: 'Christians to the lion!' What, so many to just one lion?"[23]

Many of Tertullian's rhetorical outbursts included scourging sarcasm, particularly against one heretical son of a bishop named Marcion. Marcion rejected the Jewish creator God as a "demi-Urge," a bad deity who created a material world, and he eschewed the Incarnation as a "disgrace to God" because the human body is "stuffed with excrement."[24]

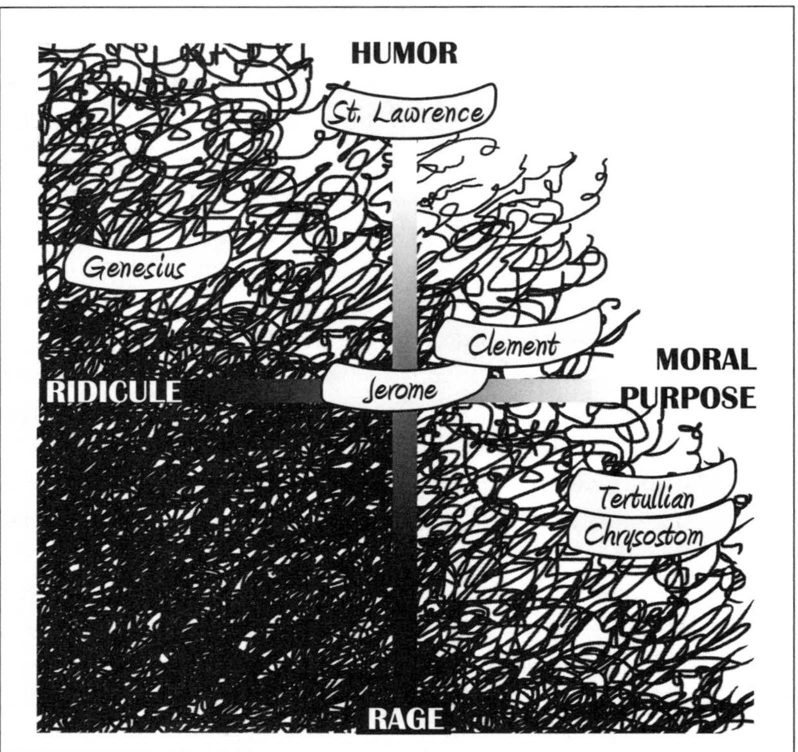

Genesius, St. Lawrence, Clement, Jerome, Tertullian, and Chrysostom on the Quad of Satire.

Tertullian emphasized that God created this entire natural world and all its wonders as good, whereas Marcion's god couldn't invent a single vegetable.[25]

The Latin apologist recognized that non-Christians laughed at the idea of the Resurrection, but he acknowledged that before he became a Christian, he found such ideas outrageous himself.[26] He met one criminal who carried a satirical image of the Christian God with an inscription describing him as "ass-begotten." The man wore a toga and carried a book, but had an ass's ears and one foot that was a hoof. Against such derision, Tertullian would unleash his own biting sarcasm. When asked what sight would give him joy, he confessed in *On Spectacles*: "I see so many great kings, . . . groaning now in the lowest darkness, and governors of provinces who persecuted the Christian name, in fires more fierce than the ones that they proudly threatened the followers of Christ with." [27] Gloating over the death of enemies sounds more like malice than satire, but such caustic derision and mordant irony were not the sole property of those who mocked God.

A trio of church fathers, Clement, Chrysostom, and Basil, championed an antigelastic view of "laughter denied; laughter deferred."[28] In other words, laughter was being kept in abeyance until the Wedding Feast when the Lord returns. While valuing much of Hellenistic culture in his *Paidagogos* (*The Educator*), St. Clement of Alexandria tried to teach Christians how to talk, walk, dress, and even laugh. He attacked the stupidity and foolishness of pagan religions, but also looked askance at laughter. "People who are imitators of ludicrous sensations, or of such as deserve derision, are to be driven from our polity."[29] However, he still found it laughable that men would pray to Zeus for beautiful progeny, when the chief god couldn't produce a comely offspring himself.

Here, again, pops up Juvenal's wicked wit toward similar targets, this time against the idolatry of Egyptians. Looking at how Roman satirists used humor for both laughing and lying, historian Maria Plaza shows Juvenal scourging the land of the pyramids and pharaohs by mocking how the cannibalistic Egyptians worshipped vegetables, finding omnipotence in onions and lordship in leeks. "O, what a holy people, in whose gardens such divinities grow!" Let us worship lettuce and kneel before corn. Plaza points out how such satire is driven by two oppositional motives—namely, to display humor and to promote a serious moral message. Juvenal thus walked in similar sandals as the church fathers.[30]

Clement distinguished among different kinds of laughter, from explosive giggling (as in the laughter of whores) to the "laughter of the wise."[31] Instruction for Christian living during times of persecution reminded converts that speech was the fruit of the mind, and that foolish discourse and buffoonery should be discouraged. Wags were to be ejected from community, as their conversation was not fit for pious ears. Pleasantry was allowable, not wagging. "Laughter must be kept in check; for when given vent to in the right manner it indicates orderliness, but when it issues differently, it shows a want of restraint." Self-control for rational animals was essential.[32]

Essentially, Clement argued for there being an appropriate condition for laughter, given that men are not laughing or neighing animals. Yet the "seemly relaxation of the countenance in a harmonious manner—as of a musical instrument—is called a smile" and is welcome. "So also is laughter on the face of well-regulated men." Clement pointed to a proverb in *Ecclesiasticus* that a "fool raises his voice in laughter."[33] Clement hesitated in finding a role for laughter in reproof. Mostly, for these saints, gravity, rather than levity, warded off "approaches of licentiousness by a mere look."[34] This did not stop them from scourging pagan idolatry with their own holy scorn. Satire does not amuse; it is a holy weapon.

The distinguished Egyptian theologian Origen (184–254 CE) wrestled against the flesh and blood of Celsus, his mocking nemesis, as well as against various principalities and powers. Celsus had ridiculed Jesus's form of execution, the cross, and how Christians had come to venerate this means of torture and death. He chided that if Christ had been "thrown off a cliff or pushed into a pit or suffocated by strangling . . . would there happen to be a cliff of life above the heavens, or a pit of resurrection, or a rope of immortality?"[35]

For Celsus, the Christian idea of a special providence was nonsense, an insult to the deity. Christians were like a council of frogs in a marsh or a synod of worms on a dunghill, croaking and squeaking, "For our sakes was the world created." Like all quacks they gather a crowd of slaves, children, women, and idlers. "I speak bitterly about this," wrote Celsus, "because I feel bitterly. When we are invited to the Mysteries, the masters use another tone. They say, 'Come to us you who are of clean hands and pure speech, you who are unstained by crime, who have a good conscience towards God, who have done justly and lived uprightly.' The Christians say, 'Come to us you who are sinners, you who are fools or children, you who are miserable, and you shall enter into the kingdom of Heaven': the rogue, the thief, the burglar, the poisoner, the despoiler of temples and tombs, these are their proselytes."[36] The great irony of Celsus is that he understood the theology of the Christians quite well. The egalitarian appeal to the poor, the weak, and the foolish was an essential aspect of Christ's ministry.

Holy Wit

One does not expect to find wit in a battle-scarred and exiled bishop from Alexandria, but Athanasius (c. 296–373 CE) challenged his persecutors with formidable satire. When Arian leaders accused him of dabbling in magic, Athanasius was called before the Emperor Constantine at the city of Tyre to face charges. They alleged that he had killed a rival bishop named Arsenius and then chopped off his hand for occult rituals.

Athanasius arrived before the emperor and his accusers confronted him with the victim's hand presented in a box. He had brought with him a cloaked figure. Setting them up, he asked his accusers if they knew Arsenius personally.

"Yes, we did know him quite well," they responded eagerly. At this point, Athanasius ushered in his mystery guest, removed his hood, and revealed his "victim" to the synod. Some still believed he had cut off the man's hand, so Athanasius uncovered the right arm. "No," screamed the crowd, "It was the other hand!"

Having punked them, Athanasius unflappably revealed the other hand and laughed at his accusers. "What kind of monster did you think Arsenius was? Do you think he has three hands?" His audience laughed and Athanasius won the day.[37]

Yet as the value of laughter waned, so did the satiric impulse. Among the desert fathers, St. John Cassian (360–435) stood as a champion ascetic, establishing an Egyptian-style monastery in southern Gaul. One parable of his life shocked fellow monks, when he was seen jesting. Asked how he could make light of life in such dire times, he pointed to the archer's bow, and asked, "Must it be continually taut?" "No," answered his critics, "as it would be weakened and ruined." "Thus," concluded St. John, "the mind and soul needs the ludicrous and jocular to loosen them lest they become too taut and break as well; the small and brief recreations of our minds should not offend."[38] Yet, these were very brief recreations.

With a stiffness of neck and an itch of lust, St. Augustine confessed to having played too much. He had dabbled in the circus and theatrical shows and enjoyed how upper-class "wreckers" would haze freshmen for their malevolent amusement. Yet his conscience haunted him, raising questions about his amusements. He wrestled with discovering how the Roman comic playwright Terence indirectly recommended Jupiter's practice of deceit and fornication, two of Augustine's favorite pastimes. In fact, Augustine called his vocation as a rhetorician a deceitful art of selling words in the market of persuasion. When he stole pears just to throw at pigs, it was "all done for a giggle pleasure in the crime itself"—as throwaway jests in a flippant life.[39]

Several events altered Augustine's views of laughter. First, he was horrified when a dying friend was baptized, and Augustine joked with him about it, only to be reprimanded by his friend.[40] Second, he discovered that God laughed at his ambition, and so he became bitingly sarcastic about those captivated by the folly of comic entertainment.[41] Mockery, he came to understand, was a chief kind of wickedness, wherein people do injurious acts to others with verbal insults, taking the "pleasure of watching other people's pain, like spectators of gladiators, or those who mock and ridicule others."[42] Somewhat suspicious of laughter and the pleasures of joking, Augustine yet relished the art of wordplay. For example, he conceived of the incarnation as a trick of God played upon Satan. In his Sermon 263, he recorded how "the Devil exulted when Christ died, but by this very death of Christ, the Devil is vanquished as if he had swallowed the bait in the mousetrap. The cross of the Lord was the Devil's mousetrap; the bait by which he was caught was the Lord's death." Christ's body is also described as the bait on a divine fishhook in which the Deceiver is deceived. Christ is the fisherman, the angler, another word for someone who does not deal in a straightforward manner, but plays the angles.[43]

One recurring question for the church fathers employing satire centered on whether Jesus laughed. While affirming his humanity, some were reluctant to concede that he laughed like a human.[44] The Cappadocian fathers, Basil of Caesarea and Gregory of Nyssa, fought for the Orthodox faith and while liberal on many issues, held to a conservative perspective on laughter. Basil wrote that "the Christian . . . ought not to indulge in jesting; he ought not to laugh nor even to suffer laugh-makers."[45] Gregory preached against the "madness" (*paranoia*) of laughter, as it was neither "a reasonable act, nor a purposeful one, but an excitation of the body," involving an "unseemly bodily loosening, agitated breathing, a shaking of the whole body, dilation of the cheeks, baring of teeth, gums, and palate, stretching of the neck, and an abnormal breaking up of the voice as it is cut into by the fragmentation of the breath."[46] He had studied the phenomenon closely, it seems.

In contrast, St. Jerome (342–420), wrestling with celibacy and his caustic attitude, championed satiric laughter. The fourth-century monk spent too many hours translating the Bible into the Vulgar Latin language, becoming known as vain, hard-headed, and downright crabby, and that by his friends.[47] He allegedly kept copies of the Roman comic playwrights Terence and Plautus under his pillow.[48] He had once convulsed in laughter in a lecture room, recognizing the tendency toward cachinnation, of getting people to crack up over such a curious text as *Testanetum Porcelli*, a piglet's last will and testament.[49] His enemies assailed him for his "very gait and his laughter."[50] Enemies called him *satyricus scriptor in prosa*, or a satirist in prose, something akin to a smart ass.

When a brash monk dared to criticize his writings and attack his intimacy with society ladies, Jerome upbraided and caricatured him as a windbag. He scolded another monk who abandoned monasticism, asking if he would go back to his mother's sagging breasts and wrinkled face to hear her hum another nursery lullaby. For Jerome, "some errors are better refuted by jeering."[51] Yet, with all his classical learning, Jerome once dreamed in a feverish nightmare that as he stood at the gates of heaven, he was denied entrance because he was more a Ciceronian than a Christian (and of all the great stylistic teachers of rhetoric, Cicero stressed the persuasive qualities of the comic, although he rejected the Stoic philosophers' assertion that noisy farts should be as free as belches).[52] Attacked for his improper relationship with the patrician Paula, who subsidized his writing and book-buying, Jerome responded to his accusers with his own accusations. He asserted that while he delighted in leanness, dieting on water and beans, one particular enemy "quaffs wine and belches as he is stuffed with duck and sturgeon."[53]

Jerome combined elements of the Hebrew prophet Isaiah and the pungency of Juvenal. In his writings, he bites, but then contritely apologizes for biting. However futile the attempt, he tries to be as wise as a serpent and as innocent as a dove, but ends up more like a cross between a toad and a crow. In a letter to Domnio, defending his use of witty polemics against critics in Rome, he protests: "Let me be granted the chance to reply to his eloquence. I can bite back, if I want to. I can leave tooth-marks. I too have learned my letters."[54] As a Christian follower of the man of peace, he shouldn't retaliate with sharp words. Yet Jerome flayed his adversaries:

> We are considered hermits because we do not wear silk clothes. And because we do not become intoxicated, or split in two with raucous laughter, men call us hard, dour, melancholy. If our tunics are not dazzlingly white, immediately a cry from the street, "Imposter! Greek!" Let men indulge in even wittier remarks, and, if they feel like it, let them parade their large paunched friends in front of us.[55]

Jerome complained about how difficult it was to be "an agent of truth." But there were dramatic precedents. Isaiah, he noted, walked about stark naked. Jeremiah was sent from Jerusalem to the Euphrates in Mesopotamia and told to discard his clothes there so that "they may be soiled and worn out among the Assyrian Chaldean enemies" (Jeremiah 13:1). Ezekiel was ordered to "devour a loaf of bread, which had been made by sprinkling human excrement and manure over an indigestible mixture of various grain" (Ezekiel 4:12). All these prophets dramatized the rebellion of Israel so that they might repent. For Jerome, nakedness, soiled clothes, and dung-flavored bread were nonverbal means to mock the wayward people of God.

Jerome, the grumpy man of God, identified with these prophets and religious satirists. He also noticed that they were not received well. Speaking truth, saints seemed like enemies to God's people. Just as many disciples lapsed and left Jesus when his words sounded hard, so Jerome reflected, "It should hardly be surprising if we too offend a good many people when we strip away their vices."[56] Jesus's own caustic words of reproof offended his fellow Jews, but they were delivered to restore them to holiness.

The wit of Athanasius, Augustine, and Jerome was spiked with salt. In an era when many clergy and ascetics questioned the validity of satiric discourse and of bodily laughter itself, these fathers found part of their holy calling in using humor as a rhetorical means to challenge both enemies and friends. Even offensive wit was fair, Jerome argued, if it helps to reform their wicked souls.

Patron Saints of Comedy

For one pagan, mocking of the Christian faith unexpectedly led to his conversion. The legendary St. Genesius became the patron saint of comedians, actors, and scoffers in an unexpected, and even comic, way. Around 303 CE, the comic playwright performed for Emperor Diocletian, presenting a farce mocking baptism and ridiculing Christian rituals. Genesius jested, "You fools, I wish to die a Christian." Allegedly, as the emperor laughed, a priest entered. The ironic Genesius quipped, "I wish to receive the grace of Christ, I long to be reborn and set free from all the sin that lies around me." The emperor hooted hilariously and lavished wine upon the performers. However, just before the water washed his head, Genesius received a vision of angels carrying a book with all his sins listed in it. The mock baptism then unleashed its true efficacy, as the hypocritical sacrament radically altered him.

Now Genesius was no longer acting the hypocrite. He began a sermon:

> Oh Emperor, listen people of Rome, especially if you have a mind of your own and know how to use it. Before today, whenever I heard the name Christian, it would make me sick and angry. I would make fun of them and encourage others to abuse them. Over and over I insulted them and encouraged others to be violent towards them. I so hated Christians, that I deserted my own family as a child when I realized that there were Christians among them. So much did I hate them, that I went secretly among them to learn their secrets.
>
> O great Diocletian, I started this play as a way to deride the Christian mysteries in which I did not believe. Yet lying on that make-believe sick bed and having an actor-priest pour water over me, I found that the words I was speaking were true. I wrote this play, these are my words. But now they are the words of my heart. I believe and when I said these words today, I saw the very angels of God surround me. The angels told me that my sins were really forgiven and that water that washed me washed away all the evil I have done.
>
> I came here today to please an earthly Emperor but what I have done is to please a heavenly King. I came here to give you laughter, but what I have done is to give joy to God and his angels. From this moment on,

> believe me, I will never mock these great mysteries again. I now know that the Lord Jesus Christ is the true God, the Light, the Truth and the Mercy of all who have received his gift of baptism.[57]

Furious at this turn, Diocletian demanded the entire troupe be punished. While his fellow actors protested they were not Christians, cursing the name of Jesus, Genesius stood and submitted to the emperor's tortures. Just before being beheaded, he confessed: "Our Lord Jesus Christ is God and we shall have life in His name."

The transformation of this scoffing pagan, aligned with the realms of ridicule, into a martyr suggests that no satirist is safe from meddling by the Divine. Today, the Internet Guild of St. Genesius exists for floundering unemployed actors and converted mockers. In a similar spirit, Our Church of St. Mary's of the Angels was constructed in Los Angeles in 1930 for contrite Hollywood actors. It is not well-attended.

Legends surround St. Lawrence, martyred in Rome around 258 CE during the era of Emperor Valerian. When the authorities demanded the treasures of the church, Lawrence asked for three days (during which he distributed whatever resources the church had to those in need) and then showed up with a great company of cripples, the poor, and the blind and told the superior, "Here are the true treasures of the Church." This led, inevitably, to his martyrdom, whereby he was stuck like a pig on a gridiron and roasted by his persecutors. After a brief period on his side, he looked at his executioners and quipped, "You might want to turn me over; I think I am well done on this side." Or, as he toasted in Latin, "Assum est, inquit, versa et manduca," causing his torturers to enjoy their work with laughter. St. Lawrence became the patron saint of butchers, cooks, chefs, comedians, and roasters, of both sorts.

The archbishop most responsible for provoking a massive shift towards the raucous Middle Ages appeared early in the tenth century in Cappadocia. Arethas of Caesarea commissioned translations of Plato and Lucian, sneaking impudent laughter into the Byzantine Christian community. Przemyslaw Marciniak suggests that the bishop saw that "the ability to laugh is as natural to a man as the ability to neigh to a horse, when he says that a man will not be seen neighing and horse laughing."[58] While not ridiculing the Christian faith itself, satirical texts would pop out of Byzantium to satirize the false worship of relics, as in the example of the monk who collected "eight legs of Saint Nestor, five breasts of Saint Barbara, and no fewer than four heads of Saint George."[59] Such saints of God were more akin to hydra and octopi than men. And in the time of the Reformation, Augustinian monk Martin Luther would take up the joke of relics and extend it with panache.

Both Hebrew prophets and Roman professionals sought to shame their targets. The Hebrews hoped, however vainly, for repentance from Israelites, while the Romans tweaked the habits of their countrymen, aiming more for wit. To salvage a soul was more crucial than scoring a point for the Hebrews, but they were not without the pleasure of puncturing the pride of fools. So, too, Jesus spoke words that seared the souls of scribes, but all the while seeking to get them to search their consciences.

Church martyrs witnessed their faith with transcending humor that rose into affirmations of God's providence, rather than utilizing true satire. Some church fathers, particularly Tertullian, borrowed as much satiric sauce from the secular culture as from their Savior. His irascible wit placed him in the lower right Quad, with caustic righteous indignation exposing enemies of the faith. So too, his fellow patriarch Jerome employed sharp and harsh wit to cut through stupidity; his Vulgate translation would soon be followed by all manner of wild and crazy vulgar laughter in the Middle Ages. Satiric impulses to reform would wane as the fun would wax. The carnival was about to begin. The professionals and the prophets would relinquish the fun of satire to the people. Reform would take a back seat.

4

Medieval Jesters and Roosters

Jesters do oft prove prophets.
—William Shakespeare, *King Lear*

While the biblical era censured the shame of religious sinners, the medieval era inaugurated a carnival of laughter, tittering at vice more than preaching for repentance. After Constantine's conversion and death, the Roman Empire declined, as licentious comedies joined gladiator fights to entertain the bread-and-circus crowds. Actually, these demanding spectators would clamor for actors to be stripped of their clothing, including the old fools playing their parts. They were to act nakedly, or as humorist Lewis Grizzard would say, "Nekkid," explaining that "in the south there's a difference between 'Naked' and 'Nekkid.' 'Naked' means you don't have any clothes on. 'Nekkid' means you don't have any clothes on . . . and you're up to somethin.'"[1] While Christianity in the Middle Ages would disapprove of the nekkid, dissolute stage, censuring what it saw as degenerate, the comedy of religious satire would be up to something.[2]

Many medieval churchmen remained suspicious of laughter. Earnestness reigned. Yet medieval satire also exhibited a high tolerance for excretory and sexual frankness, leading to what Bakhtin characterized as grotesque realism. The facts of life were, simply, the facts of life, and laughter would resound with the use of the body in all its glorious and hilarious parts, juices, functions, and emissions. Mucus, urine, spit, sweat, semen, blood, farts, and dung would mix with the spiritual aspects of humanity to make for comic juxtapositions, of which Rabelais's mixed dish of vulgar satire would be the apotheosis. Instead of a monarch's scepter, the era was ruled with a fool's *marotte*, the scepter with the carved head on top.[3]

Bakhtin identified a particular brand of folk comedy that permeated the Middle Ages as "carnival" laughter. In the Enlightenment, this laughter would be supplanted by a sneer, moving from Rabelais's belly laughter to Voltaire's sarcasm. Marked by three characteristics, carnival laughter is grotesque, ambivalent, and universal. Its grotesqueness centers on the body, with one of his most noteworthy images being that of a pregnant, senile old hag, who carries life about in her dead body. A salient quality of the grotesque is its marriage of the sublime and the ridiculous, celebrating the dual origin of the human being in earth and divine breath. The fact that God would become man stretched the comic incongruity to its zenith.

Ambivalence combines both subversion and reaffirmation. It mocks and derides, then revives and celebrates the life and faith of the people. Ideally, in breaking down the society, it is able to rebuild it. Finally, universal, or catholic, carnival laughter includes everyone, rich and poor, powerful and weak, pious and profane. It brings the larger body of people together in community, making everyone laugh and making everyone the target of laughter. Carnival laughter is ultimately a holy way of understanding life.[4] Like the promise of Mary's *Magnificat*, the laughter of the carnival would raise up the humble and bring down the mighty.

Through sermons and various writings, medieval satire showcased vices like avarice, greed, simony (both as bribe-taking and selling of religious offices), sodomy, and cow-tipping comedy that existed within the church. Clergy were frequently personified as ravenous wolves in the bestiaries. As early as the eighth century, the Venerable Bede, a Benedictine historian, complained of "those who make mirth in the dwelling of bishops."[5] It was an era when the church impiously expanded earthly power and increased wealth, corruption, and immorality. If you honored the Roman Catholic Church with your donations of gold and silver, it would welcome you into the blessings of the church and even secure salvation itself.

Mock Money Gospels, parodies of scriptural texts that substituted money for God, directed parishioners to "ask, seek, and knock" with a quest for gold and silver, rather than God's grace. The practice of monks misconstruing biblical texts for guffaws would leave a puckish habit for later seminarians.[6] A play on 1 Peter 4:8 asks the question: "What is Charity?" The answer is: "The monastic habit." "Why?" "Because it covers a multitude of sins."

Medieval literature and pulpit oratory abound with satirical commentaries on religion. As the vernacular began to spread into religious discourse, a vulgar and lively species of satire started leaking into the public spheres. While some pious members vigorously protested the flagrant contradictions within the church, it availed little. In particular, the thirteenth century introduced the goliardic Latin poetry of the *clerici ribaldi*, wandering scholars who performed rude burlesques of pulpit oratory.[7] As Nathan Schachner observes, the Confession of Golias was "a song of the open road, of the vagabond life, of taverns and hard drinking, of sport and mocking irreverence, of love, of spring, of gamesters, of poverty, of sorrow and defiance. Its gods are the pagan gods—Venus, Bacchus, and Decius, god of dice. Christianity is all but forgotten."[8]

Imitating Bishop Golias, their grotesque and mercenary prelate, these tonsured sophomores parodied everything sacred. As traveling theology students, they begged, performed, or connived for money. These impudent pups with shaven heads took licentious delight in the wine cup and subverted sacred and romantic ideas with coarse and cheerful irreverence. These wandering ribald scholars would sing the Confession of Golias with merry *esprit de corps*:

> To my mind all gravity
> Is a grave subjection;
> Sweeter far than honey are
> Jokes and free affection.
> All that Venus bids me do
> Do I with erection,
> For she ne'er in heart of man
> Dwelt with dull dejection.[9]

Disturbances at St. Remy and the University of Paris were blamed on the goliards who allegedly processed to mass, "each trailing a herring on a string along the ground, the game being to step on the herring in front and keep your own herring from being trod on."[10] Some clerks (and some priests) would sing wanton songs and dress as women. They would also eat black pudding and play dice on the altar, burning "stinking" incense from smoking old shoes, rousing laughter from bystanders. By 1289, mandates would dictate that no clerk should be a jongleur, goliard, or buffoon.

Sacred parodies (*parodia sacra*) of the Lord's Supper persisted and prospered. Cyprian's supper (*Coena cypriani*) offered a festive travesty of scriptures, as liturgies of the drunkards or gamblers (rarely accountants) were celebrated. "Father Bacchus, who art in cups, hallowed be good wine. Thy ruination come. Thy turmoil be done in the cup as it is in the tavern. Give us this day our daily drink. And send our cups to us as we send forth to fellow drinkers. And lead us not into drunkenness, but do not deliver us from wine."[11] Here appeared the great literary joke and legend of the fictitious St. Nemo, or Nobody, celebrated for having seen God and having done wondrous signs: "Nobody hath seen God" and "Nobody can do these signs that Thou dost." One marveled that "Nobody could serve two masters."[12]

Vagabond Songs

As the wheel of fortune turned the pages of the calendar, medieval vagabonds threw caution to the wind and belted out popular carefree tunes such as "Carmina Burana":

> Let's away with study,
> Folly's sweet.
> Treasure all the pleasure
> Of our youth:
> Time enough for age
> To think on truth.[13]

They enjoyed their Pastime with Good Company (in *Taberna Quando Sumus*), gathering and lustily singing a toast to anything they could soberly think of, spreading an egalitarian friendliness across class lines. First they toasted the wealth of wine, then to those in prison and those still living, to false and fickle nuns, crooked friars, troublemakers, and last to "King and Pope we all inordinately tope." In the song, everyone drinks: the mistress, the master, the soldier, and even the cleric. Swift and slothful, fair and dark, faithful and fickle, ignorant louts and men of letters drink. Even the granny and the dog drink.

Their taverns had ecclesiastical names like Mitre or Chapel-Bell.[14] They rated mendicant orders on their drinking prowess. "The Capuchins drink poorly, Benedictines deeply, Dominicans pint after pint, but Franciscans drink the cellar dry."[15]

In his collection of theological sermons, *Summa Predicantium*, English Dominican John Bromyard complained of bankruptcy of the soul. Believing that the moral purpose of satire had dissipated in these dark times. Bromyard compiled an anthology of sermons, printed in Basel in 1484, which addressed moral problems with wit. In one homiletic vision of a fair lady, assumed to be the Blessed Virgin Mary, the apparition turns its back and displays a most foul posterior. Such is the image of the church, the bride of Christ, that what is supposed to be beautiful and glorious is actually coarse. We see its backside, and it is old, wrinkled, and quite embarrassing.

Sermon tales and jests abound in *joca monachorum*, monk jokes. In one sermon entitled the "Devil's Letter," Satan greets the princes of the church, thanking them for the souls they continually dispatch to him. Friars are so greedy that they take bribes from heretics. *Everything* a Beguine nun does is viewed, tongue-in-cheek, as spiritual and pious: "if she sleeps, she's in religious ecstasy."[16] Another silly tale concerns a nun who got pregnant and excused her condition on the fact that she couldn't call out for help when the man mounted her, lest she break her vow of silence.[17]

The scheming religious hypocrite was labeled foxy, like the fox in the fable. He lay in the road pretending to be dead so that he might be put in the cart and eat the poultry; so "the hypocrites pretend to be modest, humble, compliant, and dead, as it were, to all vices and sins, especially in the eyes of those who can assist them further to the thing they are panting after, in order that they may be set in offices and promoted."[18] It comes as no surprise that monks cherished the boisterous mirth in fables like the *Romance of Renard the Fox* over the missals.

Among English antiquarian Thomas Wright's *Selection of Latin Stories* (1842), one medieval tale tells of the burial of a wolf in which a bear celebrates mass; an ox reads the Gospels; an ass brays the Epistles; a goat rings the bell; a hare carries the holy water; and then all feast. The manuscript attacks the sluggish and stinking orders of Benedictines and Augustinians, and once the animal monks begin their feast, they start looking for another funeral to conduct for their pleasure. Likewise, Sebastian Brandt's friend, the inventive and extremely popular Strasburg preacher, Jacob Geiler, defined the qualities of a typical monk as including an almighty belly, an ass's back, and a raven's mouth. Rather than pious preachers, the orders were seen as greedy as magpies, or "magpious" priests.[19]

Clergy scandalously led hounds and falcons to the chase rather than leading their congregations to devotion. In satirical sermons directed at their vices, the devil would find the monastery gate open to him because he entered with another cleric. As the prophet Isaiah had observed, it was "as with the people, so with the priest" (24:2). Many would excuse themselves from the hearing of sermons in order to hunt, attend theaters, or visit race tracks. Even the gargoyles, the grinning corbel-heads, leer from their vantage points on the high cathedrals, looking more like slothful clergy who whine about any task they have been assigned.[20] The satirists of the medieval age would therefore take their place in the upper left of the Quad, where satire celebrated humor and ridicule over substantial reform.

Jocular Preachers

Medieval preachers were conveniently compared to roosters. Both creatures rose at dawn, mounted a pulpit or hill, crowed loudly to get attention, took the best grain, and laid the hens. Satirists were loud shrill mockingbirds against these proud cocks, raucously cracking words of reproof.

The *Summa Predicandium* included many sermons making sport of the church. Several jocular preachers were known as pious buffoons of the pulpit, engaging audiences in creatively dramatic ways, such as throwing their wigs in the faces of their congregations. They flourished, according to nineteenth-century British flimflam man of humor Isaac D'Israeli, by mixing extravagant doses of illustration in their grave admonitions with a dollop of comic tales borrowed from licentious writers. During this era, everything was candidly called by its name, and even the "grossest indecency was never concealed under a gentle periphrasis."[21] Even in hell, ridicule held sway. In Dante's *Inferno*, such medieval mocking rings clearly. As the author and Virgil wander into the fifth pouch of the eighth circle of hell, they see demon claws grabbing sinners and casting them into utter darkness. Dante fears their gnashing of teeth, but Virgil consoles him, pointing to their signs of mocking: each one thrusts his tongue between his teeth towards their leader, who had made a trumpet of his rump.[22] His retort of a fart turns away their derisive wrath, even as a clever sermon would avert the boorish behaviors of uncouth congregations.

Two remarkable Franciscan preachers aiming at moral reform were the clever Oliver Maillard and the golden-tongued Michael Menot. Maillard attacked cheating in trade, castigating the rapine and usury of bankers, who charged working men exorbitant interest in order to buy their ladies unnecessary gifts. He castigated their ladies, "It is for *you* all this damnation ensues. Yes! Yes! You must have rich satins, and girdles of gold out of this accursed money. When anyone has anything to receive from the husband, he must first make a present to the wife of some fine gown, or girdle, or ring. If you ladies and gentlemen who wear scarlet clothes, I believe if you were closely put in a good press, we should see the blood of the poor gush out, with which your scarlet is dyed."[23] Maillard revived the satire of Isaiah and Juvenal, stripping dowagers of privilege.

Menot mocked the fashionable prevalence of swearing in his day, so common, he quipped, "that the child of five years can swear; and even the old dotard of eighty, who has only two teeth remaining, can fling out an oath!" Menot's sermons called all estates to account, skewering lawyers, married couples, and especially those within the church. He instructed ecclesiastics how to conduct themselves and warned girls not to be duped by them. He told the clergy to imitate the lark who "feels her pleasure in singing, and in singing, ascends towards heaven." Instead, they copied frogs that croak out day and night, and "think they have a fine throat, but always remain fixed in the mud."

Menot and Maillard set examples of satiric pulpit oratory, judiciously indulging their natural genius and bandying about humorous and lively utterances to keep the attention of their audiences. Jocular preachers were not always laughing; instead, they told bold truths "that made many a coquette blush." Such preachers possessed the art of biting when they smiled and more ably combated vice by ingenious satire than by vague platitudes, to which no one really listened. Colloquial preachers were frequently risible, imitating Horace's dictum on telling the truth with laughter, *ridendo dicere verum quid vetat*. To effectually censure the reigning vices, they willingly employed puns rather than sublime thoughts. One preacher, Father Gardeau, who solemnly declaimed against immodesty in the church, produced little effect, as the women persisted in the prevailing fashion of displaying uncovered bosoms. He exclaimed: "Cover your nakedness! At least before me. Is it necessary to tell ye, that I am made of flesh and blood, as other men?" At this everyone laughed; particularly the ladies. He then said soberly, "When I speak to you with cautious decency, and ambiguous expressions, you are deaf; and when I address you in the clearest ones, you find them ridiculous, and you laugh. What hope can there remain of your amendment?"

Medieval jocular preachers deployed *exempla*, comic stories and witticisms, "preachable conceits" for their pulpit oratory, such as the old wheeze in which an elderly woman endures a sermon on hellfire, hearing that there will be horrible wailing, weeping, grinding, and, worst of all, gnashing of teeth.But, she mutters, "Pastor, I don't got no teeth." To which she receives the disconcerting reply, "Teeth will be provided."[24]

Comic and even burlesque sermons used to attract crowds to church services were matched with dramatic presentations and passion plays of the fifteenth century, in which town guilds cooperated with church officials to enliven the stories of the Bible.[25] Entertaining characters like Noah and his shrewish wife were represented alongside the more penitential ceremonies regarding Christ's passion. While joy was elicited from scenes regarding the Resurrection, a more vulgar humor amused the crowd with the harrowing of hell episodes. On seeking an ambassador to tell the Virgin Mother of the Resurrection, Jesus rejects Adam (too many fruits might distract him), Noah (too addicted to wine and delays), and others, showing that the common frailties and follies of the patriarchs connected them with common people.[26] The provoking of Easter laughter, *risus paschalis*, was amplified through both sermons and theatrical cycles.

Rustic Sports

One particularly curious thirteenth-century religious French *trouvere*, traveling as Ruteboeuf (1245–1285), frolicked about as a master of narrative verse, singing ballads (*verse contes*), rhyming fables, and indecent songs. His specialty consisted of mocking the vices of the Mendicant orders of friars and monks, who received generous favors from Pope Alexander. As the black-friar Dominicans instigated the Inquisition, they roosted high in the political pecking order and thus suffered the brunt of Ruteboeuf's raillery. The more austere and ascetic Franciscans (and thereby somewhat more spiritually pretentious) were also ripe for the picking in his sexually oriented fabliaux.

Historian Nancy Regalado points out that the professionally virtuous are more potentially comic when they sin than ordinary mortals.[27] This principle rings true in Rutebouef's work, which often celebrates lowly peasants while ribbing religious authorities. Derived from *rude boeuf* and *rude oeuvre*, meaning "coarse ox" or "rustic piece of work," his name fits his trade well. Out of affection for the publicans and peasants, Ruteboeuf tells the sad tale of "The Peasant's Fart." A particular peasant ate so much beef with garlic and hot fat broth that his belly grew tighter than a drum skin. He was going to die unless he could drop a fart. Seeking to collect the gas in a leather bag, he was warned by a proverb that if he pushed too hard, he would release shit. However, he was able to capture his fart in the bag. The devil tossed the bag into hell, but the fart escaped the bag. All the demons scattered in frenzy and agreed never to take a peasant's stinking soul into hell. Thus, poor peasants can't go to hell because the devils find them too revolting. Their works are like dung and only grace can rescue them.[28] Ordinary people celebrated Ruteboeuf's coarse and robust series of *fabliaux*, especially as he championed them over their spiritual leaders.

Censorship of such goliards came from official church councils. The radical Council of Basel prohibited the church-sanctioned Feast of Fools, at which, among other activities, hee-haws would replace the liturgical amen during the mock services, peasants would dress as dukes, and common folk would eat and dance. The holy synod of Basel detested these abuses. It forbade clergy to allow these and similar frivolities in churches, which ought to be houses of prayer, and in cemeteries.[29]

Perhaps it was not so radical for wandering goliards to reflect what was wrong with the church during the fourteenth century, as the church itself wandered as a wastrel prodigal from 1309 to 1378, escaping the urban blight of Rome with a brief Avignon vacation. While the great humanist Petrarch leveled his more serious invectives against the religious polygamy of the church, another document cut more quickly to the heart of the matter. In fact, in 1393, little John, or more properly—Jean Petit—scribbled out his satire on the multiple popes of the Great Schism entitled "The Complaint of Lady Church," in which the Bride of Christ laments that she is the wife of two husbands (Clement and Boniface) and simultaneously a widow. So, too, the beloved Swedish St. Bridget confronts the saintly Pope Urban V, persuading him to move back from Avignon to Rome, where she had received a fantastic vision in St. Peter's. In her ecstasy, she had seen the nave filled with mitred hogs and asked the Lord what they were. He answered that they were "the bishops and abbots of today."[30]

Proverbial and Holy Fools

This carnival culture of folk humor, in comic rituals and pageants, comic verbal compositions, and wild billingsgate (derived from the raucous, foul language used by fishmongers) contributed to a festive community. It offered a madcap gala of masks and merry mayhem; people transgressed social norms and laughed.

The greatest comic celebration was the aforementioned Feast of Fools (*festa stultorum*). Mocking the rituals of church services with a topsy-turvy masquerade, revelers crowned the Lord of Misrule, the pope of unrepressed partying. The feast inverted official ways of dressing and behaving, making all monks merry and some quite wanton. When narrow-minded clerics sought to suppress the feast, the theological faculty of the Sorbonne rose to its defense, arguing that folly "which is second nature to man and seems to be inborn, may at least once a year have free outlet. Wine casks would burst if we failed sometimes to remove the bung and let in air."[31] The feast released the bung.

In this culture of feasting and foolery, beasts, like the ass, were recruited as grotesque symbols. Carved gargoyles, bestiaries, and devils adorned or rather uglified cathedrals. Tucked into the crevices and crannies of majestic churches were comic carvings of a monk making love to a nun, a wife beating her husband, and monkeys wearing bishops' mitres. Around 1140, St. Bernard inquired what purpose "these ridiculous monstrosities, those prodigies of beauties deformed or deformities made beautiful" added to their meditations. "Why those nasty monkeys, those furious lions, those animals half human?" Bernard complained that the brothers spent more time trying to decipher the marble figures and less on their books.[32] Some saw these grotesque stone monsters as evidence of "the Devil [who] broods over the vastness of Notre Dame."[33] Yet, as G. K. Chesterton so aptly noted, many of these gargoyles were not present to simply ward off evil or just to "gargle" water from the roofs. Instead, they served a more biblical purpose: if the people of God no longer praised God as St. Peter's "living stones," the very stones of gargoyles would cry out in praise.

Medieval fools (from the Latin *follis*, meaning "bag of wind") were of three distinct kinds: first, the festival fool (or motley fool, as Shakespeare would later describe him in *As You Like It*) led the community in celebration. This fool held a license to speak the truth under the cover of wit, much like King Lear's fool, costumed with bells, baubles, and ass-ears. Second, the proverbial fool (*dixit insipiens*) stumbled out of the Hebrew book of Proverbs, as the fool who said in his heart "there is no God" (Psalm 53:1). The third kind of fool was identified in St. Paul's designation of the "fool for Christ," those whose otherworldly wisdom made him appear foolish to secular audiences.

If the first category, one finds a host of fool literature (*Narren-literatur*) that culminated around 1348 with the great plague of Europe.[34] Artist Hans Holbein's later *Dance of Death* (1538) captured the end of this fool in vivid, ironic detail. For example, a mendicant friar who has just filled his begging box finds that death arrives to empty him of life. As a pretty young nun kneels at the altar, smiling at her lover playing a lute, death disguised as a hideous old hag extinguishes altar candles. Death stands in the pulpit behind a loquacious preacher, and prepares to strike him down for his long-winded sermons with a jaw-bone. Death lifts a cardinal's hat just as he hands a letter of indulgence to a rich patron. Such fools forget the mutability of time and do not count on the arrival of death.

Appearing on the vellum of illuminated prayer books came a warning to these fools: "Ecce Diabolus!"[35] By the fifteenth century, crude devilish images that threatened terror to the imaginations of illiterate devotees devolved into cunning and grotesque caricatures, like *New Yorker* cartoons. The sudden intrusion of the grim messenger into human lives became sprightly. The psalter of the bloody Queen Mary offered comic, exuberant images of devils roping kings and bishops (perhaps her father Henry VIII or his Anglican "heretics"). It wasn't long until donkeys playing harps or monkeys throwing feces would inhabit the manuscripts.

With the dance of death and the devil came a company of fat abbots, zealous preachers, and ostentatious bishops. A long catalogue of human follies in *The Ship of Fools* showed the wages of sin. Everyone must pay the piper for his or her iniquity, including clerics kneeling at prayer, knights parading falcons and yelping dogs, girls of wanton laughter "ogled by young men," and lawyers conferring with their clients.[36] These fools deserved, and duly received, the penalty of their faithlessness or folly: they died.

The third kind of fool was one that suffered for God's sake. When the Apostle Paul called himself a "Fool for Christ," he inaugurated a tradition of the holy fool, taking "the foolish things of the world to shame the wise" (1 Corinthians 1:27). Such a fool was often dressed like a court jester and so garnered the sobriquet of a silly fool. Significantly, the English word "silly" is derived from the Greek *sali*, which means blessed, similar to the Greek term for the saints who are holy fools, the *yurodivi*. The blessed are the silly ones, with "blessed" also suggesting the Beatitudes, the series of proclamations by Jesus that turn the world's values upside down. Those that mourn shall be comforted; the meek shall inherit the earth; they that weep shall laugh.

The satiric work of the fool juxtaposed apparent folly with real stupidity. As John Saward observes, "Folly for Christ's sake is always *eschatological*. The holy fool proclaims the conflict between this present world and the world to come."[37] The politics of the holy fool is redemptive *and* satirically madcap, flaunting deeds of folly and employing the absurd to revive a sense of what is right and good. The true fool reduced human pomposity back to human humility. When one sixteenth-century jester saw a prissy French ambassador kiss the pope's feet, he exclaimed: "Merciful heavens! If a representative of the King of France kisses his Holiness's *foot*, what part of the pope will a fellow like me have to kiss?"[38]

One of the greatest of these sacred idiots was the anchorite St. Simeon, the holy fool of Emesa, who lived around 570 CE and whose story typifies that of other such silly saints. Living for decades on lentils in an isolated cave next to the Dead Sea, Simeon at first struggled against temptation and then advanced to a remarkable degree of holiness. Prone

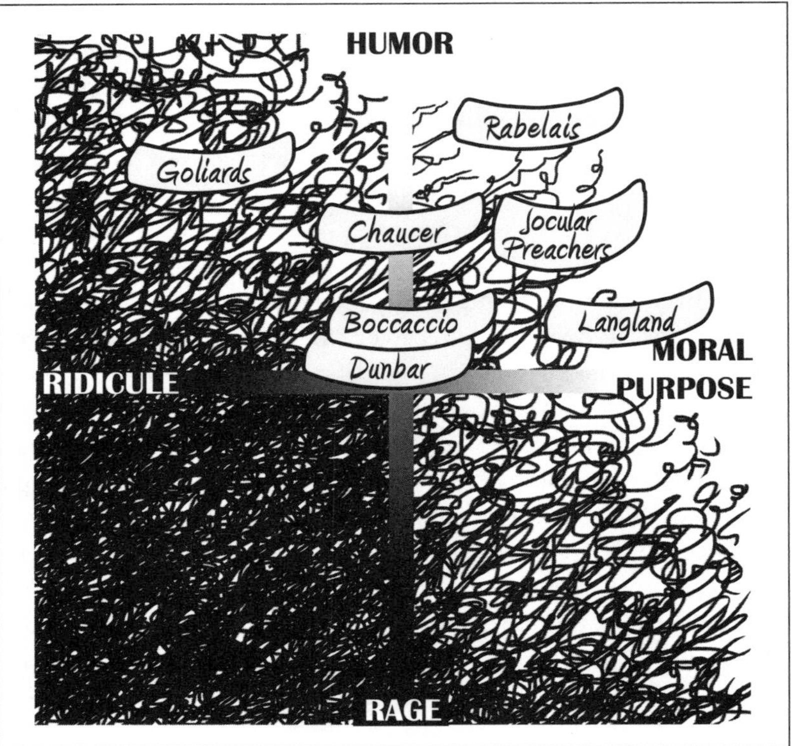

Goliards, Rabelais, Chaucer, the Jocular Preachers, Boccaccio, Langland, and Dunbar on the Quad of Satire.

to run naked through crowds or throw walnuts at clergy who preached too long, his vocation took a comic twist when he slipped out of his cave one day and visited the city of Emesa in Syria. Arriving at the city gate, he found a dead dog on a dung heap. He thereupon tied its limp leg to a rope around his waist and triumphantly entered the city, dragging the lifeless canine behind him. His prophetic message was clear: the cares of this world are like dead weight on the wealthy, as they are only carrying around a dead dog. Or maybe, the message wasn't that clear.

Such holy fools and jocular preachers were on a mission from God, but one festooned with liberal humor. Unlike the goliards whose mischief neglected any notion of reform, these satirists, and the many that followed, inhabited the upper right realm in the Quad, where their humor had purpose. However, their intention to hold up the mirror of censure did not keep them from laughing and causing their targets to laugh heartily.

Naughty, Bawdy Morals

In 1348, it didn't matter what kind of fool you were, as one-third of Europe would succumb to the Black Death. As the plague hit Florence, a young bawdy Giovanni Boccaccio (1313–1375) gathered a patrician coterie of ten attractive young people (with a very favorable ratio of seven young women to three men) and set off for the countryside to find a safe refuge from the disease. For ten days, each person told one story each night at the villa, culminating in the invention of the one hundred bawdy, ironic, and tragic stories in the *Decameron*.

Boccaccio gained a reputation for writing Latin poetry, translating a vernacular version of Livy for an emerging audience of middle-class readers. As the father of Italian prose, he drew upon the legends and tales retold by troubadours and old ladies, and he wrote his own—ultimately moral—satire. Boccaccio believed that the Black Death had been a scourge sent by "God's just wrath upon mortals."[39] Taking note of the vices of his day, he symbolized three enduring actions of God's providence among men and women: the ever-changing and capricious Wheel of Fortune, which gives gifts or takes away the same; Love; and Ingenuity, coupled with productive industry. His use of the rhetorical strategies of rhythmical medieval *cursus* (cadences in letter writing and preaching) effectively combined swift and staccato moments with his flourishing prose. Herein he imitated the famed Roman orator Cicero, who sought to use the dagger (*pugiunculus*) as well as the broadsword in bleeding his targets.

Boccaccio's aim was not merely to amuse with his one hundred novellas or to cloak his thoughts in allegory. Rather, as medieval scholar Vittore Branca shows, Boccaccio moved from comic rebuke of vice through a "carefully planned eulogy of virtue" on the last day.[40] His portrait of the human comedy led to Virtue, but only after some very frisky and bawdy tales.

The tales recount all manner of topics. Friars are continually fried for failing to live up to Christian standards. They are susceptible to carnality, as in the story of the beautiful, but dumb, girl seeking to live a Christian life. Going to an all-too-human monk, she desperately seeks how to get rid of the devil. The monk finally bids her remove her clothing. As both stand naked, he indicates that his red, angry devil must be sent to hell, which it is in her power to do, as she possesses the gateway to the lower world. (Tertullian once commented that the lusts of a woman were the "devil's gateway."[41]) She discovers her first time of "sending of the devil to hell" causes her pain, but then she begins to enjoy it immensely and looks for opportunities to keep sending that devil to hell. She wears out the monk and then complains to the old ladies of the village that she has no more devils to send to hell. They all laugh uproariously and tell her to get married to a young buck so she can continue doing her spiritual work.

As Augustan poet Alexander Pope cautioned readers, "Read each work of wit with the same spirit that its author writ." And here Boccaccio wrote with that wink-wink, nod-nod, know-what-I-mean kind of wit that made sport of naïve and gullible youth. Curiously enough, it is a joke like Boccaccio's, and not, as many erroneously believe, an admonition from the Bible, that makes the artificial connection between sex and original sin.

Boccaccio concluded his tales with a nod to the wisdom of the world exploited by religious men. The human ingenuity evident in his naughty tale about monks taking advantage of young women presents quick snapshots of Italian medieval society, capturing in dazzling rhetorical rhythms and virile wit the real behavior of fallen creatures. His rustic, vulgar fables were written "as a help and refuge for ladies in love" to evoke laughter, but also to remind his readers that there was a higher standard of virtue from which all had fallen, but to which all might still aspire. It is important to reiterate, that after his erotic tales, Boccaccio reminded his readers of more virtuous and exemplary stories. One must face and confess the facts of sin inherent in the human species before one lays down an ideal of virtue and holiness. The *Decameron* offers such delicious, titillating, and saucy confessions, and works as authentic satire.

Plowing Fields of Satire

William Langland (1330–1387) employed the medieval mode of allegory to caustically comment on corruption in the fourteenth-century church and society. As a fellow of Oriel College, Oxford, he was keenly aware of public abuses and private vices.[42] The church had suffered like the rest of society during the calamity of the Black Death. Three Canterbury bishops died as well as eight hundred priests in Norwich. But such tragedy did not mitigate the corruption Langland saw within the church. In his *Vision of William, Concerning Piers Plowman*, his prime character is a common, honest plowman named Piers, who walks the streets of London observing priests, bishops, and ordinary folk. Piers calls for his readers to respond as "pilgrymes are we alle."[43] As he naps and falls asleep on the Malvern Hills, Piers perceives a succession of twenty dreams.

In his allegorical correspondence of characters to themes, he sets forth the seven deadly sins. Avarice comes across as an old hag, with sagging leather cheeks, bleary-eyed, beetled-browed, thick-lipped, and with louse-infested hair. Her habit of hoarding extends to keeping creeping lice on her body. She is the kind of greedy old girl that would not only count sheep in her sleep, but steal sheep from other sleepers. Langland's work is a knockabout comedy, with jesting street plays and rampant vices, all of which expose his English society falling short of what it means to live according to Christian principles. This failure is due, in no small part, to the sham of church officials. Their racket to extort, butcher, and shear sheep, rather than to guide and feed them, becomes the cause of his writing.

Called a "ventriloquist for orthodoxy," Langland criticized those who spend time visiting "holy" places as sanctimonious hypocrites, rotten bores who neglect to obey the higher law of God in serving one's own neighbors. (He described one friar as a "great churl and a germ, with a face as fat as a full bladder."[44])

Langland focuses upon the female Mead (Lucre, or money), who seduces men with promises of delight, reward, and security. Ms. Mead urges religious men to compromise their virtues for her sake. She will let lords and ladies live in lechery, as long as they tithe to her.

> I'll be your friend, my friar, and never fail you
> As long as you love those lords that like lechery
> And fault not their ladies who love the same.
> It's only the flesh's frailty, as your books say,

> Nature's way of bringing us forth.
> If one avoids slander, its harm can be undone;
> It's the easiest forgiven of the seven sins.
> Be merciful to the men that persist in it
> And I'll have your church roofed and build you a cloister
> Have your walls washed and your windows glazed
> And pay those that paint and make pictures for you
> So that all men will say I'm one of your order.[45]

A good Conscience is invited to marry Mead, but refuses. Conscience accuses her of poisoning popes and impairing Holy Church; all monks and lepers, learned and rude lie with her as they please. Mead doesn't care whom she screws, as long as she keeps her influence.

> She's privy with the pope and provisors know it,
> For simony and she herself seal their bulls.
> She blesses bishops that can barely read:
> She provides prebends for parsons and upholds priests
> Who keep lovers and mistresses all their lives,
> And produce children forbidden by law.[46]

Piers Plowman develops like a corkscrew, not in a linear fashion, but like a spiraling staircase, in which the dreamer reflects on earlier moments on his journey. His journey begins with simple field workers and travels to the papal curia. The view from the steeple differs from the view in the pews, but sinners remain the same.

In the center of the journey is the Rood (or Cross) of Crucifixion. The whole work revolves around this symbol of divine love. Unlike the meditative mystics of his age (Julian of Norwich and her hazelnut), Langland, in his spare and restrained piety, did not use the cross as the primary figure of devotion.[47] Instead, he populated his work with key allegorical figures around the cross, characters like Mead, Clergy, Study, Patience, Conscience, and Hunger (who scares everybody into working), showing us the relation of all of life to this central Christian event. Like the Hebrew prophet Isaiah, Langland showed how God scours all aspects of daily life.

On the Way to Canterbury

The folly and vanity of the three estates continue in Geoffrey Chaucer's (1343–1400) *Canterbury Tales*, a rollicking portrait of fourteenth-century England. Starting from the Tabard Inn in Southwark, Chaucer's prologue describes the ripe season of sweet April showers, newly springing flowers, the refreshing breath of the west wind, and the melodies of the small birds. So, as one might think, in such a fertile spring, a young man's fancy will turn to the idea of—pilgrimages. Chaucer boldly satirized the church tradition of the holy pilgrimage to visit the "market" of St. Becket, where the church could make a lot of money from the sale of pardons, indulgences, and some very fine and odd relics. The tagline seems to be less like "come worship the Lord" than "Get your souvenirs here."

As the agonistic pilgrims set out to the Canterbury Cathedral to atone for their sins, they tell stories along the way, some serious and some bawdy, but mostly comic according to Aristotle's definition: a serious story with a happy resolution. Each traveler assumes a socially defined role, such as the Prioress, who, although a nun, imitates the dainty manners of a lady of the court with her retinue of little dogs. (Only the poor Parson seems devout, refusing to excommunicate those who can't pay a tithe.) Chaucer harvested his satire from the vineyards of Boccaccio, marketing his satires within his own special bottles of sparkling wit and humor. As jocular narrator, he offers a godlike perspective on the religiously naïve and the spiritually corrupt. When John the carpenter is cuckolded in "The Miller's Tale," it is due to the wily contraptions of hanging washtubs devised by divinity student Nicholas to save the dumb cluck from impending floodwaters.

Certain characters like the Friar or the fat Monk (glistening with an oily sheen) represent flawed aspects of their calling, seeking to justify themselves. Chaucer chiseled an awareness of what each character is and what each *should* be, and here lay the primary source of the satire, assessing characters according to moral norms. Neither the Friar nor the Monk, for example, fulfills the obligations of his order, but each embodies particular vices.

Chaucer's introduction of the Monk gives us a manly man. He owns many horses in stable and rides with his bridle jingling as loud as the chapel bell. He abandons the strict rule of old St. Benedict and replaces it with "new-world manners." He dismisses traditional texts about living a cloistered, ascetic life, finding them not worth an oyster. A monk out of his cloister is not, he argued, like a fish out of water; in fact, his holy calling might actually be hunting. Why study books in a cloistered cell like a madman or work with his hands until he sweats?

Chaucer caricatures the Friar, supposedly a mendicant devoted to the selfless vows of obedience, poverty, and chastity, as a busybody full of gossip, having ingratiated himself with all the worthy women of the town everywhere. He arranges the marriages of young women and gently absolves those who come to him for confession. In fact, "He was an easy man to give penance / When knowing he should gain a good pittance." If a man repented and gave money, the friar would forgive. "Therefore, instead of weeping and of prayer, / Men should give silver to poor friars all bare."[48] One realizes quickly that this friar, named Hubert, is a sort of goliard, singing ballads with a throat as white as lily. He gives gifts to pretty wives and frequents all the taverns, knowing every good host "and each barmaid too." Better to know them than have "poverty-stricken curs" for acquaintances. With the rich, he acts quite courteously and virtuously. As Chaucer cleverly puts it, "he was the finest beggar of his house."

A third religious scoundrel appears as the worst. The Summoner, a layman in charge of arraigning those who have broken church laws, continually scavenges for bribes. Chaucer fashions him coming from the court of Rome, with stylish disheveled hair as yellow as wax, hanging down lank over his shoulders. From his smoothly shaven face, he sings lustily, with a voice like a goat: "Come hither, love, to me."

In his lap, he holds his wallet, stuffed full of pardons from Rome. He carries a pillowcase carrying our True Lady's veil, a piece of the sail from St. Peter's boat when Jesus calmed the sea, a "latten cross set full of stones and in a bottle had he some pig's bones." Every relic one would ever need, he holds to sell. In one day he can gain more money than it takes a simple parson two months to earn. "With flattery and suchlike japes, he made the parson and the rest his apes." Chaucer ironically crowns him "a fine ecclesiast." Though lecherous as a sparrow and pockmarked with boils, there is something cherubic about the Summoner. He is spuriously generous to sinners, letting a fellow keep his concubine if he shared a quart of wine. Chaucer points out that a man could keep his soul with this rascal by using well his purse; for he knows the secrets of everyone in the diocese.[49]

In Chaucer's testy prologue, the Summoner narrates a vulgar satire in which a friar descends into hell and finds no other friars around. He boasts that they must all be godly men since none is in attendance. "Not so fast," says the angel. He commands Satan to hold up his tail and let the friar see where the nest of friars resides in hell. Numerous friars fly out Satan's *ers*, swarm about the room, and then disappear back up his rear.

In 1543, the English Parliament passed the oddly named Act for the Advancement of True Religion, which restricted everyone from reading the scriptures except nobles and bishops, lest the poor misinterpret the Bible. It also forbade plays that suggested Roman Catholic or dissenting interpretations of the Bible; however, moral plays that promoted virtue and condemned vice were permitted. The fear was that "malicious minds, intending to subvert the true exposition of Scripture, have taken upon them, by printed ballads, rhymes, etc., subtly and craftily to instruct His Highness' people, and specially the youth of this his realm, untruly. For reformation whereof, His Majesty considers it most requisite to purge his realm of all such books, ballads, rhymes, and songs, as be pestiferous and noisome."[50]

However, the act excluded books printed before 1540, such as Chaucer's *Canterbury Tales*. (This act would be repealed by Edward VI, Henry VIII's Protestant son.) Ironically, the clerics abolished English publications that might enlighten, but authorized Chaucer, who snuck in satire under cover of covert mirth. His mischief with Noah's flood and the Annunciation were quite subversive in lightening the solemnity of the English ways of interpretation.

Chaucer wrote on the eve of the Reformation, exposing many of the same abuses (from the sale of indulgences to the greed of the clergy) that Martin Luther would denounce. Since his *Canterbury Tales* and reformer John Wycliffe's *New Testament* were written in vernacular English, both opened the eyes and wits of common people to see the shortcomings of the institutional church.

Ships of Fools

Italian humanist Poggio Bracciolini (1380–1459) retrieved by hook and crook numerous Latin books and manuscripts from German, Swiss, and French monastic libraries and rescued them from layers of dust into his own safekeeping. During the delays surrounding the Council of Constance, Poggio found these neglected works and translated them for fellow humanists, opening up windows for others who were to follow, such as Erasmus. Titles of his own texts betray an underlying wit, with *On Marriage in Old Age* providing a lively jest at some old coot. His *Dialogue against Hypocrites* sets forth an unyielding moral critique of many in the religious establishment. For our purposes, however, Poggio serves as comic controversialist with his *Facetiae* (1470) and its foul, impious, and anticlerical verse. Some erotic and some indecent, the verses unsparingly showcase corrupt clergy and rampant simony.[51]

At the baptism of a baby boy, a priest reads the text from John 9:6 about how Jesus bends down to pick up dust and with his spittle makes clay to heal a blind man. The woman holding the child bends down to pick up some dust as well. As she bows, she emits a horrendous fart, at which the priest announces that the devil has departed the woman because the priest was reading the Gospel.[52] A group of churchmen are portrayed as trying to snuff out a candle (*canoner*) with flatulence; one tries too hard and shits all over the room, a telling satire on those who labor too diligently on *canon* law. Such scatological humor easily ridicules empty rituals and scholastic rhetoric as gas.

The devout Catholic Sebastian Brandt supported the ascent of Maximilian I to the throne of the Holy Roman Empire as fulfilling the divine will. Nevertheless, he remained wary of the decadence of the German people, seeking, as we have seen, to persuade them to repent of their sins and stupidity by satirizing their vices in his *Das Narrenschiff*, the *Ship of Fools*, which followed the tradition of "fool literature."[53] He was a reforming dog, barking within the camp, rebuking the faults of his neighbors. Applauded by throngs of readers, the work was republished numerous times in numerous languages, and even invited a series of public sermons from a German pulpit.

The German word *Narrenschiff* was derived from the Latin *navis*, which refers both to the nave of a ship and to a church (the central entry to the altar), and Brandt portrayed the vessel drifting without a pilot (thus being as directionless and aimless as a fool). The ship holds a circus of human fools, generally ignorant of their own destination. Oblivious of their wretched circumstances, passengers engage in silly and vain activities: they eat, drink, flirt, talk, carouse, sleep, and puke. Gluttons, drunkards, and misers are on board, as well as lascivious members of religious orders. All are deranged and mad, setting sail for nowhere in particular and certain to arrive nowhere. And as Brandt observes, the ship is fully laden with fools, and "yet forsoth I thynke, / A thousand are behynde" who cannot be received on board lest the boat sink. The Ship of Fools is suitably "Fully Fraught and Richly Laden with Asses, Fools, Jack-daws, Ninnihammers, Coxcombs, Slenderwits, Shallow-brains, Paper-Skuls, Simpletons, Nickumpoops, Wiseakers, Dunces, and Blockheads."[54] Here are the ones who display large libraries of books and cannot read, who practice unprofitable study and vain, empty prayers, who depend upon the mercies of God when they decide to sin, or those who babble too much, even in print . . .

One particularly relevant section deals with mockers and their close cousins, false accusers. These scorners ridicule those who show wisdom and sound doctrine and throw ungodly stones at the heads of the wise. They gladly practice the discipline of foolish mockers, whom wise men would eschew, for "no correction can bring them to virtue." The teacher who tries to rebuke such a fool will receive in return only the hate, slander, and defamation of the shameless mocker. For Brandt, nothing can save the mocker or alter his ways. Yet his darts will return to him and he will be sorely wounded with them: "That they that mockes alway theyr myndes cast, / Shall of all other be mocked at the last."[55]

While not particularly funny or pungent, Brandt's work is good moral satire in the tradition of the Hebrew prophets. It lays low those churchgoers who show off their new clothes or prove how respectable they are. It pinches those who make fatuous noise in the church of God and tweaks those young fools who would marry old wives for their riches. The follies of his day are impaled upon the printed page for the entertainment and moral correction of his contemporaries.

Sixteenth-century German painter Albrecht Dürer fulfilled one of his first commissions of illustrative block woodcuts by satirizing the church just prior to the Reformation. As a parody of the true ark of salvation, his motif of the floating barge of vice and stupidity echoes Hieronymus Bosch's painting (c. 1500) that captures the misshapen humans drifting through the sea of time, playing frivolous games, looking for a fools' paradise. Bosch follows Brandt in lashing out even at monks and nuns, religious personages who follow heresies (thus the owl, a symbol of heresy, and the Muslim crescent on the yellow banner) and their own lusts. Both the lute and the bowl of cherries offer erotic footnotes on the carnal desire of the clerics. Behind Bosch's demonic iconography lay a surreal preview of a Calvinist view of the total depravity of human beings, a zoo of sinners as seen in a garden of earthly delights, with corrupted images of twisted and distorted souls.

Nineteenth-century art critic Jules Champfleury described these scoundrels and fools whose manners belied their attestation to being Christian. Country buffoons would fill the basins of holy water with ink and try to steal kisses from maids in dark church corners. Champfleury also recorded one "Usurer's Pasternoster," in which the moneylender tells his wife to retrieve him from church if someone wants to borrow money. He recites his own Lord's Prayer:

> *Our Father*. Blessed Lord God, be favorable to me, and give me grace to prosper exceedingly. Let me become the richest money-lender in the world. *Who art in heaven*. I am sorry I wasn't at home the day that woman came to borrow. Really I am a fool to go to church, where I can gain nothing.[56]

Art of Flyting

The art of flyting can best be explained as a sort of medieval jousting with insults; imagine performing the dozens or a rap contest. The practice originated with a public war of words between two Scottish masters, William Dunbar (1460–1520) and Walter Kennedy (1455–c. 1518), whose outrageous verbal invention and dexterity, abusive character assassination, and extensive use of scatology marked the genius of their verbal bouts. Flyting, with its scolding and contentious quarrelling, formalized a literary exchange of taunts and ridicule. These two *makars*, or bards, had to duel in alliteration. Dunbar was, incidentally, the author of the pithy ditty condensing his view of religious life: "Man, please thy Maker, and be merry, / And give not for this world a cherry." He wrote in high courtly, middle devotional, and low *eldritch* (that is, frightful, exuberant, even eerie and unearthly) style. It was this last contribution of weirdness that earned him his place among the great comic, lurid figures of his day, and as a master of flyting.

Flyting can be called, paradoxically, "the fine *art* of savage insult," since the Scottish participants were noted authors and their works are neither repetitive nor extemporaneous, though they are a tad crude. This style fits in the bottom left hand corner of our Quad as unripe satire, marked by ridicule and playful rage. Indeed, literary critic James Kinsley surmises that the *Flyting* between Dunbar and Kennedy (which is over 550 lines long) "may have developed in a series of attacks and counter-attacks circulated in manuscript at court."[57] Poet W. H. Auden best illustrated flyting as "impromptu exchanges of truck drivers and cabdrivers" in which the literary artists are not thinking about each other, but about "language and their pleasure in employing it inventively."[58]

Dunbar was a Master of Arts, a Franciscan preaching friar full of vitality and verve, an unbridled priest in court service for a number of years, and the recipient of a royal pension from King James IV. Kennedy, who had similar academic qualifications, was greatly admired as a poet and was of the blood royal. Their rough and tumble bouts, performed in public before the court of King James, would follow a pyrotechnical pattern of vim, vigor, and vituperation, wherein Kennedy reduced Dunbar to a dwarf born of Beelzebub, lord of the flies. When Kennedy called Dunbar "a shit but wit" who would "like to throw shit by the cartload," he claimed to be one of the first to use *shit* as a personal insult.[59] Like a medieval shock jock, Dunbar returned the punches with appropriate zest and panache in this mock character assassination. (He would be the first to use the word *fukkit* in his 1503 poem, the "Brash of Wowing" as "Yit be his feirris he wald haif fukkit: / Ye brek my hairt, my bony ane."[60]) Kennedy, he accused, had intercourse with mares. Such rude verbal sparring among a Franciscan and his partner has not been equaled.

Dunbar composed general satires, called "flayers," such as the "Dance of the Sevin Deidlie Synnis," parodies of church liturgy, and bawdy comic narratives full of moral censure, such as his *Tretis of the Twa mariit Wemen and the Wedo*. In the last, the narrator eavesdrops on the Widow and two respectable married women, who share scornful secrets on how to handle one's husband. Its coarse rhetoric, coming from elegant women, taught younger women how to ruin their husbands, how to conduct secret love affairs, and how to secure their inheritance from cuckolds. It offered a scathing satire on the sensuality of the age.[61] C. S. Lewis warned those who might read Dunbar: "If you like half-tones and nuances you will not like Dunbar; he will deafen you. If you cannot relish a romp you had best leave this extravaganza alone; for it offers no other kind of pleasure."[62] Yet Dunbar was equally at home with moral and religious verse, such as his celebration of the Son of God being born on Christmas, as much as his obscene comedy.[63] Both Juvenalians, Dunbar and Kennedy entertained hearers with their scathing exchanges, but rarely reformed them.

Perhaps the fifteenth century could boast the most corrupt age of Mother Church, a time when once again one could not *not* write satire. From simony to sodomy, from greed to sloth, the range of worldly vices was deep and wide. The corruptions surely brought out the vinegar in those who cared for the church.

One odd, eccentric character emerged just before the Reformation: the ferocious but jocular parson, poet, and satirist, John Skelton (1460–1529). His glory came twofold: first, by being named poet laureate of England by Henry VII and second, for serving as Henry VIII's tutor. As humanist learning and Lutheranism spread north and Cardinal Wolsey's twisted power waxed, Skelton's own daring rhetoric found a fertile field in which to play, even while he was able to maintain his integrity as a priest.[64]

Called "beastly" by Alexander Pope, Skelton punched up the discourse with lively wit. He served as parish rector in Diss, Norfolk (where he not only visited those in prison, but was to spend some time there himself for his exaggerated satires). His diocesan bishop punished him for "having been guilty of *certain* crimes AS MOST POETS ARE."[65] Since *dis* is Latin for hell, he would merrily joke about being known as "the vicar of hell." He kept a fair wench in his rectory, and when ordered to expel her through the door, he did, only to welcome her back through a window.

Skelton's masterful poetry married his tendency for ribald, coarse entertainment; he combined erudition with satire. The latter contribution concerns us here, for the innovative poetic form known as "skeltonic" derives from his wild satirical forays against royalty and the clergy. The skeltonic format is punchy and pithy, marked by flamboyant Latin nonsense, Hebrew parallelism and repeated rhythms, and many topical allusions (most too obscure for contemporary readers). Alongside this poetical barbarism lay his pious poetry. While motley was his headdress, he was a devout jester, Mr. "Skelton Poet" in the pulpit.

What Skelton did do forcibly was hold high the banner of Christian morality against a crooked ecclesiastical institution. From a brief stint in gaol to being the *orator regius* (King's orator) in 1512 for the wife-swapping King Henry VIII, Skelton prescribed his irritating habits as a tonic for the toxic age of the ambitious Roman Catholic advisor Thomas Wolsey, the reputed power behind the English throne. Cardinal Wolsey functionally controlled British policy with his Star Chamber while the young king hunted and chased skirts.[66] Wolsey had patronized Skelton early in his career, but when he dissolved the convocation at St. Paul's in 1522, Skelton boldly attacked his old benefactor. Wolsey conveniently arranged incarceration for him several times, although Skelton would take refuge in Westminster Abbey.[67]

His writings clawed and scratched the cardinal both indirectly and directly. At first, he lambasted the sins of the general clergy through his outspoken and peripatetic rustic spokesman (and satiric mask) in *Colyn Cloute* (1522). Even before Luther took the Roman Catholics to task, Skelton excoriated the avarice, ignorance, and simony of church leaders. In contrast to the poverty of their congregations, clergy lived in luxury and built costly tombs for themselves. While they abounded in pleasure, their people suffered arbitrary taxes and unfair oppression.

A simple, ragged man, Colyn roams the countryside reporting what he hears, like American humorist Will Rogers. What he hears particularly is that the church hierarchy has done a lot of things wrong. Colyn grimly observes that the clergy don't really look after their flocks, but seek glory; however, the upstart prelates should be advised that after "*gloria, laus*, may come a sour sauce" for these spoiled geese. Punishment will come for these ignorant clergy. But, asks Colyn, what good will his observations do as sycophants blind the ignorant bishops?

Skelton catalogued the abuses of self-promoting clergy, who bought and sold church positions in the market and still complained about their lives. They vexed the poor people with arbitrary jurisdiction and took away from them the little they had with high taxes. The bishops appointed bestial and "untaught" men as priests, men who couldn't read or spell their names. Instead of finding worthy men of God, they surrounded themselves with drunkards and dissolute monks and nuns. With monasteries in disarray, the friars swarmed the country, tickling the ears of congregations, flattering silly women, and hoodwinking the gullible. For Colyn, the noblemen were partly to blame, having abandoned the people to the care of bogus clergy. For the poet, the greatest menace existed in the corrupt authority of one person, the omnipotent minister-cardinal Wolsey.

Putting together a string of pungent harangues from his catalogue of stock abusive terms, Colyn repeats what he has heard on the grapevine, reflecting on ignorant priests. Why even compile books to revile vice or exile sin or use reason in preaching when the heads of the priests are "so fat"?

> He knoweth not what nor whereof he speaks; he cries and he creaks, he pries and he peeks, he chides and he chatters, he prates and he patters, he clitters and he clatters, he meddles and he smatters, he glosses and he flatters; or if he speak plain, then he lacks brain. He is but a fool; let him go to school on a three-footed stool, that he may down sit, for he lacketh wit.[68]

Skelton also skewered the reformers themselves, contemptuously railing against those he saw as heretics and devilish dogmatists: John Hus, John Wycliffe, and Martin Luther. One perceives in his rough and ragged words how why he is called the godfather of rap and of hip-hop.

> The Churche is put in faute;
> The prelates ben so haut,
> They say, and loke so hy,
> As though they wolde fly
> Aboue the sterry skye.
>
> And some haue a smacke
> Of Luthers sacke,
> And a brennyng sparke

Of Luthers warke,
And are somewhat suspecte
In Luthers secte;
And some of them barke,
Clatter and carpe
Of that heresy arte
Called Wicleuista,
Ye are so puffed wyth pryde,
That no man may abyde
Your hygh and lordely lokes:
Ye cast vp then your bokes,
And vertue is forgotten.[69]

Therefore, Skelton advised, when you mock "reformers," do it to their faces! He doesn't speak against good clergy, but only against those who do amiss in hindering the holy church. Echoing Isaiah, he foretells that judgment will come with some preachers being sawed, some hanged, "some slain; some beaten to the brain." Finally he elects to withdraw his pen and rest a while, hoping that the grace of our Savior Jesus will be sent to rectify and amend "thynges that are amys."[70]

The signature style of Skeltonic verse is marked by "breathless rimes," a sort of vivacious and exaggerated set of grotesque images transporting one with amazement. He boldly attacked clergy (and especially Wolsey—considering the reach of his power), but acknowledged the rough quality of his own writing:

For though my rhyme be ragged,
Tattered and jagged,
Rudely rayne beaten,
Rusty and moughte eaten,
It hath in it some pyth.[71]

It is said that Skelton mellowed and even wrote more complimentary poems to his nemesis. But of all the rusty and moth-eaten poets of this era, Skelton showed pith. After all chest-thumping bravado, Skelton excused his work with a sort of Catch-22 comic trap, saying you won't be offended by his satire if you are innocent of the charges.

Around the early fourteenth century, a raucous German trickster tradition emerged from the pages of a chapbook attributed to a man named Murner and known as Till Eulenspiegel. Eulenspiegel's typical portrayal in woodcut engravings comes from the literal High German translation of "owl-mirror"; however, in Low German, the term signifies "wipe the arse," a more apt designation considering his antics. This naughty scamp plays practical jokes, often tossing in some human excrement to expose the folly of nobles, religious orders, and even the pope. He takes figures of speech literally, often turning their meanings topsy-turvy. For example, when he is instructed to teach a young ass, he feeds pages of the psalter to a dumb donkey. When ordered to repent of his sins, he repents of three sorts of tricks he had never played.

Stories of this impudent scamp of scatology are rich in pranks, with various clergy getting punked in diverse ways. In one tale, Eulenspiegel explodes with a fart so enormous that it thunders throughout the church ("what is this stuff, incense smoke?"). He bets another priest a barrel of beer that the priest can't shit in the middle of the church. After the priest dares to lay a really large pile, Eulenspiegel challenges the priest's winning, asking to measure to see if it was actually in the middle. As it isn't, the rascal wins the barrel of beer on a technicality, with the mess still to be cleaned up.

He traveled to Rome and met the pope who took him for a heretic. He tricked some rich Jewish merchants at Frankfurt by selling them tiny bits of his excrement as prophet's berries.[72] The mischief played by Eulenspiegel tweaks the greedy and vain practices of priests, merchants, and scholastics; everything they do ends up, through Eulenspiegel's own metaphorical and actual contribution, as shit. The loosely connected vignettes focus on this lazy, clever scoundrel who is always ready to expose the high pretentions and hypocrisy of the church's pompous clergy. But after spending his time reducing the sanctimonious to irreverence, legend has it that he became a "pious monk, and posthumously a saint: And of a verity is Saint Owlglass, of all the saints that be in the calendar, hath the greatest number of devout folks here on earth. For fools be there many; and upon the first day of . . . April . . . do all men honour him; for in that hour in which they accomplish any idle vain work, do they increase his glory."[73]

One Giant Movement

Franciscan friar, alchemist, leader of the French Renaissance, accused heretic, Greek scholar, and groundbreaking satirical writer, François Rabelais (1493–1553) issued his magnum opus *The Life of Gargantua and Pantagruel* as a five-book series, charting the humorous adventures of his giants in a scatological and bawdy romp, with an underlying serious examination of politics, education, and religion. Rabelais left his cloister to study law, then repented of such a wicked profession to practice medicine during a plague. Yet his writings, full of impudent Gallic wit, wedded laughter with a social conscience to birth an evangelical vision of the good life. Where Erasmus exhibited witty chastity in expressing himself on proper topics and with decorous language, Rabelais unleashed his hearty vulgarity to satirize the church, the university and the foolish citizens of his day.

In 1532, he opened his work with this famous caveat, reminding us about the proper expression of our humanity:

> Readers, friends, if you turn these pages
> Put your prejudice aside,
> For, really, there's nothing here that's outrageous,
> Nothing sick, or bad—or contagious.
> Not that I sit here glowing with pride
> For my book: all you'll find is laughter:
> That's all the glory my heart is after,
> Seeing how sorrow eats you, defeats you.
> I'd rather write about laughing than crying,
> For laughter makes men human, and courageous.
> So laugh and be happy.

To announce the propriety of human laughter in a century full of religious controversies is to announce the rebirth of a resurrected body. Mirth has its place in the Kingdom of God as the jester plays before the King of Kings. And jester Rabelais was, wearing the full costume of caps and bells in his vocation, even making his own king Francis I laugh as he scribbled his tales in the French vernacular.

Laughter, as much as reform, was Rabelais's goal as he dissected sixteenth-century society. Known as the master of prose satire, Rabelais borrowed the language of the streets and the jargon of the marketplace where a popular vulgarity reigned as the main form of communication. No subtlety or sly irony here: Rabelais's jokes are loud and belching. His satire has been called "Menippean," that Greek hybrid style of high and low culture, poetry, and prose, with its fantastic, freewheeling, and subversive comic fictions. In particular, he practiced the paradoxical encomium, a literary device used to praise anything trivial, banal, or silly, such as baldness, red herrings, professors, or later with Erasmus, folly: it would offer a model for Monty Python, except without the catholic faith.

His stories of two giants record their odd births and episodes of childhood and education while spoofing theologians of the Sorbonne and debauched ignorant monks. A significant part examines the maturation of Gargantua from gross fraternity boy to humanist philosopher.[74] *Pantagreul* champions humanist education against the monotony of scholastic books and the antiquated habits of rote medieval learning, preferring books like *Ars honeste petandi in societate* (*The Art of Farting Decently in Public*).[75] Rabelais even jokes on the last words of Jesus, with *Pantagruel*, whose name means "all-thirst," wanting a drink, announcing: "I have God's word in my mouth, 'I thirst.'"[76]

Rabelais' invention of Pantagruel's genealogy harkens back to those of the Bible (who begat Sarabroth, who begat . . .).[77] Such stylistic imitation of scriptural texts would lead to Monty Python's update, read by the Cleric: "And Saint Attila raised the hand grenade up on high, saying, 'O Lord, bless this thy hand grenade, that with it thou mayst blow thine enemies to tiny bits, in thy mercy. And the Lord did grin."[78] Oxford translator M. A. Screech points out how effectively Rabelais jested on sacred subjects. Jokes require an understanding and familiarity with scripture, and Rabelais both venerated the holy word and teased those who misused it. In a parody of the Sermon on the Mount, Pantagruel recites "blessed are the heavy for they have stumbled."

Rabelais' most polemical book, *Quart Livre*, caricatures the Mardi Gras battle of Shrovetide by juxtaposing *Charnage* (meat eating) and *Careme* (Lenten fasts) on *Quaresmeprenant* (Lent Ash Wednesday). *Careme* is portrayed as a "grotesque monster and killjoy," "abounding in pardons, indulgences, and solemn masses"—which is to say, "a good

Catholic and of great piety."[79] Its combatants are the firebrand Andouilles (the anti-Lent kosher sausages), who worship a flying, multicolored, mustard-dispensing pig, the apotheosis of Mardi Gras. These are the wild Protestants, characterized with the similar words, *Saulcisses* (sausages) and *Souisses* (Swiss—Calvinists—"fuller of shit than of gall").

The coarseness of the schoolboy antics, drinking, eating, gorging on tripe, belching, farting, peeing, wiping bottoms, and wenching has an aesthetic and moral purpose.[80] Artistically, such behaviors are meant to trigger laughter. Morally, Rabelais worked like doctors studying stool samples and applying enemas to remedy the sickness of humanity. Immorality is not in the body, but in the spirit of men and women. The reforming of a superstitious and bibulous Gargantua from foul rustic boor into a French Erasmus is a gradual process. From being an oaf who wallows in squalor, the giant becomes a sage by the next book, cured by the learned doctor Maistie Theodore and by listening to readings of the New Testament, rather than studying graffiti on lavatory walls. A new emphasis on his mind supplants an obsession with the anus.

Rabelais reserved his sharpest criticism for monks, Rome, and Bishop Big Oaf. Popimaniacs (idolaters who worship the pope over Christ) are opposed by the Popefigs (merry mockers of the Pope). Rabelais scandalized a scandalous clergy (as Gargantua could shit, piss, fart, sneeze, and dribble snot like an archdeacon) by attacking the temporal powers of the papacy. He promoted specious miracles, such as healing of hemorrhoids by touching his book's pages. The papacy's real "occult" power lay in being able "to draw immense quantities of gold from France to Rome" (that is, to collect indulgences).

Alongside his giants with their tremendous thirst for wine is the crafty scoundrel, Panurge, a knavish prankster who spends time wondering whether to marry or just seek the Temple of the Holy Bottle (his elixir of life). Few could rival his skullduggery as he gambles with loaded dice and explodes stink bombs under the benches of theologians. This horny ignoramus worries that if he gets married, he will be cuckolded and beaten by his scolding wife. When the unsavory Panurge meets a haughty lady, he publically reduces her to a "bitch in heat." He wins a debate with an earnest alchemist Thaumaste by "diddling him" and using obscene gestures. Rabelais catalogues signs of contempt such as pinching your nose, touching your sphincter, and pointing to someone as if to say, "You stink!" Panurge, in fact, puts his "left finger in his arsehole, drawing air through his mouth as when slurping oysters in their shells." Thaumaste can only wheeze like a goose. All this vulgar humor surrounds the biblical idea of hypocrites asking Jesus for a sign (Luke 11:29).[81] The sign of Jonah or the middle finger is all that this evil and adulterous generation deserves.

Rabelais listed 303 tropes for the male sexual organ and instructed Panurge on five ways to quell carnal lust: wine, anti-aphrodisiac drugs, study, hard work, and lastly, copulation. "Aha!" said Panurge. "That's what I was waiting for. Give numbers 1–4 to anyone else. I'm for number 5."[82]

While loud-mouthed and quite lecherous, Friar John is also a joyful, hilarious, and boon companion, one who shares bread and merriment with his giant friend. At the abbey of the Thelemites, monks follow the house rules of the order to "do what you will." So, they rise late, enjoy a swimming pool, and make the most of a maid service. He is "a true monk if ever there was one since the monkish world monked about with monkery."[83] And to top it off, he has an ample nose, which has since time immemorial functioned as a symbol for a healthy sex drive. Friar John celebrates his own rampant penis, recalling the words of the psalm, "I lift it up unto thee," a sort of prayer of gratitude. His laughter is coarse and boisterous, bordering on the blasphemous, but not hypocritical, as he ushers in a mood of merriment like a Friar Tuck.

Screech points out how Friar John, in the Battle for Abbey of Seville, nobly fights for the vineyard in which he rams the shaft of an ancient cross up the bums of the soldiers who are ravaging the vineyard. The enemies of God receive just deserts. "Some died laughing; some laughed dying."[84] Friar John may have enormous appetites, but he also shows deep gratitude, thanking God after rescues from storms; his ripe laughter contributes to his good doing.

The Papimaniacs and their unctuous Bishop Homenaz not only worship the pope, but hold papal decrees, the Decretals, as sacred. The text, covered with gold and precious stones, protects clerics from French civil law. Homenaz abuses the gullible, perversely tortures heretics, and justifies papal military action with the authority of the Decretals. He claims that he who reads them will be animated "with charity toward [his] neighbor, as long as he is not a heretic." The bishop elevates such human documents above inspired scriptures, as they can be used to extort more money for Rome from France than any Bible verse. Pantagruel sees the abuse conducted under the name of the church and satirizes these "sacrosanct" documents by noting that it is written that the Holy Father has got "bollocks" and that fawning fanatics would kiss his bum, expecting the pope to come to their island. The bishop's sermon does have the salubrious effect of inducing diarrhea, as it loosens the bowels of Pantagruel's friend, but it has the opposite effect upon Panurge: "Upon reading them I was so constipated that for more than four or five days I shat only a tiny ball of dung."[85] Rabelais debased this idolatry of Decretals with satirical connections to excretion.

Good Roman Catholic that he was, Rabelais still saw the idiocies and miseries caused by the institutional church. He showed how the papacy tended to destroy rather than win its neighbors. Christendom could not win when served by wicked saints.

In Book IV of *Gargantua*, a rogue Master François Villon wishes to organize a travesty of a passion play. All he lacks is a costume for his character playing the role of God the Father. The local Franciscan sacristan, Smacktail, shocked by what Villon intends, refuses to lend any church vestments for so devilish a purpose. The prankster Villon takes revenge by staging a rehearsal just as the "sacristan rides by. With firecrackers, Villon frightens the churchman's horse; the sacristan is dragged along the ground as his brains and bowels spurt out until only the stump of his foot is left in a stirrup." The mule unleashes a volley of mulish farts to punctuate the farce of the parable.

Bakhtin used this tale as a metaphor for what Rabelais does throughout his mischievous novel. Just as the character Villon derides and destroys the humorless representative of the church through his parody of a play, so author Rabelais seeks to destroy the forces of the hypocritical church in his parody. As Bakhtin wrote, Rabelais and Villon behave exactly alike in using the grotesque to satirize religious vice.

Rabelais's two great works were banned by Sorbonne academics for deriding Roman Catholic Church practices, taking liberties against the academic establishment, and explaining how to wipe your bottom.[86] Rabelais was obviously in danger of being declared a heretic for his extravagant, ribald, merry tales in search of the Divine Bottle. However, one should expect vulgarity and bodily excesses in Gargantua, whose mother ate too much tripe before he was born. Pantagruel's great journey ends with him producing a very large bowel movement, symbolizing much of the political, educational, and religious establishment of the day. As Rabelais observes, "The whole world shuns monks because they eat the shit of the world, that is, its sins."[87] Shit becomes an apt metaphor for the wickedness that comes out of a man. His comedy of farce is one of "stuffing" and its result is that it showcases the folly and feces of humanity.

Even more to the point of his overall satire, Rabelais reduces all men to their appropriate size, and he recognizes, as Bakhtin observed, that "kings and clowns have the same horoscope. It is obvious that he also knew the Gospel story of the mock crowning, uncrowning, and scourging of 'the King of the Jews.'"[88] The great irony seen in his adventures is that the humble would be exalted.

While the wild comedy of the carnivalesque medieval period celebrated the body and all its earthy functions of reproduction, digestion and excretion, it did not camouflage its targets. Unlike the crowing of goliards, the easy laughter of Chaucer and Rabelais did not neglect to pinpoint hypocrisy and folly. Jocular sermons, flytings, and naughty tales embedded criticisms in the bowels of their discourse, but they first attracted audiences through comedy. Medieval satire mocked more than preached, with roosters mounting their perches and jesters standing before kings; yet as the church descended into corruption, the comedy would need to change to something more forceful and piercing, something that would challenge it to reform itself. In the Quad of Satire, medieval satirists pointed to problems for reform, but delighted in vulgar exposure.

Medieval satire did a dance, even if it were a *danse macabre*. However, with religious corruption and immorality mushrooming, the more serious aspects of satire required a counterbalance. The Reformation would transform the dance into a march and then into a battle for ideas. The call to theological and moral reform would once again rise and confront the weakened vessel of the Ship of Fools. Brandt's ship was about to come into a port where reform-minded inspectors would challenge its seaworthiness. Salty wit would still exist, but the urgency of spiritual transformation would bring reform elements onto center stage.

5

Reformers and Fools

Who spits at heaven gets it back in his face.
—Giambattista Basile

By the sixteenth century, corruption within the Roman Catholic Church had reached a nadir of naughtiness and venality. While good and faithful Christians still served within the polluted religious system, the institutional excesses were sufficient to provoke one of the major crises of Western civilization, the Reformation. It was an era of serious reform and wild and wooly satiric battles between factions. While certain writers sought only to vent or spit, other more noble ones aimed at correcting abuses—more or less. Humor took on more of a purpose than it had held for the jesters and roosters of the previous era.

In Sir Thomas More's (1478–1535) invention of *Utopia*, the family was elevated and private property eliminated. Yet the title carried a double meaning, suggesting both a good (*eu*) place and a no (*ou*) place. Perhaps it was that no good place existed, particularly for Chancellor More. He watched King Henry VIII divorce a faithful Roman Catholic wife, Catherine of Aragon, for the sexy Protestant Anne Boleyn. But that was later. When he published his golden little book in 1516, More carried on conversations about the evils of continental society, as he inserted both wisdom and satire regarding this good place.

> Wherever you are, you always have to work. There's never any excuse for idleness. There are also no wine-taverns, no ale-houses, no brothels, no opportunities for seduction, no secret meeting-places. Everyone has his eye on you, so you're practically forced to get on with your job, and make some proper use of your spare time.[1]

In his preface, a series of greetings to his friend Peter Giles, More railed particularly against the ignorance of those who despised learning and

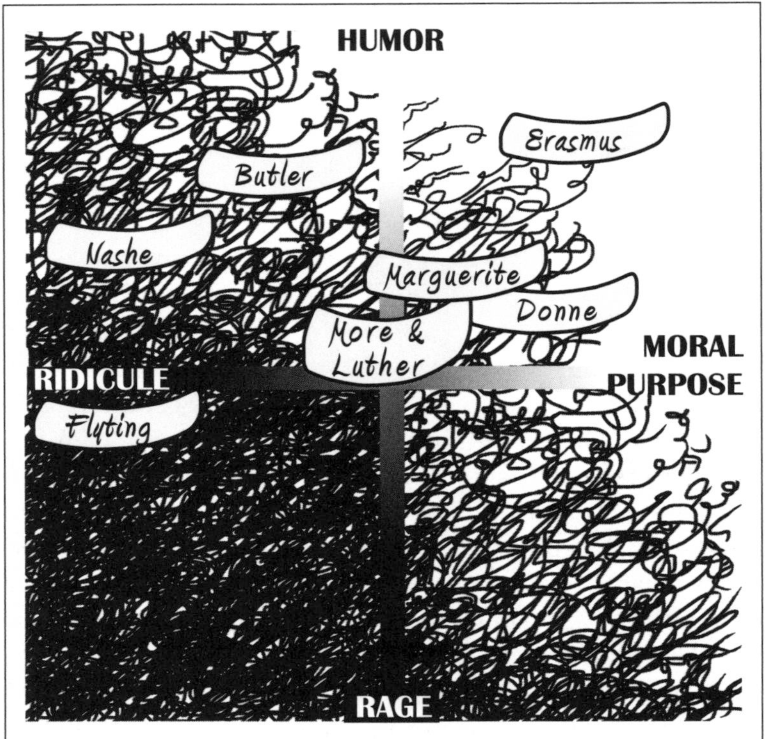

Nashe, Flyting, Butler, More, Luther, Marguerite, Donne, and Erasmus on the Quad of Satire.

lingered in taverns, pontificating over cups. These were "flat-nosed" people, or people with no noses, an image that easily conveys stupidity. They lacked any humanist learning. Some liked only ancient authors, while "many like only their own writing. One person is so dour that he cannot abide jokes; another so witless that he cannot stand anything witty. Some have so little nose for satire that they dread it the way someone bitten by a rabid dog fears water."[2] Of another garrulous preacher, he noted that "he can so roll in his rhetorick that he knoweth not what his own words mean."[3]

Writing after Columbus's recent discovery of a New World, More created Utopia as a marvelous satire. He described his own New World Island through an extended interview with a sailor named Raphael

Hythlodaeus, whose name means "nonsense peddler." Raphael peddles his tales to More. As a character, More wishes that some Utopian characteristics, like religious tolerance, were more common in Britain so that "every man might be of what religion he pleased, and might endeavor to draw others to by force of argument and by amicable and modest ways."[4] Such a wish was not followed, even by the historical More—who toasted a few dissenters himself.

In his wry travelogue, grooms and brides were forced to stand naked before marrying so that their physical compatibility might be checked. Most importantly, and comically, Utopian chamber pots were made of silver and gold, devaluing all material possessions. Erasmus wrote about *Utopia* as if it were a comic book; one critic observed that More himself classified it and Erasmus's *In Praise of Folly* as "books fitter to be burned than translated in an age prone to misconstruction."[5] As such, it is closer to Swift's *Gulliver's Travels* than to Plato's *Republic*.

Unlike his measured humanist satire against scholastic dogmatism in *Utopia*, More switched styles when attacking Martin Luther's theology and character, demonstrating a more vituperative tone.[6] He descended to the level of the German monk, characterizing Luther's protests as acts in which the reformer would "swallow down his filth and lick up the dung with which he has so foully defiled his tongue and his pen, shitting and beshitted."[7] Not quite the civil and courteous exchange one would find in Utopia. More's period was a divisive one. One did not try to win one's brother, but to cut him off. Horrific religious wars would follow and prove to be more brutal and bloody than the sword of the tongue. The satiric tongue, instead, served as the spark that set the fire ablaze.

His contemporary Edward Hall described More as a merry "man well-learned in languages and in Common Law; his wit was fine and full of imagination, by reason whereof, he was too much given to mocking, which was to his gravity a great blemish." Hall debated whether to characterize the scholar as a foolish wise man or a wise fool as his learning was "so mingled with taunting and mocking that it seemed to them that best knew him that he thought nothing to be well spoken except he had ministered some mock in the communication."[8] Scholar Constance Furey argues that More's offensive language was acceptable in sixteenth-century debate: "offensive, satirical, and condemnatory words were both dangerous and useful because they had the power to distort but also the capacity to expose the truth by piercing through appearances and challenging conventional thought."[9] Such a practice permitted a more pragmatic approach for Roman Catholic polemics.

C. S. Lewis opined that "nearly all that is best" in More's writings, "is comic or close to comedy," a sort of "satiric glass" in which we should see our own faces, sins, and avarice.[10] When describing More's "delight in the universe of folly," Erasmus mentioned that the good man "excelled in making witty remarks and even liked those directed against himself."[11] Historian Walter Gordon describes More's spirit of vitality and play that "refresheth a man much and, without any harm, lighteth his mind." As such, More's style parallels Aquinas's treatment of the Aristotelian virtue of *eutrapelia*, which refreshed the mind "where continual fatigue would make it dull and deadly."

Allegedly, More's greatest jest was his last one. Having offended His Majesty Henry VIII by not acquiescing to the king's demands for a divorce, More was condemned to death. Climbing up the scaffolding, he humbly asked the executioner to help him up. Then he added, "But getting down I can shift for myself." Even as his noble neck gave way to the axe, his humor remained intact. He entreated the executioner not to harm his beard, for it had done no treason. Erasmus noted that the virtuous More had "such a passion for jokes that one might almost suppose he had been born for them."[12] And he died laughing, or at least rejoicing in his God; for while he died the King's good servant, he was God's first.

Dame Folly

The predominant Christian humanist in the sixteenth century was Dutch polymath Desiderius Erasmus (1466–1536), whose central work picked up on the traditions of fool literature and of the mock encomium, in which one praised something insignificant, like baldness or lawyers. His masterpiece, *In Praise of Folly*, targeted the general foolishness of society and the church in particular. In fact, before Luther espoused many of his recommendations for reform, Erasmus had denounced fooleries like indulgences ("the crime of false pardons") and had made light of local utility saints who would find lost items, cure toothaches, or watch over one's cows and chickens. Still, Erasmus was Roman Catholic at his core; Luther was merely a "jumped up monk."

In Praise of Folly was written at a holiday stay at the home of his friend Sir Thomas More and dedicated to him. Explaining that kidney trouble kept him ensconced at More's house, Erasmus tinkered with Folly. As he shared his joke, others encouraged him to expand it; so he played the fool and acted out this comedy from behind the Dame's mask. Erasmus punned on his host's name. In Latin, the title *Moriae Enconium* could be read as "in praise of folly" (as in morons) or "in praise of More." More might even have become the patron saints of morons, of the fools that swallowed sermons whole and bought indulgences by the bushel.

In this classic satire, perhaps the most quintessential of all satirical literature, Erasmus attacks the practice of indulgences with barbs as stinging as any of Luther's. He mocks those mad men who buy tall tales about alleged miracles from pardoners and preachers (like Chaucer's) and ridicules those who think to cover their sins with money or escape Judgment by being buried in a monk's robe. Particularly gullible are those who would entreat priests to forge pardons for them. Folly offered good business sense, previewing showman P. T. Barnum's and comic W. C. Field's notion that a sucker is born every minute. Folly's province, like Barnum's audience, is the whole human race.

Erasmus donned the ironic persona of Dame Folly. One wonders what to take seriously and what to take tongue-in-cheek. She says, "If you ask me why I appear before you in this strange dress, be pleased to lend me your ears, and I'll tell you; not those ears, I mean, you carry to church, but abroad with you, such as you are wont to prick up to jugglers, fools, and buffoons." To those with one foot in the grave (for instance, long-winded professors), Erasmus granted the lunacy of being an infant again. Erasmus warned that if you bring a philosopher to a party (or if you give a mouse a cookie), he'll "either sit in gloomy silence or confound the company by turning the occasion into a doctor's oral lecture. Ask him to a dance, and you'll get an idea of how a camel waltzes." Erasmus followed the line with his topper gag that if you "haul him off to a public entertainment, his face will be enough to spoil the people's enjoyment."[13]

The ripest targets of his encomium were the monks. Erasmus's famous slogan in his *Enchiridion* was "Monachatus non est pietas" (Monkery is not piety), a frontal attack on those holy men who abandoned their founders' vows of poverty, chastity, and obedience to practice their opposites. A lot of frisky activity went on beneath their cowls. They accumulated wealth, tasted carnality, and maintained their own vested interests. For Erasmus, they were less "scrupulous about wine-bibbing or intimate relations with women." Monks are like donkeys in church, braying out their psalms without understanding.[14] The cocky preaching rooster of the Middle Ages was supplanted by the dumb ass.

One can judge the depth of arrogance of theologians by analyzing their diet, and Dame Folly points out that they dine on beans. They are as hypocritical as the one who weeps over the grave of his mother-in-law. Scholastic theologians teach the formal, material, efficient, and final causes of baptism, but don't baptize. They reshape scripture as if it were made of wax, and can wax eloquently on whether God could have assumed the form of a woman, a devil, an ass, or a pumpkin.

Their flocks of Christians ware equally stupid. They light candles for the Virgin, but don't imitate her sanctity. They are comparable to sheep, for "no animal is more stupid or dumb as a sheep."[15] Women like these priests, however, because they can always find a listening ear for complaints about their husbands.

For Erasmus, fools are the happiest class of humans as they alone are direct and truthful, and yet when they speak truth, even "unwelcome truths, they are received with uproarious laughter." Dame Folly ends her discourse apologizing and reminding her readers that "If I have been too cheeky or long-winded, remember you've been listening to Folly and a woman. . . . Clap your hands, live well, and drink deep, most illustrious disciples of Folly."[16]

"While I am in favor of jokes anywhere, provided they be seasoned with salt," wrote Erasmus, "I equally cannot stand those who, whenever they want to be amusing, twist words of Holy Writ for use in their absurdities."[17] His natural territory of laughter was in wit, not comedy. In fact, he seemed to object to raw laughter, such as prompted by tickling, as it wasn't quite proper to stimulate bodily pleasures, and tickling under the armpits resembled a "fit" of madness a bit too much. Erasmus explained that his taking on the voice of Dame Folly was to "admonish, not to sting; to help, not to hurt; to promote morality not to hinder it." He continued with a lesson from Plato, careful to couch his tone in a prudent and decent manner (breaking decorum for Erasmus would be like breaking wind in public): "Even such a grave philosopher as Plato approves of drinking rather freely at parties because he thinks that the merriment generated by wine can dispel certain vices which could not be corrected by sternness."[18]

When criticized for impersonating Folly, Erasmus countered that some religious people are a bit dumb in understanding what he had done: "Whoever heard of a comic pamphlet being subjected to theological scrutiny?"[19] Erasmus introduced his feast of *Colloquia* by quoting the famed Roman orator Cicero, noting that "the bottom is the most honorable part of the human body because it gets to sit down first."[20] Dutch historian Johan Huizinga defended Erasmus, explaining that looking at Erasmus is "like looking at a gallery of Brueghel's pictures," a veritable reunion of yokels and rubes in mirrors.[21]

After the death of Pope Julius, Erasmus anonymously took on the gambling, sodomizing, warlike, and secular pontiff (who took Caesar's name rather than a biblical one) with his satirical "Julius Excluded from Heaven." Locked out of heaven, Julius can't persuade Peter to let him through the gates and threatens to blast his way in with his armies and his thunderbolts of excommunication. Peter finds the bluster of this "sewer stench" to be all bombast. In their debate, Julius argues that a pope can't be excluded for any reason, including homicide, parricide, incest, poisoning, simony, sacrilege, or blasphemy. Peter refuses to open the gate to a disease as contagious as Julius; he is the salt that has lost its savor.

Standing between Roman Catholics and Protestant reformers, Erasmus found fault with both and ended up hiding in Basel. Erasmus once noted that "these paunchy monks are called *fathers*, and they take good care to deserve the name." Indeed, Luther, a stout monk himself, gave credence to a popular legend. According to some prophecies, an ex-monk and ex-nun would give birth to the Antichrist. Erasmus countered the slanderous rumor against Luther and his wife, Katie, a former nun who had been sneaked out of the convent in a herring barrel, by observing that if that tradition were true, there must have been many thousands of antichrists born before this.[22] Nevertheless, Luther did not return the favor; he called Erasmus, who did not join the Reformation, a "mere Momus," a reference to the Greek god of censure and mockery. "Whenever I pray," wrote Luther with little grace, "I pray for a curse upon Erasmus." If charity were to be a mark of the reformed man, evidence could not be found in Luther's love (of lack thereof) for his enemy.[23]

Reformed Farts

The Reformation was bathed in laughter as well as blood, both sanctioned by the church. (The Lutheran Reformation, as American writer Walter Lippmann once observed, was intended only for good Catholics.[24]) The swords of wit nicked and sliced souls as much as swords of steel slashed bodies. In terms of the Quad of Satire, more attention was given to brutal assaults on one's enemy than to a reformation of their vices.

Numerous jokes abounded regarding monks coupling with nuns, alluding to Martin Luther's marriage to Katie. However, few religious leaders equaled the outhouse humor of the rollicking German reformer himself. The angst-ridden Augustinian monk, Luther (1483–1546), wrestled with his faith and threw inkwells at the devil until he discovered in Paul's Letter to the Romans that one was justified by faith in God, not through one's own works. Confronting the manipulative practice of selling indulgences to poor, gullible people so that they might receive forgiveness of sins (and spend less time in purgatory), Luther excoriated the wicked practices of Dominican friars like Johann Tetzel. Tetzel would hop into German villages, and sing his little ditty: "As soon as a coin in the coffer rings / The soul from Purgatory springs." Against such a backdrop, Luther nailed his ninety-five theses or arguments on the door of the Wittenberg Cathedral on October 31, 1517. His fiery polemical skills were matched with the spark of wit, for he recognized that "the best way to drive out the devil, if he will not yield to texts of Scripture, is to jeer and flout him, for he cannot bear scorn."[25] And Tetzel was a devil. Luther enjoyed driving him out and confessing to tingling with pleasure from head to toe when he saw how the Lord used him, "poor wretched man that I am," to madden and exasperate his enemies.[26]

Luther found his friend Lucas Cranach an able ally in caricaturing his enemies, such as drawing a papal tiara upon the head of the Whore of Babylon in his illustrations for *The Revelation of John*.[27] In *The Passion of Christ and Anti-Christ* (1521), a famous pamphlet caricaturing the corruption of the Vatican, Cranach attacked the pope, contrasting his wealth with the poverty of Jesus. As Steven Ozment observes, "Each scene presented the pope transgressing what Christ faithfully always observed, implying that the pope was not the self-proclaimed Vicar of Christ on earth, but the anti-Christ in a clever disguise."[28] German artists Cranach and Hans Holbein's broadsides employed marvelous (albeit gross) draftsmanship and clever graphic style. One memorable caricature shows Luther, Calvin, and the pope with the two reformers pulling the ears of the pope. Luther simultaneously tugs at Calvin's beard, and Calvin threatens to throw a Bible at Luther. The scene, engraved around 1600, previews a scene out of the *Three Stooges*.

Luther borrowed stylistic turns from Lucian, easily reducing criticisms to personal attacks dealing with reeking cesspools, knavery, and sow's farts. Luther satirized Cardinal Albrecht's private collection of holy relics in a humorous pamphlet listing his supposed relics, including a piece of the cardinal's "pious heart and a large portion of his truthful tongue." Luther satirized other relics exhibited for indulgences including

> Three flames from the burning bush on Mount Sinai
> A whole pound of wind that roared by Elijah in the cave on Mount Horeb
> Five nice strings from the harp of David.
> Three beautiful locks of Absalom's hair, which got caught in the oak and left him hanging.
> A morsel of bread from the Last Supper
> Two feathers and an egg from the Holy Spirit.[29]

Luther's *Table Talk* overflowed with wit, good humor, and good honest sense: "Many a man speaks ill of women without knowing what his mother did."[30] "The Franciscans are the lice which the devil put into the fur-coat of God."[31] "Tomorrow I have to lecture on the drunkenness of Noah, so I should drink enough this evening to be able to talk about that wickedness as one who knows by experience."[32] Luther spent splendid hours in *Table Talk*, drinking German beer, squeezing his wife, and mocking Roman Catholics.

Cranach's caricatures of their opponents appeared in a series of graphic woodcut sketches.[33] For those who could not read, it was obvious what Luther thought of his adversaries. Catholic atrocities, as reformers saw them, were unmasked through scatological satire and coarse (*grobianisch*) writings. Such vitriolic critique could, for example, show peasants surrounding the pope on the throne, with their backs to the pontiff, their trousers down, and their tongues stuck out: the message being, "we fart in your face." In another, dung in the pope's hands is equated to his Decretals. To paraphrase the Apostle Paul, all the papal righteousness is counted as dung.

Luther became renowned for this scatological humor. Cursed with a bit of constipation, he would spend time in the outhouse, thinking and reflecting on what and how to say what he wanted. His world was packed down with words like *Scheisse* (shit), *Mist* (manure), *Dreck* (dirt/shit), and *Arsch* (ass). Luther wrote with uninhibited panache, offering fecal tirades against the pope as being the "cuckoo that devours the church's eggs and then craps out cardinals."[34] Most importantly, when he recognized that the pope and his minions were attending too closely to his every movement, so to speak, he boasted that "when I fart in Wittenberg, the Pope in Rome wrinkles his nose."[35] He warned the pope that no letters of indulgences could forgive the ass-pope befouling himself.

Luther's wrestled against flesh and blood and spiritual powers and principalities. He believed that "the devil has sworn to kill me; this I certainly know, and he will have no peace until he has devoured me. All right, if he devours me, he shall devour a laxative (God willing) which will make his bowels and anus too tight for him."[36] Like Thomas More, he viewed the devil as his prime accuser and a proud spirit that could "not endure to be mocked."[37] So mock him he did: "I resist the devil, and often it is with a fart that I chase him away. When he tempts me with silly sins, I say, 'Devil, yesterday I broke wind too. Have you written it down on your list?'"[38]

When his adversary Johann Eck called Luther "Herr Lugner" (Mr. Liar), Luther reciprocated by calling him "Herr Dreck," meaning "shit." Allegedly, Luther authorized Cranach's drawing of the devil excreting the pope, even as Luther was satirized in Eberhard Schon's 1530's woodcut of *The Devil's Bagpipe*, played too well by the devil.

Luther showed how self-effacing he could be as well, contritely acknowledging that "some people need a fig leaf on their mouths." In marrying his Kate, Luther showed a gentler humor: "At home I have good wine and beer and a beautiful wife, or (shall I say) lord." When asked why he got married, Luther responded, that "his marriage would please his father, rile the pope, cause the angels to laugh, and the devils to weep." Luther delighted in finding pigtails on his pillow and being seen hanging up diapers. He beamed, "let them laugh; God and the angels smile!" Hitherto, Erasmus concluded, we have "considered the Reformation a tragedy, but now, as it ends in a wedding, we know it to be a comedy."[39]

Perhaps it was in a moment of intense debate about the solemnities of the religious life that Luther rejected the dour posture of some theologians: "If you are not allowed to laugh in Heaven, I don't want to go there."[40] If the pleasures of God are forevermore, he reasoned, laughter would resound in the heavens.

Luther's satirical turn for reform too frequently dissolved into the farts of sows. Seeing the devil on his walls, his own rhetorical flourishes suggest that he may have seen his own portrait hanging nearby. His scatological excesses suggest that the image of being played by the devil sounded a familiar tune. The true reformer could also be the fool or the ass, whose tongue needed a bridle as much as the corrupt church needed his corrections.

Predestined Play

Other than a satirical, polemical poem titled "Epinicion," reformed theologian John Calvin (1509–1564) did not express much humor. In his *Institutes*, however, he acknowledged that "We are nowhere forbidden to laugh, or to be satisfied with food, or to be delighted with music, or to drink wine."[41] For all his dourness, Calvin did possess a copy of Rabelais's *Pantagruel*. In an exegesis of Psalm 104, he embraced the notion that God made "wine that gladdens the heart of man, oil to make his face shine, and bread that sustains his heart." The psalmist not only thanks God for giving those things we need to live, but thanks God for pleasures as well. "As the prophet in this account of the divine goodness in providence makes no reference to the excesses of men, we gather that it is lawful to use wine not only in cases of necessity, but also thereby to make us merry. This mirth must however be tempered with sobriety."[42] Such is the jocundity of a lean Swiss lawyer.

One might not expect wit from Huldrych Zwingli (1484–1531) either.[43] But when the weapon-wielding warrior was fatally stabbed by a

Catholic soldier at the second Battle of Kappel, he proved to be a cheerful advocate of the idea that "Wer hofft und lacht, ist nicht tot" (whoever hopes and laughs is not dead.) Although he died of his wounds, Zwingli still danced more lightly than others of the reformed persuasion. The Swiss champion of faith, shepherding his flock in the yodeling country of the Alps, showed enough mischief and spunk to serve sausages during Lent in Zurich in 1522.

In this land-locked country where Brandt's Ship of Fools had been launched, Zwingli was described by scholar Fritz Schmidt-Clausing as connecting "sincerity with joke and play."[44] He translated Paul's passage in Romans 12:8 in which acts of mercy were to be done with *hilaritas*, that eighth virtue that Evagrius identified as cheerfulness and merriment. God loved *cheerful* givers. Consequently, Zwingli would scold Anabaptists because they were too melancholy; they "could not be joyful with anyone, not even with themselves." They should rather sing Bach's song: "My believing heart: be glad, sing, joke," which is what Zwingli did. He compared the Anabaptists' teaching to hollyhock, a laxative. Zwingli's irony lacked subtlety as he found the "super-sanctimonious Baptizers" "as merry as a "wedding in hell."[45]

For Zwingli, "truth had a merry face." Joking should be employed to help make seriousness more effective. For example, he explained that a primary reason for fasting was that it enabled tubby saints to "re-fit an all too shameless pot belly back into the old clothes."[46] When challenging the doctrine of transubstantiation, in which the bread and wine of the Eucharist are miraculously transformed into the body and blood of Christ, Zwingli retorted that "Jesus ascended into heaven; He's sitting at the right hand of the Father, not on a table here in Zurich."[47]

He joked by punning on names, suggesting that his fellow reformer (with whom he could not agree on the nature of the Eucharist) Luther should speak *lauter* (louder) and not become *loutrion* (used bath water). He called the Reformers' disputation adversary, Johann Eck, by the silly name of Jeck, a carnival clown or fool. When several fellows questioned whether Christians should trade in such salty jokes (*iocis et salibus*), Zwingli retorted whether they were "customs officers over my laughter that I must give you an accounting of it?"[48]

One devout, reforming friend of Calvin, however, was known as the "laughing face of the *Eglise Reformee*."[49] An engaging and popular preacher of the Reformation, polymath Pierre Viret (1511–1571) scripted his *Metamorphose chretienne* around 1552. The humus soil of the Reformation did bear the fruitful humor of this forgotten reformer. In engraver Pierre Eskrich's satirical map, *La Mappe-monde nouvelle*, Viret is pictured brandishing books as weapons against his papal enemies.[50]

While radical bands of Roman Catholics assailed him (and even poisoned his spinach soup), he persisted by ministering in Lausanne, Switzerland, until emigrating to Calvin's city of Geneva, where he was afforded eight hundred florins a year, twelve strikes of corn, plus two casks of hearty wine. His eloquence and prolific writing attracted great audiences, including Huguenots. One shining characteristic that made him so compelling was his satirical sense of humor. On describing how to discipline or "bridle" children, a sly commentary on how to rhetorically move those to whom he spoke, he commented lightly that some will need to be coaxed, some will need no discipline, some will be motivated by liberality, some by rewards and promises, and others by honor. Treat each child according to his temperament and needs. Some will have to be treated like spirited horses, some like gentle asses, some like stubborn mules.[51]

Rabelais's influence upon the reformers issued forth in the cautiously and anonymously published *Satyres chrestiennes de la cuisine papale* (1560).[52] The Menippean satire uses rhetoric to play with the trope of the kitchen as hell (usually a topsy-turvy world ruled by women).[53] In his astute study of the vituperative satire of the Reformation period, historian Antonia Szabari explains that in his *Institutes*, Calvin pictured the papacy as being run like a kitchen in which the clergy worship by turning their bellies into their gods, with some getting "the juicy bits, others mere morsels."[54] The *Satyres chrestiennes*'s history of the theological "grand cuisines" finds no better place than this kitchen in which to serve the varied dishes of the *lanx satura*, a saucy medley of pine nuts and dried fruits. In fact, in the Eighth Satire of this culinary poem, dishes and saucepans become weapons for the papal kitchen to use against its adversaries. Nuns wash the dirty dishes in toilets in a "river of vomit" produced by the drunken priests. Their detergents are luxury and arrogance. The cooks (theologians) of the kitchen "thirst" for the "good beverage" of the scriptures; even though, says the satire, they "have never drunk from it." They serve toxic meats (doctrines and rites) rather than wholesome and joyous refreshment.[55] Those who indulge in the fare of the papal kitchen are gluttons, pleasure-seekers intoxicated with laughter (*souls-de-rire*).

The poet explains that he himself was rescued from this wicked feast while laughing at them (by reading "frivolous works," most probably like those of Erasmus and Rabelais) and vomiting at the disgusting practices of the corrupt papacy.[56] However, here a distinction should be made between the joyous, exuberant, and liberating laughter of Rabelais and the mocking, accusatory, and even angry laughter against those who satiate themselves with merriment in the *Satyres chrestiennes*.

Calvin, who charged that one should laugh at the enemies of God only with sober moderation, wasn't sure about Viret's publication of *Disputations chrestiennes*, a book celebrating laughter within the Christian life. After his conversion, Calvin retreated from "facetious writings" that once amused and now horrified him, even accusing Rabelais as a "mocker of God." However, lawyers are rarely comfortable with parables or laughter. Remarkably, Calvin did propose to write a preface for Viret "certifying that the book's satirical laughter was not merely justifiable but actually praiseworthy."[57]

Viret affirmed his faith, he said, not because of the tradition of "Tertullian, Chrysostom, or Thomas Aquinas, not *even* because of Erasmus or Luther. . . . If I did so, I should be the disciple of men. I will believe only Jesus Christ my Shepherd."[58] Viret believed that one won one's enemies not by combating them with fire, faggots, or sword, but with sound doctrine, charity, good works, and gentleness of spirit. Known for his mighty thunderous sermons, he was also remembered for the winsome charm of his humor. Yet one of the most beguiling satires came not from these merry men, but from one remarkable woman who championed gender equality in matters of mirth.

Lady of Laughter

Marguerite of Navarre (1492–1549), French queen consort and devout sister of King Francis I, wrote her own version of the *Decameron*, entitled the *Heptameron*. Intensely involved with religious reform, she demonstrated much sympathy with Protestants, although she never became one. (Her husband, Henry of Navarre, signed the Edict of Nantes, giving Huguenots freedom of religion, at least for a season.) In the sixteenth century, her support of religious renewal and reformers enabled her to protect and defend many, even John Calvin.

In her works, Marguerite makes fun of male clergy, ever ready to point "an accusatory finger at abusive and disloyal husbands and lustful men of the cloth."[59] In fact, Rabelais dedicated his *Tiers Livre* to her, conceding that many of the ladies of the French court hid their laughter behind their fans when Rabelais's colorful tales were read aloud.

In the *Heptameron*, five men and five women (a more balanced ratio than Boccaccio's) travel to the mountaintop Abbey of Notre-Dame de Serrance, when a washed-out bridge strands them on their journey. They dedicate their mornings to reading the Bible and meditating and their afternoons to telling stories. Such is the setting for the posthumously published *Heptameron*, a belle book of moral, merry, and facetious tales (with so many wicked friars seeking to lie with women). One female character opines that those clergy who "make a mockery of their vows should be burned alive."[60] Her friend Parlamente thinks that they should be exposed to public shame.

Two stories on the fifth day involve Franciscans in Flanders. During Advent, a countess requests a competent and honest Franciscan who can preach and hear confessions. The friars send their most renowned preacher, being concerned to curry favor with the wealthy noble families, but he has a weakness. Hearing the confession of a young girl, he demands an unusual penance: for her to wear a cord against her bare flesh; then the friar orders that he should tie it on.[61] Another Franciscan friar named De Vale secretly lusts after another attractive woman. But here the spirited woman gives him a kick in the stomach when he scrambles up the stairs toward her. She knocks him back down and says, "Up hill and down dale, Mr. De Vale!"

Marguerite raised the rights and honors of the woman while humiliating friars. But she mocked gullible older women who follow the wayward clerics as well, as in the calamitous story of a mother who gives her nubile daughter to Friar de Vale for "discipline." The priest rapes the daughter while the mother calls up the stairs, "Don't let her off lightly! Give it to her again! Teach the wicked girl a lesson!" When the friar has satisfied his evil desires, he goes downstairs to the lady of the house, and says, with his face all on fire: "I think, Madame, that your daughter won't forget the lesson I've just given her!"[62]

Like those of Boccaccio and Chaucer, Marguerite's stories expose sexual immorality. If such admonitions as "it is not good for man to be alone" and St. Paul's counsel that "it is better to marry than burn" were ignored, violent consequences would ensue. Her stories contrast normative values of chastity and fidelity with the twisted repressions of the church upon its male clergy. Medieval satire on gender inequality appealed to the normative ethic of the scriptures to expose the trespasses and transgressions. This brilliant hen could join the shrill voices of roosters to rouse a deaf world to the sin taking place under the sun, trying to point out to mothers and daughters a lesson on men, with or without their cowls on, which they wouldn't forget.

Marguerite's activities in the court of her younger brother, King Francis I, included spiritual concerns as well as sexual, social, and political ones. An activist for the reform and reordering of the Roman Catholic Church, she freely denounced what she saw as the evil improprieties of the men of the cloth. The voluptuous and often lurid prose of her writings did not detract from her evangelical piety in seeking reform. Her Christian humanism followed that of Erasmus and enabled her to rescue many from religious persecution, even, it is said, Rabelais. But it is in her blunt tales, and the ensuing discussions of her stories, that she worked to expose the corruption and misogyny of the religious milieu.[63]

Flights of Flyting

In 1579, Canterbury satirist (and would-be playwright) Stephen Gosson introduced a lively moral condemnation of poetry and theater in his euphuistic *Schoole of Abuse, Containing a Pleasant Invective against Poets, Pipers, Plaiers, Jesters and such like Caterpillars of the Commonwealth.* In the ornate manner of Elizabethan fashion, Gosson castigated the mischief of the sinner and the vulgar poet, trying to overthrow the bulwarks of their profane writing. He targeted those wits that capably mixed honey and gall, but were nevertheless "swine that forsake their fair fields and wallow in the mire." Gosson lamented the loss of good moral and wise poetry, as immoral poets turned the taste of the reader in a downward trajectory to "piping, from piping to playing, from play to pleasure, from pleasure to sloth, from sloth to sleep, from sleep to sin, from sin to death, from death to the devil." And yet as one who messed with scoffers, he expected to be abused himself, warning that one must be careful in judging other scoffers, as one will be judged oneself.[64]

Gosson threw his little pebbles of satire knowing some might boomerang. The rough, unpolished witticisms of seemingly insignificant wits like Gosson were akin to the little stones slung by David at the forehead of the giant Goliath. Herein, *dabar*, the word and act, were reunited in startling ways. At the end of the sixteenth century, attacks on the Church of England were made by a guerilla-style publisher who used the name Martin Marprelate ("bad prelate"). In 1588, the Martin Marprelate Wars introduced lewd catcalls into the religious debates, with rowdy haranguing replacing civil debates. The controversy revived the old practice of flyting, with inventions of novel, highfalutin language ("dissimblation") and inarticulate noises (ha-ha-ha, tse-tse-tse) to confound opponents. Stones of scoffing would be thrown with abandon.

The Marprelate Press felt obligated to expose the presumption of Anglican Church polity. In *The Learned Discourse*, Puritan William Fulke had pressed for reforms of such practices as the "sinful callings," seeking to abolish the sinecure positions given to ignorant ministers.[65] His work sought to unite all Protestants against a corrupt ecclesiastical practice.

Dean John Bridges rebuffed Fulke's invitation to debate with an "unseemly" jest, releasing "A Defence of the Government Established in the Church of Englande for Ecclesiasticale matters." Against the dean came the pseudonymous Martin Marprelate tracts, lambasting the Anglican bishops for distorting the word of God. Taking on the dramatic personae of a rustic upstart, a series of seven pamphlets starts with "The Epistle" in which Bridges is lampooned as a dunce with the brains of a woodcock. As a self-proclaimed inflated buffoon, Marprelate adapts a "decorous persona" to assault the Anglicans. His *ad hominem* arguments strip away the respectable veneer of the church offices of "petty popes." He snipes that others can "lay the ignorant sots as well as you, Brother Bridges . . . though indeed not so naturally, I grant."[66]

The tracts popularized the need for reform rather than debating it. One motive for disseminating the tracts stemmed from the need to secure an audience's attention. Even Thomas Wilson's 1553 *Arte of Rhetorique* recommended that "even these ancient Preachers, must now and then, play the fools in the pulpit to serve the fickle ears of their fleeting audience."[67] The great Roman rhetorician Cicero had put forth the proper use of liberal humor for oratory and now it could be fittingly applied to printed pamphlets. So, too, did the publishers cite Sir Thomas More, so "full of railing, gestying and baudye tales." They followed More's model from Horace's famous quotation, "Ridentem dicere verum, quid vetat?" (Why should not a jester or a merry fellow tell truth?).[68]

Marprelate whooped and hollered in his satiric epistle ("From plague, pestilence, and famine, from bishops, Priests and Deacons, good Lord deliver us").[69] However, the bishops then hired their own professional writers from among pamphleteers and playwrights (like Thomas Cooper) to respond, in a tactic that upheld Marprelate's thesis that "the bishops' cause was best suited to jesters or the stage." Cooper himself was marked as an "unskillful and deceitful tub-trimmer," best known for his excessively amorous wife.[70]

The tracts employed sneering invective as much as clever parody. Marprelate was condemned for dressing religion up in "motley" and howling like a madman in Bedlam. English scientist Francis Bacon was himself concerned that the Marprelate controversy would "turn Religion into a comedy or Satyr, to rip up wounds with a laughing countenance, to intermix Scripture and scurrility, sometimes in one sentence." This, he wrote with solemnity, "is a thing far from the devout reverence of a Christian."[71] In contrast, Puritan poet John Milton championed a strong, sinewy vein of laughter for debate, pointing to the biblical tradition of Elijah and the martyrs effectively turning "religion into a comedy to rip up the wounds of Idolatry and Superstition with a laughing countenance."[72] As scholar Raymond Anselment observes, "Throughout the seventeenth century, Elijah's reproof of the prophets of Baal in I Kings 18 remains the most popular illustration of divinely sanctioned ridicule"[73]

Unsurprisingly, the publishers were charged with improper jesting by the ostentatious Archbishop of Canterbury, John Whitgift, who opposed everything nonconformist. In 1599, Whitgift issued his ban to printers, forbidding the continued publication of snarling, biting, satirical verses.[74]

Throughout Queen Elizabeth's reign, the Act of Uniformity called for compulsory church attendance and official recognition of the Anglican Church. Whitgift set up his Court of High Commission to deal with control of the press by church bishops. It prohibited the satirical works of Samuel Johnson, Joseph Hall (the porcupine with sharp quills), and another true British character, Thomas Nashe (1567–1601), whose work Whitgift believed, "should be incinerated!"[75] However, such puny protest would not stop the outburst of excess.

From 1589–1599, the professional Oxford satirist Thomas Nashe conducted a series of public controversies known as the Pamphlet Wars. Nashe earned the reputation of being the English Juvenal, a coarse, extravagant, impudent juggler of words, who "writes with spirite." Nashe followed the traditional mix of *satura*, mingling his piety and scholarship with slang and bawdiness. He reeked of something Rabelaisian with a relish for roguery and a pungent aroma of lower class guttersnipe.

His comic flyting hit a pinnacle of reckless ridicule against one fellow in particular, Gabriel Harvey, the brother in the Marprelate controversy. The feud between these two has been unmatched in comic abuse, but it was Nashe who triumphed with his merciless wit, making Harvey the butt of his jokes, calling him Timothy Tiptoes, Braggadochio Glorioso, and Gerboduck Huddleduddle. His neologisms, which smacked of wild recklessness, could wither his opponents. "But ah! What news do you hear of that good Gabriel Huff-snuff, known to the world for a fool, and clapped in the Fleet for a rhymer?" Nashe was eventually imprisoned in Newgate for sneaking satirical materials into a devotional. Reform was rarely on his mind.

Well-Donne Wit

The dean of St. Paul's Cathedral was not only an Anglican preacher and metaphysical poet, but a subtle humorist as well. John Donne (1572–1631) abandoned his Roman Catholic faith early in his career and confessed his allegiance to the Church of England. Being made a royal chaplain and then dean of St. Paul's Cathedral in London, he wondered about his vocation.

As Jacobian poet and preacher, Donne unleashed his witty satires. In "The Will," he ironically bequeaths his spiritual legacy to various heirs who obviously need each gift. The items are superfluous: for example, his eyes he gives to Argus; his tears he leaves to women or the sea. To Jesuits, he gives his ingenuity and openness; to buffoons, his pensiveness.

His faith he gives to Roman Catholics; his good works to the schismatics. With his last gasp, he gives his physic-books "to him for whom the passing bell next tolls." Moral counsel is left for Bedlam.[76]

John Donne's "Satyre III" emphasizes the responsibility and autonomy of the individual. The poem insists that individuals have the absolute responsibility for the state of their souls. However, Donne recognizes the tendency of people to acquiesce control of the conscience to external authorities. The poet criticizes all forms of authority, Roman Catholic as well as Protestant, religious as well as secular. He identifies three temptations of the soul (the world, the flesh, and the devil) as the key battles to engage.[77] The challenge is to find the location of true religion, which was housed in Rome a thousand years ago and dwelt in Geneva for a time. He concludes that one should not trust religious men, but continually seek that which is true and good religion. Donne warns of these foes: the world, the flesh and the foul devil, the last of whom we too frequently strive to please. Nor should we love the world's self, for she wanes and becomes decrepit, and we find out we have ended up loving a withered strumpet. "And nowhere lives a woman true." The search for true religion leads back to Rome (because, as we noted, she was there a thousand years ago) or Geneva, where she is called "plain, simple, sullen, young, contemptuous, yet unhandsome." Unfortunately, many with lecherous humors judge no wench wholesome, but see them all as "coarse country drudges."[78]

The problem Donne saw is reflected in three Roman characters, Graius, Phrygius, and Graccus, who serve as allegories for the churches. First, Graius stays still at home in the established church because "some preachers, vile ambitious bawds" try to make him think that only the religion they have now is perfect; he embraces the same faith (and wife) as his godfathers. "Careless Phrygius doth abhor All, / Because all cannot be good, as one / Knowing some women whores, dares marry none." In stark contrast, Graccus blindly thinks all religions and women in divers countries with divers habits are still one kind, and thus loves all women equally.

The way to settle it all is to ask "thy father which is she," because truth and falsehood are near twins ("yet truth a little elder is"); in other words, inquire of God to find out which bride is true and right. Such questioning is not straying from the faith, but "to sleep, or run wrong, is."

Author John Peter lamented that when John Donne became a preacher, a great "writer of comedies was lost."[79] Donne was master of the metaphysical conceit, in which two ideas are juxtaposed into a single metaphor, as in his famously erotic funny poem "The Flea," a delightful jocose play on the biblical vision of the two becoming one. The lover begs that they not kill the flea because it is a symbol of three, the two of them and it. The poem is playful, amatory, and informed by biblical themes.

> MARK but this flea, and mark in this,
> How little that which thou deniest me is;
> It suck'd me first, and now sucks thee,
> And in this flea our two bloods mingled be.
> Thou know'st that this cannot be said
> A sin, nor shame, nor loss of maidenhead;
> Yet this enjoys before it woo,
> And pamper'd swells with one blood made of two;
> And this, alas! is more than we would do.[80]

However, he then asks in Satyre 3 whether satirical railing can really help find the true faith or the right female.

> Kind pity chokes my spleen; brave scorn forbids
> Those tears to issue which swell my eyelids;
> I must not laugh, nor weep sins and be wise;
> Can railing, then, cure these worn maladies?[81]

Donne warned, in his fifth "Satyre" that the Muse should not laugh so freely; for those who are extremely wretched or wicked are free from the sting of jests. What they need is a theme of charity and liberty. Thus, Donne was quite skeptical about the ability of "satyre" to actually reform a person: "to teach by painting drunkards, doth not last / Now; Aretine's pictures have made few chaste."[82]

Well-Barrowed

The most influential historical sermon on the Apostle Paul's admonition against "foolish talking and jesting" (Ephesians 5:4) was Isaac Barrow's (1630–1677) "Sermon on Evil Speaking." Awarded the Cambridge Greek professorship during the Restoration (as well as being a Professor of Mathematics, in which capacity he developed theories of calculus), Barrows was "low of stature" (which is a kindly way of saying short) and quite unkempt in his personal habits, so much so that many of his congregation left his sermon one Sunday due to his disheveled appearance.

In his famous sermon, Barrow distinguishes between playful mirth that draws friends together in community and mean and spiteful wit that divides people. Such a distinction is very timely, Barrow notes, for this particular "pleasant and jocular age."[83] Trying to define humor, Barrow explains it wears many garbs and assumes many postures, "sometimes lurking under an odd similitude, sometimes lodged in a sly question, in a smart answer, in a quirky reason, in a shrewd imitation, in cunningly diverting, or cleverly retorting to an objection, sometimes in a tart irony, in a lusty hyperbole, in a startling metaphor, in a plausible reconciling of contradictions, or an acute nonsense."[84] Such playful mirth is inclusive, inviting participants to laugh at one another and be laughed at by others.

Fighting against the image of sober Puritans as lumpish or sour people, Barrow finds all human beings to be "so irreclaimably disposed to mirth and laughter." Humor should be diverted into the proper channels. His definition of *eutrapelia* (ευτραπελια) differs from the Apostle Paul's translation of "coarse jesting" in that Barrow emphasizes ευ as "well" and τρεπω signifying "to turn." While Paul identifies it as a twisting of the good, Barrows, following Aristotle and Aquinas, explains its meaning to be "good turning," as mirth meant to generate cheerfulness or spiritual joy, one fruit of the Holy Spirit.

Barrow lists moments when such brisk felicity of wit may be practiced. Jocular discourse is allowed when it ministers harmless delight to conversation (not disturbing peace, infringing charity, or ruining piety)—for Christianity is not so harsh as to "bar us continually from innocent" wholesome and useful pleasures as life requires. As such it sweetens conversation and maintains good humor among brothers. So, too, the mind profits from the rousing exercise of wit. Christians need not "knit the brow and squeeze the brain, to be always sadly dumpish, or seriously pensive."[85] The mind must be relieved and relaxed in cheerfulness.

Second, one may speak foolishly (Μωρολογια, or foolish/moron talk) when "exposing things apparently base and vile." Ridiculous things should be derided just as Elijah exposed the wicked superstitions of the prophets of Baal. As the text says, Elijah "mocked them." "When sarcastic twitches are needful to pierce the thick skins of men, to correct their lethargic stupidity, to rouse them out of the drowsy negligence," then may such facetious discourse be applied.

Third, as salt is useful for cleansing and curing some sores (it was Quintilian who first connected *saltus* to humor, which expands the meaning of "salt of the earth"), so jesting may be "commodious for reproving some vices," as a way to pleasantly "rub" the faults of some who will not endure a direct reproof with a "jocund wipe." Some companions one can gibe into better manners. Barrow says essentially that we must "talk in their own fashion, with humor and jollity"—that we must speak their language in order to "inveigle those dotterels to hearken to us." Such humor might seem to "tickle the ear, but doth sting the heart," as a true servant of charity.

Fourth, errors that cannot be solemnly confronted may be confuted with humor. Thus one must trifle with a perverse or petulant man and dash impudence with wit. Fifth, satire provides the best way to defend against unjust reproach or slander. By fighting obloquy, argument deteriorates into yelling, but humor helps one escape personal attacks, repelling the brunt of malice.

Sixth, since such jests can be a weapon for truth and virtue, one should not surrender the sharp blades of battle that patrons of vice employ. One may impress wit for the service of truth and goodness, lest folly or impiety usurps the tool for itself. Seventh (Barrow goes on and on about good values of *eutrapelia*), as rhetoric allows us creative schemes, why not let wit instill good doctrine, excite good passions, illustrate and adorn the truth with delight? A rhetorical flourish is cousin to the jest.

Eighth, the model of sage and grave persons allows this practice. Cicero (who composed books of jests) and other patrons present us patterns for laughing. Finally, concludes Barrow, it is the abuse of jesting, wit, and fancy that is dangerous. All good things can degenerate and be corrupted, which is why the Apostle prohibited it.

Barrow forbids speaking loosely and wantonly about holy things, such as God himself. Such intolerably vain and wicked practices are marked by the "most enormous sauciness." Are the dangers of hell matters for jesting? Herein, Barrow emphasizes the importance of being comic and earnest. Those who worship flashy wit are like those who sacrifice an ox to a fly. There is also the danger of those who brazenly perform simply to be the fool. One must not fiddle with one's own soul, for as King Solomon wrote: "I said of laughter, it is mad; and of mirth, what doeth it?" But then Solomon lived with too many wives.

> All injurious, abusive, scurrilous jesting, which causelessly or needless tendeth to the disgrace, damage, vexation, or prejudice in any kind of our neighbor (provoking his displeasure, grating on his modesty, stirring passion in him) is also prohibited.[86]

Barrows lists several prohibitions. One must not prostitute laughter, nor trifle with the reputations of other men, which once cracked, are very difficult to repair. One must not damage one's neighbor. It is simply the golden rule that governs laughter. If a man offends in order to get a laugh or please himself, he is a scurvy malignity. Hurtful wanton mirth is the property of fools, and "it is the sport of fools to do mischief." Thus avoid the scurrilous and scoffing ways when they abuse piety and virtue. They become what the Greeks called pests (Αοιμουσ) or pestilent men. "Surely the Lord will scorn the scorners."

Barrow concludes by reminding his readers that they shouldn't be demure or impudent. One should use one's wits innocently and conveniently to edifying others. The field in which one can be merry is wide and spacious; "true festivity is called salt," which should give a smart, savory relish to discourse, not a sour or irritating disgust. If the salt "become insipid, it is therefore good for nothing, but to be cast out and trodden under foot."[87]

One of Barrow's playful trysts of wit occurred in the court of Charles II, with John Wilmot, the Earl of Rochester, libertine author of bawdry poetry. The earl was part of riotous company known as the Merry Gang.

The earl met his match when he and the scholar Barrow met near the king's chamber. The earl facetiously bowed before Dr. Barrow, saying, "I am yours, doctor, to the knee strings."

> Barrow (bowing lower): I am yours, my lord, to the shoe-tie.
> Rochester: Yours, doctor, down to the ground.
> Barrow: Yours, my lord, to the centre of the earth.
> Rochester (not to be out-done): Yours, doctor, to the lowest pit of hell.
> Barrow: There, my lord, I must leave you.[88]

Through the mock courtesy of the two gentlemen, Barrow's quick playfulness in a match of wits is celebrated. Yet, the exchange also demonstrates how he practiced what he preached. Here was a true man of God, his piety salted with good humor and wit.[89]

Purifying Puritans

Without an extensive, published biography, Anglican Samuel Butler (1612–1680) reigned as the ranking wit during the Commonwealth, pinching both solemn Presbyterians and cheerful Dissenters. Butler existed unnoticed in the shadows of Bunyan and Milton, yet he too aimed at reforming society, just not with as much solemnity and gravity. We may quote one of his famous lines to sum up his view of seventeenth century England: "I smell a rat."

Butler's England was pockmarked with cruel mockery and nasty amusements. Numerous attacks on Puritans portrayed them as secret lechers and austere killjoys. After the Protectorate, the ensuring Restoration ushered in an era of perverse amusement, with the gallant classes visiting chained maniacs of Bedlam and watching women prisoners flogged at Bridewell.[90] Such sadistic pleasures as bear-baiting, shooting cats with crossbows, and blinding doves in order to watch them soar in disordered and suicidal flight engrossed a bored leisure class. Taunting of religious difference was just as pronounced, as Anglicans danced about maypoles mocking Dissidents once the Church of England had been reestablished.[91]

Growing up under the strict guidance of Sir Samuel Luke, a Puritan justice, Butler would go on to ridicule his Puritan superiors as "praying and babbling apostates." Luke had oppressed the clerk so much that Butler's coil would spring back, with a vengeance. The civil war between the Cavaliers and the Roundheads offered him sufficient material for a grand burlesque.[92] Once the Restoration unleashed its winds, Butler began his revenge on unsuspecting Roundheads. His extravagant mock-heroic verse concerned the witty parody romance of *Hudibras*, the "chief of Domestic Knights and Errant who never bent his stubborn knee to anything but Chivalry."[93] He mingles broad, slapstick humor with sneering mockery to undermine the Puritan character.

Built on conflicts raging between Cromwell's Puritans and British society, Butler finds the church more bellicose than peace-making and describes his Presbyterian hero, Hudibras as follows:

> For his religion it was fit
> To match his learning and his wit:
> 'Twas Presbyterian true blue;
> For he was of that stubborn crew
> Of errant saints, whom all men grant
> To be the true Church militant;
> Such as do build their faith upon
> The holy text of pike and gun;
> Decide all controversies by
> Infallible artillery,
> And prove their doctrine orthodox,
> By apostolic blows and knocks.[94]

Hudibras parodies the picaresque chivalric romance, made internationally famous by Cervantes' *Don Quixote*. What almost appears as a road vaudeville team, symbolizing a battle between Lent and Carnival, or Quixote and Sancho Panza, is matched by Hudibras, a zealous and ignorant Presbyterian justice, and Ralpho, the cheeky and disputatious Inquisitor and Dissenting Puritan. They are "allies at each other's throats"

Having witnessed the fraudulent ways of some saints, Butler directs his primary focus on hypocrisy. His burlesque mocks the knight errant tradition of heroic actions during the Civil War and Interregnum. Reform-minded, supercilious Puritans are

Compound for sins they are inclin'd to,
By damning those they have no mind to;
Still so perverse and opposite,
As if they worshipped God for spite;
All piety consists therein
In them, in other men all sin;
Rather than fail, they will defy
That which they love most tenderly;
Quarrel with minc'd pies, and disparage
Their best and dearest friend, plum porridge;
Fat pig and goose itself oppose,
And blaspheme custard through the nose.[95]

Hudibras is a greedy, counterfeit opportunist, an impoverished colonel who tries to arrange a marriage with a wealthy widow. The knight attempts to separate her from her "jointure," just as the Puritans sought to separate England from her inheritance. In this allegorical civil war, the conflict is over the soil/soul/sole ownership of England and her property. Bears, which suffer that medieval practice of bear-baiting, represent the monarchy, and the synods parallel the control of the state by religious governments. The Restoration will unite Royalists (including the widow) with the Presbyterian Saints, for better or worse, till death they do part. Yet Hudibras is outdone by the clever lady—who confronts the knight with his hypocrisy. The widow laughs at Hudibras and his comic sidekick Ralpho in the stocks:

Democritus ne'r laugh'd so loud
To see Bauds carted through the crowd,
Or Funerals with stately Pomp,
March slowly on in solemn dump;
As she laugh'd out, until her back
As well as sides, was like to crack.

For now the War is not between
The Brethren, and the Men of sin:
But Saint and Saint to spill the Blood
Of one another's Brotherhood. [96]

Adventures of the two deluded protagonists involve a carnivalesque confrontation with a motley crew of stave-wielding commoners, led by a disabled fiddler with a wooden leg and his miserable bear. Religious tropes illustrate immoral or criminal behavior, such as lay sisters shown as whores and a pimp disguised as a Roman priest. For Butler, the reforming religious mind is obsessed and unhinged, and all dissenting religions appear similar: put them all in a bag and shake them, and you would mistake them, not knowing which is which.

The colloquial and spritely adventures do, however, demonstrate a key Calvinist doctrine, that all men are indeed depraved. There are none righteous. Noble human actions can be reduced to selfish greed and self-gratification. Appropriately, both Hudibras and Ralpho end up in stocks.[97]

Butler enjoyed his writing with boyish pleasure, sneaking in strange rhymes and bizarre tropes (for instance, "Greek and squeak," "Hick-up and prick-up," "magician and piss in"). As carnival and popular misrule provide a release valve for dangerous energies, so Butler offered relief for a strained political Commonwealth. For Butler, the body, as honored in the Incarnation, was good. To quote twentieth-century comedian Lenny Bruce, "If God made the body and the body's dirty, the fault lies with the manufacturer."[98]

The notion of Bakhtin's carnival is reborn, with hierarchies of humans and beasts, men and women, turned upside down and made topsy-turvy. Women, for Butler, accept who they are, unlike Hudibras who lives in illusion. The widow recognizes that a cunning and wily bride can

> reduce the most imperious Brace to be her Drudge, and utensil,
> And Slave; to husband takes the Idiot during life
> And makes him but a Helper to his wife.[99]

However, after the Commonwealth, the licentious Restoration erupted. Reflecting after 1667 upon the Restoration inversion of Commonwealth hypocrisy, Butler wrote that twice men have "turned the World / The wrong Side outward, like a Juggler's Pocket." In other words, even with hypocrisy gone, the other sides of sin returned to England. Now instead of hiding their damned souls in private holes, wearing masks of hypocrisy to steal and slink away in masquerade to hell, sinners bring their crimes into the open.

One final contribution of Samuel Butler to religious satire occurs in his invention of polemical prose characters who captured the essence of types. He drew the ecclesiastic figures of "a Hypocrite" and "Hypocritical Nonconformist." For Butler, extremes like a Popish Priest and a (Puritan) Fanatic are identical. Fanatics look like puppet saints, who will suffer for religion, but do nothing to help their neighbors. For the Zealot, his zeal is "never so vehement as when it concurs with his Interest. . . . He is very severe to other men's Sins, that his own may pass unsuspected."[100]

In his essay "On the Hero of Hudibras: Butler Vindicated," critic Isaac D'Israeli argued that Butler, like Cervantes, but unlike Rabelais and Sterne, never wrote a single word of "indecent ribaldry." Such "trash" might have made him more popular. What D'Israeli found most fruitful was that Butler not only attacked the villainy of religious/political hypocrisy during the Commonwealth, but that when the world changed with the Restoration and its profligate Cavaliers (who became "as obnoxious to public decency as the Tartuffes"), Butler turned his arrows in this new direction, against the wretched court and the licentious age of Charles II. "This then is the greater glory of BUTLER, that his high and indignant spirit equally satirized the hypocrites of Cromwell and the libertines of Charles."[101]

A significant aspect of *Hudibras*'s success stems from its illustrator, engraver William Hogarth (1667–1774), who produced twenty-odd plates. These, like the icons of the early church, made ideas and controversies accessible to the illiterate, even as Hogarth's subtleties escape many today. His caricatures strike the eye as cutting visual satire. Few have skewered the hypocritical excesses of his era more than Hogarth. But he will reappear in the coming golden age of satire.[102]

The age of Reformation emphasized, as one would expect, the reforming aspect of satire. Nevertheless, it did not neglect the comic vulgarity of the medieval period to elicit laughs while satirizing. On the extreme side of ridicule, practitioners of flyting like Thomas Nashe subtracted a motive of moral or spiritual reform from the equation. However, they were more than compensated with the apotheosis of true satire in the humanist Erasmus and his celebration of folly. Reformers like Luther sought to purify a corrupt church, using satire alongside other polemics. Their satiric purpose was not merely savage joy, as contemporary poet Joseph Salemi described it. For him, such satirists "lambaste stupidity for the sheer joy of doing so. . . . If satire is going to be worth a damn it has to be *destructive*, period."[103] Not so for these reforming satirists of the sixteenth-century. For them, satire was important only because it would save people from damnation. Of course, it had to be destructive, but only so one could build a constructive and orthodox theology. That this satire was coarse and wonderfully vulgar was because its practitioners were wonderfully vulgar. But this would change with the onset of the Enlightenment, with the ascent of wit, even at the expense of losing shit.

6

Augustan Poets and Pundits

If Faith itself has diff'rent dresses worn,
What wonder Modes in Wit should take their turn?
—Alexander Pope

In 1660, the Restoration of the English monarchy ushered in the House of Stuarts with the monarchy restored in all its lavish and licentious glory. While merry King Charles II reigned, John Dryden (1631–1700) scrambled about making his mark as a great English poet, teetering between the Metaphysical and Romantic periods and tiptoeing between eras of thought and emotion. During this time, the cosmopolitan Roman Catholic Dryden established himself as the pontiff of British poets, holding court at Will's Coffeehouse, where he once entertained the young Alexander Pope. In 1668, Charles elevated him to become the first poet laureate of England. His critics accused Dryden of earning money by flattering patrons ("pleasing not himself, but other men"[1]), and so he was seen as the palace lap dog, barking at the king's foes.

During the English Enlightenment, literature became occupied with politics and religion, engaging contemporary struggles and driving Augustan satirists into mock-heroic battles. A spirit of "party and faction" shaped the emergence of satire as a dominant literary form in the late 1600s.[2] Dryden stepped up as a civic poet, seeking to tidy up thoughts and controversies with his talent. He held a "Layman's Faith that Reason grows pale at Religion's sight"; it dies and "dissolves in supernatural Light."[3] The rhetorical weapon of reason was not enough to confront his adversaries. In contrast to the brilliance of the sun, reason was like a "nightly taper," or flickering candle, which could only bring a little illumination. Nevertheless, his iambic pentameter poetry of satire shone upon dark corners of corruption, briefly flashing like lightning across the emerald isle.

Dryden surgically diagnosed the source of satire's strength in his *Discourse Concerning the Original and Progress of Satire* (1693). It was

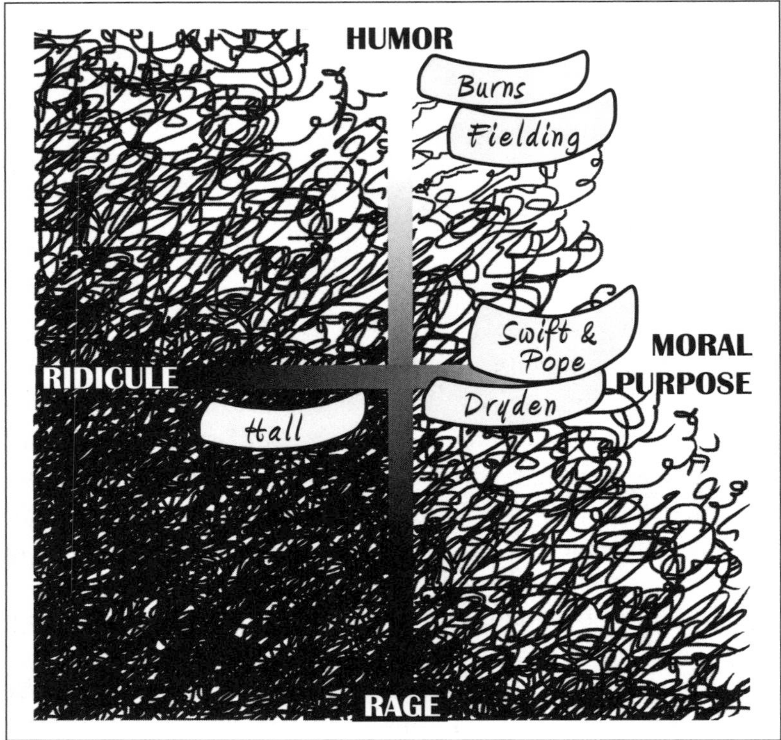

Hall, Burns, Fielding, Swift, Pope, and Dryden on the Quad of Satire.

corruption; bad times are good times for the poet of mockery. Horace's disadvantage was that he lived under the golden age of Rome, "better for the Man, but worse for the Satirist."[4] Old acerbic Juvenal, on the other hand, lived under tyranny and all manner of vice; thus his zealous satire and sharp, incisive sword fit with the times. Rather than slash with Juvenal's sword, Dryden skillfully applied his finely sharpened scalpel in cutting and slicing. He knew that "there is still a vast difference between the slovenly butchering of a Man, and the finesse of the Stroak that separates the Head from the body, and leaves it standing in place."[5] For Dryden, satire had risen from the ill-mannered, ribald comedy of the satyr to the smorgasbord of choice bits in the *lanx satura*. To serve such a satiric banquet, Dryden's menu prescribed focusing upon one theme, a refusal to lampoon or attack individuals (inconsistently obeyed), and a calling to give the reader a precept of moral virtue that cautioned against some particular vice. It was a classic, even Augustinian, feast.

Dryden took his inspiration from the classical poets thriving under Caesar Augustus. The literary elite of his era, brimming with numerous classical allusions, emulated that era of Roman prosperity, hoping their verse would publically contribute to a golden age. With order as a chief virtue, Dryden wrote with clarity, solidity, and, especially, chameleon-like flexibility. Where he once praised Lord Protector Oliver Cromwell, now he praised King Charles II. It was his job to take on the enemies of the leader, whether protectorate or king.

In 1666, that *annus mirabilis*, when war against the Dutch broke out and a great fire ravaged London, Dryden wrote his prophecy of rebuilding a decimated capital, a new Rome, using decasyllabic lines to establish a national poem. He thus became the nation's Poet Laureate. His was a life in capital letters.

Although a lumpy, portly, and short poet squab, Dryden collaborated with the king, even strolling about in conversation inquiring about what he might write to mar his majesty's enemies. The underlying question was who was to rule England, either the king or Parliament. Dryden found his bread buttered on the side with Charles II. One key problem was the spurious popish plot of 1678, manufactured by Titus Oates during a period of rabid anti–Roman Catholic hysteria. And Dryden was marked with papist tattoos.

Against this alarming mood Dryden directed his satirical magus opus, *Absalom and Achitophel*.[6] He composed this political satire against Lord Anthony Ashley Cooper Shaftesbury and his opposition party, using the biblical story of King David and his rebellious son Absalom as an allegorical blueprint to ridicule the king's enemies.[7] The poem exposed the names and the characters: Charles II was the tranquil old King David, while the king's popular son James, the Duke of Monmouth, paralleled David's usurping son Absalom, and the Earl of Shaftesbury (accused of high treason) was the brilliant but treacherous Achitophel, David's sneaky counselor and old friend who stirs up the son against the father. Yet as readers of the Bible know, Achitophel finds his strategic advice undercut by another deception.[8]

Shaftesbury, with intrigues against both the court and Roman Catholics, propagated his deist notion of virtue as the general good for humanity. Dryden, the Roman Catholic, characterized him as "sagacious, bold, and turbulent of wit." (It was *his* "great wit that to madness surely was allied."[9]) Shaftesbury insisted that one should practice only good humor that was "moderate," as in the "sharp, witty, and felicitous language" of Christ's "Humorous pleasantry."[10] Jesting about grave matters was for him "the devil's work."[11] He conceded that satire could ridicule fanatical beliefs, but that, of course, did not refer to him. He disapproved of such "peevish and wanton wits" as Dryden.[12]

A fear of despotism arose from Roman Catholic influence in the court of Charles, as Catholic monarchies tended to affirm absolute power, with the king falling under its spell. The suspicion of Charles as a secret Roman Catholic didn't help.[13] Against such a suspicion, the text of Dryden's poem curiously sets off two groups of "chosen people," the "headstrong, moody" Jews and the Dissenters (the "Elect" saved by "Grace," their doctrinal shibboleth or code name that set them off from Papists and Anglicans).[14]

The poem satirized certain individuals camouflaged under the guise of the chosen people of God. One prominent Whig gentleman, by the name of Slingsby Bethel, was represented as the annoying Shimei. When King David had been ousted from Jerusalem by his son Absalom and was fleeing the city, Shimei popped out of the hills and began cursing David, throwing dirt, stones, and mocking epithets at Israel's king. Bethel, it seems, as a Dissenter, had supported the beheading of Charles I.

Dryden tweaked the character by adding qualities of avarice, an obsession for Sabbatarianism, and the typical Dissenter attitude against sin. The religious hypocrisy reflected here had its counterpart in politics. Dryden insinuated that Bethel practiced a political casuistry about his oath of office, awkwardly having to defend his convenient conversion from republicanism. Thus Bethel was set forth as the general target against which the Roman Catholic Dryden could shoot his sharp arrows against the Whigs.[15]

> Shimei, whose youth did early promise bring
> Of zeal to God and hatred to his King,
> Did wisely from expensive sins refrain
> And never broke the Sabbath but for gain:

The City, to reward his pious hate
Against his master, chose him magistrate
His hand a vare of justice did uphold,
His neck was loaded with a chain of gold.
During his office treason was no crime
The sons of Belial had a glorious time.[16]

Dryden twisted the biblical story into a political allegory, skewering the enemies of the king (and himself) in the process. All the good men align themselves with David, and thus with Charles II. In contrast, mischief percolates in the character of Achitophel, who, as a smooth-tongued tempter, radiates "demonic energy."[17] The miserly Shimei, who "loved his wicked neighbor as himself," joins the villainous company of Absalom.

Although Dryden employed this literary device to veil his attack, his intent was obvious. For example, readers easily recognized the portrait of King Charles II reflected in the nobility of King David. However, Dryden's wily innuendo also suggested the philandering ways of both lusty kings. Charles II, a sex-crazed monarch, was "divinely endowed with procreative power," and like King David, scattered "his Maker's image through the land."[18]

Dryden reiterated the classic definition of the "true end of Satyre" in his preface to *Absalom and Achitophel*, namely "the amendment of Vices by correction. He who writes Honestly is no more an Enemy to the Offendour than the Physician to the Patient, when he prescribes harsh remedies to an inveterate Disease." To stop the spread of the vermin, the physician must operate. "A satirical poet is the check of the laymen on bad priests."[19] Satirists keep the clergy honest, or as honest as they can be kept. Dryden expanded this theme in his *Discourse*, where he proposed that diseased corruption provides an opportunity to demonstrate poetic skill so that it might lead to a cure of one's moral sickness. He believed that the poet was obliged to give readers some "one precept of moral virtue; and to caution [them] against some one particular vice or folly."[20]

In seeking to make "examples of vicious men," Dryden gave us scapegoats who would suffer for our crimes and follies, goading others to be better and do well. However, Dryden discovered the consequences of being a prophet and daring to expose knaves and rascals. The dangers of writing satire for Dryden led to one of the most "notorious beatings in literary history" on December 18, 1679, when he was the victim of retaliation by one of his targets.[21] Now alienated from the new society, Dryden would continue, however gingerly, to aim high at his enemies, until his passed his baton on to a shorter heir, Alexander Pope.[22] But other quills were sharpened before Pope would reign.

Prickly Satire

During the late 1590s, a free-for-all flyting took place, thanks to a most provocative and self-publicizing satirist. Marked by what historian Chris Boswell termed a "fraternal competitiveness of the Inns of Court," a revival of public quarreling in formal prose arose among men of letters.[23] The prickly nature of their quarrelling was summed up very neatly by the irenic Joseph Hall (1574–1656), who was son of a strict Puritan mother and an English bishop and who was also a controversialist and author of the appropriately titled *Of Toothlesse Satyrs* (1597) and *Of Byting Satyrs* (1599).[24]

> The *Satyre* should be like the Porcupine,
> That shoots sharpe quils out in each angry line,
> And wounds the blushing cheeke, and fiery eye,
> Of him that heares, and readeth guiltily.[25]

Also a writer of devotional and moral works, Hall tried to unify Calvinist and Arminian tendencies in the Church of England through his *Via Media* (1619), uniting those who believed in predestination and in free will. The intolerant Archbishop of Canterbury, John Whitgift, had ordered that Hall's satires be burnt, along with those of the licentious Thomas Nashe and others. Although a reprieve seems to have stayed their destruction, the prissy prelate Whitgate aimed to punish all satires. Hall, on his part, incensed by the devastation caused by religious zealotry, brought his switches to bear on religious hypocrites and even those who inserted erotic images into religious verse.

In his hot-blooded rage, Hall broke his spleen in laughing, as he tried to prick the conscience of anyone who read his stuff "guiltily."[26] Like

Thersites, the lame soldier in Homer's *Iliad* who ridiculed Agamemnon and Achilles as greedy cowards, Hall sensed a calling to be a satirist. It was a spiritual vocation. Yet, he recognized that Thersites not only ridiculed others, but was himself an object of mockery. Hall claimed to be the first English satirist, and called upon any other daring soul to spar with him, to slur and provoke the dialogic exchange of wits:

> I first adventure, with fool-hardie might
> To tread the steps of perilous despight:
> I am the first: follow me who list,
> And be the second English Satyrist.[27]

Hall summoned Juvenal's ghost to "stamp and stare that Caesar's throne is turned to Peter's Chair."[28] He laughed at how mongrel saints ran houses of prostitution and how the wealthy were buried in the brown garb of St. Francis to trick their way into heaven. In the house of Hall, many religious mansions would be exposed as facades, houses of sticks and cards, and properly demolished. Yet his lacerating discontent with the human condition allowed little laughter. Like his serious satire *Mundus alter et idem*, describing a voyage to the South Pole where an inverted world existed (for example, in the province of Ivronia—drunkenness—citizens were censured for sobriety), Hall turned satire into a saturnine expression of malcontent, almost as if he had given up hope for human redemption. Even though passionately Christian, his satires became woodenly moralizing and didactic. To his credit, he did target how low the salaries are for teachers and mocked their need to publish any irrelevant novelty for prestige.

Novel Satires

When the Archbishop of Canterbury banned the printing of all verse satires in 1599, his persecution tended to raise the bantering spirit rather than quench it. Censorship does not rid the world of laughter; it only challenges it to find a new disguise. A decade later, King James would outlaw "pasquillis, lybellis, rymes, cokalanis, comedies, and sickly occasionis" and maneuver to have a satirist living in Poland executed for a few pounds.[29]

Over a century later, in 1737, Parliament stamped its Theatrical Licensing Act on all new plays through the Lord Chamberlain's office. The spritely plays of Henry Fielding (1707–1754) had succeeded on the English stage, with his "squibs and crackers" that made audiences laugh. His works metaphorically set fire to the stage until the law banned their performances. With a family to support, Fielding left off writing plays to the dim reflection of William Congreve's Restoration comedies (*The Tragedy of Tragedies: or The Life and Death of Tom Thumb the Great* [1731]) to find a new vocation.[30] He did so by writing epic comic prose novels, declaring, none too modestly, that he was the founder of a new province of writing—namely, novels of the comic class.[31]

Fielding was vexed by the phenomenal success of a short, pompous rival's success. Samuel Richardson's melodramatic novel *Pamela*, designed to "inculcate the principles of virtue and religion," concerned a young and virtuous woman in dire straits. The maid successfully resists the hot assaults of a horny master until he marries her. Virtue triumphed and a literary sensation ensued. Fielding responded with his own naughty parody entitled *Shamela*, about a lascivious and frisky Methodist lady who actively seeks to seduce Squire Booby. In *Shamela*, Fielding attacks the moral hypocrisy of his contemporary's novel with gusto. Shamela, who feigns chastity, has a limited library that includes the notorious French pornographic volume *Venus in the Cloyster: Or, the Nun in her Smock*. The irreverent novel follows the correspondence of two clergymen, the gullible Parson Tickletext and the wiser Parson Oliver. Fielding showcases a third pastor, the antinomian Parson Arthur Williams, as the worst clergy model, false, hedonistic, and an ardent disciple of Methodist evangelist George Whitefield. *Shamela* "rationalizes her frequent fornication" with Williams by "frequent and sincere repentance."[32] Fielding's parody of the false piety of the era satirized religious and erotic "enthusiasms."

In the Augustan satiric tradition of cutting with the caustic knife as a good physician, Fielding's satiric drama spoofed Richardson and lampooned the social and religious climate of London. His *Shamela* rips open the bodice of the "notorious falsehoods and misrepresentations" of *Pamela* while striking out at the corruption of clergy, with its nadir in Parson Williams's debauched character and his self-serving interpretation of the scriptures. In his lecture to Shamela on the Flesh and Spirit,

Williams avers they are two distinct matters that have no relation to each other. "As the Spirit is preferable to the Flesh, so am I preferable to your husband. I say these things to satisfy your conscience." "A fig on my conscience," responds an over-eager Shamela, "when shall I meet you again in the garden?"[33]

Fielding's novel is one of the purest literary parodies of the period. Shamela tries to remember Parson Williams's sermon on the text of "Be not righteous over-much," but tends to hear what she wants. By showing her stupidity, Fielding also skewers the applauding readers of Richardson's book and audiences of the clergy who sold such sentimental claptrap from their pulpits. Shamela remembers the Parson preaching, "That to go to Church, and to pray, and to sing Psalms, and to honor the Clergy, and to repent, is true Religion," but she interprets the sermon according to her own carnal desires.[34]

Fielding distinguished between burlesque and comedy: the former, like caricature, "distorts its subject in grotesque fashion, whereas the comic artist strives for the exactest copying of nature."[35] George Meredith, champion of a genteel tradition of humor of "thoughtful laughter," interpreted Fielding's satire as fundamentally purposeful.[36] For him, "the only source of the true Ridiculous is affectation," particularly with characters marked by vanity and hypocrisy.[37] Parson Williams strikes poses as when he recognizes that "contempt of the clergy is the fashionable vice of the times; but let such wretches know, they cannot hate, detest, and despise us, half so much as we do them."[38]

In his sequel, *Joseph Andrews* (the ersatz brother of Richardson's *Pamela*), Fielding championed a manly, good-natured Anglican priest, Parson Adams, who takes on Methodists and all manner of disreputable clerics. While Parson Williams is a ridiculous burlesque, Parson Adams is a veritable creation of good and honest humor. While the young hero is deliciously set upon by predator Lady Booby, a calculating minx, it is the story of the irrepressible Parson Adams, wearing an old tattered cassock and an odd wig, who takes center stage. With his miraculous escapes and common wisdom, he is affectionately represented as a quixotic Anglican rector, an innocent and absent-minded moralist, an apt precursor to Chesterton's Father Brown. He has a sermon for every wrong passion, including that "silly one of vanity." And he has one on marriage. When his wife thinks he might have a sermon on loving one's wife too well, she counters, "If I knew you had such a sermon in the house, I am sure I would burn it."[39]

In his preface, Fielding identified two sources of affectation, hypocrisy and vanity. Scholar Paul Baines emphasizes that because religion in *Joseph Andrews* is concerned with virtue, one necessarily must look at characters' ethical behavior. Vices, he observes,

> are satirically exposed in a succession of innkeepers, snobs, lawyers, doctors, beaux, fine ladies, . . . and clergymen. Since Adams contrasts with all these people and is obviously virtuous, his religion is the one the novel recommends. He is unorthodox and undoctrinaire, untainted by corruption, honest to a fault, and not usually inclined to preach except from the pulpit.[40]

In Fielding's work, everyone becomes a figure of fun, from judges to Lady Booby herself. Parson Adams may end up fouled by the mire of a pigsty or drenched with the contents of a chamber pot, but his genuine spontaneity and goodness prevail.

Fielding targets the villainy of the times, the venal, the avaricious, and especially those exhibiting an arrogant pomposity, all apt objects for ridicule.[41] The real battle occurs between the charitable and the uncharitable. Adams is portrayed as a generous and charitable man of good Christian character, who gives not a whit what one's official religion is, just so the man is also generous and charitable. Other clergymen, such as Parsons Barnabas and Trulliber, are degenerate and crooked, and in their hypocrisy, they judge Adams as irreligious, only to get their comeuppance at the end. Critic James Work, suggesting that Fielding's morality was not far from that of Adams, observed that "Fielding was the major moralist of his day, determined to preach Christianity as a solution to social problems. . . . He thought it far more important to express one's religious duty in everyday social situations, to be kind to other people, to help them out of tight spots if you could, to lend them money if they were poor, to share your food with them if they were hungry, in any event to do something rather than talk piously."[42]

Fielding relished mocking enthusiastic Methodists, considered by many to be the hypocrites of the era.[43] In *The Female Husband*, his character Mary is identified as a Methodist, a religious opportunist who used the "justification of the faith doctrine to do whatever she wanted." In *Shamela*, the heroine's (whore) mother sends her daughter the enthusiastic sermons of evangelist George Whitefield to study. In *Tom Jones*, we discover that the earthy Tom decides to stay at the House of Entertainment at Bells' Inn, which turns out to be owned by the brother of the great preacher Whitefield. Fielding playfully assures us that the inn remained "absolutely untainted by the pernicious principles of Methodism, or of any other heretical sect."[44]

In contrast, the Reverend Mr. Twackum, a sadist and slanderer, tries to beat religion into the young Tom Jones. However, good people can also put up a good fight. In *Tom Jones*, Parson Adams is a pugilistic marvel, ready to engage in knock-down fisticuffs (while another character, Molly Seagrim, has the brazen temerity to fight outside a church). Fielding playfully orchestrates a mock-heroic battle in a tavern scuffle with bustling earthy characters punching each other. In his dedication to his mock-heroic tale, Fielding laid out his purpose: "I have employed all the wit and humor of which I am master in the following history; wherein I have endeavored to laugh mankind out of their favorite follies and vices."[45]

Roman Catholics as well as Methodists take a beating in Fielding's comic prose. In recognition of contemporary Jacobite rebellions, characters react negatively to Roman Catholics. Tom Jones keeps his Protestant faith against a suspicious "popish priest" and Partridge, a secret Jacobite sympathizer. Squire Western is a quite ignorant Jacobite. But Fielding mostly objects to all corrupt clergymen who accumulate wealth, satisfy their own appetites, and seek their own fame. As an ironic narrator observing Tom Jones's adventures, Fielding pinpoints a particular distaste for the greedy and utterly selfish Thwackum. In contrast, he lauds those, like Parson Adams, who do good works, comfort the sick, counsel the sad, and preach (even if nobody buys his sermons).

Fielding saw the satirist as a physician, as one who brought health to the social body, even if there might be some pain in treating the disease. "Satire on vice or vicious men," Fielding pointed out, "though never so pointed, is no more a sign of ill-nature than it would be to crush a serpent or destroy a wild beast."[46] Fielding's benign and amiable humor remains incarnated in his parson Adams, a quite loveable and quirky character. In his own "Apology for the Clergy," Fielding set forth an ideal character of man, who turned out to be an Anglican, and not unlike Parson Adams.[47]

Wee Bit of Devilish Satire

If one were to look for a mix of comedy, laughter, religion, and love in the Scottish highlands, one would espy quickly the favorite poet of the Scots, Robert Burns (1759–1796). An old Scottish joke revolves around the mistaken authorship of Psalm 121, where the poet speaks of lifting one's eyes to the hills as referring to "Rabbie Burns." "Ye've never heard o' Rabbie Burns?" bawls an old Scottish farmer to an ignorant tourist. "Awa', man, 'an read yer Bible!"[48] Another old joke tells of a Scottish man buying a picture of the pope because he "thought it was a picture of Rabbie Burns in his Freemason's apron."[49] Scotland's national satirist stands as a universal satirical poet of pubs and devils and as an all-too-human saint.[50]

One of the freshest legacies of inspired comic religious verse gushes out of Burns's endearing and bawdy treatment of God, the devil, and hell. This canny Scot almost belches his poetry out with a burp and a laugh, as he toys with topics of drink and the too, too earthly flesh. He is both saint and sinner, who although "homely in attire may touch the heart."[51] Writing in a variety of accents, from vernacular and unlettered rustic to elegant literary English, Burns served a friar's roast of haggis (tasting like savory cardboard and being "monstrously productive of the wind.") for hard drinkers and hard lovers.[52]

After the distinguished Englishman of letters Samuel Johnson described Scotland as a vile country, his companion asserted that God made it. Johnson retorted, "Certainly He did, but we must remember that He made it for Scotchmen; and comparisons are odious, but God made Hell."[53] And for the Scotch, when God made Burns, he made him in his own image.

Burns's wit combined comic observations with simple scolding. In his broadside "Address to the Unco Guid, or the Rigidly Righteous," he paraphrased Solomon's maxim in Ecclesiastes 7:16 and mocked those who are so "guid yoursel', sae pious an' sae holy, ye've nought to do but mark an' tell Your neebour's fauts an' folly!" Such rigid righteous ones are lumped as fools, even those "high, exalted, virtuous dames, Tied up in godly laces." He would chide rival ministers who preach against one another, rail against cold churches, and complain of how women ruled men while the devil ruled women. In "To a Louse," he reproached a woman who goes to church to show off her new bonnet rather than to pray. Unbeknownst to the self-satisfied lady sitting in her pew, a louse has crawled up the back of her bonnet and spoils the effect. To which Burns draws out a universal lesson: "Oh wad some Pow'r the giftie gie us To see oursels as others see us!"[54] Should we be given perspective on the lice in our lives, we would be humbled and most blessed.[55]

Accordingly, he credited his ability as an astute theologian (and as a great drinker) to his long acquaintance with the devil. He knew old Slewfoot too well to be fooled by him.

> Satan, I fear thy sooty claws
> An' now, auld Cloots,
> I ken ye're thinkan,
> A certain Bardie's rantin, drinkin,
> Some luckless hour will send him linkan
> To your black pit: But, faith!
> He'll turn a corner jinkan,
> An cheat you yet.[56]

Quizzed about their understanding of the devil, Scottish children responded in Burns's style. One wee girlie asked her friend, "Do you believe in the devil, Tam?" "Ach No," the laddie replied. "It's just like Santa Claus; it's yer Faither." The great preacher Charles Spurgeon taught his graduate students a similar lesson: "When you speak of Heaven, let your face light up, let it be irradiated by a heavenly gleam, let your eye shine with reflected glory. But when you speak of Hell, your ordinary face will do."[57]

In the eighteenth century, an austere Calvinism filled Scottish Presbyterian souls with terrifying nightmares of a hell of sulfurous brimstone, a vast bottomless pit populated with roaring demons, the blazing fires and furnaces of Milton and Dante, and heated-up Burns's satires on hell. Like Irishman C. S. Lewis, Burns reduced the devil to a more comic figure, more associated with drinking and wenching.

Burns' address to the devil subverts the image of Milton's tragic and malignant Satan, who, as Lewis described him, acted more like a petulant child or spoiled celebrity with his sense of "injured merit." Instead of cowering before this chief of many thrones who led embattled seraphim to war, Burns renamed him with whatever titles suited him: "Auld Hornie, Satan, Nick, or Clootie." The Devil is less majestic and angelic, appearing more ridiculous and wily; he not only resides and lurks in the human breast, but looks like a Scottish man. The mirror of satire looks back. In a "Poem on Life," Burns laughed at his particularly Scottish devil, with a cavernous gargoyle-like grin, playing bagpipes and indulging in reels and high jinks. Burns confessed to learning of the devil from his nurse's knee, where he learned her collection of fairy stories, witches and brownies, elves and wraiths, and "other trumpery, all of which cultivated the latent seeds of poetry."[58]

As the devil distracts Burns's ability to write poetry with temptations of whiskey and women, he still toasts old John Barleycorn for the sins that so easily beset him. As Lord Byron puts in the mouth of Don Juan, "Man, being reasonable, must get drunk."[59] But dissipation cannot be separated from its reckoning. "Let us have wine and women, mirth and laughter, / Sermons and soda-water the day after."[60] For Burns and for Byron, sin has its mate.[61]

In Burns's comic masterpiece, "Tam O' Shanter," the blustering drunken babbler (having gotten drunk after hours in the pub) has a weird encounter on a stormy night with an orgy of witches in an old haunted church where a comic devil plays squealing bagpipes. In this black mass of wizards and witches, everyone dances jigs, and everything is revealed, including the rotten hearts of three priests and lying tongues of lawyers. Yet, the witches are withered, old, and wizened hags who would turn a stomach. One young witch wears a very short skirt that, when she dances, kicking up her legs into the air, reveals "a vision scarcely heavenly." Pursued by the devils, Tam escapes by crossing a running stream, which they cannot follow because of the water's association with baptism; however, his mare Maggie is caught by her rump and left scarce a stump.[62] Burns warns that if any man or mother's son feels inclined to drink, remember Tom O'Shanter's mare.

When his patron and friend, Gavin Hamilton, was censured by the church for Sabbath desecration, Burns leveled his satire of "Holy Willie's Prayer" at the hypocrisy of the Reverend Mr. Auld's session. The specific target was a sanctimonious and humorless elder in a parish church in

Ayrshire, the farmer Willie Fisher, a pompous moral spy who tattled on other people's waywardness. Willie attacked those not attaining his level of piety. In the poem, Burns skewers those posturing self-righteous people who lord their piety over others.

> O Thou that in the Heavens does dwell,
> Wha, as it pleases best Thysel,
> Sends ane to Heaven an' ten to Hell
> A' for Thy glory,
> And no for onie guid or ill
> They've done before Thee![63]

Like the Pharisee praising God in public, Holy Willie trumpets his steady presence before the Lord as a "burning, and a shining light" to his generation. Although he acknowledges that he deserves a just damnation for many broken laws, he stands in exaltation. As sin marked him since falling from his mother's womb, he could have been plunged deep into hell, to gnash his gums, weep, and wail in burning lakes, "whare damned devils roar and yell, Chain'd to their stakes." But he is a model Christian and a pillar of God's temple as he shows God's grace is great and ample. Of course, he must confess a few little sins, mostly lust of the flesh, but he points out to God that He must remember he's only dust. He then comically lists his sinful trespasses:

> O Lord! yestreen, Thou kens, wi' Meg—
> Thy pardon I sincerely beg—
> O, may't ne'er be a living plague
> To my dishonour!
> An' I'll ne'er lift a lawless leg
> Again upon her.
>
> Besides, I farther maun avow—
> Wi' Leezie's lass, three times, I trow—
> But, Lord, that Friday I was fou,
> When I cam near her,
> Or else, Thou kens, Thy servant true
> Wad never steer her.[64]

He ends his prayer focused upon himself, but gives the glory to God. In this parody of a Presbyterian prayer (with adoration, confession, assurance of pardon, praise and thanksgiving, intercession, petition, benediction, and the amen and amen), Burns merrily attacks the old light of Calvinism, which, with its doctrine of predestination, is pleased to "send one to heaven and ten to hell, all for thy glory!"[65] Elder Willie lambastes those who drink, sing, dance, and swear, yet he himself fornicates. Like Jacob in the book of Genesis, he tries to bargain with God, hoping to buy absolution for fornication in bulk. He would fornicate three times for the Trinity.

The Scottish Church became alarmed and convoked several meetings to examine these profane rhymes. (Since Burns already stood accused of impregnating one woman, exile in Jamaica became a possible option.) In "The Holy Fair," minister Moodie preaches so much hellfire and damnation that the congregation flees to the pub. Where the Lord's one trumpet toots, the congregation unfortunately sleeps due to an excess of drink rather than responding to true religion and morality. Goodness is not to be found in stern, severe Calvinism or in the alehouse.

The poem earned the church's censure as Burns described a downward trajectory after religious conversions.

> How monie hearts this day converts,
> O' sinners and o' Lasses!
> Their hearts o' stane, gin night are gane
> As saft as only flesh is.
> There's some are fou o' love divine;
> there's some are fou o' brandy;
> An monie jobs that day begin,
> May end in Houghmagandie [fornication]
> Some ither day.[66]

Even with a scathing satire on what Burns sees as the cowardice of suicide ("Here lies in earth a root of Hell, / Set by the Devil's ain dibble; / This worthless body damned himself, / To save the Lord the trouble"), biographer Raymond Grant yet views the poet's range of laughter "informed by one basic and underlying motif, gentle laughter at human weakness, gentle laughter born of the poet's ability always to see the humorous side, the human, forgiving side of every moral question."[67] Grant quotes the former Archbishop of Canterbury Michael Ramsey to make his point: "If a man must be aware of himself it is a happy thing if he can *laugh at himself*, for that is a way of coming near to God."[68] As he stood between the New Light of Arminianism and the "Auld Licht" of Calvinism, Burns could laugh. He may not have been an ideal practitioner of the Presbyterian tradition, but he was delightfully devout in his own way, with a wee bit of ale of course. The satirist who does not scar with sarcasm still hopes to move people to amend their behavior, and to do so cheerfully. And then they would all sing Burns's "Auld Lang Syne."

Pope of Satire

> Know then thyself, presume not God to scan;
> The proper study of Mankind is Man . . .
> Created half to rise and half to fall;
> Great Lord of all things, yet a prey to all;
> Sole judge of truth, in endless error hurl'd:
> The glory, jest, and riddle of the world.[69]

In his *Essay on Man*, the diminutive Alexander Pope (1688–1744) situated human beings both at the glorious center of God's creation and as its comic tail-end joke. Perhaps his own life could be summed up in the words of his own ninth beatitude: "Blessed is the man who expects nothing, for he shall never be disappointed."[70] Pope was born the same year as the Glorious Revolution, which ushered in a Protestant government under William and Mary. As a beleaguered but crafty Roman Catholic, he was partly responsible for this period becoming known as the Augustan Age, a golden era of British literature and culture in the eighteenth century.[71] The revival of learning and wit sparked some of the best religious satire for a growing and literate audience who would buy subscriptions and pay to read.

The poet's worst scandals involved an accusation that his father was a linen merchant who had converted to Catholicism and that he himself was a closet Roman Catholic. Banned from attending the Anglican universities of England, Pope educated himself by learning numerous languages and translating the works of Homer, Horace, and Juvenal. With gentle prodding, he updated the genial Roman Horace so that he could speak to his own age. During the reign of George II and his prime minister, Robert Walpole, Pope explained why he used Horace's satire to critique the incompetent government in his *First Epistle of the Second Book of Horace*. As Horace addressed his poems to his patron Caesar Augustus, so Pope slyly dedicates his work to King George II, who hated to read, and whose second name conveniently was Augustus.[72]

Pope ridiculed those in positions of authority, especially in the church, who did not attend the poor (as Jesus said, "the poor will be with you always") because God made them that way. "The grave Sir Gilbert holds it for a rule, / That every man in want is knave or fool."[73] Pope also satirized the softening of traditional Church doctrine among the Anglican bishops: "To rest, the Cushion and soft Dean invite / Who never mentions Hell to ears polite."[74]

When a friend argued with the poet that his muse, Horace, was so nice and delicate, not lashing out at vice, Pope replied, "But shall the vicious swear without rebuke? Virtue occupies both high and low, dwelling in monks or lighting upon a King. Not so with Vice; if it is great, she is not mean or low. Her Birth, her Beauty, Crowds, and Courts confess, Chaste Matrons praise her, and grave Bishops bless."[75] Pope holds that villainy is sacred to all, except for the satirist, who holds vice in disdain. Pope cleverly challenged the corruption of the church:

> Friend: Spare then the Person, and expose the vice.
> Poet: How Sir! Not damn the Sharper, but the dice?
> Should one name the reverend Atheists?
> Or keep quiet about their names?
> Could I expose a Dean, provided I spare a Bishop?[76]

Ironically, one church dean, who sat with his current mistress at his table, had been indicted for rape in 1730. When a friend recommended that he stigmatize only poor wretches, Pope refused and aimed at higher targets. In one of his most famous set of couplets, he explained,

> Yes, I am proud; I must be proud to see
> Men not afraid of God, afraid of me:

> Safe from the Bar, the Pulpit, and the Throne,
> Yet touch'd and sham'd by *Ridicule* alone.[77]

For Pope, satire was his calling, even a spiritual vocation, directed at exposing and censuring a wayward clergy. In his *Essay*, Pope found "A vile Conceit in pompous Words exprest, / Is like a Clown in regal Purple drest." His portrait of the clerical blockhead is built to slam how folly has invaded the sacred churches:

> No Place so Sacred from such Fops is bar'd,
> Nor is Paul's Church more safe than Paul's Church-yard;
> Nay, fly to Altars; there they'll talk you dead;
> For Fools rush in where Angels fear to tread.[78]

Satire requires its priests to be martyrs, witnessing and railing against any betrayal of moral standards, wherever it may hide.[79] In his claim to be an enlightened humanist like Erasmus, Pope argued that he was only providing the middle ground of reason and moderation between papist and Protestant, while honoring the great designer, the one who divinely ordained order.

One stinging biblical allusion was directed against those who sacrifice piety for secular success, leaving God in their wake. Pope portrayed "a citizen of sober fame, a plain good man, and Balaam was his name; / Religious, punctual, frugal, and so forth."[80] Balaam is offered a reward by Moab if he will curse his own people. He capitulates and sells out, for his religion is merely a tissue of outward self-righteousness. He exchanges his birthright, replacing the care of God, for the pride of self-made autonomy. "What late he call'd a Blessings, now was Wit, / And God's good Providence, a lucky Hit."[81] On Sundays, such a man goes to his counting house and seldom attends church. He becomes a minister of Parliament and buys his son a commission in the army where he "drinks, whores, fights, and in a duel dies." He buys his daughter a viscount for a husband, who bestows on her "a Coronet and Pox for life." Satan, who seduced him, wins, and "sad Sir Balaam curses God and dies."[82] In the Faustian option, this modern man gives up his soul for the specious promises of the world. If only he had had an ass like the biblical Balaam had to warn him of his folly.

One engaged in satire must be ready to be ridiculed, and so was Pope by those who envied, feared, or just disliked him. As a debilitating Pott's disease had stunted his bone growth, restricting his height to four and a half feet, he was ripe for cruelty of the most sophomoric kind. One disdainful enemy, John Dennis (described as "deaf to every merit but his own"), laid a scalding iron to Pope's soul, searing not only his literary output, but his personal life, especially his crippled appearance. Dennis fastened himself like a giant tick to Pope, and jeered at him for being as "stupid and impotent as a hunch-back'd Toad."[83] Deformed in body, but not in soul, Pope physically resembled Homer's contemptible figure of Thersites in the *Iliad*: Thersites "was the ugliest man who came to Troy: bow-legged, lame in one foot, his humped shoulders stooping over his chest, with a pointed head above on which a thin stubble grew."[84]

Pope made his enemies the old-fashioned way: he earned them by his barbs and stings. As he once quipped, "A person who is too nice an observer of the business of the crowd, like one who is too curious in observing the labor of bees, will often be stung for his curiosity."[85] His keen sight and insight invited the buzz of pests. In his great work, *The Dunciad* (1729), Pope attacked the dullness of his society, wanting to swat to death insect rivals who sucked the literary blood out of culture and aspired to the artistic gutters of becoming sycophants of George II.

In his *Imitations of Horace*, Pope protested that "satire's my weapon, but I'm too discreet / To run amuck, and tilt at all I meet." Actually, he wasn't. Everyone was fair game, especially when Pope got a whiff of the reeking stench of pride. In looking at power grubbers and preferment seekers, Pope's friend Dr. Arbuthnot pointed out that his belief in the sinfulness of all human beings had empirical evidence. He had opportunity to "calmly & philosophically" consider "that treasure of vileness & baseness that I always believed to be in the heart of man," exerting their insolence and baseness. However, instead of being surprised or grieving him, such instances "improve my Theory." Arbuthnot warned his friend Pope to refrain from mentioning actual names like Walpole in his satirical writings, lest he incur the wrath of that disgruntled and offended person.[86] Pope responded that "general satire in times of general vice has no force. . . . It is only by hunting one or two from the herd that any examples can be made."[87]

Thus a central question concerned whether to attack individual persons or assail general vices. Was one more effective in focusing on the individual or in extending satire to larger measures? Given that general satire in times of general vice lacks the power to reform, Pope insinuated that preventive action is preferable. If perhaps one or two are hung up or pilloried, the example might arrest others in their folly. Use satire to make an example of a few, and the rest will attend. Such was Pope's pipe dream.

Too easily the hunter becomes the hunted; the satirist can become the object of derision or danger. According to biographer Maynard Mack, during this time of anti-Jacobite sentiment, some saw Pope's hump as a "mark of God and Nature upon him, to give us warning that we should hold no Society with him."[88] An anti-Pope industry did grow up around the little man from the caterwauling crowds of hireling writers on Grub Street. Publication of *The Dunciad* stirred up opposition, and at first Pope wrote to Swift, believing—naively—that "this poem will rid me of those insects."[89] Yet Pope felt sufficiently afraid that he walked around London protected by two loaded pistols and a very Great Dane named Bounce.

Worse yet were his estrangement from, public quarrel with, and romantic rejection and scorning by the distinguished Lady Mary Wortley Montagu, a married woman who incidentally helped to introduce the practice of small pox inoculation from Turkey into Britain.[90] A great portion of Pope's malice towards courtier and politician John Hervey may have stemmed from his conspiracy with this great lady. She herself had been pitted with the disease's scars upon her face. Her words, "Satire should, like a polished razor keen, / Wound with a touch that's scarcely felt or seen," take on a special irony, for both male and female wits were marked with deformities.[91] In the famous painting of *The Rejected Poet* (1863) by William Powell Frith, she stands throwing her head back in laughter after Pope had declared his ardent love for her. He sits stubbornly forlorn. This was a wound that was felt, keenly. Regarding Pope, the sunshiny Joseph Addison advised Lady Montagu: "Leave him as soon as you can, he will certainly play you some devilish trick else; he has an appetite to satire."[92] The former friends traded gross and insulting words between the *Dunciad* and other anonymous pieces, with many less-than-subtle accusations.

Pope found fellowship of likeminded friends in the Scriblerus Club, which provided him with protection from a wary public and slanderous adversaries. Pope was buttressed by that divine safeguard against raillery, friendship. The Scriblerus Club joined together a handful of jovial fellows and spirited Tory wits, mainly Pope, Jonathan Swift, John Gay, and John Arbuthnot (probably the originator and most focused leader of the group), whose purpose it was to puncture the pretentious pedantry of British society. Their joint work was a mock biography of Martin Scriblerus, a lunatic philomath who "dipped in every art and science, but injudiciously in each."[93]

This generous fellowship filled their lives with cheer and mischief. Their joint invention, Martinus Scriblerus (a "*swift* writer") mocked hack writers. Like the later Tolkien, Lewis, and Charles Williams, these poets both stimulated and contributed to each other's ideas. Book III of Swift's *Gulliver's Travels* with its flying island of Laputa and Gay's *The Beggar's Opera* grew out of the interaction and friendly suggestions to one another. Pope's own *Peri Bathous* would erupt out of this merry association.

Writing to his friend Jonathan Swift, Pope sang, "I see no sunshine but in the face of a friend." And thus in the "Epilogue to the Satires," Pope would offer the advice:

> Laugh then at any but at fools or foes;
> These you but anger, and you mend not those.
> Laugh at your friends, and if your friends are sore,
> So much the better, you may laugh the more.[94]

These friends cultivated laughter throughout their lives. Swift impishly offered Pope twenty guineas (as opposed to thirty pieces of silver) to convert to Anglicanism. Pope replied that the bribe to get Pope converted to the Church of England would break the Lord Treasurer's bank. Pope bantered with Swift that the Irish dean was one who "by his own Confession, has composed more Libels than Sermons. If it be true, what I have heard often affirmed by innocent People, that too much Wit is dangerous to Salvation, this unfortunate Gentleman must certainly be damned to all Eternity. . . . Be it as it will, I should not think my own Soul deserved to be saved, if I did not endeavor to save his."[95]

The satire of Pope harkened back to a Roman tradition that Wallace Jackson refers to as a sort of "bastard genre, a farrago, a mixed dish, a hastily set down affair without the style and unity of the more elevated genres."[96] Where it was best baked and served was on the dessert menu of *The Dunciad*, a work called "a giant raspberry of a satire," laughing with outrageous cheekiness.[97]

In two versions of the work, Pope derided two writers, Lewis Theopold and "Comedian" Colley Cibber. While Pope recognized Theopold's prestigious status as a literary figure, he saw Cibber as a coxcomb, an undistinguished organization man and (worse) a mediocre comic. Cibber's father had been a sculptor who created two statues at the gates of a hospital for lunatics, a sure sign of the connection between poetry and madness, Parnassus and Bedlam. Cibber supplanted Theopold in 1743 as poet laureate and continued to snipe at Pope. Thus Pope viewed the royal position of an endowed Chair for the King of the Dunces as a dull post. Dunces may work tirelessly, but they still bore readers: "While pensive poets painful vigils keep, / Sleepless themselves to give their readers sleep."[98] Their works are "born in sin" (from being conceived in an alehouse). Herein we find a purpose of satire to be that universal mirror of man, and especially of his fall from God's presence. By contrast, these writers prostitute the craft of writing; so Pope puns on their smutty works being sold on the street, but destined for hell (those works "purified by flames" will find their destiny).

The work parallels and parodies Milton's *Paradise Lost*, but instead of portraying an overweening and tragic Satan, it crowns King Dunce and thereby mocks contemporary pedantry and pseudo-scholarship. For Pope, dunces are groveling and servile writers who suck up to pretentious toads. In a grotesque confederacy of dunces and devils, all are interchangeable, with sin's gravitational pull drawing all dunces into darkness and chaos. Dunces are even transformed into the demonic forces of the Antichrist, with Colley Cibber being crowned on a throne on the Seven Hills of Rome as the "Antichrist of wit."[99] Where Milton began Book II of *Paradise Lost* with an invocation to light, Pope prays to darkness.

The influence of the Bible and Christian sacramental themes percolates in *The Dunciad*, forming a significant theological context.[100] As literary critic Robert Griffin observes, there is an anagogic dimension to the poem: on the level of religious meaning, "Dulness, as nonbeing, is presented as a blasphemous, satanic version of the Christian God." Dunces are viewed as rebellious Israelites who have forgotten their Lord or as false prophets prostituting the word. What is required here is a comic as opposed to a solemn reading. "Irony and serious vision are not by necessity mutually exclusive. There is no compelling reason to choose between comic 'Dunciad' and tragic 'jeremiad.'"[101] With mock-epic irony compatible with moral prophetic indignation, Pope places Cibber as a worshipper of Baal in contrast to Elijah and makes him a joke. As the Hebrew prophets saw worshipping false gods as a peculiarly dunce-like activity, indeed, as true folly, they castigated their own people for forgetting the Lord, seeking after money, and perverting justice for the poor. Here were shepherds who fattened themselves by flattering patrons; they were sorcerers who "seduced the people into abandoning the true God."[102] Thus this false Elijah became what Pope once recognized: "The worst of madmen is a saint run mad."[103]

Pope scholar Maynard Mack has demonstrated how a print engraving entitled the "Festival of the Golden Rump" (lampooning those who kiss the rump for profit) shows "A Walpole wearing a wizard's robe embroidered with dragons," a not so subtle allusion to Jerusalem as a den of dragons (Jeremiah 9:11). The yawning of Dulness "permeates the entire society, from the churches and the schools to houses of government." References point to Jeremiah's depiction of the drunkenness of princes and wise men and Isaiah's "spirit of deep sleep, visions of impending darkness" (Isaiah 29:10). Dunces cause the darkness covering the face of Britain and usher in its imminent destruction. Pope's prophecy is masked by a lighter touch of mock-epic comedy. Griffin concludes that even with a vision of renewal from Moses's song in Deuteronomy being implicit, a worse fate awaits the denizens of *The Dunciad*: "It shall come to pass, when many evils and troubles are befallen them, that this poem shall testify against them as a witness."[104]

By the time the second edition came out, Pope was ensconced in Twickenham, his grotto retreat outside London, retired and distinguished. The many malicious cartoon figures that the gutter press put out fell flat. Called the "wicked wasp of Twickenham," Pope could sting friends and enemies alike with his sharp pen. As Mack concluded, "To be a great satirist, a man must have, literally and figuratively, a place to stand, an angle of vision. For Pope . . . the garden and the grotto supplied this."[105]

Poets are as useful to the state as soldiers, for both teach children and foreigners. While Joseph Addison set passion on the side of truth and poured human virtue into hearts and Swift upheld Ireland's cause with wit and helped the poor, it is Pope who showed the importance of the satirist for society, as well as the moral dangers he risked.

Pope acknowledged that the free habits of satirical poets led to license, where taunts are mixed with jests. And when the age grew corrupt, malicious words triumphed with their stings, bringing strife among friends and family. An appeal to law and justice brought forth the dreadful potential of statutes against the poets; so they learned again to please and not to wound. While some wandered into flattery, others freely and nicely avoided the vice. To this wavering between extremes, Pope explained that "Hence satire rose, that just the medium hit, / And heals with morals what it hurts with wit."[106] One can put up with the surgeon or dentist if the final prognosis is good health.

Finally, Pope's assessment of his audience reveals how they had descended from being a thinking community to become a mob gratified by visual farce:

> There still remains, to mortify a wit,
> The many-headed monster of the pit:
> A senseless, worthless, and unhonour'd crowd;
> Who, to disturb their betters mighty proud,
> Clatt'ring their sticks before ten lines are spoke,
> Call for the farce, the bear, or the black-joke.
> What dear delight to Britons farce affords!
> Farce once the taste of mobs, but now of lords;
> (For taste, eternal wanderer, now flies
> From heads to ears, and now from ears to eyes.)
>
> With laughter sure Democritus had died,
> Had he beheld an audience gape so wide.[107]

Even Democritus, the laughing philosopher, as opposed to Heraclitus, the melancholy one, would be surprised with the poor quality of the laughing art. What Pope and the Scriblerians demonstrate is that the rhetorical art of satire remains grounded upon normative values and that moral law is a mirror, reflecting the ridiculous nature of man. Augustans believed that the fall from Eden was a satiric event, because henceforth we could see from whence we came and what gullible suckers and knavish fools we had become.

As far as summing up his own critical work, Pope wrote a letter to Swift in 1737 defining their crafts: "You call your satires libels. I would rather call my satires epistles. They will consist more of morality than of wit, and grow graver, which you will call duller." Pope's epistles brought vice into the light.[108] Or as he would put it in a more modest way, "Fools rush into my Head, and so I write."[109]

Dean of Satirists

Of all the satirists gathered at this table, the most well-known and notorious may be Jonathan Swift (1667–1745), primarily because of the baby-back ribs menu for cooking Irish children he provided in his "A Modest Proposal." He realized that while it was difficult to define his art ("What Humor is, not all the Tribe / Of Logick-mongers can describe"[110]), he felt called to practice it with vim. A member of the Scriblerus Club, he hung around with his little, even Lilliputian, friend Alexander Pope, who once wrote to him about their options as satirists, asking whether they would "choose Cervantes' serious air, or laugh and shake in Rabelais' easy chair."[111] Swift opted for the latter, drawing his knight-errant satire in gargantuan images and finding something theological in the vulgar. For Swift, all our righteousness is as dung, so much so that he considered that the best symbol for sin to be shit. And one could tell the emotional/political state of a person by examining their excretory deposits. As Swift wrote in *Gulliver's Travels*, "Men are never so Serious, Thoughtful, and Intent, as when they are at Stool."[112] One might even discover conspirators of a coup by checking the constitution of public excrement.

The Anglo-Irish author would be exiled in Dublin as the dean of St. Patrick's Cathedral, but not before he had made a mark on the literary world. Swift put to flight that old Victorian prejudice that one could not be both a caring clergyman and a satirist. Faith and conscience were wedded to his bark and his bite. Both clergy and satirists are called to pull down appearances, to expose evil, and to hold up virtue. As both a Christian and comic poet, Swift tried to elevate God while humiliating those men who would not be humble.[113] Of course, an anonymous source posted a poem on the door of the St. Patrick's Cathedral on the day of his institution, which read in part:

> Look down St. Patrick, look we pray
> On thy own church and steeple
> Convert the Dean on this great day
> Or else God help the people.[114]

As we have seen, the friendship among the Tory scribblers bore much satiric fruit. The offspring of this convivial community—the faux-travel novel of *Gulliver*, the ballad opera of Gay, and the mock epic of the *Dunciad*—made their papas proud. Each sought to entertain, but also to instruct through humor. For example, Swift pointed Gay's attention to the trulls, rogues, and riffraff of the London back streets. So, Gay composed the light verse for his burlesque of the heavy Italian opera. After *The Beggars' Opera* was produced by the entrepreneurial John Rich and became a phenomenal mutual artistic and financial success, one wag quipped that the play made "Gay rich and Rich gay."[115]

The play was not bereft of ecclesiastical satire, as Gay ridiculed the all-too-hypocritical estates through Polly Peachum's singing,

> All Professions be-rogue one another
> The Priest calls the Lawyer a Cheat
> The Lawyer be-knaves the Divine.[116]

Swift would be-rogue both the priest and the lawyer in his satires. While living with his patron, Sir William Temple, Swift penned his most explicitly religious satire, *A Tale of a Tub*, during a time of controversy between High and Low Church.[117] The mock book (even beginning with "once upon a time") catapulted his reputation and became an instant bestseller. Swift cleverly "sartorialized" church doctrine into what three sons do with their inheritance of their father's cloth. The three brothers, too clearly identified as Peter (obviously Roman Catholic), Martin

(Anglican) and Jack (Nonconformist, Calvinist), quarrel over the coats bequeathed to them by their father.

The coats have two virtues. One, that with good wearing, they will "last you fresh and sound as long as you live." Second, they will grow in proportion to how their bodies grow, "lengthening and widening of themselves, so as to be always fit." Father encourages them, "Wear them clean and brush them often." He also bequeaths to them a will, dictating as it were, the will of the father on how to wear and manage their coats, how to avoid the penalties for every transgression or neglect upon which their future fortunes depended.

The father tells them, "I have also commanded in my will that you should live together in one house like brethren and friends; for then you shall be sure to thrive and not otherwise." For seven years, the brothers follow the will of the father, travel extensively, encounter several giants, and slay dragons. However, on returning to town, each falls in love with a lady, but then finds himself rejected. Determined that they need to transform themselves according to the world, the brothers begin immediately to pick up on the good qualities of the town. They rhyme and rally and write and sing; as Swift writes, they "drank, and fought, and slept, and swore, and took snuff. They went to new plays on the first night, haunted the chocolate houses, beat the watch, . . . ran in debt with shopkeepers and lay with their wives; they killed bailiffs, kicked fiddlers down stairs. . . . Above all, they constantly attended those committees of Senators who are silent in the House and loud in the coffeehouse, where they nightly adjourn to chew the cud of politics."[118] Still, the women do not respond according to their desires.

Romanist Peter argues for his primogeniture as first, sole, and primary heir and usurper of all rights. He adds ceremony and fancy decoration to his coat—silk, satin, and all manner of embroidery. Satirizing the ostentatious Roman Catholic ecclesiastics, Swift shows how Peter ascends from being Brother Peter to Father (papa/pope) Peter to My Lord Peter; even later he signs pardons as Emperor Peter. Finally as God Almighty, and sometimes Monarch of the Universe, he wears a three-tiered hat.

The Anglican Martin, who comes off best (no surprise), strives for the unity recommended by the father, but Martin appears infrequently. Calvinist Jack, braying like a donkey, with ears erect and tongue up his nose, is "dog-mad at the sound of music" and subject to carnal forces. Modern, severe, and lawyerly, Jack calls his hatred of Peter "zeal," suggesting that one can disguise one's vice by dressing it up in religious language.

Jack is vexed with Martin's patience regarding Peter: "Ah, good Brother Martin, do as I do, for the Love of God: Strip, Tear, Pull, Rent, Flay off all, that we may appear as unlike the Rogue Peter, as it is possible."[119] The book reveals the various wrangling of churches over doctrines, the overweening vanity and pride of the clergy, and the church's search for fame and fashion. "In conclusion, Swift observed that he was trying an experiment very frequent among modern authors, which is to write upon nothing," as if he were writing for Seinfeld.[120]

These three foolish fops follow fickle fashion by adding ornamentation and gilding to goodness, disguising it beyond recognition. Swift echoes the preacher of Ecclesiastes in lamenting, "Vanity, vanity, all is vanity," and drawing on the word's meaning both self-absorption and futility. For Swift, the religious mind that is "entubbed" is separated from its moorings and drifts and bobs on its own. So a new utopian religion wafts about, emanating out of the freethinking Descartes and Hobbes. In *The Fringes of Belief*, Sarah Ellenzweig observes that a strand of eighteenth-century freethinkers, while suspicious of revealed religion, were not so antagonistic to the institutional Anglican Church. Swift and Pope resisted those who openly denigrated official Christianity; they defended its moral system. However, overly pious churchman remained a staple for satire.[121] On Gulliver's travels to the floating island of Laputa, he finds learned citizens obsessed with mathematics and music, lacking all imagination, fancy and invention, and always in danger of tumbling down precipices because of their preoccupation. Other freethinkers might have an open mind, but it was like an open sieve through which all thoughts passed.

In *A Tale of a Tub*, questions of doctrine become arguments over clothes. The boys are more interested in the ladies and worried about being unfashionable. They forget the father and become Hogarthian gallants, taking snuff, swearing, going into debt, dueling, whoring, killing bailiffs, and rhyming. Adrift in the tub, they follow the sect of Aeolists as inspired admirers of the wind, that heavenly spirit or breath. But it is all hot air and exhaust for them. In the end, the Anglican Church is the most sensible, useful cloak, albeit a bit stained, but a "right application of liquid" helps. Swift constructed an "Apology" defending his work, as a "satire that would be useful and diverting." However his nod to Horace's *utile et dulce* resulted more in wicked delight than in renewal. As these vapors enter human organs, women were doubly blessed "better disposed for the admission of those oracular gusts."[122]

Swift spoofed the innumerable gross corruptions in both religion and learning rampant in the seventeenth-century. In particular he targeted those theologians/philosophers who, as Peter Leithart writes, "mangle in order to understand."[123] Seeking to defend the stature of British statesman (and Swift's employer) William Temple after his inopportune and ill-conceived essay on ancient and modern learning, Swift entered the controversial fray with more effective rhetorical wit. Temple promoted what he saw as that humanistic tradition that "abhors rigid absolutism consumed with pride and devoid of charity," which marked an emerging enlightened club of progressive intellectuals.[124] One of Temple's most vocal critics was William Wotton, who contended that satire blasphemes Christian tenets; although keen and piquant satires existed in the Reformation, Wotton feared that ridicule would undermine faith and spur atheism. He contemptuously dismissed those "ill-placed Cavils of the Sour, the Envious, the Stupid, and the Tasteless."[125]

Three "oratorical machines" through which men might gain the attention of the public by rising above them (namely, the pulpit, the ladder/gallows, and the stage) provide images of the satirist as preacher, hangman, or actor.[126] Each earns his celebrity by rising above the crowds with dramatic panache. Swift's satire added an effective fourth machine for arresting the interest of his readers, inventing an independent rhetorical voice that mimicked other writers and muddying their motives with intentional ambiguity. Swift could unmake and unmask both author and reader, twisting the former and tricking the latter.

Supposedly, Swift's career in the church was stymied by *A Tale of a Tub*; perhaps it was why he was sent back to Ireland. Swift conceded "youthful lapses of improprieties," but his apology smells of a ruse. He asks how there could be any offense: "Why should any Clergyman of our Church be angry to see the Follies of Fanaticism and Superstition exposed, tho' in the most ridiculous Manner? Since that is perhaps the most probable way to cure them, or at least to hinder them from spreading."[127]

Along with his *Tub*, Swift scripted *The Battle of the Books*, a contest between the classics and the moderns. In the preface, he penned his famous definition that "SATIRE is a sort of glass wherein beholders do generally discover everybody's face but their own." This is the reason, Swift opined, why very few are "offended with it."[128] The satire contains the parable of the Bee, in which the ancients gather honey, sweetness, and light, showing a productive nature, while the Modern Spider, which catches the bee in its web, spins traps and spews out poisons.

Swift defended himself with the argument that the "noblest and most useful Gift of humane Nature" is wit and "the most agreeable is humour."[129] He pointed to how his own mirth helped to mingle Divinity and Wit.[130] As Swift expressed with panache,

> For Wit and Humor differ quite,
> That gives surprise, and this Delight;
> Humor is odd, grotesque, and wild,
> Only by Affectation spoild,
> 'Tis never by Invention got,
> Men have it when they know it not.[131]

Such practice laughs rather than lashes men out of their follies and vices through its peculiarly exuberant, robust, mirthful character. While his humor could be playful ("My nose itched, and I knew I should drink wine or kiss a fool"), this was not his usual mode. More frequently, his satire was biting and incisive. In "A Modest Proposal" he recommends the roasting of small and tasty Irish Roman Catholic children, which could "greatly lessen the number of papists among us." For Swift, such diversions were a form of fighting. He wanted not merely to amuse, but to irritate and disturb as well. In a letter to Pope, Swift confessed that the chief end of all his labors was "to vex the world rather than to divert it."[132]

Gulliver's Travels offers one truly extravagant examination of the anatomy of human nature, seen under the microscope of Swift's sardonic imagination.[133] Gulliver is a naïve and vain *eiron*, given the privilege of seeing human nature through both ends of the telescope, first reducing, then magnifying the follies of the species. The most pernicious and pervasive vice in all the adventures is pride. In fact, most all of Swift's thinking is shaped by this idea of original sin, which he called the "foundation of the whole Christian religion."[134] Even the good body is corrupt; it looks ridiculous when you reflect on it as it gets old, wrinkles, and decays.

Lilliputians are buried upside down so that on resurrection day they will be right side up. Swift exaggerates the perspectives of size to mock human vanity. Giants have pores in their noses big enough to drive a honey wagon through. And when Gulliver is set upon the breast of one of these Amazons, a Brobdingnagian nurse, her enormous breasts are spotted with pimples and freckles, and her nipple looms half as big as his head. Swift shows the grossness of humanity seen from below, mocking us as a pernicious race of little odious vermin that nature ever suffered to crawl upon the surface of the earth.[135]

Swift mocked and shocked those who would worship the female form and make beauty into idolatry with his scatological poems titled "Lady's Dressing Room;" while in "Beautiful Young Nymph Going to Bed," a whore takes off all her false adornments. His misogynistic satires on women caricature them as given over to trivia, cards, and their own decay. As Jonathan Vickers observes in his *World of Jonathan Swift*, with the "unscrupulous ingenuity" of women in their disguising powers, they cover themselves with "artificial hair, crystal eye, false eyebrows, false teeth and a whole galaxy of contrivances to pad out the cheeks, breasts, hips, legs of any other deficiency, predating much plastic surgery."[136] Swift is the child of Isaiah and Juvenal.

However, he allowed ladies one last laugh on him. In *On the Death of Dr. Swift*, he ridiculed his own egotism by asking what his friends might say of him. When card-playing ladies receive the news they respond, "in doleful dumps, / 'The Dean is Dead; pray what are trumps?'"[137]

Accused of being misanthropic, Swift explained that he detested the group but loved the individual. "I hate the tribe of lawyers, but I love councilor Such-a-one. . . . But principally I hate and detest that animal called man—although I heartily love John, Peter, Thomas, and so on."[138] Most people fell into groups similar to his bestial Yahoos, those hairy, backward, humanoid creatures. Actually, Swift delighted in seeming worse than he was, becoming what Jonathan Vickers described as an "inverted hypocrite."[139] Calling himself a "hypocrite reverse," Swift concealed his religious observances, prayers, and exemplary piety. "I look upon myself," he said, "in the capacity of a clergyman, to be one appointed by Providence for defending a post assigned to me, and for gaining over as many enemies as I can."[140]

Swift's reputation during the Victorian era was to suffer the slings and arrows of a respectable society. In the 1856 *Scottish Review*, one writer found it ridiculous that anyone would even suggest that Swift was a Christian. He was rather a man of contempt, a "minor Satan, who surprised man naked and asleep, looked at him with microscopic eyes, ignored all his peculiar marks of fallen dignity and of incipient godhead, and in heartless rhymes reported accordingly."[141] The archbishop of York whispered to Queen Anne that he thought the Reverend Swift a great writer, but "not, I think, a Christian."[142]

Satire is indeed so thoroughly concerned with justice, morality, and virtue, that it shares striking resemblances to the basic ethical viewpoint of Christianity. Both satire and Christianity believe strongly in the fallen nature of man. Both hold that reason itself possesses authority, but that when men pretend that enlightenment can solve all problems and be the sole arbiter of all truth, moral disaster is imminent. Edward and Lillian Bloom also mandate that the satirist must love or at least care for humanity to take the trouble to attack and (hopefully) correct our wickedness.[143] And religion needs satire, for religion itself can be a false god. Swift observed that "We have just enough religion to make us hate, but not enough to make us love one another."[144] Christianity provides an answer, but it is not one that most want to try.

The Christian Swift was firmly convinced of the fallen nature of man. Such a view propels his satire, pushing folly out into the open so that it might be purged, cleansed, and corrected. This belief in human depravity is not misanthropy; it is realism along the vein of Chesterton's maxim that only the one who is truly honest about his miserable condition has hope of being helped.

In that way, Swift aligns with Voltaire, against the fluffy-headed optimism of the Leibnitz lemmings of the world, blindly believing that this is the best of all possible worlds and blindly leading others off into a ditch. Satire stops the fall, or attempts to arrest the effects of the Fall, with good sense and good humor. In a tidy little essay on the "gloomy satire" of Swift, Pope, and the other Scriblerians, scholar Louis Bredvold carefully distinguished between the realistic and somewhat miserable recognition of human sin and folly and the misanthropy, melancholy, and even insanity of which the Tory satirists have often been indicted. For Bredvold, their incisive satire must have "at its core a moral idealism expressing itself in righteous indignation. The *saeva indignatio* which Swift suffered from is radically different in quality from a morbid *Schadenfreude*."[145] Such darkness, then, necessarily implies light; and the darker the gloom of their satires, the more ennobling the classical and Christian ideals against which they measure their contemporaries.

The misery of their satire harkens back to a phrase in the Book of Common Prayer with an invocation for God to have mercy upon such *miserable* sinners, with the root of "misery" denoting that which desperately needs and begs for mercy. Such misery is graciously given. But the clergy do not fulfill that giving of mercy. Although he reputedly gave strong popular sermons ("plain, honest stuff") at St. Patrick's, Swift had little regard for many serving in sinecure pulpits. He viewed the clergy as too ignorant, servile, and pragmatic. Rather than moving their congregations, Swift found the "clergy have almost given over perplexing themselves and their hearers with abstruse points of Predestination, Election, and the like."[146] Clergy were ripe for ridicule, but only because they had succumbed to the wiles of this world. "But Satan now is wiser than of yore, and tempts by making rich, not making poor."[147] (Swift mockingly suggest that we may judge Heaven's attitude toward riches by looking at those particular people upon whom it "has been pleased to bestow them."[148]) Yet with so many complaints, he defended the church, even if ironically. In his poem "Cadenus and Vanessa," Swift warned that those using irony should include a hint or key as to their purpose:

> But those who aim at Ridicule
> Shou'd fix upon some certain Rule,
> Which fairly hints they are in jest,
> Else he must enter his protest:
> For let a Man be ne'er so wise,
> He may be caught with sober Lies.[149]

The Test Act of 1673, imposing penalties upon Roman Catholics and dissenting nonconformist religious groups, inspired "An Argument [against] the Abolishing of Christianity in England," in which Swift attempted to make objections to Christianity look ridiculous. With poker-faced irony, Swift mockingly conceded that mutable opinion molded by those in power is against the system of the Gospel; for fashions against it have descended from those of high minds to the vulgar common people, culminating in the idea of the "Majority of Opinion" as the new voice of God. Now, he argued that he was not trying to get rid of *real* Christianity, that faith that actually "had an influence upon men's beliefs and actions." Swift's shifting arguments against the nominal religion of his day yielded insights such as "what wonderful productions of wit should we be deprived of from those whose genius by continual practice hath been wholly turned upon raillery and invectives against religion."[150]

How ironic was he being when he defended a nominal Christian faith, garnering a collection of utilitarian arguments on how it was good for society, not on its truthfulness or historical reality? Churches were good for complaining about; if you didn't have them, you might have to deal with the government. And one could find plenty of good uses for churches, as places for a business appointment, an amorous rendezvous and flirting, or simply a quiet place to sleep. They could be used as "Theatres, Exchanges, Market-houses, common Dormitories, and other public Edifices."[151] He also pointed out that "I never saw, heard, nor read, that the clergy were beloved in any nation where Christianity was the religion of the country. Nothing can render them popular, but some degree of persecution."[152] And abolishing Christianity would give us an extra day for business and pleasure.

Swift is funny, recommending how a "superior Power" could be "of singular use for the common People, as furnishing excellent Materials to keep Children quiet, when they grow peevish; and providing Topics of Amusement in a tedious Winter Night."[153] Religion will help keep the peace, at home and throughout the nation. It is an expedient argument, one that parasite nations will encourage. Swift snuck in a clue to his own thought by suggesting it would be a wild project to restore "that *real* Christianity, such as used in primitive times."[154] Of course, he acknowledged that the abolition of Christianity would insure the collapse of the Church of England, which might only mean the growth of Roman Catholics and Presbyterians, Lord help us. And who can put up with the propaganda of the parsons, who on Sundays rail against what everyone does the other six days? Swift suggested that such a taboo makes doing these wicked things only a little more exciting and keeps life from becoming too boring. And if you got rid of these preachers, whom would we have to mock and ridicule? Where would we get our entertainment?[155]

In defending this work (which is as self-critical of the church as a non-Christian institution as it is of secular society), the hack author had to apologize for misleading readers, and then pointed them to his other publications, such as "A Modest Defence of the Proceedings of the Rabble in All Ages," ironically celebrating those who had stormed the Bastille or chopped off the head of King Charles I and his mock encomium on "A History of Ears," with its symbolic rise and fall of ears (or genitals) of dissenting Puritan preachers.[156]

Swift had the

> Sin of wit, no venial crime;
> Nay, 'tis affirmed he sometimes dealt in rhyme;
> Humor and mirth had place in all he writ,—
> He reconciled divinity with wit.[157]

Writing of how a house was being robbed, he pointed out that it often "happens that the weakest in the family runs first to stop the door." As such, with the house of God being robbed, he was "in the case of David, who could not move in the armor of Saul; and therefore I rather chose to attack [an] uncircumcised Philistine with a sling and a stone."[158] The satiric tradition of the Hebrews had been bequeathed to an Augustan Age of English letters.

With his volcanic rage against injustice and stupidity, Swift left us with a simple truth for religious reflection: "Men are happy to be laughed at for their humor, but not for their folly."[159] But it is in recognizing and confessing folly that men once again find their holy laughter. One final couplet summarizes each of these Scriblerus rascals in this Augustan Age: "Yes, while I live, no rich or noble knave / Shall walk the World, in credit, to his grave."[160] He shall be a prophet until the end. As Søren Kierkegaard observed, there is an irony in Swift's fate that "in his old age, he entered the insane asylum he himself had erected in his early years."[161] Yet he found his place among the true satirists in the Quad. His satiric mirror reflected not only the ills of England, but of his own soul that he knew too well. He was one with his targets, sharing both the tub and the stool with fellow sinners.

Medicine Goes Down

Samuel Johnson (1709–1784) was not fond of Swift's *topoi* and rejected those "general lampooners of mankind." He suspected that satire was born "of an unholy cohabitation of Wit and Malice." However, he recommended that a "man should pass a part of his time with the laughers, by which means anything ridiculous or particular about him might be presented to his view, and corrected."[162] In his 1773 *Dictionary of the English Language*, Johnson defined satire as "A poem in which wickedness or folly is censured." One might add stupidity to the list, particularly of the biblical pedant, the scholar who exegetes the Bible for some odd interpretation. Writing against blockheads and coxcombs, Johnson gave good advice to Mrs. Macaulay, who wrote a history she wanted him to read. She first sought to excuse its faults by claiming that she had a great many irons in the fire, to which the learned doctor coolly replied, "Then, I recommend you, Madam, to put your history where your irons are."[163]

Looking back on this era of Charles II's easy and loose living wits, the devout Anglican Johnson critiqued their tendency to showcase immorality in his *Prologue Spoken at the Opening of the Theatre in Drury Lane Spoken by Mr. Garrick in 1747*:

> Themselves they studied, as they felt they writ;
> Intrigue was plot, obscenity was wit.
> Vice always found a sympathetic friend;
> They pleas'd their age, and did not aim to mend.[164]

A jest may have broken no bones for Johnson, polymath and genius of his age, but he recognized that of "all the griefs that harass the distrest, sure the most bitter is a scornful jest."[165]

In 1779, a somewhat melancholy poet bothered by bouts of insanity, William Cowper (1731–1800), joined with former infidel and slave trader John Newton to compose the Olney Hymns, a collection of evangelical songs for the poor, ragged, and illiterate. Among them was Newton's famous sweet-sounding "Amazing Grace." While even writing of his own "Contrite Heart" ("if it not be broken, break"), Cowper sought to break the fraud of his age with Christian common sense.[166] Having been converted by his Wesleyan cousin, Martin Madan, Cowper relied upon common sense as the standard of his satire, even against the man who brought him into faith.

> Defend me, therefore, common sense, say I,
> From reveries so airy, from the toil
> Of dropping buckets into empty wells,
> And growing old in drawing nothing up![167]

Cowper's problem with the Wesleyan Madan was that he wrote an offbeat work called *Thelyphthora*, translated as the "undoing of womankind," in which he argued that polygamy was acceptable for society. Allegedly concerned that promiscuous men were not held accountable for their wild lifestyle of adultery, fornication, and visits to prostitutes, he advocated for its decriminalization. Madan argued that people mistakenly imagine promiscuity to be sinful, but God does not condemn it anywhere in the Hebrew Scriptures. Such people who judge sexual promiscuity to be immoral, Madan argued, are prejudiced and vulgar in their errors.[168] What is needed, he suggested, is simply a means to make libertine men responsible for their actions: let them financially and socially support all the women they enjoy.

Cowper laughed at the spiritual egotism of his mentor in a satirical fantasy entitled *Antithelyphthora*, based in part on Butler's *Hudibras*. Challenging Madan's foolish substitution of the sacred texts with his own peculiar interpretations, Cowper invented a daring knight, "Airy del Castro," who ventures into a knotty forest of error and "Hypothesis."[169] Scripture, wrote Cowper, is "warp'd from its intent." With tongue-in-cheek, he wryly remarked about Madan's thesis in the *Thelyphthora*, "If I had a Wife of whom I was weary, and wish'd to be indulged with the liberty of taking another, I would certainly Read it, and Study it too."[170] Cowper's gently pungent words were based on his understanding of the role of the satirist, who could not reform his audience unless he had earned the right to be heard and had clothed his instruction in wit and delight. He expressed such sense in his poem "The Flatting Mill":

> Alas for the poet! Who dares undertake
> To urge reformation of national ill—
> His head and his heart are both likely to ache

With the double employment of mallet and mill.
If he wish to instruct, he must learn to delight,
Smooth, ductile, and even his Fancy must flow,
Must tinkle and glitter like gold to the sight
And catch in its progress a sensible glow.
After all he must beat it as thin and as fine
As the leaf that enfolds what an invalid swallows,
For truth is unwelcome, however divine,
And unless you adorn it, Nausea follows.[171]

Cowper understood how that spoonful of sugar helps the medicine go down; satire requires a sweet and sour tanginess, particularly when coming from a pious reformer. As for his sharper satirist peers, he raised the question of whether satire even works:

It may correct a foible, may chastise
The freaks of fashion, regulate the dress,
Retrench a sword-blade, or displace a patch;
But where are its sublime trophies found?
What vice has it subdued?[172]

This question framed a central debate of the era: Could satire actually subdue vice? Did satire work, especially in an illiterate society? But if a written text could address only a select audience, there would be other ways to communicate persuasively, to utterly reduce folly and stupidity to a memorable graphic discourse. From the engravings of artists like William Hogarth and the dramas and discourses of the Continent, an onslaught of fresh satire would castigate religious hypocrisy with all the pith and vinegar of a Swift, but with a swift and powerful visual immediacy.

In the medieval period, when Rabelais's Pantagruel was deep in thought, he would fart under the strain. In this enlightened period, Dryden and his disciples would think wittily, but rarely strain. Enlightened wit made for light satire, opting for a learned, stable, and articulate society. One might even say that religious satirists posed more, showcasing conceits and witticisms, pleasing audiences more than pushing them to amend their behaviors. Many of these poets unintentionally revealed how knowledge had the tendency to puff up, to elevate the poets' own esteem and station in life. In the Quad of Satire, they straddled the line between ridicule and reform, generally being more concerned with their own expressions of well-formed phrases. Of course, exceptions like the unbridled genius of Robert Burns, deriving his satire from both Augustans and the ribald, flyting tradition of Dunbar, held up the mirror to the self. He employed satirical humor not only to castigate hypocritical neighbors, but to confess his own sins as a jolly beggar. Repeating his admonition "O wad some Pow'r the giftie gie us / To see oursels as others see us!," [173] we see the power of heaven using the gift of the satirist to provide such perspective. Unfortunately, as we move to the enlightened wit of continental Europe, the ability to see the comic earthy side of our humanity will be overshadowed by the sneer of Voltaire's wit.

7

Continental Wits, Rakes, and Ironists

But satire, ever moral, ever new,
Delights the reader and instructs him, too.
—Nicolas Boileau

In Presbyterian reformer John Calvin's adopted home of Geneva, the Estienne family had established a dynasty of Renaissance scholars, engravers, and printers. Henri Estienne II (1531–1598) and his brother translated a Latin New Testament (with a thesaurus of Latin vocabulary) and the church history of Eusebius. However, the flowering of French humanism with the pollen of Rabelais and others wafted over the borders into the Swiss city-state. Here Henri crafted his *A World of Wonders*, with apologies to Herodotus, as an independent Lucian satire. The conservative elders in Geneva needed to investigate his tendency toward salacious stories; but his intellectual acumen and sly, opinionated polemics took on the priests and monks of the Roman Catholic Church, a political move that would have agreed with the Calvinists (as Estienne was a good friend of reformer Conrad Badius). In particular, Estienne subversively compared the Eucharistic doctrine of transubstantiation to cannibalism, which fit in tastily with the previously mentioned satire of the papal kitchen.

Estienne turned his society inside out, as he demonstrated how European culture and customs were just as wild as those of ancient Greece. He ridiculed French King Henry III of the Medici mafia for his effeminate affectation. While gleaning tales from the jocular Menot and Maillard, Estienne's writing remained more gossipy. Estienne would be arrested and required to edit out the more scandalous segments; thus, he is not discussed much here. But it is worth noting that his family became renowned for their excellent publishing house and that he himself dabbled in religious satire. His work augured numerous Continental contributions that mirrored British practices, but aimed their sharp pens more at the Roman Catholic Church than at Anglicans or Puritans.

The business of publishing would augment literacy and help to usher in an Enlightenment that would radically alter the tone of religious satire. Wit would crowd out humor, and the sardonic sneer would supplant the belly laugh. Irony would reign above all.

As a member of a cluster of French Renaissance poets, Joachim du Bellay (1522–1560) mastered the art of poetic irony, expressing his disenchantment with both the Roman Catholic Church and Protestant reformers. He served as one of the secretarial assistants of his cousin Cardinal du Bellay in Rome, wryly observing Roman life and culture. Influenced by classical models recommended by Horace, du Bellay formed a stellar group of like-minded poets, called the Pléiades, to imitate Latin authors. In his personal writings, du Bellay tackled his own church and the misconduct of her priesthood with panache.[1] In Sonnet 78, he wrote of the Holy See, "which makes idleness its richest treasure and which, under the pride of the triple crown of gold [that is, the pope's three-tiered crown as opposed to the crown of thorns], breeds ambition, hate, and dissimulation." Two sonnets later, he chronicles his descent in the Holy City:

> If I go up to the palace, I find nothing there but pride, but dissimulated vice, but pomp, but a noise of drums, but a strange harmony, and a vainglorious show of scarlet apparel. [2]

In the exchange things weren't much better, with endless usury and a sharp division of Florentines and Sienese. Joining them was "Venus's great lascivious gang, displaying on every side a thousand amorous charms." In contrast, old Rome, as in director Federico Fellini's *La Dolce vita*, displayed only a stony heap of old monuments.[3] When a new pope was elected, du Bellay mischievously observed what went on in the crowded conclave of cardinals. In the walled-up palace, the godly troops scheme, with some moved by ambition, some by publicity, and some just out of spite. Outside people shout, "The pope is made," giving out false alarms. What is most fun to see is who "boasts of one, who another, who bets on this one, who bets on that, and for less than an ecu, ten cardinals for sale."[4]

For du Bellay, the Vatican, unlike Mount Olympus, had only mortals to run the show. Contrasting Peter and Jupiter, du Bellay finds that from their high perches both throw thunderbolts, but the pope only when some king has stirred his resentment. The Greeks "boast of the heavenly Jupiter's Ganymede. The Tuscan Jupiter has more than fifty of them. One gets drunk on Nectar; the other on good wine. Both claim the eagle for their escutcheon. But one hates tyrants; the other favors them."[5]

Du Bellay then placed himself as a champion—however laughable—of satire, based upon that old Roman statue:

> I used to be Hercules, but now I call myself Pasquino—Pasquino, the people's laughingstock—though I still perform the same labor I did before, in that now with my verses I beat to death so many monsters. My true calling is thus to spare no one, but to sing out vices with a public voice. And yet, however strong I may be, I can still not overcome the rage of that Hydra of Rome. I bore on my shoulders the great palace of the gods to ease Atlas, whose broad, strong back, tired and worn out, bent under the weight of the heavens.
>
> Now, instead of the heavens, I bear on my back a fat Spanish monk who bruises my bones and weighs much more than my original load.[6]

He suggests that those who would clean out the dirty sewers of the Vatican are too often choked by the terrible stench. So he promises that "whoever brings that task to completion will be able to boast that he has done much more than the man who purged the Augean stables."[7] Hercules cannot tackle such a labor of cleansing the church of filth; so one must be Pasquino and ridicule it all instead.

However, across the lake in Geneva, where Calvin lectures as the titular head, du Bellay finds a holy place of fools, guilty fugitives, slanderers, the envious, the greedy, and all manner of reprobates, all with "repentance painted on their brows," but "there is no return, and they will wail in the underworld."[8] He accuses Genevan reformers of being guilty of hypocrisy, for they had abandoned the mother church and could no longer speak to its shortcomings and intrigue. He also denounces the austere moral zeal preached from the pulpits, which is not always matched by the behavior of its Swiss citizens. The Catholic Church may be a whore, but it is his whore, and woe to anyone who neglects her.

Du Bellay defended his method of comic discourse by showing that it is not doctrine that he attacks, or even the propriety of the church, but that which is by its nature risible, that which invites laughter within the congregation:

> I do not reveal here the sacred mysteries of the holy priests of Rome. I do not want to write anything that a blushing virgin would be ashamed to read. I want to touch lightly on less hidden vices. But you will say that I misname these Regrets, seeing that most often I write in a comic vein. But I say that the sea does not always roar out its anger and that Apollo does not always shoot his arrows at the Greeks. So if you encounter some laughter here, do not label as false complaints the poems I sigh out. If I laugh, it is as one laughs in company.[9]

While ruing the state of the papacy at the time of the Reformation, du Bellay shows the state of satire within the Church, and while no less critical than Luther's, his version is sadder and more resigned to endure the present occupation by corruption.

Sátira de España

The dangers of satire were felt more keenly in Spain, particularly under the shadow of the Spanish Inquisition. In "La elección de los alcaldes de Daganzo" (Election of the mayors of Daganzo), a political candidate is asked whether he can read. He says, "You won't find among my relatives any-one-so stupid as to set himself to learn those wild fancies that lead men to the brazier."[10] The brazier refers either to the place where the Inquisition burnt heretics at the stake or a method of torture used by the Inquisition whereby the victim's feet were rubbed with fat and held close to a brazier of live coals. Religious satire was closely monitored and censored. And yet in the midst of tyranny and oppression, laughter would subversively break out of the prisons.

The man who led Spain a giant step forward, Miguel de Cervantes (1547–1616), was known as the "Prince of Wits" and erstwhile father of the Spanish language. His superb work, *Don Quixote de la Mancha*, opened a literary golden age while satirizing the chivalric tradition of romance and war, with a sly humor regarding religious institutions underlying his romance. As Lord Byron opined, "Cervantes smiled Spain's chivalry away."[11]

The grand knight would achieve his immortality through madness, with a cry of *Ecco lunatic*. The Man of la Mancha has presumably lost his mind through a lack of sleep and from reading too many books. Poetic philosopher Miquel de Unamuno finds the madness of Quixotism similar to a madness at the cross; the "greatest height of heroism to which an individual, like a people, can attain is to know how to face ridicule."[12] Quixote overcomes the world by becoming a laughingstock, for he has heard divine laughter and echoes it by crying aloud in the wilderness. When we pity Don Quixote, Coleridge once observed, "We reflect on our own disappointments; and when we laugh, our hearts inform us that he is not more ridiculous than ourselves, except that he tells us what we have only thought."[13]

Don Quixote's misadventures obliquely twitted the grand institution of the church. At midnight, Don Quixote and Sancho blunder into the town of El Toboso. Everyone is asleep and all is quiet except for dogs barking, an ass braying, pigs grunting, and cats mewing. In the darkness of the night, the enamored knight and Sancho stumble upon the church near where Dulcinea lives. The church tower of El Toboso is an unusually massive and conspicuous one. Where an English translation of the *Don Quixote* text has Don Quixote announcing, "It's the church we have lit upon, Sancho," the original Spanish says, "Con la iglesia hemos dado," which means something more like, we have "run into" or "come up against" the church. The popular Spanish saying derived from the text is "Con la iglesia hemos topado," with the term *topar/topado* conveying more of the sense of "come up against."[14] This saying is used whenever an individual encounters opposition from a powerful, unyielding institution.

So, when Sancho tells Don Quixote that they've come to the church, Don Quixote concludes they've come to their graves. After debate about whether a palace can be on a dead end street or not, they turn right around and go back the way they came (no use trying to continue when you've come up against the church and its Inquisition). The misperceiving, but prescient, knight, observes, "We have run into the church [a brick wall] and might as well turn around."

Using pithy wordplay called *conceptismo*, Spanish baroque and Roman Catholic poet Francisco de Quevedo (1580–1645) captured the flair of his age, tilting his lance at its follies and foibles. His *Sueños*

(*Dreams*) were saucy moral satires, full of caricatures, exaggerated stereotypes, and epigrammatic conceits. He rose as the lively wit of the Counter-Reformation, a clever and more cheerful counterpart to his spiritually disciplined countryman, Ignatius Loyola, founder of the Society of Jesus.

Quevedo's bread was buttered on the side of the traditional authorities of Spain—the military government, the aristocracy, and the Roman Catholic Church. His view of the nature of man, deeply Augustinian, saw sin rooted everywhere in the soul, with humans being "fundamentally dishonest and hypocritical." For this satirist, "not only are things not what they seem, they are not even what they are called!" So, he invented his *Dreams and Discourses*, or *Sueños y discursos*, and provided direct, and privileged, access to dreams and revelations from God, and also from hell.[15]

In Quevedo's satiric vision of hell, he placed didactic messages in the mouths of devils, as in his *The Devil upon Two Sticks* (1641). What might be viewed as scorn or withering contempt for corrupt clerics and worldly aristocrats was leavened by dexterous wit and laughter. Quevedo found the worldiness and spiritual hypocrisy of ignorant priests to be ripe targets. Simultaneously, the Church of Spain sought to reform its own clergy and willingly acquiesced to his mischief. While his satire supported the church's position rather than subverting it, it exposed spiritual disease.

Although connected to Spanish Castilian nobility, Quevedo was comparable to Alexander Pope in that he was physically handicapped. He was overweight, had a clubfoot, and suffered from extreme myopia, prompting him to wear a pince-nez. He studied theology with the Jesuits and acquired a zeal for challenging heretics and atheists, which included writing a treatise on *God's Providence*. Like Pope, he collected good literary friends, particularly Cervantes, but also like Pope, he made enemies.

Quevedo's keen polemic writing *Sueños y discursos* is composed of five fantastic dream discourses. As he falls asleep, he is transported to hell (that is, seventeenth-century Spain), with chapters including "Last Judgment" (a peek into hell similar to that of Dante and Lucian), "A Vision of Hell," and "The Dream of Death." Each exposes the duplicity of human nature. Inhabitants from hell speak forth bluntly and sarcastically, exposing the vices of all the estates, such as the cynicism and avarice of ministers in the court of Madrid, along with their sycophantic flatterers. The true nature of each sinner is held up to pitiless mockery.

Controversial and full of verbal gymnastics, the *Sueños* ridicule stupidity and vice in detail, and offer a moral vision for a society in which much religion has become formalized. In one of his best satires, "The Bedeviled Constable," he goes to St. Peter's Church. There he finds Licenciado Calabres, a "a rosary-waving, heavy-booted, hard-dealing churchman indeed, who wore his spiritual discipline like a badge."[16]

This alleged man of God is slow to start Mass, but very quick to finish his table. "He was known to set bones and perform cures all the while giving thanks to God and blessing his patients with signs of the Cross made with the exaggerated fervor of an adulterous sinner. He made slovenliness a virtue and was forever recounting revelations,"[17] which he elevated to the status of miracles. The priest Calabres symbolizes the Lord's "*whited sepulcher*—immaculate on the outside and rich with carvings, but worm-eaten and rotten within. Outwardly he gave the impression of being chaste and honorable, but in the depths of his soul he was dissolute and unprincipled, an obvious hypocrite, a fraud, a walking lie and a talking fabrication of tales."[18]

In one of his wild exorcisms, a man is tied with the priest's belt and is jerking his limbs in frenzy. However, the evil spirit trying to possess the man cries out, "This isn't a man; it's a constable!" Infernal spirits do not really want to inhabit constables. "You can strike a bargain with a devil far more reliably than with a constable. We at least flee before the sight of the Cross, while they simply use it as a cover for evil doing. . . . Rest assured that constables and demons are indistinguishable one from another, save only in that they belong to a somewhat lax order of devilry, while we are members of a most strict fraternity of law officers, and follow a hard regime in Hell."[19]

Quevedo closes his vision with a tale of how he found many devils traveling a road, driving a great throng of souls *out of* Hell, prodding them with sticks and spears. What amazes him is that the crowd includes mostly beautiful women, priests, and lawyers.

Puzzled, Quevedo asks why Satan would want to banish these people from the infernal regions. One devil replies that "they were of infinitely greater benefit in gaining more inmates for Hell on the Earth above—the women through their features, their beauty and virtuous appearance which masked their dishonesties, the priests through selling absolution, and the lawyers through their honest faces and crooked dealings. They were therefore being flung back into the world to deceive people."[20]

Quevedo sought to drive such corrupt company to see themselves in his satirical mirror, to humbly laugh at their hypocrisy, and to reform their ways. Not that he had much hope of such fruit, but it was worth trying. In one of the last words in the *Dreams*, an angel-like voice from a cloud announces, "He that rightly comprehends the morality of this discourse shall never repent the reading of it."[21] Not only is the satire funny, with its portrayal of an impending apocalypse of a pestilence of chaperones, but it aims toward reminding readers of their own sin. Such a motive of comically exposing the vice of religious and legal leaders was being paralleled in seventeenth-century neighboring France as well.

French Hypocrites

In the hilarious satire on hypocrisy in *Tartuffe*, Molière (Jean Baptiste Poquelin, 1622–1673) doubles the pleasure of looking at and identifying with the affectation of pompous religious characters. When one character observes, "She is laughing up her sleeve at you," it is a happy recognition that Molière is also laughing at his audiences, both in the provinces and at court. When the imposter Tartuffe, a houseguest of Orgon and his wife, Elmire, plays upon the gullible nature of his bourgeois host, his confessions only mask illicit, lascivious lust (for Elmire). "Although I am a pious man," he utters, "I am not the less a man." He feigns both Christian charity and virtue, only to sneak a peek and gratify his desires.

Tartuffe admonishes Dorine, the saucy housemaid: "Cover that bosom that I must not see." Her retort provides one of the funniest lines of the play:

> Your soul, it seems, has very poor defenses,
> And flesh makes quite an impact on your senses.
> It's strange that you're so easily excited;
> My own desires are not so soon ignited,
> *And if I saw you naked as a beast,*
> *Not all your hide would tempt me in the least.*[22]

Other family members plan to expose the imposter. With her husband hiding under a table in the room, Elmire unveils the true character of the horny scoundrel Tartuffe. In response to Elmire's concerns about the wrath of heaven for such an adulterous affair, Tartuffe counsels,

> Madam, forget such fears, and be my pupil,
> And I shall teach you how to conquer scruple.
> Some joys, it's true, are wrong in heaven's eyes;
> Yet heaven is not averse to compromise.
> . . . .
>
> If you're still troubled, think of things this way:
> No one shall know our joys, save us alone,
> And there's no evil till the act is known;
> It's scandal, Madam, which makes it an offense,
> And it's no sin to sin in confidence.[23]

He essentially argues that what happens in Vegas, stays in Vegas: sin is not sin until it is publicized.

Molière's play was banned twice by ecclesiastical authorities from any public performance, primarily for linking sex with religion.[24] He sought to rid the minds of his audience of spiritual cant by chastening the double standard of his world with ridicule. In his defense against an irate Roman Catholic hierarchy, Molière played with the definition of a sacrament in defining the "comic" as "the outward and visible form that nature's bounty has attached to everything unreasonable, so that we should see, and avoid, it. To know the comic we must know the rational, of which it denotes the absence and we must see wherein the rational consists. . . . Incongruity is the heart of the comic."[25]

The battle between flesh and spirit is complicated by the duplicity of the hypocrite Tartuffe. The body and its desires are not bad, for they were created good, but everything created good can go bad, be spoiled, ruined, and bent. Molière mocked not the created flesh, but the specious arguments Tartuffe employs for gratifying his lust.

Molière's challenge was to make the gentry laugh, and make them laugh, he did. He exploited the comic vein in Tartuffe's rhetorical mix of piety and sin. Since Tartuffe would be transformed from a cleric to a man of the world, his initial appearance may even have suggested a Jesuit. In fact, a pun by Dorine ("Ce Monsieur Loyal porte un aire bien deloyal") may allude to anti-Jesuit propaganda, as there was a stock allegation that Jesuits acted quite "disloyal" to their host countries (such as France and Britain).[26] Following Molière, another Frenchman attacked Jesuit casuistry as a mode of rationalizing one's vices and ridiculed their order.

According to scholar F. H. Buckley, *Tartuffe* was directed against the clever and pious Jansenist sect in Port Royal that had condemned the "lax morals at the court of Molière's regal patron."[27] This Jansenist response came from the philosopher, mathematician, and scientist Blaise Pascal (1623–1662), who, in his *Provincial Letters*, under the pseudonym of an ingenuous provincial character, Louis de Montalte, waged a war of satiric words against the Jesuits, especially for their purveying of cheap grace and their sophistic use of casuistry. As a Jansenist, Pascal adhered to Augustinian doctrines of original sin and the efficacious grace of God. Condemned as heretical by Pope Leo X in 1655, due in part to their Calvinistic emphasis on predestination, Jansenists found their greatest advocate in Pascal, a clever provincial *eiron*. Against the Jesuitical idea that one who committed acts in ignorance of God's laws could be excused, Pascal ironically celebrated, how delightful this was, as more people can now be saved by ignorance rather than by God's grace.

Pascal's letters were ostensibly a series of correspondences from a Parisian telling a friend in the provinces what was happening, with the correspondence slyly mocking the Jesuits' moral presumption and laxity. Having been charged with "turning sacred things into ridicule,"[28] Pascal lampooned their machinations in devising easier ways to get through confession and repentance, or finding shortcuts to Heaven, indirectly accusing them of indulging in all kinds of pleasure under the cloak of ignorance or temporary dispensations. For instance, if a monk wants to visit a whore, he could "temporarily defrock" himself. In his eleventh *Provincial Letter*, Pascal puckishly spoofed the idea that "a monk is not to be excommunicated for putting off his habit, provided it is to dance, swindle, or go incognito into infamous houses." It is "impossible to refrain from laughing" at such idiocy. And here, Truth properly has a "right to laugh, because she is cheerful, and to make sport of her enemies, because she is sure of the victory."[29] Charity obliges us to laugh at each other, that we may be induced to laugh at our errors and renounce them. The best satire is laughing at each other. For Pascal, "two faces which resemble each other make us laugh, when together, by their resemblance, though neither of them by itself makes us laugh."[30] One finds the best laughter in a community of faces and souls side by side. Those who point out our faults and folly do us a favor; they mortify us with mirth.[31]

On the issue of usury, Pascal wrote that "according to our fathers, it consists in little more than the intention of taking the interest as usurious. Escobar, accordingly, shows you how you may avoid usury by a simple shift of the intention." Under the slippery tactics of casuistry, of using previous cases for justifying one's actions, one could excuse one's vices by showing that the intent to do evil was not there, even though the poor suffered. Where Molière used his satire to attack the foibles of a particular type of religious hypocrite, Pascal aimed at discovering the ultimate truth, pricking all "balloons of vanity, even all pride in knowledge," so that we might laugh at the self, even as we see the reedy limits of reason.[32]

His constructive humor for the human reed lurks as well in those scattered scraps of reflections gathered in his *Pensées*. Various fragments of his thoughts, like a collection from the Hebrew books of Proverbs, offer insight into the Christian life and faith. His own musings gently satirize human frailty and folly. For Pascal, "men never do evil so completely and cheerfully as when they do it from religious conviction."[33] Pascal sums up his discovery that "all human evil comes from this: man's being unable to sit still in a room."[34] When asked why he wrote with such a comic tone, Pascal explained, "Had I written in a dogmatic style, only scholars would have read the letters, and they did not need them."[35]

Another Frenchman, Bible lecturer, missionary to the Huguenots, and Roman Catholic rhetorician, François Fénelon (1651–1715), sought to reform the Court of Louis XIV, even as he served as tutor to the spoiled and seemingly intractable dauphin. Upon becoming a Jesuit priest, Fénelon sedulously preached to stubborn Protestants—enough of a trial to frustrate one into becoming a satirist. Yet his calling led him to write treatises (such as *Dialogues sur l'éloquence*) on the existence of God and on educating young girls.[36] It was during his teaching of the king's grandson that Fénelon wrote his *Dialogues* on the education of a prince and his pedagogical romance, *Telemachus*, a satire emphasizing morality, religion, and the good of the people. The book, not surprisingly, received a papal condemnation, even though Fénelon had abandoned Menippean satires, those wicked verses of Lucian, for a more gentlemanly tone.

When this amazing *Les aventures de Télémaque, fils d'Ulysse* (*The Adventures of Telemachus, the Son of Ulysses*) was published in 1699 (most likely without Fénelon's public approval), the king reacted furiously, banishing the author from Versailles, as the work slyly challenged the divine right of kings. A cause célèbre, it stood as a thinly disguised exposé of an absolutist monarchy. Fénelon argued that the work was merely a vehicle for his political thoughts and a "learned parable." It is satire at its gentlest, but most forceful, mirroring the method of moral teaching through personal guidance that sought to raise Telemachus, the son of a great man, to the "highest pitch of glory."

The fantastic adventure story follows Telemachus's search for his father, accompanied by his appropriately named tutor and sage, Mentor (actually Athena, goddess of wisdom in disguise).[37] His advice is clearly didactic, seeking to cultivate the character of the sixteen-year-old, as when he instructs his charge: "He who has not felt his weakness and the violence of his passions is not yet wise; for he does not yet understand himself and does not know how to distrust himself." The son is tempted by Eu, a nymph on Calypso's island. Mentor, in his numerous speeches, holds up an ideal of quiet and simplicity, qualities that marked the work of Fénelon's actual friend Madame Guyon and her controversial teaching on prayer and Quietism. For Mentor, "How rare it is to find a soul quiet enough to hear God speak."[38]

By focusing upon universal human rights and clear personal responsibilities, Fénelon gently goads and pricks his readers into a biblical morality. For example, the art of forgiveness is couched in Mentor's observation that "if we were faultless we should not be so much annoyed by the defects of those with whom we associate."[39] As one of the most noble and exemplary Christian satirists, Fénelon set out a classical model of moral education. However, the work fails as satire in its lack of humor. While it provides moral direction, it does not trigger laughter. However ironically, the publicists for King Louis XV would exploit Fénelon's work to laud their monarch as Telemachus. The postscript for his satire indicates the typical troubles that follow one whose tongue is quick, even if it is very quiet, as an enraged Louis XIV forbade Fénelon from leaving his diocese. Voltaire would later undermine the church's hypocritical posturing by using Fénelon as his evidence.[40]

"Laughter and truthfulness" found fertile ground in another Horatian-trained satirist, the French poet Nicolas Boileau-Despreaux (1636–1711), who sought to unite the pleasing and the instructive elements of poetry. His discussion of classical satire appeared in *Art Poetique*, where he argued that one of the best ways of freeing minds from errors came through the Latin satirist's strategy of *redendo dicere verum*, speaking the truth through laughter. Scholar Howard Weinbrot pointed to how Boileau mingled the pleasantry of Horace and the fire of Juvenal so effectively that other poets would praise him for his genius that "as tickles us at once and bites." [41] Boileau echoed Juvenal's lament over the moral malaise, for what the Roman had written "with all the physical and spiritual decadence described there—[it] was as vividly appropriate to seventeenth-century Paris as it had been to ancient Rome."[42]

While Boileau lamented the "terrible burden of having nothing to do," he slyly wrote satire. In *Le Lutrin*, his burlesque work against the clergy, Boileau audaciously ridiculed "the manners of a set of fat and lazy ministers," as Julian White observes, by "insert[ing] the language of the heroic epic into the mouths of common people."[43] He grounded his fiction on actual characters, yet avoided any isomorphic correspondence between actual people and his characters, lest some enterprising lawyer find a ripe case of slander. The grand old deadly sin of Sloth dwells in the Abbey of Citeaux, with indolent canons rushing to the chapel when they are awakened by a rumor that a sumptuous feast has been prepared. One particular gourmand, Evrard, furiously protests at the idea of having to read at his advanced age. Boileau writes that he reads the Bible as much as he reads the Koran. His sole concern is to know "what annual rents are due to the chapel from the tenants on its lands. His arm alone, without the benefit of Latin, is strong enough to overturn the lectern, after which they may eat and drink."[44]

In this ancient abbey, dwelling in ease and with the "melting Pleasures of Fraternal Peace," the abbots bask in fat and bless themselves "in sweet Repose of Sacred Idleness." They stretch out on downy featherbeds to chant their matins, never having to lift up their heads. But their noses are lifted high as they can smell the kitchen aromas and be wakened from their sleep (even though they are deaf to the prayer bell). Although they always arrive for meals in person, these monks praise God by proxy, "pawning the Chanters and Poor Singing-boys,"[45] who are usually condemned to the lowest drudgeries. Boileau rued that discord and villainy perch on proud magnificent cathedrals, with prelates lounging on stately beds with gilded posts, sumptuous crimson quilts, and double curtains that scorn the light of the mid-day sun (so they can sleep quite late) and counterfeit night. If any prelate is tempted by an unseasonable zeal to spend time in prayer, for shame, allay that desire. All the learning that suggests this is Lent or any Saints' Days' Eve should be put aside, because you should remember that "Meat heated twice, is not worth half a Groat!"[46]

The worst indignation comes because the world is "set agog on Reformation." Boileau pointed out empty names had set the world on fire; those who pleaded conscience (while making a "heavy Din") are saucy dissenters who will not give blind obedience to Holy Mother Church. Boileau lamented that preaching mendicant friars were busy traveling, "exercising their toes in Dust and Gravel" and keeping such a coil [trouble] that even the narrator's head aches so much that he can "get no wink of Sleep!"[47]

Holy Mother Church had become a bank, a house of sloths and gluttons. Boileau's satires on the Jesuit casuistry followed Pascal's, with his hope that laughter and truthfulness would wed to bring about reform. He advanced morality, even as he confessed his own "Shame," a communicable disease from which all humanity suffers, and a slipping into the slough of vice. He remained, like Horace, sympathetic to the follies of man.

One other playful Frenchman of the seventeenth century adapted numerous fables to satirize the church—namely, Jean de la Fontaine (1621–1695), whose *Fables choisies* amused many a child (his first edition was dedicated to the six year old dauphin) and perceptive adult. Many, such as "The Fox and the Grapes," "The Tortoise and the Hare," and "The Ant and the Grasshopper," linger as delightful moral tales, but others carried the weight of more theological criticism.

As a vibrant member of the famous quartet gathering at an apartment of the Rue du Vieux Colombier (including Molière, Boileau, and

Racine), Fontaine boldly took on the avarice of the clergy. In one tale entitled "The Curate and the Corpse," a priest partakes in the funeral procession of a man and fantasizes about the money he is earning and how he is going to spend it, rather than tending to the mourners. While he daydreams, the funeral coach crashes, cracking the priest's head and killing him. Death interrupts the greedy daydreamer, just as in the woodcuts of Dürer. As scholar Gregory Carlson observes, for Fontaine "fable and image have worked together well to satirize the human being whose religion is a cover for greed."[48]

More frequently, Fontaine dressed his humans in animal skins. In "The Rat Who Retired from the World," he tweaked the life of the religious anchorite. Wanting to escape the worries of the world, a rat decides to take a vow of seclusion, hoarding all he needs to spend his days as a hermit. He lives in abundance and leisure, eating and getting fat. One day, however, the citizens of Ratopolis seek his aid during a cat attack. The secluded rodent dismisses them saying that "earthly affairs no longer concern me." His vow of seclusion precludes him from assisting them.

The analogy was clear: Fontaine mocked those monks who sought to remain aloof from the sufferings of others and remain in seclusion for their own comfort. At the end of his fable, Fontaine added a sarcastic commentary: "Whom have I in mind, do you think, when I speak of this rat, so sparing of his help? A monk?—Oh, no! A dervish rather, for a monk, I suppose, is at all times, charitable." As Carlson so aptly puts it, "La Fontaine's last lines ironically deny exactly what the fable portrays: selfishness in the name of religion."[49]

Fontaine and Boileau dwelt under the shadow of the cathedrals; on the other side of the alley was a wit who allegedly described God as a comic playing to an audience too afraid to laugh. He would form his own audience and laugh, or at least smile, with smug superiority.

Best of All Possible Satirists

Voltaire assumed a nom de plume derived from the French verb *volter*, to turn abruptly, masking his original name François-Marie Arouet (1694–1778). While he greatly admired Alexander Pope, Voltaire objected to Pope's ideas in *The Essay on Man* that suggested that one could trust God.[50] Although Votaire's *Candide* primarily skewers Gottfried Leibnitz's idea that this is the best of all possible worlds, Pope's work on God's sovereignty was implicated as well. In contrast to their religious optimism, Voltaire invented the word "pessimism." In *Candide*, Voltaire employed the voice of the Turkish Dervish to question how the deity of the cosmos could actually take a personal interest in insignificant humans. "When his highness sends a ship to Egypt, does he worry about the comfort or discomfort of the rats?"[51]

What Voltaire could not understand was how Pope could advocate laughter as a means to deal with the enormous evil that existed in the world. Voltaire's life had legitimately been darkened by evidence of suffering and evil: the Lisbon earthquake, the Seven Years' War, imprisonment in the Bastille, and bittersweet quarrels with his Prussian sponsor Frederick II. It was the difference between an agnostic, for whom this is all there is to life, and a Christian, for whom religious doctrine bolstered hope for a grander, more joyous perspective.

Early in his life when clubbing with freethinkers, Voltaire wrote a daring verse on "The True God," mocking the idea of a "god killing himself for the sake of sinners."[52] Not believing in the foolishness of the cross, Voltaire nevertheless championed social justice. His cause célèbre stemmed from his campaigns on behalf of victims of religious hysteria and persecution, such as the Protestant Jean Calas, who was falsely accused by Roman Catholic authorities of murdering his own son lest he leave his father's Protestant faith. Voltaire's clarion call was "Écrasez l'infâme!" or "Crush the infamy!" alluding to the Roman Catholic Church. Voltaire's biographer Theodore Besterman argues that Voltaire accused Jesuit priests of sexually abusing him as a child—an experience that supplies its own evidence for a not-so-good world.[53] In Voltaire's later satire, God becomes a monster who created men in his own image so he could abuse them.

Candide was not one of Voltaire's *contes* of philosophic tales, but possessed an ulterior motive. As a missile of assault, it waged war against beliefs he wished to demolish. The kind, generous character James the Anabaptist rescues a brutal sailor who tosses him overboard to drown, an ironic ending for an Anabaptist. The gullible Candide and his German tutor, Dr. Pangloss, stumble into numerous catastrophes, from shipwrecks to earthquakes. The novel plays with the idea that the Inquisition with its spectacle of burning people over a slow fire, was seen as an infallible antidote for earthquakes. Candide and friends endure the auto-da-fé, the ceremonial procession in which they wear paper crowns (of painted devils and inverted flames) on their heads and are forced to listen to long sermons. The Grand Inquisitor himself ogles Candide's lady friend, Cunegonde, during Mass and then takes her for a mistress.

Accused of instigating the earthquake, Pangloss is hanged, and Candide robbed and whipped (paralleling Voltaire's own thrashings and incarceration). Later he is conscripted as a galley slave. In Paraguay the native poor are consigned to eat coarse Indian corn from wooden bowls, starving, while the priests live in luxury, dining from golden bowls. Throughout the book, Pangloss (who we discover did not die), stands as the woefully inadequate ventriloquist for Leibnitz's doctrine of optimism. He tries to explain the origins of his own miserable condition of syphilis (it all comes from the pleasures of love). His account traces the history of his personal venereal disease with parallels to biblical genealogies, with the clergy being the root of all sexual evil, as Pangloss "received this present from a very learned Franciscan monk . . . who owed it to a marquise . . . who caught it from a Jesuit who had it in a direct line from one of the fellow adventurers of Christopher Columbus."[54] He escapes death and being eaten by cannibals because he is *not* a Jesuit. Their final escape is to a little farm where each contributes his or her skills. Candide discovers that the best thing in the world is to cultivate one's garden, even as he marries the ugly, ravaged, flat-chested Cunegonde.

Voltaire reserved his harshest criticism for those clergy who were called to serve people, but through their own egoistic casuistry, served only themselves. In a collection of sardonic essays compiled in his 1764 *Dictionnaire philosophique* Voltaire belittled the ancient history of the Bible with his ironic pose, not attacking the Church directly, but showing how much society had been misled, revealing "how ridiculous are many things alleged to be respectable," and letting readers draw their own conclusions. For example, in his entry on Abraham, Voltaire suggests that of the patriarch's Jewish and Muslim offspring, God must have surely preferred the latter, as both are thieves, but the Arabs are much better at thieving. The Jews, he intimates, sell their old fables to Christians, Muslims, and anyone who will buy them, just as they sell old clothes.

Voltaire unfrocked the *infâme* of the clerics, challenging them to live up to their name of *abbé*, a name signifying a poor man who led others in the vow of poverty. But now these same poor spiritual fathers had incomes of two to four hundred thousand crowns, while some in Germany even had regiments to guard their money. As Voltaire writes,

> The word *abbé*, let it be remembered, signifies father. If you become one you render a service to the state; you doubtless perform the best work that a man can perform; you give birth to a thinking being. In this action there is something divine. But if you are *Monsieur l'Abbé* only because you have had your head shaved, wear a clerical collar, and a short cloak, and are waiting for a fat benefice, you do not deserve the name of *abbé*.[55]

Fattened on the substance of the unfortunate, these clerics, warned Voltaire, sounding like a secular Hebrew prophet, should "tremble for fear that the day of reason will arrive!"[56] For Voltaire, those who assumed authority over others, whether wearing "green robes, turbans, black robes or surplices, cloaks and clerical bands,"[57] were wretched, ignorant, and impertinent human beings, the same who condemned Galileo or challenged the circulation of the blood. Voltaire caricatured the church as anti-science with such judgments. But it was their hypocrisy that vexed him most.

Voltaire formulated an axiom that came to underlie most Marxist thought: namely, that the institution of religion exists "only to keep mankind in order." Thus the Roman Catholic Church, according to Voltaire, controlled the masses through superstition and fear:

> Instruction, exhortation, threats of torments to come, promises of immortal beatitude, prayers, counsels, spiritual help, are the only means ecclesiastics may use to try to make men virtuous here below, and happy for eternity. All other means are repugnant to the liberty of reason, to the nature of the soul, to the unalterable rights of conscience, to the essence of religion, to that of the ecclesiastical ministry, and to the rights of the sovereign.[58]

However, for Voltaire, even the institutional church was a lie at its core. The Roman Catholic religion was not only superstitious, but "the most ridiculous, the most absurd, and the most bloody that has ever infected the world." He targeted the chasm between the rules and doctrines of the various orders and their actual practice. Zeroing in on ascetic practices, he pointed out that nowhere in the Gospels do we read that "Jesus Christ forbade omelets to His apostles; on the contrary He said to them: 'Eat such things as are set before you.'"

> Why, on days of abstinence, does the Roman Church consider it a sin to eat terrestrial animals, and a good work to be served with sole and salmon? The rich Papist who has five hundred francs' worth of fish on his table shall be saved, and the poor wretch dying with hunger, who has eaten four sous' worth of salt pork, shall be damned. Why must we ask permission of our bishop to eat eggs? If a king ordered his people never to eat eggs, would he not be thought the most ridiculous of tyrants? How strange the aversion of bishops to omelets![59]

Although a champion for religious toleration, Voltaire disliked Jews, not because he was typically anti-Semitic and believed they murdered Jesus, but because they seeded Christianity, which he despised. His hatred for Christians thus propelled him to pour his "hot lead upon the Jews" and their barbarous history.[60]

Voltaire was a nimble wit. As one trained by Jesuits, he carried on a scholastic tradition of logic and argument, but added sarcasm. He mocked the ranting of certain preachers who banned opera, comedies, Sunday concerts, and even card-playing. He was amused by Anglicans who seemed so serious about collecting tithes, by Presbyterians "who look as though they were angry and preach with a strong nasal accent," and by Quakers, "who go to church and wait for inspiration with their hats on their heads"[61] Voltaire compared Christians cursing Jews to children beating their fathers. He confessed to praying only one prayer in his life: "Oh Lord, make my enemies ridiculous. And God granted it."[62]

Voltaire himself was exiled. Even after he died, the Bishop of Paris refused him a Catholic funeral, and he was allegedly buried half in a church courtyard and half out. He couldn't quite find his place, although the French Revolution would extol him and bury him in the national heroes' pantheon.

Human Epigram

As a proponent and practitioner of incongruous and ironic comedy, Søren Kierkegaard (1813–1855) was an odd duck, even for Denmark. He wore hats and costumes out of fashion, popularizing the name Søren as a term of derision, suggesting "kook" or crazy man. "My whole life," he would explain, "is an epigram to make people aware."[63] As a sort of Don Quixote/Socrates, he wrote and lived like an ironic clown, wearing various pseudonyms or comic masks to speak his mind.[64]

Called the father of existentialism, Kierkegaard was more a misunderstood reformer for Christianity. He spoke of himself as an auditor for the established church in Copenhagen since an auditor was called to reveal counterfeits (this he could do, he confessed, for he was once a counterfeit person). His comedy would reside in part in that great absurdity of God becoming human, *credo quia absurdum*, which one could know only by becoming personally, or existentially, involved in the seemingly improbable Incarnation of Christ. He perceived such incongruities of life, from his own predicaments to the doctrine of God becoming man, as foundational for the comic: "Where there is life there is contradiction and wherever there is contradiction, the comic is present."[65] Kierkegaard lampooned everyone, including himself. As a congenital and somewhat schizophrenic melancholic, he teetered between being the Happy Prince and Hamlet. His early pseudonyms are replete with comic forms: John the Seducer, Hilarius Bookbinder, the Fashion Designer, Nicolaus Notabene, and a young man known only as "A." By entering into a character role, he lived "audaciously" with his ironic voices hinting at the coming of the comic.

He grew up in a conservative Lutheran home with a dour, guilt-ridden merchant father, who had acquired enormous wealth. His father felt like Faust, as if he had made a pact with the devil for riches and honor, having once, as a shepherd boy out on the cold heaths, cursed God. His life had been hard and he shook his small puny fist at God. He also seduced the housemaid, when Kierkegaard's mother was dying. Having become rich, he retired to brood over sins and practiced a stern fear of God. Due to his own sins, he bestowed upon his son a morbid consciousness of sins of the flesh. In this oppressively religious household, guilt was compounded in a series of family deaths in a very short time.

When in early manhood, Kierkegaard stumbled upon the human sinfulness of his beloved parent, his childhood idol was broken, and he entered a crisis of earthquake proportions. He ran off to university—where in Luther's language, he sinned boldly—living a debauched and disorderly existence until his twenty-fifth birthday. Then, like the proverbial prodigal, he returned home and was reconciled with his father.

Kierkegaard was marked by conflicting emotions, with two moods alternating: first, he was gregarious, with a grand, lively enjoyment of diverse company, a glass of wine, and a pretty girl. Yet an underlying tension would surface: "I was the life of the party; wit poured from my lips—all toasted and celebrated me. I went home and wanted to kill myself."[66] He felt called to make a great sacrifice like Abraham, who sacrificed his beloved Isaac. Falling deeply in love with a young girl named Regine Olsen and becoming engaged to her, Kierkegaard broke off the engagement, due mostly to his call to be a religious author. Instead of getting married, he wrote twenty volumes of philosophical, devotional and satirical books. He received a large inheritance, but spent and gave it all away by the day he died.

Denmark in the mid-eighteenth century was ostensibly a Lutheran nation. However, Kierkegaard found it full of hypocritical illusions and pretentions; it had compromised its integrity for social and political relevance. "Danish Christianity was reduced to the three experiences of being HATCHED (born), MATCHED (married) and DISPATCHED (buried). In this nominal state religion, three things were thrown at you: water at Baptism, rice at marriage and earth at burial," observed Kierkegaardian scholar Howard Johnson.[67] Kierkegaard's calling was to make people aware of what was essentially Christian, "the reintroduction of Christianity into Christendom." For this, he needed the indirect modes of communication afforded by irony and satire.

In one of his parables on "untouched food," Kierkegaard lays down the contradiction between what Christians say they are and their actual behavior:

> If there was a certain kind of food, an article of food which, for one reason or another, had such significance for a man that it was completely tied up with his most intimate feelings (we may imagine a national dish, or a food which has religious significance), and as a result of this it was impossible

> for him to remain silent of this food if this food was scoffed at or even referred to disparagingly: then it would be natural that, if this happened in his presence, he would admit and confess his own emotions. But let us imagine that the relationship is somewhat altered. We imagine that this man gathered in company with several others, and this food is set before them. When it is offered them, each of the guests says personally: "This is the most excellent and precious of all foods." Certainly, if that man of whom we are speaking discovers with astonishment, or believes that he discovers, that the guests do not eat of this dish, that they leave it untouched, that they confine themselves to other foods, while they still say that the food is the most excellent and precious: is the man in that case required to acknowledge his own conviction? There is no one indeed who contradicts him; no one says anything other than what he says.[68]

For Kierkegaard, people may well say that they believe in the Christian faith; however, they may not partake of it or live it in a full sense. Church people offer lip service to the most excellent sacred meal of the Eucharist, but then do not eat or even taste it.

Kierkegaard was brutally lampooned by a comic periodical called the *Corsair*, which portrayed him with spindly legs, in trousers of different sizes, a large nose, and a hat worn down on his ears—as a bizarre little figure, a kind of comical monk, a human gargoyle looking down at absurd world.

Yet even as an object of ridicule, Kierkegaard made a discovery that he must "find a truth which is true for me, the idea for which I can live and die." He wrestled with what it meant to be a Christian in Christendom. Sadly, he saw that "there are many people who reach their conclusions about life like schoolboys: they cheat their master by copying the answer out of a book without having worked out the sum for themselves." Faith must be lived: it must be subjective about its object. Yet Kierkegaard's lived faith seemingly came in against his own will: "If Christ is to come and take up his abode in me," reflected Kierkegaard, "it must happen in accordance with the title of today's Gospel in the Almanac: 'Christ came in through locked doors.'"[69]

For Kierkegaard, theologians and philosophers had built beautiful castles and lived in shacks next door. Like stupid geese, Christians gathered every Sunday to hear a goose preach.

> The gist of the sermon was as follows: What a high destiny geese have, to what a high goal the creator—and every time this word was mentioned the geese curtsied and the ganders bowed their heads—had appointed geese.
>
> It was this way every Sunday. Afterwards, the assembly dispersed and each one waddled home to his family. And so to church again next Sunday, and then home again—and that was the end of it. They flourished and grew fat, became plump and delicate, were eaten on St. Martin's Eve—and that was the end of it.[70]

Kierkegaard ironically faulted the one goose that took seriously the business of flying, which made him look like a fool, as he grew thin and suffered the torments of traveling and hunger; this kind of bird, quacked the other geese, would assuredly lose the grace of God, reserved for those that become plump and fat. So, too, Kierkegaard slyly suggested, just let Christian worship be a sort of Sunday daydreaming.[71]

Kierkegaard satirized such geese and church-goers as having "a bourgeois love for God," which began, as he observed, "when vegetable life is most active, when the hands are comfortably folded on the stomach, and the head sinks back into the cushions of the chair, while the eyes, drunk with sleep, gaze heavily for a moment towards the ceiling."[72] The venality of clergy and stupidity of their parishioners appears in this bit of dialogue:

> Parson: Thou shalt die unto the world. The fee is one guinea.
> Neophyte: If I must die to the world, I shall have to fork out more than one guinea. I have but one question: who gets the guinea?
> Parson: Naturally I get it; it's my living. It's really very cheap. To preach that one must die to the world, if it's done seriously and with zeal, takes a lot out of a man. So I really have to spend the summer in the country with my family to get some recreation.[73]

People are not given true Christianity but an inadequate dose of it. Imagine, Kierkegaard wrote, "a kind of medicine that possesses in full dosage a laxative effect but in a half a dose a constipating effect. Suppose someone is suffering from constipation. But—for some reason or other,—he is given, with the best of intentions, a half dose: 'after all, it is at least something.' What a tragedy!"[74] Herein we find echoes of Swift, and comic rejoinders to atheists like Christopher Hitchens who see Christians as full of shit: "Yes!" Kierkegaard would, like Swift, not only concede, but celebrate: we are full of it, and it needs to come out, lest we remain full.

Kierkegaard's inexorable mockery of Hegel for his dialectic and his hubris revealed his philosophy of the comic, wherein one is not cruel or abusive, but merely exposes the absurdity of a position. For Kierkegaard, the most authentic humorist around was J. G. Hamann (1730–1788), a true eccentric who preferred exceptions to rules. Hamann's famous answer to Hegel was a roar of laughter, the most apt and debilitating reply that could be given. Socrates, on the other hand, was the supreme ironist. Neither humor nor irony compromises with the world. Humor doesn't give two hoots about appearances; the humorist is like a duck in water. When it is laughed at by the world, it goes under and then rises above it and laughs. What Christianity needed, Kierkegaard recommended, was its own Cervantes.

Kierkegaard and the Comic

Kierkegaard did not hesitate to push his comic analogies to gross extremes: he imagines a man who pretends to let "himself be skinned alive in order to show how the humorous smile is produced merely by the contraction of a particular muscle—and thereupon follows this with a lecture on humor"[75] The comic incongruity lies in the contrast between the safe setting of the lecture hall and a man presumably being skinned alive in order to demonstrate that an involuntary contraction of a tiny muscle appears to be a smile. For Kierkegaard, understanding comic consciousness requires understanding human nature in its three existential stages: aesthetic, ethical, and religious. It is fairly easy to locate the stage in which one is currently operating if one understands comic sensibilities. And it is easy to see where a person stands in the "stages on life's way" by looking at how that person experiences and understands the comic.

Take, for example, the contrast of the aesthetic (pleasure) and ethical (moral) stages in regard to a decision to marry in *Either/Or* (a satiric title contrasting with Hegel's dialectic Both/And formula). In the aesthetic, we experience erotic love; in the ethical, a loyal covenant and commitment to fidelity. In the first, Kierkegaard introduces the papers of "A" or the Young Man; in the second, the wise experiences of Judge William. While "A" pursues immediate personal pleasure, the Judge recognizes the importance of marital vows and raising children. The comic tension arises from the fact that the aesthete young man tries to avoid the frightful decision, seeking only self-serving gratification, while the Judge sees the eternal dimension of marriage, the irrevocable choice that binds two people together. Incongruities appear as one makes a transition from one stage to the next.

Kierkegaard invites his readers to a banquet in which aesthetic young men debate approaches to marriage. They rationalize, complicate, and bungle, avoiding commitment. Why buy the cow when the milk is free? Trying to maximize their pleasure and avoid all pain, they waver in a liminal state of indecision. Yet the charge to become more fully human, and humorous, occurs in making the decision, choosing in an either/or predicament that which will bring suffering, but also humanity. Irony reveals a problem, but it does not resolve it. The ethical stage of Judge William presents a perspective on eroticism that is fulfilled, happy, passionately satisfied in the marriage covenant, and so may flash forth with hilarity to the limited life of the bachelor.

Human existence juxtaposes extreme opposites to produce comic awareness: the body and soul are combined into one being; the human is a creature who is both temporal and eternal; humans are both saints and sinners; humans are free with imaginative possibilities, but finite with necessity; God has divided his nature into both male and female, two beings so divinely alike and so frustratingly different. These ongoing relations of opposites create both suffering and the possibility, even the necessity, of a comic perspective. Human life lived out is torn and mended by these incongruities, always making things comic. Tragedy comes from a painful contradiction, while comedy comes from a painless, or pleasant, contradiction, fully conscious of suffering, pain, and the tragic, but able to rise above it.[76] "The more one suffers, the more, I believe, one has a sense of the comic. It is only by the deepest suffering that one acquires the authority in the art of the comic."[77]

According to John Libbitt, Kierkegaard's"humor presupposes a radically Christian conception of things earthly and heavenly," which suggests that Lenny Bruce might have worked for God.[78] In religious consciousness, one becomes aware of human limitations, but also finds that God intervenes in human drama. The tragic trajectory of sin inevitably draws downward, but the grace of God interrupts and unexpectedly recreates. The incarnation, as Augustine realized, produced the most humorous and unexpected reversal, one that paradoxically leads toward death and ends with resurrected new life. The proper response to this astonishing turn of events is laughter, even as the apocalypse ends in a banquet and a wedding. Who could have anticipated such a feast for fools?

Key to Kierkegaard's understanding of the comic is that it is always based on an experienced *contradiction* or incongruity. The comic resides in this omnipresent category of contradiction. Even the religious individual will have to confront the tension between inwardness and external activity.[79] Something is not right with the world, and Christianity recognizes that. Thus, faith is blessed with many such incongruities: the infinite God appearing in finite time; joy erupting out of suffering, as birth out of labor; and the most despicable sins being forgiven. Christianity hides its truths in mysteries and paradoxes, such as "My yoke is easy and my burden is light." Hence, for Kierkegaard, Christianity offers "the most humorous view of life in world history,"[80] and being earnest at the wrong time about religion and philosophy is "comical." As G. K. Chesterton would put it, a printer or editor could express an eternal truth by making a simple mistake of leaving out one letter and make the whole cosmic universe a comic universe. Humorists develop a divine perspective on an upside world.

For Kierkegaard, struggles with the world are a jest, for the joy of faith overcomes the world. Instead of joining masses of mimickers or a crowd of copycats, the individual subjectively sees himself or herself in light of eternity. Misfortunes are to be seen as comic contradictions of life. The immorality of our laughter is not in the laughing itself, but in laughing flippantly when we should be repenting. In a cuckolding comedy, for example, a man suffers demoralizing loss, and so to sit with the man and laugh is not fitting. Secular comedy tries to hide despair, suggesting that everything is phony, so let us laugh. Herein, humor can become blasphemy or folly, thinking existence is all a joke.[81]

> It happened that a fire broke out backstage in a theatre. The clown came out to inform the public. They thought it was just a jest and applauded. He repeated his warning, they shouted even louder. So I think the world will come to an end amid general applause from all the wits, who believe that it is a joke.[82]

Teutonic Gravity

In 1794, German philosopher Georg Friedrich Meier demonstrated heavy Teutonic solemnity in his "Thoughts on Jesting": "We are never to jest on or with things which account of their importance or weight, claim our utmost seriousness. There are things . . . so great and important in themselves as never to be thought or mentioned but with sedateness and solemnity. Laughter on such occasions is criminal and indecent. . . . For instance, all jests on religion, philosophy, and the like are important subjects."[83] Thus, jokes on German philosophers are especially out of bounds. Of all cultures that believe that neither animals nor sages laugh, this Teutonic land of self-perceived wise men seems to repress and deny laughter. No doubt, this foreboding language would give rise to Sigmund Freud seeing more than laughter repressed.

The curious perception of German culture as non-humorous extends back to 1578, when George Whetstone constructed a hierarchy of descending lasciviousness in his "rehearsal of the use and abuse of Commedies" that he might "checke in others which I cannot amend in my selfe." From the most unrestrained comedy of the Italian, he marked the Frenchman, the Spaniard, and then the "Germaine [who] is too holye, for he presents on every common Stage what preachers should pronounce in Pulpets."[84] Germans have had a bad rap for laughter ever since, being seen as grave (heavy, sad, *and* solemn) wits.[85] By the time Englishman Ronald Knox appeared in the early twentieth century, he concluded that no one ever "ventured to congratulate the Germans on their sense of humour."[86]

Johann Wolfgang von Goethe (1749–1832), the German "non-Christian" author, wrote early introspective novels full of "storm and stress."[87] Within his tormented and solemn psychological novels of young men growing up, or *Bildungsroman*, he could yet insert some religious comedy. In his great tragic novel of *Faust*, his devil, Mephistopheles (whose Greek name translates as "the spirit that denies" or "not a lover of the light") is a suave comedian who makes a bet with God that he can tempt one of God's chosen men, Faust, a student of divinity that has despaired of ordinary knowledge (Satan had failed earlier with Job). The devil first appears as a sort of poodle, who persuades Faust to wage his soul for knowledge and power.

In the first part of Goethe's *Faust*, a manager and dramatic poet interact with a Jester who wants Folly in the play. Mephistopheles appears in the "Prologue in Heaven" and mocks three archangels (Raphael, Gabriel, and Michael) with ironic, self-effacing humor. "Pathos from me would make your sides with laughter shake, / Had you not laughter long ago forsworn."[88] He tells God that man is so wretched that he finds himself reluctant to torment him. When God offers him Faust to tempt, he confesses he does like to take on full fresh cheeks, and feels like a cat going after a mouse. Hence, when God and his angels disperse, Mephistopheles muses on God:

> I like to see the Old Man not infrequently,
> And I forbear to break with Him or be uncivil;
> It's very pretty in so great a Lord as He
> To talk so like a man, even with the devil.[89]

At the end, when he must pay for his blood pact with the devil, Faust dismisses hell as one of Mephistopheles' "foolish tales." Mephistopheles dismisses his naiveté and warns that "you may think so still until experience changes your mind."[90]

The devil descended on the Continent from around 1870 to 1914, when, according to François Boespflug, a "large-scale anti-Christian offensive took place."[91] Partly engineered by anti-clericals and freethinkers in France, a war of ideas escalated in illustrated satirical magazines, in which "everything was laughed at: the Bible, the Ten Commandments, Jesus, dogma, the sacraments."[92] In the past, mockery and satire had aimed at religious characters, their folly and hypocrisy. Now God himself was attacked with sarcasm. In 1878, a Belgian caricaturist, Felicien Rops, scandalized Europe with an illustration of a naked woman on a cross, wearing a crown of flowers and substituting the traditional INRI inscription with EROS.

The image of a dull, institutional church in Germany, a condition that Kierkegaard called Christendom, provided fodder for the rebellion of Friedrich Nietzsche (1844–1900). "I like not these coquettish bugs that in their insatiable desire to smell of the infinite make the infinite smell of bugs." In his bestiary, he employed the spider as an apt metaphor for how the creature ensnares the unsuspecting into its web, even as the Christian worldview would weave a web of interpretation that draws the vulnerable believer into the same fate as the spider's victims.[93]

For the Super-Philosopher and "religious desperado," laughter was the gay science, light-hearted scholarship, and Thalia was its comic muse. He rejected the "gravity" of thought that weighs humans down. (Thus Dionysian frenzy was preferred over the Christian emphasis on sin, as the latter weighs one down.) Considering the bad reputation that the solemn Englishman Thomas Hobbes tried to attach to laughter, Nietzsche once suggested ranking philosophers "according to the importance of their laughter, right up to those who are capable of *golden* laughter." The *petit fait* (the small fact) that under Plato's pillow on his deathbed was no holy or philosophical book, but a copy of Aristophanes, partially redeemed the ponderous writer.[94]

Authors Robert Solomon and Kathleen Higgins argue that Nietzsche promotes the human use of "the comical as a therapy against the restraining jacket of logic, morality and reason. He needs from time to time a harmless demotion from reason and hardship and in this sense laughter has a positive character for Nietzsche."[95] He contrasts the blessings and wonders of laughter with the curses and condemnation of religion, exclaiming that "Laughter blesses where god curses. Unlike god, humanity isn't condemned to condemn. Laughter can be filled with wonder if that is what humanity wants it to be—it can be light and it *itself* can bless. What if I laugh at myself?"[96] He recognized the negative tendency in the comic being used to express delight in the misfortunes of others, the old classic practice of *Schadenfreude*. For him, religion was for the rabble. "After coming into contact with a religious man, I always feel I must wash my hands."[97] Laughter could help subvert this solemn "Christian" society. Much of Kierkegaard's Christendom comes under attack, for who could live in a society in which one did not dance? And every truth uttered should be discarded as false if it is not accompanied by at least one laugh.

Nietzsche's use of hyperbole in self-mocking becomes evident in the chapter titles he selected for his very tongue-in-cheek *Ecce Homo*: "Why I Am so Wise;" "Why I Am so Clever;" and "Why I Write such Good Books." His sly ironic tone corresponds to his fear of collecting disciples. "I have a terrible fear of being declared holy one day. . . . I don't want to be a saint, and would rather be a buffoon."[98] He sought to lighten up philosophy with his own instructions that we "should consider every day lost on which we have not danced at least once. And we should call every truth false which was not accompanied by at least one laugh."[99]

In an epigram he expressed a notion that would subvert the modernist idea of inerrancy emerging out of the Scofield Bible, quipping that "it is subtle that God learned Greek when he wanted to become a writer—and that he did not learn it better."[100] He struck at the heart of an outward piety in another epigram, noting that it was not their love for humanity, but "rather the impotence of their love for humanity that keeps today's Christian from—burning us."[101]

In *Thus Spake Zarathustra*, Nietzsche accused Satan as the one who remained "serious, thorough, profound, and solemn."[102] As an anti-god, Satan was the "spirit of gravity, through whom all things fall." (Corpulent Roman Catholic Chesterton would argue that he fell from the force of gravity, because he took himself too seriously.) Nietzsche saw that the only hope for the future lay perhaps in the only true human original *invention*, to be buffoons, dancers and wildcats of God,; in fact, the only thing that may have a future is our *laughter*.[103] It would make sense that Nietzsche found his society to have put God to death, as it had rejected laughter as well. Unfortunately, Nietzsche's laughter would go mad, sounding like that fiery crackling of thorns of Koheleth (Ecclesiastes 2:2).So, too, would Nietzsche go mad, tended to in his last days by kind, patient, and good-humored nuns.

America's first professor of drama, James Brander Matthews, observed that most German wit does not tempt us to mirth; in fact, it often "arouses a feeling almost of inimical contempt. The sallies of Schopenhauer and of Nietzsche recently reminded Professor William James 'half the time of the sick shriekings of two dying rats.'" So, too, according to Matthews, George Eliot cut open Goethe's saying that "nothing is more significant of men's character than what they find laughable," and exposed the dreariness of German satiric works that may yield laughter in the homeland, but offer "little for the palate of other lands."[104]

One Swiss German, however, laughed at himself more robustly. Theologian Karl Barth (1886–1968) challenged the liberal theology of his day, with his 1919 commentary on Paul's letter to the Romans falling like a bomb in a dull German classroom. He laughed at the "notion that complete impartiality is the most fitting, and indeed the normal, disposition for true exegesis, because it guarantees complete absence of prejudice. For a short time, around 1910, this idea threatened to achieve almost a canonical status in Protestant theology. But now, we can quite calmly describe it as merely comical."[105]

In his friendly epistolary exchange with Carl Zuckmayer, another earnest Christian who viewed the grand and small moments of life *sub specie aeternitatis*, the two laughed, especially at the fleeting moments of congratulatory awards: "We are both people, are we not, who can have a good laugh at such things?"[106] They commiserated on the grotesque comedies of their bodies wrinkling, leaking, falling about, and shutting down. Commenting on his failing health in his eighties, Barth spoke of his body, like the Church body described by St. Paul in his first letter to the Corinthians, as being "unavoidably controlled by the less honorable members of my body." So, too, Zuckmayer had bladder and kidney problems, which he dealt with cheerfully.

Barth laughed at his body *and* his mind, which tended to take things a bit ponderously. Confronted with his own tendency to keep writing, Barth repeated the story about Pablo Casals who, at the age of ninety, still practiced his cello four or five hours each day. When he was asked why he did this, Casals answered, "Because I have the impression I am making progress."[107]

For Barth, true humor is primarily self-directed, particularly in confessing the incongruity between being sinners and saints. "Humor is the opposite of all self-admiration and self-praise."[108] Standing against humorless Nazis and refusing to salute the flag, Barth told the German court that he deserved a reward, just like Socrates, for doing right. He acknowledged "laughter amid tears," which presupposed the knowledge of suffering, rather than excluding it.[109] He distinguished genuine humor from false humor by the former's awareness of the reality of suffering.[110] One confronts evil injustices of the world and refuses to resign oneself to defeat by giving it the last word. The last laugh will be a sign of liberation, of resurrection, grace, and the fulfilled promises of God. As Daniel Migliore expressed it, "humor for Barth is rooted in the glory and beauty of God and is an expression of the delight and pleasure which the God of the gospel evokes in human life."[111] Beyond the irony and satire in this life, Barth found that God speaks of an eschatological joy, an almighty "Yes" of a new creation to the No of sin and death.

However, Barth also warns that while a witty analysis of the times may be a fine gift, "the task of bringing the gospel to light is more urgent than manifesting that earnestness and bringing this gift into play. He to whom this positive task is not absolutely the supreme task, who first of all wants to shout at, bewilder, or laugh at men on account of their folly and malice, had better remain silent altogether."[112] Satire is a penultimate concern. Thus for this old theologian, the laughter that relieves and liberates and does not administer gall and poison is the worthy one. Only those who laugh at themselves will be able to laugh at others; only those who satirize their own folly can satirize the folly of others.

The Unknown Comic

In a post–World War II publication in the satirical *Candido* magazine, Giovanni Guareschi (1908–1968) introduced his comic voice, the hotheaded priest Don Camillo. Modeling him on a real Roman Catholic priest, Don Camillo Valota, who endured the concentration camp of Dachau, Guareschi focused the adventures of the priest on his relationship to his friend and nemesis, Communist Mayor Peppone. The two pull practical jokes on each other, with Peppone repeatedly painting the hind end of the priest's dog, Ful, a bright Communist red.

The pugilistic priest converses with Christ from a crucifix above the altar. In one scene, after Peppone acknowledges in the confessional that he beat up Camillo in the dark and knocked some eggs out of his hand, the priestly Confessor Camillo wants to pummel his enemy while the Marxist Catholic is kneeling at the altar rail. He asks Christ if he can beat up Peppone up for him. God says no because he had forgiven him and so must Camillo. The priest still wants to whack him with a candle. "No," replies Christ, "your hands were made for blessing." To which Camillo mutters, "My hands, but not my feet." So Christ allows him to land a thunderbolt kick to Peppone's underside. To which, a penitent Peppone remarks, "I've been expecting that for the last ten minutes. I feel better now." "So do I," exclaims Don Camillo, and it seems that even Christ is pleased too.[113] The gentle and very endearing humane satire shows two flawed men of good will from radically different political positions engaged in trying to do what is right.

Don Camillo is wonderfully human; he regularly loses his temper, engages in fisticuffs and brawls, earns reprimands for impatience and lessons on self-control from the crucified Christ, who continually chides his servant. Christ rebukes him, and not his adversary, when he is sarcastic toward his enemies. The novels illustrate the spiritual dimension of ordinary people, incorporating "satire as a branch of morality"[114] as the tales revolve about the proper love of one's neighbor as a reflection of the love of God, in a telling Horatian satire for a divided country of *paisans*.

As one who fought in the war and endured the hardships of a German POW camp, Guareschi saw satire as humor's weapon, like the canon to the science of artillery. Guareschi explained that "When the alarm sounds, humor dons a uniform and arms itself. It becomes satire."[115] As such, the effect of satire is prompt and instantaneous. The humorous vignette endures, poking fun and demolishing an adversary. It is not a simple trite comic story (the "preferred drink of slower minds"), but a perspective in which the humorist looks calmly at the serious condition of the world, which many see as cataclysmic, and sees "the funny side of the issue."[116] Like Viktor Frankl in Auschwitz and Aleksandr Solzhenitsyn in the Gulag Archipelago, Guareschi found a deepening of faith and humor in the camps.[117]

After the war, Guareschi attacked Communists and capitalists as much as he did Fascists. Dictatorships were the institutional negation of humor and thus social enemies. He viewed humor as a cure to power politics, as leveling the playing field and combating pompous rhetoric of oppressors: "Humor is the declared enemy of rhetoric because, while rhetoric puffs and flares everything up, humor takes rhetoric down and strips it to the bone with vicious criticism. Against rhetoric's power to enflame egos with its depiction of war as glorious flag-waving, sustained by the allegory of ghostly heroes mounted on white horses, humor describes war in such a way as to calm hearts and awaken reason."[118]

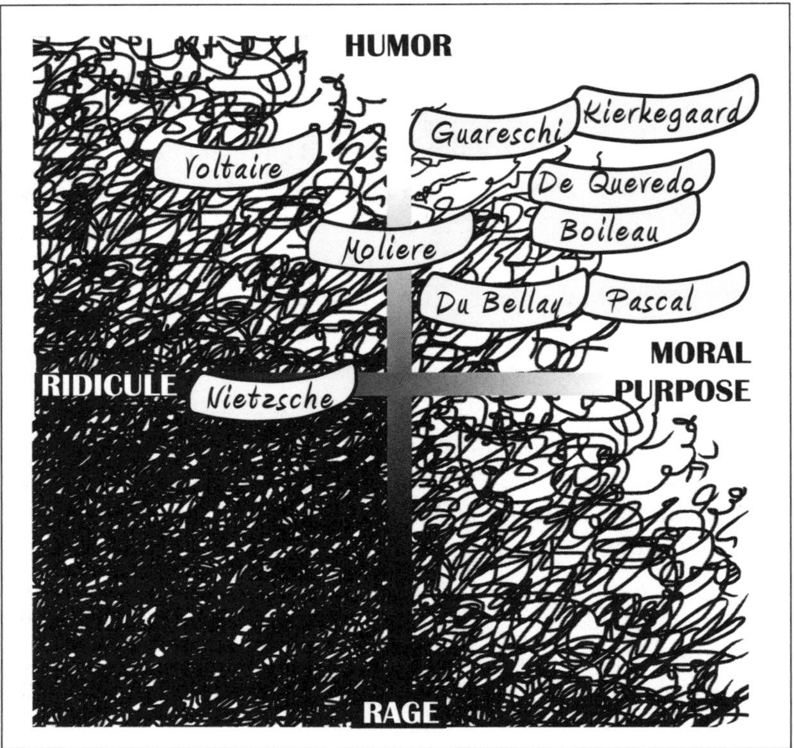

Voltaire, Nietzsche, Molière, Du Bellay, Guareschi, De Quevedo, Boileau, Pascal, and Kierkegaard on the Quad of Satire.

In a column against liberal changes wrought by Vatican II in the Roman Catholic Church, the reactionary Guareschi expressed his sarcasm in palpable ways: "A very wise decision was to abolish the famous 'Index.' Doing that kept some liberal Conciliar Fathers from proposing to put the Gospels on the Index." With tongue firmly planted in his cheek, he presciently spoke of "replacing the traditional altar with the cordial 'buffet-table' designed by Lercaro; substituting Gregorian chants with catchy modern tunes; and introducing microphones in church along with loudspeakers and other electronic mechanism—useful only if the power doesn't go out—to remove from what was once the Mass that austerity and magical air of mystery that gave it the cold feeling of a religious rite."[119] Not only a satirist, Guareschi was a prescient prophet.

Trying to get Italians to take themselves less solemnly and to be humorous, Guareschi admonished: "The person who doesn't know how to laugh doesn't know how to rule. We Italians, we're serious. We're so serious we provoke laughter. . . . Let's become more serious. Let's learn to laugh." The key is to love and forgive one's enemies, even as one laughs with them.[120] In fact, laughing stood as a sure sign of forgiveness.

Continental satire evolved from the sparkling wit of Molière and Voltaire, who skewered hypocrisy with caustic abandonment, into a more humane Italian humor. From those who mocked saints from outside the community of faith, it was like "aller à la pêche dans un tonneau." The Christian fish were easy targets. Secular satire on spurious saints loitered in the outer upper left courts of the Quad, leaning toward ridicule and humor. Nietzsche, in his will to power, called "higher men" to learn to laugh, with a laughter that took men and women beyond good and evil. For Nietzsche, laughter was howling against traditional morality, a ridicule mixed with rage. The truest religious satire came from writers within the Christian Church. Kierkegaard, Guareschi, and Barth kept a fresh orthodox faith at the center of their comedy. They saw that the angels laughed at all mortals and so joined in that mocking mellowed by mercy. They could strip off the cloaks of Christendom. While making himself a laughingstock, Kierkegaard strove to let the readers in on his irony, enabling them to enjoy the derision that ricocheted from this awareness. He lifted up a distorted mirror and urged them laugh and repent. However, over in the former British colonies, after an uptight beginning, American satirists showed a tendency to sacrifice all for laughter.

8

American Naifs and Agnostics

Against the assault of laughter, nothing can stand.
—Mark Twain

The Puritan legacy of William Prynne did not encourage much laughter in the colonies. With plow or powder in your hands, little time was permitted for play or pranks. The American sense of humor evolved over time, with geographical expansion into the Southwest and frontier lands.[1] Manifest destiny would make room for several American species of satiric laughter.

Concerns about the dangers of laughter arrived as English exports. William Prynne's one-thousand-page harangue against the theater, *Histriomastix*, was published in 1633. In this lengthy diatribe, full of solemn quotations from the scriptures and dour church fathers, Prynne not only preached against stage plays and their actresses ("notorious whores"), but took a stand against the wanton laughter elicited from audiences.[2] He sought repressive state control to protect the gravity of the Puritans, respecting their burden of being God's chosen people. Jesus, he noted, was "never laughing."

Even if Prynne was not funny, he became a primary instigator of repressed Anglo-American laughter. The Bay Colony of Massachusetts followed his lead in 1712, when they passed "An Act Against Impertinence, Immorality, and Profaneness, and for Reformation of Manners," which focused mainly on "any filthy, obscene, or profane song, pamphlet, libel or mock sermon, in imitation or in mimicking of preaching, or any other part of divine worship."[3] All of this probably meant that some rascals were finding the grim preachers unintentionally funny. Yet under Prynne's inspiration, humor could lead to the pillory; stock jokes could lead to the stocks.

The Puritans' desire for independence suggested a rejection of reverence for the past; however, they kept certain genteel British attitudes, even those espoused by a non-Christian like Lord Chesterfield (1694–1773), who condemned all manner of laughter in his *Letters to His Son*. Allowing that his "son may smile often," Chesterfield advised him to "never [deign] to laugh while you live." Such behavior was "characteristic of folly and ill manners, so illiberal, and so ill-bred." With arrogant prejudice, Chesterfield rejected the indecorous and bragged that "since I have had the full use of my reason nobody has ever heard me laugh."[4]

Polymath Samuel Johnson commented on Chesterfield, saying that in hoping for a lord of wits, he found only a small wit among the lords. Johnson also judged him to be a selfish prig, who taught his son the manners of a dancing master and the morals of a whore. This "genteel tradition," as George Santayana called it in 1911, involved shallow good manners, prissy decorum, politeness, and prizing of propriety. It would make ripe fodder for satire when Yankee cracker-barrel humor would crack open such posturing and pretentions.[5] The hicks of America would disrupt the proper manners of New England with raucous guffawing, crude tall tales, and wild travel stories.

One early American colonist made a subversive mark of mirth against the Separatist Pilgrims. Thomas Morton brought laughter into the colony of Merrymount (now Quincy, Massachusetts) in 1624. At that time, Governor William Bradford denounced colonial dancing and frisking about with Indian women, who were like "so many fairies or furies," in some mad Bacchanalian feast.[6] He was referring, according to Nathaniel Hawthorne's later account of "The May-Pole of Merry Mount," to the old English custom of imbibing barrels of beer and making good cheer on Mayday, which, in this case included Native Americans. Everyone celebrated the revels of a New Canaan, including Morton, who penned a lusty singsong poem:

> Drink and be merry, merry, merry boys,
> Let all your delight be in Hymens joys,
> Iô to Hymen now the day is come,
> About the merry Maypole take a Room.[7]

Captain Miles Standish of Plymouth marched to Merrymount and arrested Morton, bringing him back to face Puritan justice. Standish couldn't stand the man who had put the moniker of "Captain Shrimp" upon him. Morton, auspiciously deported, published his *New English Canaan*, a panegyric of a place flowing with "milk and honey" and blessed by God, unlike the bleak Plymouth with its pickle-faced citizens.

Morton's vision of "harmless mirth" provided an early model of a multicultural utopia. The disciplined citizens of Plymouth were later depicted as morose by Hawthorne in such stories as "Young Goodman Brown," whose titular character laughs at discovering the sinfulness of his entire sainted community and then ends in mad despair. In *The Scarlet Letter*, Hawthorne lamented that the art of gaiety had been forgotten in those days, allowing "no Merry Andrew to stir up the multitude with jests, perhaps hundreds of years old, but still effective."[8] The laughter of the Puritan theocracy required that humor be moral (even allowing satirizing of wicked living) and dignified (usually coming from the pen of a witty minister).

Dissenting churchmen found that the vernacular style of speaking would "strike home to the capacity and humor of the multitude."[9] It would make congregations laugh. Satire leaked out of nonconformist Nathaniel Ward's *The Simple Cobbler* (1636), a pungent attack on King Charles I. In the text, an ordinary craftsman lectures the crown on excessive toleration—so excessive that England allows "room for Hell above ground." In Boston, Harvard colonial wit Joseph Green spontaneously composed four lines on finding that a school was being torn down so a new church wing could be constructed. He sharply condensed the decision to a verbal whipping:

> A fig for your learning! I tell you the town,
> To make the church larger, must pull the school down.
> "Unluckily spoken," replied Master Birch;
> "Then learning, I fear, stops the growth of the church."[10]

The free-wheeling scallywag George Alsop arrived in Mary-Land in 1659 and thought it an oasis despite being employed as an indentured servant; then he returned to England as an Anglican minister. His frank, extravagant, and vituperative wit lashed out at the "constipated" roundhead Puritans he had met during his American jaunt. Scholar Howland Kenney identifies Alsop, a refreshingly democratic merrymaker, as "the

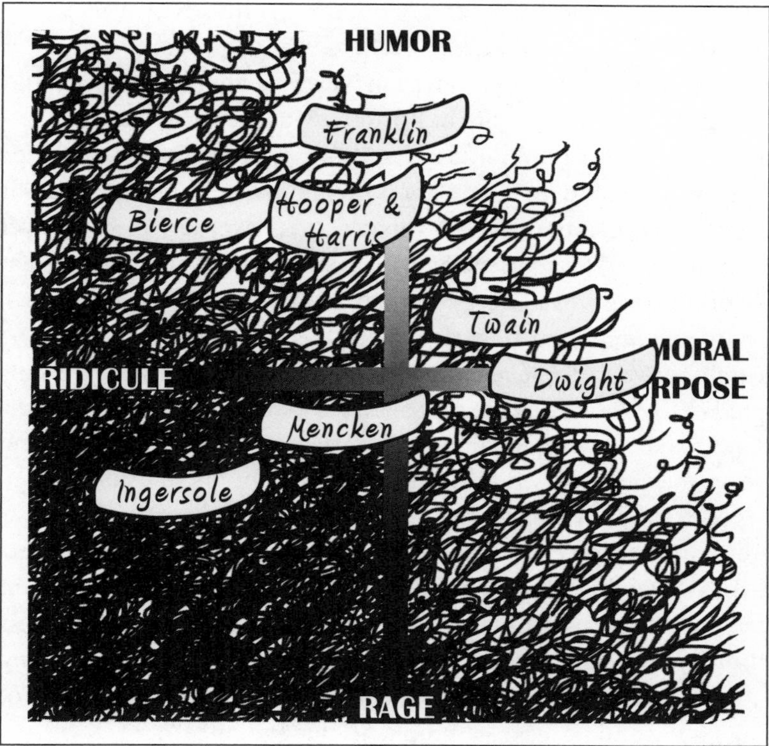

Bierce, Ingersole, Hooper, Harris, Franklin, Mencken, Twain, and Dwight on the Quad of Satire.

first writer in British America to elaborate the engaging stereotype of the uncouth but shrewd American who used his image of ignorance and stupidity to 'scalp' snobbish and unsuspecting British merchants."[11] His *Character of Maryland* masked satire of his beloved England.

For many, the wonderfully practical American "humor" originated with Benjamin Franklin, who rightly observed the nature of phenomena like "an Empty bag cannot stand upright."[12] Even sitting down, Franklin could surprise, as can be seen in the recent collection of his works edited by Carl Japikse, entitled *Fart Proudly*.[13] He wrote proverbs so good that even Deists mistake them for biblical sayings: quipping in his 1733 *Poor Richard's Almanac*, "God helps those who help themselves."[14] While Franklin found writing humorous pieces to be challenging, he developed that peculiar American brand of humor that historian Walter Blair calls "hoss sense," which edified his readers.[15]

Such horse sense didn't cotton well in New England, however. Franklin's first jabs at the elite families of Boston invited censure. Puritan Cotton Mather deplored the Franklin family's sensational newspaper for its jesting at his expense. "Some good men are afraid," he intoned, "it may provoke Heaven to deal with this place as never any place has yet been dealt withal."[16] Franklin went on to lampoon Harvard College, that "temple of learning where clergy were formed," as the house of Plagius, where students were hard at work copying passages.[17]

The gullibility of people regarding witchcraft and other superstitions prompted one of Franklin's great hoaxes. He exploited the suspicion directed at Quakers, along with Cotton Mather's 1693 treatise defending his role in the Salem witch trials, *The Wonders of the Invisible World*, with his own spoof, *A Witch Trial at Mount Holly*. According to scholar Richard Amacher, witches were feared for, among other things, their shape-shifting ability and capacity for turning into animals. Franklin reported that the accused Quakers "had been charged with making their Neighbors' Sheep dance in an uncommon Manner, and with causing Hogs to speak and sing Psalms, to the great Terror and Amazement of the King's good and peaceable Subjects in this Province."[18]

Along with a trial by water, the accused were also subjected to a weighing contest with a Bible. Franklin wrote: "To the great surprise of the Spectators, Flesh and Bones [of a suspected witch] came down plump, and outweighed that great good Book by abundance," even though "a chapter out of the Book of Moses" had been read over him before he stepped onto the scales. "After the same Manner," the account continues, using mock biblical language, others were weighed, and their "Lumps of Mortality were too heavy for Moses and all the Prophets and Apostles."[19] After the accused swim in the cold water, making them suspect, several men in the jury recommend that the women be thrown in the water again, during warmer weather, but this time, *naked*.

Just before fleeing Boston, Franklin defined his task as lightening the spiritual load of the colonists, espousing the view that "pieces of pleasantry and mirth have a secret charm in them to allay the heats and tumults of our spirits, and to make a man forget his restless resentments. They have a strange power in them to hush disorders of the soul and reduce us to a serene and placid state of mind."[20] For example, as one who valued industry and diligence, he recommended a cure for sloth: "Every morning, as soon as the sun rises, let all the bells in every church be set ringing; and if that is not sufficient, let cannon be fired in every street, to wake the sluggards effectually, and make them open their eyes to see their true interest."[21]

Franklin skipped out of town to the safer environs of Philadelphia to publish his famous *Poor Richard's Almanack*. In it he observed that "Religious knaves, of all knaves, [are] the worst." Jefferson and Adams refused to trust the mischievous Franklin to write the Declaration of Independence, lest he insert a snappy little joke into that austere document.

Franklin, as vanguard for what would later be characterized as southwestern humor, provided a frontal attack on the pretensions of gentility. Franklin made the American public laugh "as a mother makes a child laugh before inserting the medicine spoon." Imitating British humorists like Joseph Addison, Franklin frequently employed the construct of a feigned person's report to make his point. In fact, in his *Studies in Classic American Literature*, D. H. Lawrence saw the poker-faced Franklin as the "master of the art of disguise."[22]

Franklin adhered to a practical Deist religion with Puritan virtues, yet tolerant toward all. Many found his Poor Richard morality quite oppressive, and his folksy aphorisms, such as "early to bed and early to rise," at odds with Franklin's own reputation as a wine-imbiber and connoisseur of good-looking ladies.[23] He was an odd, somewhat "generic" believer, although he enjoyed the rhetorical flourishes of George Whitefield's enthusiastic preaching. Once, while listening to an old cross-eyed minister (dubbed "Dr. Squintum"), Franklin stood determined not to give an offering. Then, when the stentorian evangelist challenged the crowd to donate to an orphanage, Franklin relented and decided to contribute some copper coins; a little later, he became willing to part with his silver. By the end of the eloquent and remarkably persuasive sermon, Franklin was emptying his pockets of gold and was glad he had no more money.

Franklin embodied the idea of the self-deprecating *eiron*, a reverse hypocrite, tending to make himself look worse than he was to "befool" others. He sniped at pretentious preachers who too frequently polished "the Art of saying Little in Much."[24] Franklin tried to help Gospel expositors who wove a "Discourse of considerable Length," but whose thoughts on various topics were not well stocked, such as those tending to "divide and subdivide as far as *Two and fiftiethly*."[25]

Demonstrating some witty irreverence, Franklin's epitaph even read:

> Like the cover of an old book
> Its contents torn out
> And stripped of its lettering
> And gilding,
> Lies here, food for worms.
> But the works shall not be wholly lost;
> For it will, as he believed,
> Appear once more,
> In a new and more perfected edition
> Corrected and amended.
> by the Author."[26]

Light Art of Dwight

In 1699, Ned Ward, an English satirist (and tavern owner) who never set foot on American soil, warned his fellow British about the New England colonists, "though they wear in the Faces the Innocence of Doves, you will find their Dealings as Subtile as Serpents."[27] The devil was very active in the troubled early days of the American Republic, especially at Yale University, where he has since set up permanent residence in its School of Divinity.

Poet and evangelical clergyman Timothy Dwight (1752–1817), later to be a president of Yale, challenged the devil who appeared in the guise of enlightenment philosophers David Hume, Thomas Hobbes, and Lord Shaftesbury.[28] Dwight's verse satire *The Triumph of Infidelity* was sarcastically dedicated to Voltaire, who had devoted himself to the "elevation of his character" above his creator. The book ushered Dwight to the forefront of a spiritual battle in the midst of the American Revolution. His literary warfare fit in with the trend of Connecticut wits who wrote satires in the Augustan mode, packing their poems with specific allusions. Clergymen satirists employed "instructive satire, true to Virtue's cause"; thus, "When churchmen scripture for the classics quit, / Polite apostates from God's grace to wit."[29] Against the ordination of the likes of "Tom Brainless," Dwight's friends unmasked the bankrupt faith of the Unitarians, who summoned "moral dunces" for their disciples in their "infidel philosophy."

Like Pope's attack on the literary dunces, Dwight's American *Dunciad* pounced on a naive Unitarian faith in innate human goodness and progress for progress sake. He composed his "mock-epic" in the satiric style of Pope and Swift, and filled it with Augustinian theology that emphasized sin. Reviving the metaphor of satire as a mirror, the Connecticut wit hoped that when it reflected the image of vice, truth would drag forth sin and bring self-hatred on "her own deformity." Healing comes through the surgeon's diagnosis and his skillful wielding of his satiric knife.

Calvinism had found its literary Pope, and finally the Reformed movement produced a viable wit that aimed at reform.

> With her, brave Ridicule, 'twixt ill and good,
> Falsehood and truth, satanic umpire stood.
> He, Hogarth like, with hues and features new,
> The form of providence, persuasive drew:
> Round its fair face bade hells black colours rise.
> Its limbs distorted, blear'd its heaven-bright eyes.
> At the maim'd image gaz'd, and grinn'd aloud—
> "Yon frightful hag's no semblance of a god."[30]

Dwight suggested that by railing against God, philosophers inadvertently helped blockheads (like Yale divinity students) devote themselves to foolishness. They "Help'd fops to folly, and help'd rakes to sin." He caricatured Voltaire as drawing cobwebs over the minds of his malleable readers, using the Jesuitical arts of casuistry. The history of the scriptural texts was debunked as fiction, with agnostics believing everything else around the world except the truth in Palestine. Voltaire saw "Gospel truths" as "airy dreams, the shades of nonsense, and the whim of whims," and if the Romans "proved the Gospel," they lied. In his realm of lies, all mortals gathered:

> Here shall you, raptur'd, find there is no hell;
> A priest shall teach it, and the gospel tell

'Twas best, he said, mankind should cease to sin;
Good fame requir'd it; so did peace within:
Their honours, well he knew, would ne'er be driven;
But hop'd they still would please to go to heaven.
Each week, he paid his visitation dues;
Coax'd, jested, laugh'd; rehears'd the private news.
To him all things the same, as good or evil;
Jehovah, Jove, the Lama, or the Devil;
Mohammed's braying, or Isaiah's lays;
The Indian's powaws, or the Christian's praise.
With him all natural desires are good;
His thirst for stews; the Mohawk's thirst for blood:
But his dear self, choice Dagon! to adore;
To dress, to game, to swear, to drink, to whore;
To race his steeds; or cheat, when others run;
Pit tortur'd cocks, and swear 'tis glorious fun.[31]

Dwight's exposure of the tendencies to merge all religions into one, to dismiss any historical evidence of the Jewish and Christian scriptures, to insinuate that all knowledge simply seeks to justify delight in the own pleasures of drinking and whoring, and to celebrate Man, "that illustrious brute of noblest shape, / A swine unbristled, and an untail'd ape," as the new god adumbrates the modernist theologies of the late nineteenth century. He ridiculed their idea that "Hell is no more, or no more to be fear'd"; thus those wicked rogues who persecute widows and exploit orphans need not worry: "this is no hell." Dwight concluded that what Unitarian philosophy reaps is an unmoored man.

Dwight's ingenious style, when eviscerated of its apologetic Christian vision, would become the aloof, almost supercilious humor of Ralph Waldo Emerson, whose essay on "The Comic" revealed the perpetual game of humor to be not only moral and supposedly "droll to the intellect," but dull to the reader. In 1876, Emerson tried to transcend the comic, explaining that "the perception of the comic is a tie of sympathy with other men." Wit had the potential to level distinctions among human beings. Comedy could be centripetal, open, and sharing. To demonstrate such an egalitarian cooperation, Emerson quoted the squirrel who sought to be equal with a mountain:

Talents differ;
All is well and wisely put;
If I cannot carry forests on my back,
Neither can you crack a nut.[32]

Cracking nuts became the play of more squirrelly wits.

Frontier Rowdies

In contrast to the nuanced intellectual satire of Timothy Dwight, an exaggerated and earthy American brand of humor known as Southwest or frontier humor spilled from the pen of Johnson Jones Hooper (1815–1862). Hooper's *Adventures of Captain Simon Suggs* welcomed the Alabama conman and scoundrel Simon Suggs onto the American stage.[33] Suggs, whose motto was "it is good to be shifty in a new country," caught the frisky spirit of the new land, wandering into trouble, hoodwinking and cozening many victims. Suggs shared an affinity with Old Hickory Jackson and the bombastic southern conmen who ruled the highways and byways. Attending a backwoods Methodist-type camp revival meeting, Suggs devises a way to earn a little money from the gullible congregants. As he watches the "big dog," an amorous and eloquent preacher, who claims to be just a "poor worrum of the dust," but who nevertheless leads the bumpkins into an enthusiastic worship, someone in the crowd shouts out the question, "Who was behind all his evil ways?" "SATAN!" is the laconic judgment of the oldest preacher present (sounding like the Church Lady of *Saturday Night Live*), who thus informs the congregation that the devil had attacked Suggs in the shape of an alligator. When the congregation feigns its own generosity but resists giving the freshly redeemed brother any funds, Suggs realizes he must approach them a bit differently. Instead of appealing to their Christian charity, which is nonexistent, he exploits their competitive nature.

Meanwhile, the lusty minister shows an excess of affection for a bevy of pretty girls and lavishes his holy caresses on them, even as they all affect piety. "Keep the thing warm, breethring!—come to the Lord, honey!" he adds, vigorously hugging one damsel he seeks to save.

> "Well now," said the observer [Suggs] as he watched the lusty brother "officiating" among the women, "that ere feller takes *my* eye! thar's he's been this half-hour, a-figurin amongst them galls, and's never said the fust word to nobody else. Wonder what's the reason these here preachers never hugs up the old, ugly women? Never seed one do it in my life—he sperrit never moves 'em that way! I judge ef I was a preacher, I should save the purtiest souls fust, myself!"[34]

Living by his wits, the rascally Suggs steals the money, prays over it in a swamp, and skedaddles off on his horse. Hooper ends with his own palinode, a sort of passage of repentance once the book is over, indicating he meant no disrespect to any Christian denomination. However, according to his biographer, Hooper was so identified with his scoundrel, that he forfeited his standing in the community due to his vulgar work.[35] Hooper supplied us with a bright satiric look at revival religion, through eyes of one very rascally frontier roughneck. Here, the grand American tradition of native shrewdness beating book-learning wins every time.

George Washington Harris (1814–1869) likewise invented a disreputable, unrepressed scalawag with the comic moniker of Sut Lovingood, whose *Yarns* would become the most popular humorous book of the antebellum period. The wily Sut didn't trust lawyers like Stillyards, preachers like Parson John Bullin (the "infernal, hypercritical, pot-bellied, scaley-hided, whisky-wastin', stinkin old ground hog" who catches Sut and a girl "frisking horizontally in a huckleberry bush"), Clapshaw the circuit-riding preacher, and especially Yankees, as all they ever contribute are "rat-traps, mantraps, and new-fangled doctrines for the aid of the devil."[36] Sut is a true American character, full of backwoods sass and subversive schemes; yet he is also a bit of a reformer. For example, in dealing with an adulterer, Sut gets his own revenge by taking on the voice of Satan to "skeer" the fellow back into church. The rascal tries to both terrify and edify, engineering his reformation while reaffirming the sanctity of marriage.

Sut Lovingood speaks bluntly, like a coarse Will Rogers: when asked about a political friend, Sut replies, "Ef he haint in Congriss, he's gone tu h—l." He also performs the role of trickster, even during a revival church meeting in "Parson John Bullen's Lizards." When Parson Bullen raves on his tiptoes and pounds his fists on the pulpit, Sut lets loose with "seven-ur-eight big pot-bellied lizards" and empties them under the bottom of the preacher's britches. The lizards climb his legs like squirrels, and the inspired parson stops preaching right in the middle of the word "damnation." Realizing what is happening, he screams and howls and twitches and squirms and rubs his back like a hog scratching himself against a stump. Finally, he summons his congregation, begging that they "pray for me right now, brothers and sisters, for I am a wrestling with the enemy right now."[37] As the three-hundred-pound Bullen squirms and gyrates, he begins to strip, until wearing nothing but shoes and short woolen socks, he runs wildly and "nakidly" into the woods, as if possessed of the devil.[38] The true hypocrisy of the sanctimonious parson is fully exposed.

Sut's conniving is sometimes cruel and vicious, but very funny. Self-described as a "nat'ral-born durn'd fool," Sut makes satiric observations and plays tricks that make a lasting impression. He sees the world and its "universal unregenerate human nature" without illusions, observing that "bishops eats elders, elders eats common people, they eats such cattle as me, I eats possums, possums eats chickens, chickens swallers worms, and worms am content to eat dust, and the dust am the end of it all." The author of Ecclesiastes couldn't have said it any better. He continues with an early Smokey Mountain version of *Schadenfreude*, saying "if anything happens sum feller, I don't care if he's your bes' friend, . . . there's a streak of satisfacktion 'bout like a sewin thread a-runnin all thru your sorrow. You may be shamed of it, but durn me if it ain't there."[39]

The raucous, raunchy escapades of such humor revealed sparks of divinity in good old American mud and shared the eighteenth-century ridicule of affectation (especially as derived from Fielding).[40] One locates these rascally satirists primarily in the Quad section of humor and ridicule. Calls for reform were shunted off to the side; although moral purposes were implicit in their writings, they was overshadowed by the sheer pleasure of laughter. Slang permeated the American vernacular enabling it to triumph over the genteel tradition (where everyone smiles knowingly, but no one really laughs) and cultural refinement. These characters would make their mark as the "most vulgarly unrepressed of all the southwestern scalawags," exposing the dirty undergarments of humanity, with eating, drinking, and staying awake with the "wimen" all night.[41] The genteel tradition of educated gentleman laughing down at "the uneducated boors of the frontier" is upended by Suggs and Sut, who recognize the natural folly of all sinners and saints, laughing at each other and themselves.[42] As philosopher George Santayana observed, Americans compulsively laugh; they have a predilection for "joking."[43]

Fireside Satire

Trying to capture Yankee and frontier dialects of native types, humorist Artemus Ward (a.k.a. Charles Farrar Browne, 1834–1867) defined the nature of comedy as an uneven grindstone, one of the most useless things in the world. In a San Francisco lecture dealing with "Bigamy, Trigamy, and Brighamy," Ward related how he walked about Salt Lake City on the morning before the lecture and "met Elder Kimball. Well, I most imprudently gave him a family ticket. That ticket filled the house, and left about a dozen of the young Kimballs howling in the cold. After that I limited my family tickets to 'Admit Elder Jones, ten wives, and thirty children.'"[44] Brigham Young tells Ward that he once married four young daughters from New Jersey, their mother, and their two grandmothers, agreeing to "swallow the two old venerable antiquities as a sort of sauce to the other five." As Ward saw it, any Mormon menu included soups (Matrimonial Stews, with pretty pickles) and desserts (Apples of Discord and a great many Pairs).

An early editor of a failed *Vanity Fair*, Ward moved on to contribute shrewd, good-natured, humorous pieces to *Punch* magazine and to his president, Abraham Lincoln. Frontier humor spoke lightly of serious and sacred themes, joking about sin, preachers, heaven, and hell—common *topoi* of early rural America. It was through stories and parables that a moral message would be conveyed, rather than by ramming points down throats of audiences.

Oliver Wendell Holmes Sr. (1809–1894), a patrician founder of the *Atlantic Monthly*, composed his light poem, "Deacon's Masterpiece or the Wonderful One Horse Shay" as a satirical image of an intricately built, polished system of Calvinism, which just collapses. The Deacon, with his twangy New England dialect, is "working his Sunday's text" in preparation for his Sabbath sermon. In accordance with Puritan principles (it has five points), the one-horse shay breaks down on the one-hundred-year anniversary of the Lisbon earthquake, which punctuates an ironic commentary on those predestined for destruction. The Shay is a wonder, and nothing less, but both the buggy and Calvinism fall apart with ironic art, dismantling the same "airtight logic that Jonathan Edwards worked out in his essay *On the Freedom of the Will*."[45]

Holmes was quite mischievous in lecturing his all-male Dartmouth medical students, often using bawdy and vulgar references. In teaching on female genitalia, he prefaced his remarks with "My subject this afternoon is one with which I trust you young gentlemen are not familiar." He took on religious fanaticism in "The Moral Bully," where he reproved abolitionists and members of the emerging temperance movement as whey-faced, timid, spectacled, and frowning Protestants.

> Though he never swears,
> Nor kicks intruders down his entry stairs, . . .
> Feels the same comfort while his acrid words
> Turn the sweet milk of kindness into curds,
> Or with grim logic prove, beyond debate,
> That all we love is worthiest of our hate.[46]

Such moral bullies were souls from Bedlam on parole. Does such a tyrant really have the right to "stick us with his cutthroat terms, and bait his homilies with brother worms?"[47]

Henry Wheeler Shaw, better known as the Phunny Phellow lecturer and humorist Josh Billings (1818–1885), looked at the quaint character of ordinary Americans and found that their "piety is a good kind of disease for a man to have, but when he has so much of it that he has to go behind the door on Sunday to drink his whiskey it will do to watch him the rest of the week."[48] His father and grandfather were United States congressmen from Massachusetts, but that didn't deter him from stealing the clapper from the church bell at Hamilton College (and being expelled). His gentle humor brought laughter (which he defined, using "flatulent words," as "Anatomikally konsidered . . . the sensashun of pheeling good all over and showing it principally in one spot"), as well as insights for sinners and saints in such aphorisms as "It is much easier to repent of sins that we have committed than to repent of those we intend to commit," and "the time to pray is not when we are in a tight spot but just as soon as we get out of it." Chiding his readers gently, he reminded them that while humans were created a little lower than the angels, humans have been getting "a little lower ever since."[49]

In Billings's "Beau Bennet's Supplikashun," the supplicant prays for copious morality and a shirt collar that's stiffer than china and whiter than snowballs. He requests both a good moustache and the wisdom of Solomon. "Take away from me all vanity, but grant that mi Sunday panterloons may fit me, even as korn fitteth the kob. Remove far from me, O gentle Fortune! all pride and ostentashun, but grant that mi name amung wimmin may ever be spoken in acksents of gladness."[50] Billings realized his real gift, explaining that satire "that iz seazonable and just iz often more effektual than law or gospil."[51] His placid, honest style of waking his readers up to their vanity and tiny hypocrisies remains a most effectual reproof.

In 1851, Herman Melville launched out to find some good whale jokes. "A good laugh is a mighty good thing," he wrote in *Moby-Dick*, "and rather too scarce a good thing: the more's the pity. So, if any man, in his own proper person, afford stuff for a good joke to anybody, let him not be backward, but let him cheerfully allow himself to spend and be spent in that way. There is more in that man who has anything bountifully laughable about him than you realize." Ishmael reflected upon the joke of existence. "When a man takes this whole universe for a vast practical joke, though the wit thereof he but dimly discerns, and more, than suspects that the joke is at nobody's expense but his own . . . [that even] death itself, seem to him only sly, good-natured hits, and jolly punches in the side bestowed by an unseen and unaccountable old joker."[52] When such laughter becomes solitary, as it does for Pip in *Moby-Dick*, Young Goodman Brown in Hawthorne's Puritan "comedy," or in Edgar Allen Poe's "The Oblong Box," it becomes lonely, desperate, and haunted.

Twenty years later, the prestigious *Saturday Review* solemnly wrote:

> Comic perception is not quite compatible with the possession of the highest Christian virtues. A humorist may be a thoroughly excellent and amiable person; but he is hardly likely to be a saint. We cannot imagine the loftiest spiritual nature having the full appreciation of a joke. We have known some very good men who liked puns and small witticisms, but we have found them rather shocked even by the innocent varieties of humor.

> The humorist, in fact, has just that tendency to look at the seamy side of things, and to delight in bringing high emotions to the test of some vulgar or grotesque association, from which the man of saintly nature characteristically shrinks.[53]

In the late nineteenth century, *Saturday Review* sounded more like Sunday Morning.

Hearts of Darkness

Thematically and theologically, the book of Job underlies the dark comic poetry of Stephen Crane (1871–1900), brooding on the tragedy of life. Crane mocked the notion of the good pilgrim seeking truth and goodness; most people ran from such an encounter and chose to wallow in dark suffering rather than in a piercing light.

> In the desert
> I saw a creature, naked, bestial,
> Who, squatting upon the ground,
> Held his heart in his hands,
> And ate of it.
> I said, "Is it good, friend?"
> "It is bitter—bitter," he answered,
> "But I like it
> Because it is bitter,
> And because it is my heart."[54]

Crane's flashes of perception into the human heart aggravated despair. In the natural world, without a loving and gracious God, one saw only moments of vanity and futility. When told that he should laugh at his misery, Crane responded: "It *is* ridiculous, but it doesn't make me laugh."[55] Crane perceived the paradoxes of the human predicament with quick, terrible flashes of insight, and expressed them in terse, concrete language.

Crane described his poems as "pills," bitter but necessary medicine for the disease of being human. Growing up as the son of a preacher, Crane confronted what he saw as the cruel injustice of the world and awarded badges of cowardice and pretention to society. Critic Gerald McDonald explains that Crane's diction derives mostly from the bible, due to his Methodist upbringing.[56] Crane practiced a sort of *katastasis*, a standing outside the self and objectively observing the general suffering of men and women and the social pressures to conform. Yet in his premature end, he saw the dark grins of a fallen, but shared humanity.

Exploring the darkness within religion became the mission of another late nineteenth-century satirist. "Christianity has made more lunatics than it has ever provided asylums for." So spoke one of America's most scathing advocates of agnosticism, orator Robert G. Ingersoll (1833–1899), son of an abolitionist and intellectual Presbyterian preacher. However, the prejudice against his father shown by narrow-minded parishioners poisoned faith for Ingersoll. At a ridiculous trial in Madison, Ohio, Ingersoll senior was accused of lying and of conduct unbecoming a minister; unfortunately, the prosecutor was his third wife. Ingersoll was noted for his energetic warfare against what he saw as the savagery of Calvinism and the "gloomy insanity of Presbyterianism."[57]

Poet Walt Whitman considered Ingersoll a specimen of "leaves of grass," a truly independent individual, "spreading, giving, demanding light."[58] Ingersoll's bellicose spirit led him to challenge Christian orthodoxy and religious practices of "ignorance and faith" at the fin de siècle.[59] He mocked the founding of the Church of England in terms of Henry VIII's ulterior motive of getting a divorce. "For a while the new religion was regulated by law," Ingersoll quipped, "and afterward God was compelled to study acts of parliament to find out whether a man might be saved or not."[60]

Rather than engaging in witty satire, Ingersoll unleashed a rant on the mindless slavery of Christians. "Whoever has an opinion and honestly expresses it will be guilty of heresy. Heresy is what the minority believe; it is the name given by the powerful to the doctrine of the weak. This word was born of the hatred, arrogance, and cruelty of those who love their enemies, and who, when smitten on one cheek, turn the other." For him church history taught that "unbelief is the blackest of crimes. God is supposed to hate, with an infinite and implacable hatred, every heretic upon the earth, and the heretics who have died are supposed at this moment to be suffering the agonies of the damned. The church persecutes the living and her God burns the dead."[61]

Ingersoll pointed out that a Christian is not better than his God, is he? So, "Why should the church pity a man whom her God hates? Why should she show mercy to a kind and noble heretic whom her God will burn in eternal fire?" For Ingersoll, intolerance was the primary mark of the God's people, with an "undying hatred of all who think for themselves" and an ignorant eagerness to crush that brain. And if that were not bad enough, Ingersoll seethed about "drowsy, idealess, vapid sermons" and "moldy wonders and stale miracles."[62]

Rage tends to dissipate humor, and Ingersoll's rhetoric percolates with terms like "ferocity," "savagery," "inflicted," "unsheathed sword," "hating heretics with every drop of their bestial blood." For this agnostic, God is an infinite fiend, demanding genocide of those who are different, putting to sword even the "prattling, dimpled babe." Who could worship such a God? Ingersoll fumed over the deity who threatens "torment in eternal fire the moment death allows him to fiercely clutch our naked helpless souls."[63]

Ingersoll's doubts allegedly evolved from his rejection of hell and the idea of eternal punishment, not, he says, from the oppressive atmosphere of his childhood home and paternal authority. In fact, according to biographer David Anderson, he read widely "in the standard Calvinistic classics: *Institutes*, Edwards' *The Will*, Bunyan's *Pilgrim's Progress*, Foxe's *Book of Martyrs*, and a good many more. But their designed impact, to reinforce the dominance of a Calvinistic faith, had just the opposite effect on young Robert. Like Benjamin Franklin a century before, he rejected orthodoxy partly as a result of inept attempts to support it."[64]

Ingersoll's hatred of cant shows him to have been an allied spirit with Voltaire, as both embodied skeptical rationalism against the wild men of God. The weakness of religion lay in superstitious faith in a deity who would not only allow disrespectable behaviors, but who practiced them himself. God did not act according to his Victorian idea of decorum.

At his death, a paper's headline simply announced: "Ingersoll Dead: Great Infidel Called to Meet His God." He could almost quote Robert Frost's prayer, "Forgive, O Lord, my little jokes on Thee / And I'll forgive Thy great big one on me," but that would have taken a more humble sense of humor regarding the jests and justice of Jehovah.

Satirist in the White Suit

> So you see, the quality of humor is not a personal or a national monopoly. It's as free as salvation, and, I am afraid, far more widely distributed. But it has its value. The hard and sordid things of life are too hard and too sordid and too cruel for us to know and touch them year after year without some mitigating influence, some kindly veil to draw over them, from time to time, to blur the craggy outlines, and make the thorns less sharp and the cruelties less malignant.[65]

Before ending his life swirling in pessimism about that damned human race, Samuel "Mark Twain" Clemens (1835–1910) thought laughter could expose falsehoods and thereby liberate the mind. His satire attempted to arouse indignation in his fellow creatures at some of the injustices of life.

His earlier work held on to a stubborn huckleberry-bush hope. In *Tom Sawyer*, the rascal finds himself in a Sunday school and a revival. Tom, who is "not the Model Boy of the village," exhibits boyish mischief. Eating forbidden fruit jam, he is caught by his aunt and exposed as a fraud in Sunday school. When asked to name the disciples, he proudly identifies David and Goliath. *Huckleberry Finn*, advertising a "laugh on every page," makes Huck a Sunday school scholar to his raft buddy, the runaway slave Jim. Huck elaborates on the story of King Solomon's harem, to which the wise Jim responds that not only would there be a racket in the nursery, but "I reck'n de wives quarrels considerable; en dat 'crease de racket. Yet dey say Sollermun de wises' man dat ever live'. I doan take no stock in dat. Bekase why would a wise man want to live in de mids' er sich a blimblammin' all de time?"[66] In a dilemma contrasting institutional Christendom and the spirit of Christ, Huck is confronted with the choice of turning Jim over or facing damnation. He opts for the latter.

Twain caricatured religious characters like the Grangerfords and Mrs. Watson. The former are kind people who attend their reformed church regularly, but have to listen to "very ornery preaching—all about brotherly love, and such-like tiresomeness; but everybody said it was a good sermon, and they all talked it over going home, and had such a powerful lot to say about faith, and good works, and free grace, and preforeorderstination, and I don't know what all."[67] After sitting through the homiletic ordeal on brotherly love, they practice the opposite when getting into a fight with the Shepardsons, with their boys shouting out, "Kill them, kill them!"[68] Mrs. Watson, Huck's guardian, is portrayed as quite knowledgeable about her Bible stories; Huck declares he learned about Moses through her. However, knowledge puffs her up and turns her judgmental, as when she suggests that his friend Tom Sawyer wouldn't make it to heaven. Reflecting on the possibility that Tom wouldn't be there, and that heaven must thus a bit boring, Huck decides he doesn't want to go either.

Attacking sham, Twain observed the irreverence of Roman Catholics to Protestants, Protestants to Roman Catholics, and all to Thomas Paine, who justly deserved it. He asserted that in dealing with all such controversies, "all you need is ignorance and confidence and the success is sure. Against the assault of laughter nothing can stand."[69] Early in his career, he stood as "God's fool," championing the cleansing properties of American humor.[70] Its greatness lay in its contribution to mental health. "Humor is the great thing, the saving thing. The minute it crops up, all our irritations and resentments slip away and a sunny spirit takes their place."[71]

As the international missionary movement found its vigor and vision, Twain caricatured missionaries as busybodies. In "King Leopold's Soliloquy," the king brags that he used Christianity to further his own cause in the Congo. On being accused of cannibalism, he protests that he should be viewed not only "with my crown on my head, munching human flesh," but also saying grace, mumbling thanks to Him from whom all good things come. As a vociferous critic of missionaries, Twain contrasted their work in foreign lands with the undone business of American racism and injustice. "If you want to do good, come home from China and stop lynching in America." Then, crying out like a Hebrew prophet, he lamented, "O compassionate missionary, leave China! Come home and convert these Christians."[72]

One special, affectionate, and nostalgic target was the fundamentalist Presbyterian Church in which he grew up.[73] On his mother's church, First Presbyterian of Hannibal, he quipped, that one never saw any Presbyterians "getting in a sweat about religion and trying to massacre the neighbors."[74] They were too slow for that. No ranting, shouting, or tearing up the ground. Instead, they sat quietly in church, looked at the hymn book, and checked off the verses to see if they don't shirk any of the stanzas. During the sermon they furtively counted bonnets and caught flies. They were content with the tried and safe old regular religions and took no chances on wildcat religions.

Twain was an underground moralist, acknowledging that humor can both teach and preach.[75] He wrote several perverse stories of the "Good Little Boy" and the "Bad Little Boy," brilliant parables on Victorian sentimental religion, showing the impracticality of being "good" by noting that the good little boy who did the best he could perished while the bad boy prospered. Unlike the overly pious Sunday books of the nineteenth century in which everything turned out upbeat for the righteous, nothing worked for those who sought to be righteous. Twain's was more akin to the story of Job than of the promises of King Solomon's Proverbs. Satires on the treacly religious literature of the day, where everything turned out optimistically, contrasted the realistic biblical narratives where scoundrels like Jacob and cowards like Peter triumphed. Twain indirectly castigated the American dream of civil religion that asserted that one could manage one's own manifest destiny. In an era when industrial magnates controlled monopolies and exploited workers, the story of James, the bad little boy, resonated more than the specious success of the good boy stories.

Twain did, however, initiate a delightful habit of telling benign satiric stories of a dog in church, tales that Methodist minister Will Willimon ("My Dog, the Methodist") and the *Wittenburg Door* ("Dogs that Know the Lord") would comically emulate.[76] Like Augustine, Twain's dog confesses to the most vulgar of deeds, succumbing to the temptation of the flesh of spaniels. In a most "depraved moment of carnality, only the blast of water from a cold hose was sufficient to separate me from my shameful congress with Duchess, the West Highland terrier next door."[77] Tuffy begs his beloved master not for a snack treat, but for forgiveness.[78]

Later in life, as he experienced old age and the tragedies of losing his beloved wife, Olivia, and a daughter, Twain's satires began to "burn with conviction," albeit pessimistically. Where once everything he touched had turned to comedic gold, now in the beginning of the twentieth century, everything he touched "turned to ashes."[79] As a *fabulator*, he foreshadowed existential or black humor and took on a nihilistic cast, in which he saw that "reform is neither suggested, nor for that matter, even possible." The writing of satire with the intent to reform wanes, and an empty, helpless, but hilarious laughter ensues. What satire needs in its humorous intent to reform is hope, and hope was evaporating. He lamented what humans had become since they fell into corruption. "Everything human is pathetic. The secret source of humor itself is not joy, but sorrow. There is no humor in heaven."[80]

Twain skewered the optimism of certain sects of Christianity. Raised a Presbyterian, he got stuck in Methodist Sunday school, a "religious *dis*-order." When he once entertained the thought of becoming a minister, he soon realized that "a preacher could be damned" as much as anyone else.[81] His subtle but blistering sarcasm with regard to Calvinism and God's sovereignty comes out in such quips as "I never count any prospective chickens when I know that Providence knows where the nest is." In Twain's "Letters from the Earth," Satan writes his fellow angels Gabriel and Michael, sneering at "man's hubris at believing he was made in the image of God, when he is just an experiment." Satan translates the Beatitudes as a set of "immense sarcasm." Twain's obsession with the caustic quip carries over to his description of the human being in "Satan's Letter" as a sort of "marvelous curiosity. When he is at his very, very best he is a sort of low grade nickel-plated angel; at his worst he is unspeakable, unimaginable; and first and last and all the time he is a sarcasm."[82]

Satan's masterpiece of satire occurs on the topic of celestial music, the same exquisite sound that Dante heard as he followed Beatrice into Paradise. However, for Satan,

> In man's heaven *everybody sings*! The man who did not sing on earth sings there; the man who could not sing on earth is able to do it there. The universal singing is not casual, not occasional, not relieved by intervals of quiet; it goes on, all day long, and every day, during a stretch of twelve hours. And *everybody stays*; whereas in the earth the place would be empty in two hours. The singing is of hymns alone. Nay, it is of *one* hymn alone. The words are always the same, in number they are only about a dozen, there is no rhyme, there is no poetry: "Hosannah, hosannah, hosannah, Lord God of Sabaoth, 'rah! 'rah! 'rah! siss!—boom! . . . a-a-ah!" Meantime, every person is playing on a harp—those millions

> and millions!—whereas not more than twenty in the thousand of them could play an instrument on the earth, or ever wanted to. Consider the deafening hurricane of sound—millions and millions of voices screaming at once and millions and millions of harps gritting their teeth at the same time! I ask you: is it hideous, is it odious, is it horrible?[83]

In 1904, Twain constructed *The War Prayer*, in which he took on the jingoistic conspiracy of politics and religion.[84] During a time when the country was engrossed in the Spanish-American War, every breast was burning with "the holy fire of patriotism" and "the drums were beating, the bands playing," Twain used his pen as an alternative to the sword:

> O Lord our Father, our young patriots, idols of our hearts, go forth to battle—be Thou near them! With them, in spirit, we also go forth from the sweet peace of our beloved firesides to smite the foe. O Lord our God, help us to tear their soldiers to bloody shreds with our shells; help us to cover their smiling fields with the pale forms of their patriot dead; help us to drown the thunder of the guns with the shrieks of their wounded, writhing in pain; help us to lay waste their humble homes with a hurricane of fire; help us to wring the hearts of their unoffending widows with unavailing grief; help us to turn them out roofless with their little children to wander unfriended the wastes of their desolated land in rags and hunger and thirst. . . . Lord, blast their hopes, blight their lives, protract their bitter pilgrimage, make heavy their steps, water their way with their tears, stain the white snow with the blood of their wounded feet! We ask it, in the spirit of love, of Him Who is the Source of Love, and Who is ever-faithful refuge and friend of all that are sore beset and seek His aid with humble and contrite hearts. Amen.[85]

Finally, wearing his trademark white linen suit and holding a cigar, Twain facetiously offered prizes for the best newspaper obituary on himself. He characterized humor like his own life, as "only a fragrance, a decoration. . . . Humor must not professedly teach and it must not professedly preach, but it must do both if it would live forever. By forever, I mean thirty years. . . . I have always preached. That is the reason that I have lasted thirty years."[86] Twain's remarks on religion could fill a book of quotations with gems such as "Nothing so needs reforming as other people's habits" and "In the first place, God made idiots. That was for practice. Then He made School Boards."[87]

To a dying man who couldn't make up his mind about going to heaven or hell, Twain noted that both places have their advantages: "heaven for climate, hell for company!"[88] Another time, at a dinner party, he was accosted by his hostess on the subject of eternal life and punishment. "What is your opinion, Mr. Twain? Why do you say nothing?" Twain replied gravely, "Excuse me, Madam, I am silent of necessity, for I have friends in both places."[89]

For Twain, humor was a vocation, as he indicated in an 1865 letter to his brother:

> And now let me preach *you* a sermon. I never had but two *powerful* ambitions in my life. One was to be a pilot, & the other a preacher of the gospel. I accomplished the one & failed in the other, *because* I could not supply myself with the necessary stock in trade—*i.e.* religion. I have given it up forever. I never had a "call" in that direction, anyhow & my aspirations were the very ecstasy of presumption. But I *have* had a call to literature, of a low order—*i.e.* humorous. It is nothing to be proud of, but it is my strongest suit.[90]

Twain was less surprised at what God knew than what He didn't know; so much so one apocryphal quote attributed to him concluded that "It's not the things in the Bible that I don't understand that bother me; it's the things I do understand."[91]

Devil's Own Satirist

Should the devil ever need a darkly comic and cynical work, Ambrose Gwinnet Bierce (1842–c.1914) could supply it with panache. *The Devil's Dictionary* erupted out of Bierce's diabolical imagination to counter cant and obfuscation. As a *San Francisco Examiner* reporter, Bierce turned Webster's standard tome on its binding, covering a legion of religious as well as other comic topics.

Escaping the Bible belt of Ohio, where his family worshipped at the First Congregational Church of Christ, Bierce left the fire and brimstone revivals and set out for parts unknown. Growing up as the youngest of ten children (all of whose names started with the letter "A"), Bierce endured constant "praying, hymn-singing, and Bible reading" with his fanatical parents.[92] Sundays were so oppressive with righteousness that in *The Devil's Dictionary*, he defined "Sabbath" as "a weekly festival having its origin in the fact that God made the world in six days and was arrested on the seventh. Among the Jews observance of the day was enforced by a Commandment of which this is the Christian version: 'Remember the seventh day to make thy neighbor keep it wholly.'" His calling as an avenging angel was to uproot hypocrites, poseurs, the smug, and the stupid.

Known for his disturbing tale of "An Occurrence at Owl Creek Bridge" (a dream short story about a man about to be hanged, which has an unexpected twist) and Civil War stories, Bierce was also an epigrammatist, essayist, and poet. Armed with idealism, he wrote for an antislavery newspaper in Indiana, preferring journalistic clubbing (even with Hearst reporters) to literary posing. By the first decade of the twentieth-century, Bierce would scribble out his "word book for cynics," *The Devil's Dictionary*. His bitter and funny lexicographical writings earned him the moniker of the "laughing devil." Brilliant epigrams and definitions of sundry religious terms created satire in miniature as in the definition of "clergyman" as one "who undertakes the management of our spiritual affairs as a method of bettering his temporal ones," and preachers as "birds of pray." The clergy's enthusiastic brother, the "evangelist," appeared as "a bearer of good tidings, particularly (in a religious sense), such as assure us of our own salvation and the damnation of our neighbors."[93]

Reflecting on "The Passing of Satire," Bierce recognized he was swimming upstream against the tide of American culture. "Satire," rued the melancholy author, "is punishment. As such it has fallen into public disfavor through disbelief in its justice and efficacy. So the rascals go unlashed. Instead of ridicule we have solemn reprobation; for wit, we have 'humor,' . . . why sir, the American reading public hardly knows that there ever was a distinctive kind of writing known, technically, as satire—that it was once not only a glory to literature, but, incidentally, a terror to all manner of civic and personal unworthy."[94] Any Aristophanes or Swift who appeared would be put in a sanitary prison, with churches praying for him and women seeking to marry him.

Bierce argued that the "true function of wit is not to make one writhe with merriment, but with anguish . . . it is something to make a man cry."[95] A witty combination of the absurd and the tragic emerged in one column: "Last week was the best week for dead babies we have ever had. Of the seventy-four deaths occurring in the city, more than half were of infants under two years of age. Thirty were under one year. Whom the gods love die young, particularly if their parents get drunk and neglect them." To those who protested against such strident humor, he ironically agreed, responding: "O certainly humor should be 'delicate.' Every man of correct literary taste will tell you that it should be delicate; and so will every scoundrel that fears it. A man who is exposed to satire must not be made unhappy—O dear, no! Don't mangle the man like that coarse Juvenal, and that horrid Swift, but touch him up neatly, like Horace or a modern magazinist."[96]

Bierce articulated three principles for his "lashing of rascals," who, in spite of his efforts to reform them, "manifested a deplorable and doubtless congenital propensity to continuance in sin." His principles contrasted wickedly with traditional ones. First, one should attack specific individuals, not mere abstractions. Second, satire should serve as a form of punishment. Finally, it should have a lasting significance as literary verse; for "if the verse is good it *makes* the victim known" (as in "Leland $tanford").[97] Bierce didn't quite agree with the idea that one should condemn the sin, but spare the sinner. Just slice them all. His pen was a sharp weapon with which to bleed targets. The church hierarchy was *zany* with its hierarchy of "the curate, who apes the rector, who apes the bishop, who apes the archbishop, who apes the devil."[98]

One of Bierce's most venomous quills pricked the idea of the Incarnation, of God becoming human. In defining "piety," he explained that it involved "reverence for the Supreme Being, based upon His supposed resemblance to man," as captured in this epigram of "Judibras": "The pig is taught by sermons and epistles / To think the God of Swine has snout and bristles."[99]

Bierce targeted what he saw as the Christian presumption that God would choose the human form through which to communicate his presence. So Bierce reduced the doctrine of the "holy scriptures" to the "sacred books of our holy religion, as distinguished from the false and profane writings on which all other faiths are based."[100] Yet his wickedly clever writings were more than merely funny and shocking rants. In an insightful study, Lawrence Berkove finds a "prescription for adversity" in Bierce's moral art, connected to the satiric moral tradition of Juvenal and Swift.[101] For Berkove, this irascible character inherited the realistic observations of the author of Ecclesiastes and remained unwavering in his skepticism of pious Calvinists.

Bierce noted that while one pious man came to an untimely death while penning an irreverent book, so too might a holy man annotating the scriptures be hit by lightning. So it was that he engraved his own revised version of the Decalogue, "a series of commandments, ten in number—just enough to permit an intelligent selection for observance, but not enough to embarrass the choice." But even these are driven by Bierce's secular moral concerns as three will show.

> Thou shalt no God but me adore:
> 'Twere too expensive to have more.
>
> Take not God's name in vain; select
> A time when it will have effect.
>
> Don't steal; thou'lt never thus compete
> Successfully in business. Cheat.[102]

In his poem "Christian," a dreamer meets a tall spare figure wearing a white robe.

> "God keep you, stranger," I exclaimed. "You are
> No doubt (your habit shows it) from afar;
> And yet I entertain the hope that you,
> Like these good people, are a Christian too."
> He raised his eyes and with a look so stern
> It made me with a thousand blushes burn
> Replied—his manner with disdain was spiced:
> "What! I a Christian? No, indeed! I'm Christ."[103]

When he turned his pen to the underworld, Bierce included the clergy as citizens of hell—with the exception, of course, of Universalists, who declined "the advantage of a Hell for persons of another faith."[104] But redemption would come for some, bringing deliverance of sinners "from the penalty of their sin, through their murder of the deity against whom they sinned. The doctrine of Redemption is the fundamental mystery of our holy religion, and whoso believeth in it shall not perish, but have everlasting life in which to try to understand it."[105] To his definitions and epigrams, Bierce added his own waspish fantastic fables, attacking revivalists, heathen, itinerant preachers, and holy deacons.

In the era of a zealous Temperance movement, Bierce poured out his definition of "wine" as "Fermented grape-juice known to the Women's Christian Union as 'liquor,' sometimes as 'rum.' Wine, madam, is God's next best gift to man," and of "rum" as "generically," referring to "fiery liquors that produce madness in total abstainers." Bierce would bequeath his drink and acerbic wit to another American heir of brilliant jesting, a man from Baltimore.[106]

Last Glass of Satire

Few Americans have attacked so many with so many linguistic weapons as newspaperman and satiric commentator, H. L. Mencken (1880–1956), master of the English language and crisp wit, in the lineage of Twain and Bierce. An autodidactic who never went to college, he learned to write by listening to people, especially in his own bourgeois environs of Baltimore. Though streaked with racist and anti-Semitic remarks, his misanthropy was captured in an aphorism, that a cynic was "a man, who when he smelled flowers, looked for a coffin." However, as one who suspected that religion was a tool for manipulating credulous masses, he was best known for his classic definition of Puritanism as "The haunting fear that someone, somewhere, may be happy."[107] A clergyman was merely a "ticket speculator outside the gates of heaven." Yet Mencken was an equal opportunity mocker, ridiculing the office of an Anglican bishop as being that of "a Christian who has attained to a higher ecclesiastical status than Jesus Christ."[108]

In his independent, good-humored style (he confessed to being in "permanent opposition" to everything), Mencken expressed impatience with uplifters, quacks, rubes, and the "booboisie" ("No one ever went broke underestimating the intelligence of the American people"). In his creed, he averred, "I believe that religion, generally speaking, has been a curse to mankind—that its modest and greatly overestimated services on the ethical side have been more than overcome by the damage it has done to clear and honest thinking." Laughter, he thought, was the only antidote to melancholy, and he practiced it while writing.[109]

His satiric take on all religion, but especially Southern fundamentalism, marked him as a true iconoclast, who felt it his calling to tear down all superstitious idols. He believed that

> the liberation of the human mind has been best furthered by gay fellows who heaved dead cats into sanctuaries and then went roistering down the highways of the world, proving to all men that doubt, after all, was safe—that the god in the sanctuary was a fraud. One horse-laugh is worth ten-thousand syllogisms.[110]

He would elicit guffaws with his descriptions of "Holy Clerks," who are not necessarily religious. Even though most of us cower and become self-conscious in the presence of a rector, he is actually "less pious than the average right-thinking Americano." The way to expose this fraudulent religiosity is to follow the trail of a young man taking holy orders. "The young theologue," reflects Mencken, "studies theology instead of medicine or law because it offers a quicker and easier route to an assured job and public respect." He becomes distinguished the moment he is ordained, and is deferred to even by those who "question his magic." While everyone else works, the priest lives in a fine house, attends all birthday parties, and enjoys baseball games on summer afternoons. Even bootleggers had no such leisure. The "young Methodist *dominie* in his Ford sedan, flitting about among the women while their husbands labor down in the yards district, a clean collar around his neck, a solid meal of fried chicken in his gizzard, and his name in the local paper every day."

These young clergy are not really pious, only realistic. Their job is similar to that of the "general manager of a corporation." Such men become anaesthetized to religion, even hostile to it. For example, to see a bishop "fall on his knees spontaneously and begin to pray to God would make almost as great a scandal as if he mounted his throne in a bathing-suit." However, Mencken concluded, "If the higher clergy were actually religious, some of their own sermons and pastoral epistles would scare them to death."[111]

Mencken was a conservative contrarian, playing the "role of public immoralist, the heaver of dead cats into the sanctuaries of America,"[112] but not a mere "sower of doubt." He believed in rationalism and morality and was a faithful practitioner of secular virtue, even as he was a satirist and mocker.[113] His writing expressed a loud defiance, but his satire was meant to make men laugh.

Mencken invented the moniker "Monkey-Trial" for the Tennessee Scopes court case. As part of his reporter's commentary on the cultural event of July 1925, he wrote about a revival on the edge of town. His dispatch, "The Hills of Zion," was scribbled out when he was in his BVDs, wearing no shirt, on one of those hot, humid Tennessee afternoons. The "bad boy of Baltimore" sauntered to Dayton to see "something of evangelical Christianity as a going concern." He reported that religion was wasting away in the big cities, where "Sunday-school superintendents, taking jazz from the stealthy radio, shake their fire-proof legs; their pupils, moving into adolescence, no longer respond to the proliferating hormones by enlisting for missionary service in Africa, but resort to necking instead."[114]

Deep in the buckle of the Bible belt, where a revival mob prepared to execute Scopes before the trial, Mencken sniffed "a strong smell of antinomianism. The nine churches of the village were all half-empty on Sunday, and weeds choked their yards. Only two or three of the resident pastors ('wowsers!') managed to sustain themselves by their ghostly science; the rest had to take orders for mail-order pantaloons or work in the adjacent strawberry fields; one, I heard, was a barber."

Mencken described how "sweating theologians debated the darker passages of Holy Writ day and night" on the courthouse green. He observed the local faithful, "while interested in their exegesis as an intellectual exercise, did not permit it to impede the indigenous debaucheries." The scene is reminiscent of Ambrose Bierce's definition of a "Christian" as "one who believes that the New Testament is a divinely inspired book admirably suited to the spiritual needs of his neighbor.

One who follows the teachings of Christ in so far as they are not inconsistent with a life of sin."[115]

Mencken meets a kindred spirit, a newspaperwoman who offers him a glimpse into the old-time religion of the hills. The reporters sneak in like snakes in the grass to get a peek of the tall, thin mountain preacher, whose rumble of exhortation on the Day of Judgment broke the silence of the woods. The preacher paced and thrust his arms in the air, roaring that the "high kings of the earth would all fall down and die," all doomed to Hell. His congregation consisted of both elderly and younger folk, of girls, mothers, babies, and an immensely huge mountain woman who rolled on her heels at every "Glory to God!"

Various people testified. One woman with her hair pulled back into a little tight knot denounced book reading, for everything one needed was already in the Bible. The preacher warned that education was a snare, the gift of tongues was real, and beyond all that, lay only "infidelity and damnation. Sin stalked the cities. Dayton itself was a Sodom. Even Morgantown had begun to forget God."

After other sermons and hymns, the mood changed, with the music becoming a monotonous, unintelligible chant, followed by exultations. An anxious-bench was established, and a half-grown girl threw herself upon it, asking for prayers. All the faithful crowded up to the bench, fell on their knees, and began to pray over the penitent. Words spouted from the lips of the preacher "like bullets from a machinegun, appeals to God to pull the penitent back out of Hell, defiance of the demons of the air, a vast impassioned jargon of apocalyptic texts. Suddenly he rose to his feet and began to speak in the tongues—blub-blub-blub, gurgle-gurgle-gurgle. His voice rose to a higher register. The climax was a shrill, inarticulate squawk, like that of a man throttled. He fell headlong across the pyramid of supplicants."

Mencken keenly observed the gyrations of Pentecostal enthusiasms of squirming, jerking, cavorting, and convulsing. He described the caterwauling and leaping "discreetly," and left the interpretation of the lady's subjective sensations to "infidel pathologists," who read Freud. Whatever these moments of religious enthusiasm were, he confided,

> they were obviously not painful, for they were accompanied by vast heaving and gurgling of a joyful and even ecstatic nature. And they seemed

> to be contagious, too, for soon a second penitent, also female, joined the first, and then came a third, and fourth, and a fifth. The last one had an extraordinary violent attack. She began with mild enough jerks of the head, but in a moment she was bounding all over the place, like a chicken with its head cut off.[116]

Other worshippers were not so expressive. One man put on his spectacles and read his Bible. A young mother suckled her baby "through the whole orgy." Others, on the margins, stood aloof, and one even loosed a "bray of laughter." Finally, the two reporters returned to Dayton, where the whole town, awaiting the Scopes trial, was attending to the disputes of the theologians.

After describing the whole scene as "better than a circus," Mencken ended his journalistic satire on the wild country of Tennessee with a curious epilogue. He conceded that authentic devotion was not found in Dayton, where the "faithful" could slip off to the drug store for a Coca-Cola. "The real religion was not present. It began at the bridge over the town creek, where the road makes off for the hills."[117]

His savage indictment of southern fundamentalism earned him the title of a "serpent in Eden." Given his castigating of the Methodist and Baptist barbarism of the South for his northern elite friends, it may be understandable why he was denounced as a sort of satirical carpetbagger.[118] However, in his description of the "Hills of Zion," Mencken aligned himself not with the pretentious fundamentalists in Dayton, whom he viewed as the southern Puritans and Philistines, but with the wild Pentecostals in the hills. His own task was to comfort the afflicted and afflict the comfortable. He was a man in revolt against his own time and place. Assuming the skeptical mantle of Swift, he held up the glass of satire to show America its own image.[119]American satirists were primarily humorists, with a dominant trend of their writing being entertainment. Benign comic creations like Captain Simon Suggs and Sut Lovingood could point to American excesses in religion and morality, but they were harmless amusements that brought the democracy together in laughter. Popular writers like Twain, Bierce, and Mencken were outside observers of the stupidities of the American booboisie. They sliced parishioners of counterfeit evangelists like Sinclair Lewis's Elmer Gantry with their keen blades. They inhabited the left side of the Quad of Satire, where success on the public stage would be marked by dollars and yuks. The satirical pens of American scribblers were supplanted in the early twentieth century with the cinematographic camera. American satire would move from the hills of Zion to the hills of Hollywood. But across the channel, the British were reviving a hearty and reasonable satire of the Christian faith.

9

British Catholics and Curmudgeons

I can set a braggart quailing with a quip,
The upstart I can wither with a whim;
He may wear a merry laugh upon his lip,
But his laughter has an echo that is grim!
—W. S. Gilbert

Dry humor in damp weather invents its own incongruities. British wit traverses diverse religious terrain, due in part to its mixed religious traditions. The Roman Catholic umbrella of Chaucer is broad enough to cover those who followed, from the Anglicans and Scottish Presbyterians to the moderns. Englishmen may declare that it takes a surgical operation to get a joke into a Scotchman's head, but this may be not because of a lack of humor, but because cultural boundaries tax the import of certain kinds of laughter. But for all the British, author Samuel Butler identified the overriding theme as "Hypocrisy's the universal calling, / The only saints-bell that rings all in." One ordinate response sprouted from English cleric Charles Colton: "Where Mammon Church and State triumphant rules: / Let Satire then her keenest Sickle wield."[1] Colton exalted Swift, Pope, and Gay (while dismissing Voltaire) as the model artists of satire to reform England.

Among nineteenth- and twentieth-century British satirists, wit and humor would be raised as merrily and frequently as a glass of ale. Letters, essays, and prints deal with the follies of Anglican and Methodist clergy. A common image of venal Anglicans is that of the gluttonous "tythe pig," taking the money of the poor for his own luxury. Too many clerics are more concerned that their books be purchased than read. Even the good and kindly Parson Adams vainly tries to sell his sermons. Some "would print the Bible backwards—if't would sell."[2]

The jocular progression from impoverished university student to corpulent, indolent bishop was captured in "Mustard," George Moutard Woodward's clever 1791 illustration. With growing economic gaps be-

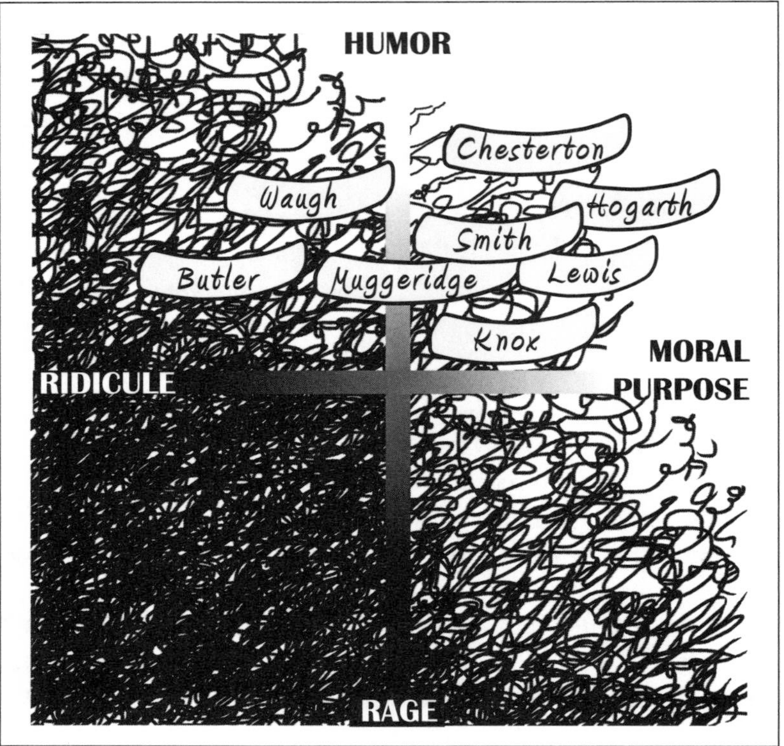

Butler, Waugh, Muggeridge, Smith, Chesterton, Knox, Lewis, and Hogarth on the Quad of Satire.

tween the higher clergy and their poorer parishioners, one finds men of God eating and drinking parish funds. Not practicing what they preach, they have become voracious pigs wearing pearls and wigs.

Caricatures also deflated the authority of the clergy with images of drunkenness. However, the theme of anti-Catholicism spawned more rhetorical ink as irrational fears of papal political control persisted. As a pamphleteer, Daniel Defoe (1661–1731), of *Robinson Crusoe* fame, observed the ignorance of many anti-Catholics, describing them as "stout fellows that would spend the last drop of their blood against Popery that do not know whether it be a man or a horse."[3]

In *The Shortest-Way with the Dissenters*, Defoe depicted a society that had traded freedom of religion for a pressure to conform. Assuming the mask of a Church of England fanatic, who seemingly hates the treasonable schismatic Dissenters, he calls them "church-devouring malignants" who should be treated like an "infectious plague."

Unfortunately, Defoe succeeded too well, and readers failed to detect his ironic tone. Defoe's "High-Flyer" persona *ironically* condemned the obstinacy of dissent ("Let us crucify the thieves," he wrote, "let the obstinate be ruled with the *rod of iron*"); however, some rabid Anglicans read his opinions literally. Defoe explained it was a joke in "A Brief Explanation."[4] As is the habit of explanations, however, the result was to raise the ire of both sides, neither being quite sure what Defoe was saying. Defoe attempted to make sure his readers understood that he wasn't ribbing the monarchy or the Protestant faiths. Confronted with the potential tyranny of popery, there was little distinction between the Church of England and the various Dissenters. Both were safer than the encroaching authority of the Roman Catholic Church. As he quipped, "That of all Plagues, with which Mankind is Curst, / Ecclesiastical Tyranny's the worst."[5]

On the other hand, his "True Born Englishman" provided a comic caricature of the stiff-upper-lipped Brit's Anglican religious practice:

> Wherever God erects a house of prayer
> the Devil always builds a chapel there;
> And 't will be found, upon examination,
> the latter has the larger congregation.[6]

At one point, Defoe was punished in a pillory and thus responded with "A Hymn to the Pillory," recommending that his privileged place in the stocks should be bestowed upon drunken priests. During his arrest, citizens did not assault Defoe with rocks and rotten vegetables, but rather pelted him with flower petals. The people understood when the authorities were ridiculous.

For the great materialist philosopher of the despotic *Leviathan* state, human nature was best described as "solitary, poor, nasty, brutish," and much too short. Living between the turbulent era between the Glorious Revolution and the Thirty Years' War, Thomas Hobbes (1588–1679) viewed the utter selfishness of humans and tendencies of men to war with one another, especially over religious beliefs, as fundamental to their nature. His own father, a vicar, had to leave his parish after brawling outside a church.

Hobbes' perspectives on laughter centered on a roar of triumph, or as he put it, "a sudden glory" accompanied by elated feelings of superiority over others. In his *Treatise on Human Nature*, he wrote that "the passion of laughter is nothing else but *sudden glory* arising from some sudden conception of some *eminency* in *ourselves*, by comparison with the infirmity of others, or with our own formerly; for men laugh at the *follies* of themselves past, when they come suddenly to remembrance."[7] We discover with a distortion of the face the absurdity of nature and so feel free to laugh at the infirmities of others.

Both laughter and weeping were for Hobbes, "sudden motions." So, he argued, "no man laughs at old jests, or weeps for an old calamity." Old jests could never surprise Hobbes. This "Monster of Malmesbury" slyly disparaged Christianity by defining religion as "fear of power invisible, feigned by the mind, or imaged from tales publically allowed."[8] However, if the tales were not permitted, they were simply *superstition*. "And when the power imagined is truly such as we imagine, [this is] *true religion*."[9] His proper distinction between religion and true religion, however, occurs only on the surface; looking closely, one sees he grounded both kinds of religion in imagination rather than truth.

Hobbes busied himself with readings of the scriptures, arguing that no sovereign king in the Bible was ever removed by a priest, thus establishing a *Leviathan*-inspired precedent for rulers standing over the religious authorities. For Hobbes, the kingdoms of darkness were ruled by the political bodies of Roman Catholics and the Presbyterian clergy. He compared the papacy with a kingdom of fairies. Ecclesiastical figures, as spiritual men, have their cathedral churches, just as fairies have enchanted castles. And, remarkably, opined Hobbes, both clerics and fairies "marry not; but there be among them *incubi* that have copulation with flesh and blood."[10] The analogy is quite comically clear, with Hobbes tiptoeing closer to Boccaccio's monks who sneak maidens into their cells, social contracts and religious oaths notwithstanding.

Challenging Hobbes was Francis Hutcheson, whose *Reflections upon Laughter* denounced the pompous philosopher for reducing everything to self-love. Championing incongruity over superiority as a more inclusive explanation of laughter, Hutcheson celebrated the cheerful contagion of laughter and its tendency to bring reconciliation. He believed that criticism, couched as a joke, can more effectively alter a person's foolish behavior. Good-natured ridicule of a friend's minor faults could actually improve him or her and reunite friends in common love, as a result of the ridiculous having been intentionally "implanted in human nature" by the almighty.[11] Yet, Hutcheson warned, "Ridicule, like other edged tools, may do good in a wise man's hands, though fools may cut their fingers with it or be injurious to an unwary bystander."[12]

Hutcheson protested the abuse of turning satire into meanness. He found a valuable purpose for ridicule in "relation to smaller vices, which are often more effectively corrected by ridicule than by grave admonition. Men had been laughed out of faults which a sermon could not reform."[13] In his refutation of Hobbes, Hutcheson celebrated the pleasant, happy state that laughter implants. It is, he observes, "very contagious," and even when it arises from a jest of ridicule, as in Elijah's mocking the false gods, it offers hope that wrongs may be corrected.

In this vein, he preceded Chesterton, who also questioned whether Hobbes's explanation of the sources of laughter in cruelty or in exultation over the pain of an enemy is really applicable to children. For Chesterton grinned at the idea that "It is a very hard even for the most imaginative psychologist to believe that when a baby bursts out laughing at the image of the cow jumping over the moon, he is really finding pleasure in the probability of the cow breaking her leg when she comes down again."[14] (Humorist Max Eastman extended the challenge to theorist Henri Bergson who attributed hostility to babies' laughter by wondering not only whether Bergson had ever seen a baby, but also whether he had ever been one.[15]) For it all, Hutcheson concluded that it is "impossible to conceive of anything better ordered than human laughter for pleasure and for kind reproof."[16]

Thousand Words of Satire

Preaching in the mid-seventeenth century was best described as talking in someone else's sleep, but wit did inhabit pulpits and spur the somnolent to attend to the sermon. Sermons were packed with epigrams, conceits, puns (such as contrasting those who pray from those who prey), paronomasia (as in John Donne's Son of God and the Sun setting and rising again), paradoxes, oxymorons, and ingenious texts. What preachers strove for was vivid visualization for the imaginations of their audiences.[17]

Few satirists could match the universal and vivid visual appeal of William Hogarth (1697–1764), a "comic history painter" who produced some of the most compelling narrative images with piquant comic details. Known primarily for his series of moral engravings on *The Rake's Progress*, Hogarth produced a broad range of satires. One sportive caricature shows Button's coffee house, which other satirists like Pope and Addison frequented. In this merry burlesque, Hogarth audaciously tosses in a naughty background bit of a dog sniffing up a poet's coattail. A similar joke occurs in his self-portrait, *Hogarth Painting the Comic Muse*, where he allegedly painted a small dog urinating on a pile of paintings by the old masters.[18] Here was a trickster ready to play with art.

Alongside his moral engravings and religious oil paintings (*Paul before Felix*), Hogarth showed his genius in etching some fantastic and complicated visual satires.[19] In *The Gate of Calais*, he exacted vengeance on the French after a visit to Calais. Two contrasting groups, starving and ragged French soldiers and a fat, gluttonous friar in a pompous parade of religion, look at a side of roast beef being transported.[20] The worship of the beef, with the servant bending his knee before the friar and a drunken Jacobite with hands clasped in a supine posture of prayer, is contrasted with a scene of the Roman Catholic Eucharist being conducted in the background.

Hogarth's engravings of eighteenth-century religious controversies reveal a stinging wit. *The Fat Pluralist and His Lean Curates* portrays a corpulent bishop carried by six "meager and wretched curates." Analyzing the caricature, James Parton describes how a fat priest grasps a "large church under one arm and a cathedral under the other." Tagging along beneath his feet are pigs, hen, and a goose. His proud words are self-explanatory, as Hogarth ironically twists Jesus's words on the Sabbath, "The Church was made for me, not I for the Church."[21]

Hogarth attacked the Latitudinarian tendency of Anglicans to rely on reason and practical religion in *The Sleeping Congregation*, a jolly juxtaposition of the biblical text and the congregation. The moral teaching tends to produce deadly dull and tedious sermons. Citing Matthew 11:28, "Come unto me all ye that Labor and are Heavy Laden, and I shall give you Rest," Hogarth shows a literal application of the word of God, as only a clerk and preacher possess consciousness. Critic Allan Cunningham describes a scene in Hogarth's Catalogue of "the heavy parson promoting, with all the alacrity of dullness, the slumber of a respectable auditor."[22] Hogarth's depiction brings to mind the opinion of Anthony Trollope, that "there is, perhaps, no greater hardship at present inflicted on mankind in civilized and free countries than the necessity of listening to sermons. No one but a preaching clergyman has, in these realms, the power of compelling an audience to sit silent, and be tormented."[23]

One engraving undermines the religious enthusiasm of Methodists. Hogarth's *Credulity, Superstition and Fanaticism: A Medley* (1762) links the new holiness movement with contemporary deception.[24] The hoodwinking of a gullible congregation happens under the ranting Methodist preacher, who holds devils and witches aloft to frighten the congregation. He crowds many inside jokes (bogus reports of Mary Tufts giving birth to rabbits) and allusions (to a pipe-smoking Muslim peering in the window, little devils whispering in sleeping parishioners' ears) into his print, both legion and damning.[25] Most hilarious is the presence of a spiritual barometer, which registers the religious emotions of the congregation.[26] In its reading of the scene, rooted in the heart of worship, it detects a mood of "lukewarm" spirituality, while a couple in the pew who are fondling one another sparks readings of "lust" and "ecstasy."

In 1762, Bishop William Warburton lambasted Hogarth for this print as a "horrid composition of lewd Obscenity & blasphemous prophaneness" which he thought fortunately would not be understood by the people. How right he was, for Bernrd Krysmanski identified him as a "keen antagonist of deism, atheism, and Methodism," and Warburton was one of the people who missed the satirical target of the print.[27] The hidden reference was to that of an enthusiastic Methodist congregation gone wild, with an allusion to George Whitefield's bull roar style of preaching, with a hand typically raised and dramatic repetitions like "Blood, Blood, Blood, Blood" fervently made. The minister is cross-eyed as "Doctor Squintum," the common caricature of a flamboyant Whitefield, whose sermons lie under the pulpit in the engraving.[28]

Between 1660 and 1740, the church existed in an "age of danger," with its creeping deism and corruptions.[29] While punning and jocularity were on the ascent during this era, witty religious satire waned.

Hogarth, however, kept his humor and his moral censure together in holy wedlock. One target who did not mind being caricatured by Hogarth, Horace Walpole, explained that "mirth colored his pictures, but benevolence designed them."[30] Fielding, whose portrait Hogarth was to paint, applauded Hogarth by observing that his characters "appear to think"—that is they seems to be drawn from actual observation rather than merely caricatured.[31] The nature of caricature as form of graphic satire is that it deflates the object of ridicule, imprinting in the imagination an enduring image. Hogarth took advantage of putting comedy in painting, but a comedy that instructed on the follies of humanity. His works reaffirm a "moral tendency, by painting Vice in those true and disgusting colors which, by leading the mind to reflection will induce it to embrace with zeal the cause of Virtue."[32]

In *The Snarling Muse*, Vincent Carretta points to diverse ways that satire deploys iconography. It strikes or tickles the imagination of spectators through decks of cards, pageant wagons, graffiti, puppet shows, chapbooks, engravings, and pantomimes.[33] It offers a graphic rhetorical tradition that illustrates its verbal counterparts and frequently makes more indelible impressions. Biblical imagery can satirize folly with gusto equal to prophetic words. Such nonverbal signs as the vomit of fools, the spit, the gaping mouth, the slapped face, and the gnashing of teeth convey attitudes of stupidity and mockery alike.[34] Art humiliates by exposing.

Hogarth's caricatures belonged to this enduring satire, which, in eighteenth-century in Britain lampooned religious belief unmercifully through "Sacred Satire." It demonstrates how both graphic artists and their literary counterparts "seized on anti-clerical themes with fresh vigor" during the age of reason.[35] Visual satirists found much to caricature, from the dull old Anglican clerics to the enthusiasm of populist field preaching and missionary societies.

The sexual sins of the clergy took center stage, with the naughty suggestiveness of "Love Feasts" showing enthusiastic (that is, erotic) inner movements of the spirit in mixed company. Bits of eighteenth-century satire inhabit John Dunton's *The Hazard of a Death-Bed Repentance* and touch upon the immorality of saints. Dunton confessed a belated remorse after serious reflections on his adulterous life, repenting with an essay on whoredom called "Conjugal Perjury," addressed to *other* "husbands of Quality that keep MISSES." He astutely observed how sickness alters a man and summons penitence, but wellness allows him to return to his lewd waywardness:

> The Devil was sick,
> The Devil a Monk wou'd be;
> The Devil was well,
> The Devil a Monk was he.[36]

He confessed that those who attend playhouses never think of going to church until breath "goes out [their] nostrils."[37]

Emerging evangelical denominations like Methodists and Quakers introduced more somatic religious experiences like shouting, weeping, quaking, shaking, speaking in tongues, falling into fits, and even barking. One of the most damning print engravings came from a Bernard Alsop woodcut of 1650 caricaturing the dissenting cult known as the Ranters. In *Ranters Ranting*, the alleged promiscuity of the sect is suggested by a female welcoming a stranger into an orgy of eating, mirth, and numerous other men dancing with erections. One sexually perverse image shows a woman kissing the ass of a leader under the caption of "Behold, our love to our Fellow Creature."[38]

The caricaturists who followed Hogarth spilled out more venomous and scurrilous ink upon their victims, even in the realm of religion. In his 1791 etching of *Transubstantiation Satirized*, Samuel Ireland shows the Holy Mother sending her son through the hopper of a windmill, essentially a meat grinder, to be transformed into the wafers for the Eucharist.

The pleasures of visual satire in Georgian England tended even more toward the lewd, the rude, and the perverse nude. Various artists like Thomas Rowlandson, James Gillray, and George Cruikshank, the spirited satanic descendants of Hogarth, would employ grotesque and sexual imagery to skin victims alive. Cruikshank and the more misanthropic Gillray grew up with devout Dissenting parents against whom they rebelled. They came to disparage outsiders like Methodists and Quakers, and, as historian Vic Gatrell argues, they "castigated religious pronouncements as 'cant' and clergymen as 'canting.'"[39] As Charles Colton wrote succinctly in his satire on hypocrisy, "No more should cant for sound Religion pass, / Degree defend, nor wigs conceal an ass."[40] In Cruikshank's *Interior View of the House of God*, a black-winged devil hovers behind the uncouth and sanctimonious congregants listening to the "fire-and-brimstone" preacher Elias Carpenter, or more likely, ignoring him. Using literary and cultural quotations within the images, Cruikshank shows one man holding on to a "dirty ditty" song from "Capt. Morris Hymns" while another teases a comely lass with a copy of John Cleland's erotic novel, *Fanny Hill*. A poster announces that tickets for pews in heaven are for sale. Above the image is the spiritual message from 1 John 4:1 to "believe not every spirit, but try the spirits whether they are of God because many false prophets have gone out into the world." The message is clear. Rowlandson's more obscene print, *The Sanctified Sinner*, portrays a sanctimonious clergyman saying his prayers while a harlot massages his lower extremities.[41]

There were, according to some, too many clerics wiling away their leisure with wining, dining, wenching, and even "hiccoughing" like laymen overindulging in worldly pleasures. Rich grease dripped from their chins while napkins covered their overripe bellies. Richard Savage's *The Progress of a Divine* follows the Hogarthian lead in ministerial training. The sporting parson follows a downward arc from his selfish habits to masturbation, procuring abortions, wife-beating, homosexuality, and finally to becoming a bishop.[42] In describing the clergyman's relation to his wife, Savage describes her dying in childbed with a broken heart, while he mourns her by wishing her to *depart* in peace.

> He weeps, and weeps-Oh, how he weeps-for joy!
> Then cries, with seeming grief, Is Nelly dead?
> No more with woman creak my couch or bed!
> 'Tis true, he spouse nor doxy more enjoys;
> Women farewell! He lusts not—but for boys.[43]

Savage's indictment of the self-absorbed clergy did not extend to all clergy since he sought to protect himself from accusations of slander (which, alas, did not succeed). He concludes *The Progress of a Divine* with:

> This priest, ye Clergy, not fictitious call;
> Think him not form'd to represent ye all.

Should satire quirks of vile attornies draw;
Say, wou'd that mean to ridicule all law?
Describe some murd'ring quack with want of knowledge,
Wou'd true physicians cry—You mean the college?
Blest be your cloth!-But, if in him, 'tis curst,
'Tis as best things, corrupted, are the worst.[44]

Samuel Johnson inaugurated his *Lives of the Poets* with the "Life of Savage," painting the man called a dissolute libertine with sympathy, "a noble piece of truth" built upon the fraud of Savage's own testimony.[45]

The inexpensive mass production of graphic caricatures by watercolor illustrator Thomas Rowlandson (1756–1827) removed the moral reform element from the Hogarth school of engravings. Rather than satirize, Rowlandson was more likely to amuse and titillate. Obscene material was used to vilify, not to correct or instruct. Rowlandson had begun as an artist, even illustrating a hand-colored aquatint frontispiece for Goldsmith's *The Vicar of Wakefield*, but after inheriting a fortune from an aunt, became quite a dissipated artist.

In particular, Rowlandson's commercial prints explicitly illustrating genitalia may have shocked, but he intended more than pornographic amusement. The prints were bold and brazen, with obscene images that opposed the aesthetic and social cant of the era. The key word here again is "cant," the sanctimonious piety of his age. Two of his best prints (and least offensive to later Victorian sensibilities) were both entitled *The Man of Feeling*. In the first, a lascivious parson, carrying in his coat pocket a copy of one of the dirtiest pamphlets of his day, John Wilkes's "An Essay on Woman," has strategically laid his hand upon the breast of his lady.[46] With his church looming in the background, the man of the cloth feels beneath the cloth of the bosom. His transgressing hand is frisky, even as the church tower looms only a little in the backdrop. The drawing's title also mocked the sentimental Scottish novel of Henry Mackenzie, *The Man of Feeling* (1771), about a naïve innocent being fleeced (the protagonist visits Bedlam like the Methodists and weeps for an inmate). It is possible that some of the primary men of feeling were the enthusiastic Methodists, who would visit prisons, tend to the prostitutes, and exhibit sentiment. In Rowlandson's second illustration, the cleric has gotten a bit further with his ministry, watching the water for tea heat up while he feels up his own enthusiasms.

The satire of the eighteenth-century spurts out in rude, nasty, and malicious pranks, like the toilet humor of drunken frat boys, with engravers deploying "buttocks, chamber pots, enemas, farts, urine, and turds as recurrent elements in their symbolic language."[47] Few prints aimed so high as social reform, but instead were coarse observations upon human folly. Bodily functions, from sexual intercourse to fart jokes, reigned until decorum was reinstituted by the ascent of Queen Victoria, when sermons would supplant obscene jests. Evangelical movements, reform acts, and improved manners would hide the indecencies of grandfathers' portfolios of naughty prints, which remained out of sight and out of reach.

Cant Rebels

As the eighteenth-century drew to a close, one finds Evangelical enthusiasms and enlightenment skepticism forming two poles. Deists rose to prominence, giving rise to Cromwell's Chaplain John Howe's characteristic epigram, that "there shall be a God, provided he does not interfere."[48] And if their self-created and convenient god displeases them, they can think him back to nothing. When not sailing with an albatross, poet Samuel Coleridge (1772–1834) dabbled with the devil and wives in his cheery chauvinism. His devil was dressed in "his Sunday best": "His jacket was red, and his breeches were blue, / And there was a hole where his tail came through."[49] When he sees a lawyer killing a viper on a dunghill, he smiles because it reminds him of Cain and his brother Abel.

In Coleridge's short poem, "Giles' Hope," a henpecked Giles bemoans his biblical fate; while in "Job," the devil is tricked by his own shortsightedness with regards to due punishment for the beleaguered schlemiel. Thinking of rising again with all his bones, Giles wants to go to heaven without his rib. Sly Beelzebub takes everything from Job—except *his spouse.*

> But Heaven, that brings out good from evil,
> And loves to disappoint the devil,
> Had predetermined to restore
> *Twofold* all he had before;

> His servants, horses, oxen, cows—
> Short-sighted devil, *not* to take his spouse![50]

The nineteenth century brought forth a crusade against moral, religious, and sentimental cant, which Johnson's *Dictionary of the English Language* defined earlier as a "whining pretention to goodness."[51] While many reformers like William Wilberforce were jolly men and happy imbibers of wine, the apparent killjoys of the century were the Methodists. The anonymous *A Missionary Society Meeting* (1826) portrays a sour group of men and women, sitting up straight, listening to a haranguing minister (whose own huge portrait adorns the wall), along with an engraving showing missionaries reaching out their arms to natives. The evangelical minister's red nose and one parishioner's sneaking leer at a modest lady reveal the hypocritical prudery in such joyless religion. Moral societies to abolish slavery, to establish rights for animals, to promote Sabbath rest, to suppress vice, and to send Bibles and pamphlets and missionaries to the untutored savages of foreign lands, dominated the anti-vice era, as well as attempts to repress obscene laughter.

Anticlerical prints, like Rowlandson's *Cash* or the anonymous *The Vicar and Moses*, teased out the prevailing images of lecherous, drunken, or incompetent clerics (one shows a vicar leisurely on the way to bury a corpse, which "can't run away"). Even more damning is the 1777 engraving of *Wolves in Sheeps' Clothing*, with corpulent and debauched Anglican clerics sitting around a table laden with wines and meats, hosting courtesans on their laps.

This mocking onslaught against perceived religious humbug and hypocrisy, against "The March of Morality" and "The Progress of Cant," and against the likes of Sunday reformers and religious tract societies would not be sustained. As historian Vic Gatrell chronicles, Evangelicals protested that such that was "neither sprung from Christian love nor compatible with it." Mirth had been excited without a sense of a correcting vice or stripping folly of its masks, but merely seeking to strike.[52] Just a few years after the ascent of George IV, one of the last religious blasphemies arrived in Richard Carlile's *The God of the Jews and Christians: The Great Jehovah* (1825), which literalized descriptions of Jehovah from the Hebrew scriptures and the book of Revelations. Carlile's portrait of

God paints his eyes "as a flame of fire." Social historian Vic Gatrell described it vividly:

> Smoke comes from his nostrils and from his mouth fire so hot that "devoured coals were kindled by it." His mouth projects "a sharp two-edged sword," while horns emerge from his hands and burning coals from his feet. This was an extraordinary invention expressing an outrageously parodic disbelief that could be more easily depicted than spoken.[53]

Satire had descended to the depths of the inferno, wanting only the laughter of ridicule. The Victorian era was to introduce a revived respectable morality; for when the Queen is not amused, it is time to tidy up.

Satirist Named Smith

As the age of respectability emerged, the Anglican reverend Sydney Smith (1771–1845) of St. Paul's Cathedral decisively won the title of Canon of Wit, with his genial mirth and Falstaffian girth.[54] Chesterton, no small man himself, called him a court jester for kings.[55] Originator of the phrase "a square peg in a round hole," Smith himself was frequently mocked, both for his appearance ("an odd-looking man Sydney Smith is, with a mouth like an oyster, and three double-chins!") and his behavior of being "naturally coarse and a lover of scurrilous language."[56] Smith was actually wonderfully convivial and captivating; his rejoinders brought the pompous and proud back to earth. (His sayings even made Queen Victoria convulse in fits of laughter.) One freethinking squire who belittled the vocation of the church told Smith that if he had had a son who was an idiot, "I'd make him a parson." To which Smith quickly added, "Very probably; but I see that *your* father was of a different mind." His independence and irreverence kept him from an appointment to a bishop's bench. When he acknowledged his belief in apostolic succession for clergy, he pointed out that there was "no other way of accounting for the descent of the Bishop of Exeter from Judas Iscariot." When theater managers sent him free admission tickets to their plays, Sydney sent back tickets for free admission to hear him preach at St. Paul's Cathedral.[57]

The wit and wisdom of Smith were well-wedded, and his satire was often self-directed. For example, not that he worried about romance, but Smith pondered how a bachelor bishop could ever get married. "How can he flirt? The most he can say is, 'I will meet you in the vestry after service,'" which may be why Smith quipped, "There are three sexes—men, women, and clergymen." He brought his wit and jeering against the citizens of Noodledom and the hypocrisies of colonial rule and missionary work:

> If the Bible is universally diffused in Hindustan, what must be the astonishment of the natives to find that we are forbidden to rob, murder and steal; we who, in fifty years, have extended our empire . . . and exemplified in our public conduct every crime of which human nature is capable. What matchless impudence to follow up such practice with such precepts! If we have common prudence, let us keep the gospel at home, and tell them that Machiavelli is our prophet, and the god of the Manicheans our god.[58]

Smith was famous for his preaching, with standing room only for his Sunday sermons, advocating the abolition of slavery, Roman Catholic emancipation, and the education of women, although he did once describe one woman who looked "as if she had walked straight out of the ark."[59]

"Preaching," he lamented, "has become a byword for long and dull conversation of any kind; and whoever wishes to imply, in any piece of writing, the absence of everything agreeable and inviting, calls it a sermon."[60] In fact Smith suggested that many fellow preachers sought to take evil out of their hearers "as Eve was taken out of Adam, by first putting them 'into a deep sleep.'"[61] So, too, he devised an apt and satisfying judgment for the church hierarchy, that a "bishop ought to be preached to death by wild curates."[62]

Smith, the mocking cleric, was accused of being a disciple of Voltaire, but his orthodoxy and charity demonstrated otherwise. In a communion of levity, he warned his friends and enemies not to think of him as "necessarily foolish because I am facetious, nor will I consider you necessarily wise because you are grave." His own rule came from a part of his rhyming recipe for salad dressing, which remains an apt description of a method for satirical prose: "Let onion's atoms lurk within the bowl / And, scarce suspected, animate the whole."[63] Smith's satiric dressing tastily reeked with sweet onions.

Victorian Wit

Victorian satirists were viewed mostly as innocent and cheery. William Thackeray hinted in *Vanity Fair* that "A good laugh is sunshine in the house." One of the ablest masters of good humor, Leigh Hunt (1784–1859), recommended that the Bridgewater Treatises, usually concerned with elucidating the nature of God, should deal with the subject of laughter. "That highest, holiest men, great reformers and martyrs, have obtained their irresistible influence over their fellow-men by their skill in wielding the weapons of humor-rousing even to the very mirthful views of things—who can doubt?" Hunt counted Pascal, Thomas More, and Luther as saints who combined wit and reverence.[64] It was not inappropriate to join subjects both "grave and gay," in spite of William Hazlitt's argument to Hunt and Charles Lamb that certain things should not rouse laughter, at which the two laughed immeasurably. When the heart and the brains are wedded, gravity and levity married, then "the man whom we might have feared as a satirist, we think we might count upon as a friend."[65]

Riding the Victorian era into oblivion, Oscar Wilde (1854–1900) notoriously played the flamboyant fool for his age. His friend Richard Le Galliene believed that Wilde made waning Victorianism "laugh at itself." What serious reformers had labored to achieve, he "did in a moment with a flash of an epigram; gaily, with humor and wit for his weapons."[66] Laughter was a primeval attitude that Wilde believed survived only in artists and criminals, and his life would prove him both. His was a grotesque and fantastic pose that would undercut the hypocrisies of his "civilized" society.[67]

In Wilde's *A Woman of No Importance*, Lady Hunstanton can't remember if a character was a clergyman who wanted to be a lunatic or a lunatic who wanted to be a clergyman. It didn't matter, as the character with straws in his hair was declared quite sane. While lecturing in America, Wilde reported that he discovered the absolute stupidity of the English people one Sunday at the Oxford University Church, when a preacher misunderstood Wilde's ideas, taking "our epigrams as earnest and our parodies as prose."[68]

For Wilde, to "be either a Puritan, a prig, or a preacher is a bad thing. To be all three at once reminds me of the worst excesses of the French revolution." When asked at his trial if he thought his epigram "Wickedness is a myth invented by good people to account for the curious attractiveness of others" were true, he answered, "I rarely think anything I write is true." His ironic poses provided the masks he needed to speak the truth. With growing notoriety, he landed in gaol; Wilde realized a bit too late that "If you want to tell people the truth, make them laugh, otherwise they'll kill you."[69]

His *Ideal Husband* recognized that when "the gods wish to punish us they answer our prayers." Regarding missionaries, Wilde explained: "Don't you realize that missionaries are the divinely provided food for destitute and underfed cannibals? Whenever they are on the brink of starvation, heaven in its infinite mercy sends them a nice plump missionary." Wilde suspected that in creating human beings, God may have "somewhat overestimated His ability." In his great moral novel, *The Portrait of Dorian Gray*, the converted revivalist is seen as one who warns people of all the sins of which he has grown tired. Yet, in spite of his cynicism, and out of devout curiosity, Wilde went to the pope and was blessed not once, but seven times. He feared that when he went before the Holy Father with a blossoming rod, it would "turn at once into an umbrella or something dreadful of that kind. It is absurd to say that the age of miracles is past. It has not yet begun." The master of wit converted on his deathbed.

One can say that Wilde threw lilies at his audience, letting the religion of art have its way (as it did effectively in his children's story "The Selfish Giant"). But his ironic voices did not arrive at satire. Satire, requires, as with Swift, a sort of benevolent bullying, knocking someone down for their own good, as Chesterton says the Irish do to their own countrymen. Feathers are not part of the arsenal of satiric weapons.[70]

Sarcastic Son of a Bishop

To be the son of a son of a bishop sounds like a curse. Samuel Butler (1835–1902) was born to an Anglican clergyman and dutifully followed the family tradition, studying for holy orders at Cambridge. However, doubts undid the plans of the fathers, as Butler grew disillusioned with the stuffy, formalized religion of the established church. In fact, Butler came to bitterly resent his Victorian upbringing. In an 1864 picture painted by Butler, entitled "Family Prayers," a stiff family sits around a table, upright and wooden, revealing the façade of the Victorian family.

In his classic *Erewhon* (anagram for "nowhere"), Butler challenged the national Victorian religion. The people of Erewhon are concerned with mercantile matters, and in the chapter on "Musical Banks," ladies dress up with their purses to go the epic edifice, which allegorizes the Church of England as a commercial banking corporation. *The Way of All Flesh* carries semiautobiographical caricatures of Victorian parish life through four generations of the Pontifex family. Bachelor Edward Overton offers cynical, irreverent musings on the vicissitudes of the family, bridging the Pontifex ancestors to the guileless son Ernest. The self-righteous and domineering father, Theobald the Rector, along with his wife, Christina, who is unfortunately the daughter of another clergyman, hover over the family tree like heavy fruit. Theobald vents his spleen and believes in curbing the will of boys with whippings. His lack of grace is evident in that he refuses to reassure the dying of their place in heaven.

Another clergyman hoodwinks Ernest out of his money. Descending from the high church, Ernest becomes a low-church evangelical trying to live out the Gospel among the poor, even attempting to save a "prostitute." After beginning with missionary zeal, Ernest suffers doubts, loses his faith, and descends into despair like a Hogarthian rake. He is finally redeemed with money from an aunt, only to return to his malignant parents. But, by now, Ernest has become a notorious author. Butler's satire blames church catechism for unhappy parent-child relations. His wickedness from birth was, unfortunately, imperfectly wiped out at baptism and exacerbated by legalistic religious instruction. Seeing himself as an *enfant terrible* of literature, Butler satirizes his experiences of a humbug church with demonic vindictiveness.

In his poem "A Refusal," Thomas Hardy (1840–1928) discharged similar anger at the same Victorian religion, blistering the Dean of Westminster Abbey for not honoring Lord Byron in Poet's Corner, due to the man's licentious lifestyle. When the Bishop of Wakefield allegedly burned a copy of Hardy's *Jude the Obscure* (a.k.a. Jude the Obscene), Hardy thought he might have really wanted to burn the author. Hardy went on to castigate a preacher "In Church" who doesn't pay as much attention to God as he does to the rhetorical effects of his sermons:

> "And now to God the Father," he ends,
> And his voice thrills up to the topmost tiles;
> Each listener chokes as he bows and bends,
> And emotion pervades the crowded aisles.
> Then the preacher glides to the vestry-door,
> And shuts it, and thinks he is seen no more.
>
> The door swings softly ajar meanwhile,
> And a pupil of his in the Bible class,
> Who adores him as one without gloss or guile,
> Sees her idol stand with a satisfied smile
> And re-enact at the vestry-glass
> Each pulpit gesture in deft dumb-show
> That had moved the congregation so.[71]

Not all satire was heavy-handed rage against the inhumane religion of the fathers. Two men would jolly up satire with wild and hearty laughter.

ChesterBelloc

Laughter expanded throughout the universe in the rollicking delight of G. K. Chesterton and his friend poet Hilaire Belloc (1870–1953). Dramatist George Bernard Shaw described their partnership as that of a sort of Siamese mythical beast, the ChesterBelloc.[72] This monster of wit shared a lively and playful Roman Catholic faith and a robust whimsy that opened the gates of both heaven and hell, even as Chesterton and Belloc would regularly debate their counterparts of Shaw and H. G. Wells on the British stage. Belloc would later draw much laughter from Monty Python's audiences, whenever his name was mentioned.[73]

Known for his French and European histories, Belloc was a blunt Roman Catholic humorist, who viewed satire as a weapon of truth for the defense of the faith.[74] In an introduction to his verses by poet

Joyce Kilmer, Belloc was accused of flipping from "rollicking burlesque to shrewd satire; merrily jesting with a bladder on a stick, he suddenly draws a gleaming rapier and thrusts it into the heart of error."[75] For example, he scribbled a bit of doggerel on the specious promises of modern Scientism, and exposed its absurdity by stating its philosophy of materialism so nakedly:

Life is a veil; its paths are dark and rough
Only because we do not know enough:
When Science has discovered something more
We shall be happier than we were before.[76]

With wry morbid wit, he penned *Cautionary Tales for Children*, which garnered praise for its macabre ditties about "Jim, who ran away from his nurse, and was eaten by a lion"; "Rebecca, who slammed doors for fun and perished miserably"; and "Matilda, who told lies and was burnt to death." A falling marble bust of Abraham arrests the rude behavior of Rebecca and knocks her flat:

Her funeral Sermon (which was long
And followed by a Sacred Song)
Mentioned her Virtues, it is true,
But dwelt upon her Vices too.[77]

The wickedly clever poetry squeezed the sentiment out of children's literature and "showed the Dreadful End of One / Who goes and slams the door for Fun."[78] In a coda, Belloc explained that children brought to hear this awful tale must be impressed so that they "never more would slam the Door. / —As often as they had done before."[79] He wrote drinking songs in which all good fellows would drink ale in heaven with him, and then,

And may all my enemies go to hell!
Noel! Noel! Noel! Noel!
May all my enemies go to hell!
Noel! Noel![80]

Another "Drinking Song" celebrated a German bishop who debated Pelagian heretics and with his stout episcopal staff so thoroughly "thwacked and banged the heretics all, both short and tall [that] they rather had been hanged." For "Old Thunder," the task set before him was to debate the world. He castigated those, who in his view, held "wrong" opinions: "Heretics all, whoever you be / . . . You never shall have good words from me / *Caritas non conturbat me*." One such heretic whom Belloc challenged was Wells, whose social Darwinism was apparent throughout his *Outline of History*. In a clever review, Belloc praised the book as well-written until the appearance of man, somewhere about page seven. Wells complained that debating Belloc was like "arguing with a hailstorm." At his funeral, Monsignor Ronald Knox eulogized that "no man of his time fought so hard for the good things."[81]

An enjoyment of life was deeply rooted in Belloc's his faith. As he wrote,

> But Catholic men that live upon wine
> Are deep in the water, and frank, and fine;
> Wherever I travel I find it so,
> Benedicamus Domino.[82]

In many of his hymns, Belloc sang praises of his faith, mixed well with the fruit of the vine: "Wherever the Catholic sun does shine, there's love and laughter and good red wine." One particular sonnet upon God, the Wine Giver, was created for Easter Sunday. It observed that God made man in his own image, and part of that blessed image was an ability to make good wine, to share in creation the fermentation of the grape.[83]

"The Christian ideal," quipped G. K. Chesterton (1874–1936), "has not been tried and found wanting; it has been found difficult and left untried." Few satirists exhaled such fresh air as this giant, a noted Fleet Street journalist, detective-story writer, and hilarious Christian saint. Not only did he write with uncommonly good sense and spontaneous wit, but he wrote about satire, humor, and jokes as well, particularly from a theological perspective. In his preface to *Charles Dickens*, Chesterton quipped that "a good joke is the one ultimate and sacred thing which cannot be criticized. Our relations with a good joke are direct and even divine relations."[84] But the idea of the joke is that it recognizes our common humanity, even our vulgar humanity.

> I believe firmly in the value of all vulgar notions, especially of vulgar jokes. When once you have got hold of a vulgar joke, you may be certain that you have got hold of a subtle and spiritual idea. The men who made the joke saw something deep which they could not express except by something silly and emphatic. They saw something delicate that they could only express by something indelicate . . . [and] in order to understand vulgar humor it is not enough to be humorous. One must also be vulgar, as I am.[85]

And not only are we vulgar, we are diseased with sin. Or as Chesterton said, "Not only are we all in the same boat, but we are all seasick." It is this vulgarity of human life—literally its commonness—that unites, allowing all to understand each other and to satirize each other.

> [We should] defend grotesquely what we believe seriously. It is that all grotesqueness is itself intimately related to seriousness. Unless a thing is dignified, it cannot be undignified. Why is it funny that a man should sit down suddenly in the street? There is only one possible or intelligent reason: that man is the image of God. It is not funny that anything else should fall down; only that a man should fall down. No one sees anything funny in a tree falling down. No one sees a delicate absurdity in a stone falling down. No man stops in the road and roars with laughter at the sight of the snow coming down. The fall of thunderbolts is treated with some gravity. The fall of roofs and high buildings is taken seriously. It is only when a man tumbles down that we laugh. Why do we laugh? Because it is a grave religious matter: it is the Fall of Man. Only man can be absurd; for only man can be dignified.[86]

Chesterton's celebration of divine frivolity gently satirized the somber tones inhabiting much of Christendom. When various clergymen reproached him about making jokes about religion, citing the second commandment that one should not take the name of the Lord in vain, Chesterton argued that to make a joke out of something is not to take it in vain. "It is, on the contrary, to take it and use it for an uncommonly good object."[87] The people who do take the name of the Lord in vain, he countered, are the clergymen themselves. "The thing which is fundamentally and really frivolous is not a careless joke. The thing which is fundamentally and really frivolous is a careless solemnity." God's truth, he argued, can be expressed in long sentences or short jokes, just as it can be expressed in French or German. Of course, Chesterton conceded, wherever you have hilarity, you will have some dangers, but at least men and women will be alive and awake, unlike when they listen to ponderous sermons.[88]

In illustrating the mirror of satire, he referred to himself as a proper object of laughter. In fact, he was renowned for self-effacing humor. When the three-hundred-pound satirist had trouble getting out of a taxi, a woman recommended that he get out sideways. "Unfortunately," Chesterton pointed out, "I have no sideways." But this was just the point of his self-deprecation in defining satire: "Satire may be mad and anarchic," he conceded, "but it presupposes a standard. When little boys in the street laugh at the fatness of some distinguished journalist, they are unconsciously assuming a standard of Greek sculpture. They are appealing to the marble Apollo."[89]

Referring to the works of Rabelais, Swift, and Pope, Chesterton distinguished among three kinds of noble practitioners of satire, men who could laugh without losing their souls. The first kind was Rabelais, the man who first, enjoys himself and then enjoys his enemy.

> In this sense he loves his enemy, and by a kind of exaggeration of Christianity he loves his enemy the more he becomes an enemy. He has a sort of overwhelming and aggressive happiness in his assertion of anger; his curse is as human as a benediction. Of this type of satire the great example is Rabelais. This is the first typical example of satire, the satire which is voluble, which is violent, which is indecent, but which is not malicious.[90]

The second type of satiric mind is "embodied in the satirist whose passions are released and let go by some intolerable sense of wrong. He is maddened by the sense of men being maddened; his tongue becomes an unruly member, and testifies against all mankind. Such a man was Swift, in whom the *saeva indignatio* was bitterness to others, because it was bitterness to himself." Finally, the third type of satirist rises superior to his victim, but "in the only serious sense which superiority can bear, in that of pitying the sinner and respecting the man even while he satirizes both." So it is Pope who can take pleasure in "pointing out his enemy's strength before he points out his weakness. That is, perhaps, the highest and most honorable form of satire."[91]

Chesterton combined all three, and added the art of paradox to catch readers off guard. In such epigrams as "Moderate strength is shown in violence, supreme strength is shown in levity" and "If there were no God, there would be no atheists," Chesterton played with the topsy-turvy nature of rationality.[92] He would have given fits to Voltaire, by playing outside the box, but trying to bring him into the Church at the same time. To those seeking to follow the golden rule of his faith, he reminded, and he reminded more than he preached, "The Bible tells us to love our neighbors, and also to love our enemies; probably because they are generally the same people."[93] For Chesterton, however, the appeal to satire was an appeal to common sense; for such a background allowed figures to look "comic and sprawling like caricatures." But what is important for revolutionary satirists, for good satirists, is the fight for something, even as no man "will risk a revolution unless he trusts a rule or hopes for a republic."[94] The good satirist uses vivid purple prose to bring about some improvement through his comedy. For the satirist not to bear his sword in vain, it is essential that he bear it with ease: "that for the wit the weapon should be light if the blow be heavy."[95]

The cheeky but accurate generalizing of Chesterton, who missed the facts but captured the essence of a man or a moral, stood in fat juxtaposition to the slim respectability and propriety of the Victorian age. He highlighted a whole new thing in Victorian literature, "a thing called nonsense," from the odd asthmatic and epileptic Lear to the mad-hatter cartoons of Lewis Carroll. Chesterton pointed back to the new chapter started by Rabelais, who treated intellectual things with the "energy of high spirits" and physical exuberance. With Chaucer, who gave us personal sketches in which we could laugh at people and like them simultaneously, Rabelais gave a genial mirror for all of us; just before, Cervantes gave us "that grand and very Christian quality of the man who laughs at himself." The satirical humor and wit bequeathed to human beings from such artists are divine gifts, the chief antidotes to pride, and they remain, ever since the Book of Proverbs, "the hammer of fools."[96]

Among comic saints like Chesterton and Belloc, theologian Dudley Zuver saw "comedy keeping company with the Church." For both saw the way that things should be and the way that things actually were. Like Presbyterian Frederick Buechner, one must start with the real, the tragic, the inescapable and inevitable pain of reality, but then see that unexpected comedy (and a real fairy tale) will ensue.[97] In his *Salvation by Laughter* (1933), Zuver pointed out that the church would do well to show mercy and kindness, which he saw as manifestations of both the holy and the comic spirits.

Like Chesterton, Zuver pointed to the contradictions of demanding tolerance for all religious views, as tolerance was merely "a cloak which conceals a rapier."[98] Satire would strip the passive-aggressive disguise of tolerance and demand a struggle to find out what was true or right; the committee shouting for tolerance are those who "choose not to fight in the hope that they may win without a fight." The inherent contradiction is that the tolerant will never be tolerant of what they see as intolerance. In dealing with people, one must show love and magnanimity; however, in dealing with ideas, one fights, mostly with satire. As Zuver jested, he was once informed that "intelligent men the world over profess one and the same religion, and when I eagerly inquired what that religion was, I was told that intelligent men never say."[99] For Zuver, God, too, has a sense of humor, and those made in his image, however corpulent or lean, should laugh as well.

Hard Knox

A Roman Catholic chaplain at Oxford, Monsignor Ronald Knox (1888–1957) was more than a mere humorist, which he categorized as a satirist out of a job, "a clock without hands." Knox distinguished two comic pursuits as the "humorist runs with the hare; the satirist hunts with the hounds."[100] In his *Essays on Satire*, Knox argued that a satirist not only had a laugh up his sleeve, but medicine in his pocket. In contrast, the merely ironical writer turns cynical and tends to throw up his hands and walk away. The satirist is eager for the challenge, being a witty controversialist who doesn't really want the dust to settle. "Let us scourge our vices like Juvenal," Knox counseled, "and purge our consciences like Hogarth." Satire not only depends on critical abilities to deflate error and folly, but, for Knox, requires sympathy as well. Knox would vent his spleen; nor would he scorn or mortally wound his victims, but did seek to make them a tad uncomfortable.[101]

Satire, he continued, is "a normal function of the human genius and humor that has no satire in it is a perversion of the function. Our sense of the ridiculous is not a child's toy, but a weapon, entrusted to us for exposing the shams and hypocrisies of the world."[102] The humorist, in short, must grow up to be a satirist and find gainful employment. Knox grieved that the modern "habituation to humorous reading has inoculated our systems against the beneficent poison of satire." While the satirist may borrow weapons from the humorist, he must be careful not to surrender to the trifling pleasures of evoking laughter. Knox pointed out that while other ages "stoned the prophets," his pelted them instead with the "cauliflower bouquets of the heavy comedian."[103] One must remember that Rome was not amused by Juvenal.

The Roman Catholic father, whose first duty as a priest was the salvation of souls, would gleefully spoof ponderous theologians, pretentious psychoanalysts, windbags of ecumenical coexistence, and higher textual critics (for example, in the parodic *Studies in the Literature of Sherlock Holmes*). Thus, while making fun of the liberal theology of Schleiermacher, Knox penned the following:

> A man so broad, to some he seem'd to be
> Not one, but all mankind in effigy . . .
> When suave politeness, temp'ring bigot Zeal,
> Corrected "I believe" to "One does feel."[104]

Against such foolish types, Knox recommended satire as one of the better cures: "Satire has an intensely remedial effect; it purifies the spiritual system of man as nothing else that is human can possibly do."[105] It was not scorn that shaped his work; rather, he enjoyed a delightful calling to make his colleagues and congregations squirm. In fact, Knox believed that there dwelt less contempt in satire than in irony; the latter keeps something up its sleeve—namely, an attitude of superiority.

Knox's frothy essay on "The New Sin" never tells us what it is, but Professor Laileb (Belial) remonstrates with the reader for having such a wicked curiosity for such things. Knox knocked the press's and the public's voracious appetite for scandal and skinned them with their own insatiable curiosity for this new sin, as if the other seven deadly sins were not enough. Some people see something apocalyptic while others look for novelty. The Christian Scientists see it all as illusion, and the spiritualists try to find out the secret from mediums, but they all get it wrong. As they gather at the public event when Professor Laileb is to disclose his secret, he refuses to do so so because they really don't care to be naughty, but only to hear something naughty. "Curiosity," wrote Knox, "is the easiest of all sins to punish, for it carries with it its own worst punishment when it is ungratified." So Professor Laileb tells them all to go to hell; then they all want to enact the "old conventional sin of murder."[106]

One of Knox's cleverest arrows to zip the modernist "new church" of the "indifferent" Anglicans was his mischievous essay entitled "Reunion All Round." Taking on the pose of the ultra-tolerant and supercilious Anglican, he recommends accepting everyone as members, from atheists and Buddhists to Muslims, all for the sake of coexisting in unity and good fellowship. He suggests that anyone "arrogantly styled *Orthodox*" could have no part in the church of the future. "How can a man proclaim his own tenets to be orthodox, without thereby implying that other people's opinions are less likely to be true than his own?" Such ecumenists would sacrifice the creed, but would find difficulty in dealing with lifestyles. "In the days of theological enlightenment, it was diet, not dogma, which divided the church and disrupted potential unity." For example, the Muslims unfortunately held it "sinful and unclean to eat the Flesh of the Pig, or drink fermented Liquors. And though, Anglicans might be prevailed upon to abandon whatsoever else in the interests of Peace, there are two Privileges they will never relinquish except at sword's point, and namely, Bacon and Beer!"[107]

Biographer Robert Speaight crowned the 1939 "Let Dons Delight" as Knox's supreme literary achievement. As eavesdropping pseudohistory, it covers a series of conversations among imaginary professors at an imaginary college (Simon Magus), spanning a period from 1588 to 1938, drawing on the Oxford Common Room that Knox so affectionately knew. One overhears droll conversations:

Mr. Savile: We were not talking of Rome, but of the Church of England as she is and ever has been a part of the Catholic Church.

Dr. Greene: I must beg of you, Mr. Savile that you will not refer to the English Church as if it were some female of your acquaintance. I tell you, I cannot digest my dinner if you will talk so.[108]

Speaight explains that "Where the weapon of satire is exaggeration, the virtue of history is exactitude. This is the way dons talk; this is the way they have always talked; these are the subjects they discuss; these are the kinds of men they are." "Let Dons Delight" echoes a little ditty familiar to all British urchins in Eton collars. It starts, "Let dogs delight to bark and bite, for God hath made them so." What happens is that bright and eager young dons bark and bite and age and each generation wilts into "elderly Provosts asleep by the fire." By the end of the chronicle, theology has been fully eradicated from the curriculum.[109]

In his vocation to secure the foundation of the faithful and orthodox, Knox was ever too ready, like a rascally schoolboy, to topple the loose stones of modern theology. Yet Knox remained humble like a sheep-dog chasing after sheep, and sometimes rudely barking his sermons. "Wherever there is a joke," he confessed, "it is Man, the half-angel, half-beast, who is somehow at the bottom of it."[110]

The literary executor of Ronald Knox's estate was author Evelyn Waugh (1903–1966). As Knox's friend, Waugh secured permission to write the biographical *Life of Ronald Knox*. As a devout fellow Roman Catholic and a very wry satirist in his own right, Waugh merrily followed in the mold-breaking image of early twentieth-century Christian authors. Like Chesterton and Knox, he played with the world, ushering in fresh, indirect perspectives on orthodox dogma. He pointed out that "He is only a very shallow critic who cannot see an eternal rebel in the heart of the Conservative." He would revolt against modernity in all its plastic and superficial postures of progress.

Waugh practiced what James Carens called an "adjectival incongruity" (such as a "lovely College meeting") with a bit of low burlesque satire. Like T. S. Eliot, Waugh rebelled against the modern wasteland. He rejected behaviors of the hollow men and women as inadequate, pompous, and to use one of his favorite words, "bogus."[111] Introducing innovative forms for his dialogues, such as a telephone conversation,

Waugh satirized the modern lifestyle and communication of spoiled English youth. In *Vile Bodies* he exposes the emptiness of luxury and lax morality, playing a satirist who critiques his world. He caricatures a grotesque, plotting Jesuit clergyman in the character of Father Rothschild, who wears a false beard. Balancing this satiric portrait is that of the American revivalist evangelist, "a damned impudent woman," Mrs. Melrose-Ape, whose dubious female angels and others, are obviously less consumed with a passion for God than men. One named Chastity ends up a whore.

Waugh was renowned for exploiting atrocious material for his spoofs; here was the satirist as verbal butcher, a mortician of metaphors. *Vile Bodies* spotlights one of the bright young people running around England, who gets drunk, steals a racing motor car, crashes, and hosts a cocktail party in her hospital room; then dies. In a subplot, an unscrupulous religious filmmaker is trying to make a profit on a movie about John Wesley (with a script inventing a duel with George Whitefield and a battle with American Indians). Wesley, an icon of enthusiastic religion, is a most fitting choice for a Hollywood exploitation film.

However, Waugh's reform or reaffirmations of a moral world is buried more deeply under the low burlesque of his writing. Waugh converted to Roman Catholicism, which gave him a tradition that would sustain him and a standard against which to hold up the effete banality of contemporary life. Just as Juvenal remembered the good old days in his acidic attacks on a corrupt Rome, so Waugh celebrated the British world by stripping the mask from its face with acute, witty craftsmanship.[112]

Waugh's 1930 conversion was "like stepping across the chimney piece out of a Looking-Glass world, where everything is an absurd caricature, into the real world God made."[113] At such a point, one could begin the delicious process of exploring its wonders; for Waugh this change ushered in themes of faith. In *Brideshead Revisited*, he demonstrated that once God has a hook in his catch, he holds on, but lets the tether extend to the ends of the earth. At the end, he almost leisurely reels in his child. By hook or by the shepherd's crook, God keeps his own. In "making a choice between Christianity or chaos," Waugh "saw in Europe's increasing materialization a major decline" and bankruptcy.[114] He satirized the unfathomable ignorance of British people about the Christian faith as a significant cause of cultural deterioration.

In one particular passage of this evocative novel, a man of the world wishes to marry the Roman Catholic daughter of an affluent and titled grande dame. She stipulates that he must become a convert if he wants to marry her. So he anxiously resigns himself to the catechism of a priest. When the priest asks if anything troubles him, he bursts out:

> "Look, Father, I don't think you're being straight with me. I want to join your church and I'm going to join your church, but you're holding too much back."
>
> [When the priest] asked what he meant, he said: "I've had a long talk with a Catholic—a very pious, well-educated one, and I've learned a thing or two. For instance, that you have to sleep with your feet pointing east because that's the direction of heaven, and if you die in the night you can walk there. Now I'll sleep with my feet pointing any way that suits Julia, but d'you expect a grown man to believe about walking to heaven? And what about the pope who made one of his horses a cardinal? And what about the box you keep in the church porch, and if you put in a pound note with someone's name on it, they get sent to hell. I don't say there mayn't be a good reason for all this," he said, "but you ought to tell me about it and not let me find out for myself."

It turns out that the thirteen-year-old sister of his fiancée had punked him, pulling the leg of the credulous suitor, and filling his head with nonsense. So, too, Waugh has fun with his readers, poking his finger in the brains of uninformed but "educated" men of affairs, like journalists. The secular mind for Waugh will believe anything preposterous and outrageous regarding the Christian faith without truly investigating it.

Brideshead Revisited, a poignant satire on bright young things between the wars, has been viewed as deeply, or widely, Chestertonian. One key underlying motif concerns the redemption of lost souls, and its source has been attributed to one of the Father Brown detective stories. The reference of "the unseen hook and invisible line—the twitch upon the thread" floated out of Chesterton's pool of thought. As Waugh noted,

> The Roman Catholic Church has the unique power of keeping remote control over human souls which have once been part of her. Chesterton has compared this to the fisherman's line, which allows the fish the illu-

> sion of free play in the water and yet has him by the hook; in his own time the fisherman by a "twitch upon the thread" draws the fish to land.[115]

Waugh, however, denied that he wrote satire, which he viewed as "a matter of period." He argued that satire flourished in stable societies, which presupposed homogeneous moral standards—as in the early Roman Empire and eighteenth-century Europe. "It is aimed at inconstancy and hypocrisy. It exposes polite cruelty and folly by exaggerating them. It seeks to produce shame. All this has no place in the Century of the Common Man where vice no longer pays lip service to virtue."[116]

Such a pronouncement is itself an understated, sly mocking of the contemporary era as one without virtue. In one apocryphal literary anecdote, author Nancy Mitford once approached Waugh and inquired how he could "behave so abominably and yet still consider himself a practicing Catholic." Waugh responded: "You have no idea how much nastier I would be if I were not a Catholic. Without supernatural aid I would hardly be a human being."[117] Perhaps it was a divine joke that Waugh should die in the water closet, purged of his sins and cleansed fully.

One final British couple deserves honorable mention. Authors and publishers, husband and wife, Frank Sheed and Maisie Ward used tremendous humor to articulate the Christian faith and speak it forth on soapboxes, not only in the grand public venue of Hyde Park, but in backwaters like Clapham and Pimlico, notably sites that properly belong in comic British monologues. Their organization of the Catholic Evidence Guild delighted in rough-and-tumble debates, trying to explain the meaning of the Christian faith to onlookers and hecklers.

According to scholar Dana Green, from the earliest days of the guild, they "refused to enter political debate. Maisie, and especially Frank, insisted on principle that their statements be apolitical."[118] Sheed had determined "not to fight for anything that wasn't worth fighting for." It was a question of using time wisely. According to their son, "his tongue was a weapon like a fighter's fist, to be used only when the purse was right. And the purse had to be a human soul. He was damned if he'd alienate one of those precious things in some dingy political scuffle."[119]

He playfully confronted issues of contemporary sexual morality. Sheed argued that "there is no sophistication or maturity in doing what any alley cat can do, no mastery in being mastered, no virility in being unable to say no."[120] Sheed laughed at those that viewed the sex act as love's highest expression. He explained, "the ruling purpose in their own intercourse seemed to be the enrichment of their partner's personality. One wondered how refinedly he might bear the discovery that she did not want her personality enriched that night. I mentioned this particular point to a couple thousand women at a luncheon in Los Angeles. They laughed and laughed. I got the impression that each of them was seeing one special face, not looking its best."[121]

The satirist's temptation was that his or her humor could easily veer into effrontery. Sheed stressed that jokes and amusement should never result in personal diminishment: "To have raised a laugh at a man's expense is a sure way to make him loathe you. You have acted against your whole purpose in being there! To whatever barriers there may already be between him and God, you have added your own smiling self."[122] In the same vein, he counseled, "to make a questioner look foolish is to push him further away from the Faith, thus cutting right across our whole reason for being on the platform."[123] Conversely, Sheed advised, messengers needed to have thick skins, and "if a joke is made at your expense, do not be annoyed. If it is a good joke, enjoy it."[124]

For Sheed, the hecklers were, in fact, a kind of mirror in which the speaker might catch a glimpse of himself. If they were bigoted and prejudiced, Sheed inquired, then "what about ourselves?" This would be a salient question for all satirists.

Satirist to the Skeptics

Oxford don C. S. Lewis (1898–1963) was shaped by men like Chesterton, Knox, and children's author George MacDonald, who once quipped that "it is a heart that is not sure of its God that is afraid to laugh in His presence."[125] After a youthful infatuation with atheism and other fashions of the 1920s, Lewis found assurance in the orthodox God of Christianity. Lewis picked up ideas about three possible explanations for the identity of Jesus (an imposter, a mad man, or the Son of God telling the truth) and the image of a man who thought he was a poached egg from the Roman Catholic apologists.[126] Lewis would appropriate these ideas for his famous trilemma in *Mere Christianity*.[127] In fact, before Lewis had become a Christian, he had read Chesterton's *Everlasting Man* and been convinced that Chesterton was the "sanest man alive" (apart from his Christianity).[128] When Lewis met Knox for lunch through a mutual friend, he assessed Ronnie to be "possibly the wittiest man in Europe."[129]

In his famous little book, *The Screwtape Letters*, which landed him on the 1942 cover of *Time* magazine, Lewis explained that "humor involves a sense of proportion and a power of seeing yourself from the outside."[130] Lewis was adept at communicating his own faith in topsy-turvy style by having his devil inversely articulate the doctrines he believed. God is thus defended by unlikely apologists, much like the Misfit in Flannery O'Connor's "A Good Man is Hard to Find" or the sociopath Pinkie Brown in Graham Greene's *Brighton Rock*.[131]

In the eleventh epistle addressed to his dumb-and-dumber nephew, Wormwood, old demon Screwtape categorizes laughter along four lines, Joy, Play, the Joke Proper, and Flippancy. Between the two categories of the Joke Proper and Flippancy resides the realm of Satire. The devil Screwtape describes jokes as turning on a "sudden perception of incongruity." For Screwtape, Flippancy is best.

> In the first place it is very economical. Only a clever human can make a real Joke about virtue, or indeed about anything else; any of them can be trained to talk as if virtue were funny. Among flippant people the Joke is always assumed to have been made. No one actually makes it; but every serious subject is discussed in a manner which implies that they have already found a ridiculous side to it. If prolonged, the habit of Flippancy builds up around a man the finest armor plating against the Enemy that I know, and it is quite free from the dangers inherent in the other sources of laughter. It is a thousand miles away from joy; it deadens, instead of sharpening the intellect; and it excites no affection between those who practice it.[132]

In these diabolically light letters, Lewis evinced keen psychological insights that satirized humanity. For example, Screwtape writes about how to tempt the "patient" after he has become a Christian and goes to church: "When he gets to his pew and looks around him he sees just that selection of his neighbors whom he has hitherto avoided. . . . Provided that any of those neighbors sing out of tune, or have boots that squeak, or double chins, or odd clothes, the patient will quite easily believe that their religion must therefore be somehow ridiculous."[133]

What is most telling about this brief passage is that it echoes Lewis's own prejudices—namely, his dislike of poorly written hymns and bad poetry. Thus, the passage is a satirist's attack on his own pride; the satire is actually that Swiftian mirror in which Lewis mocks his own sins even before he sets his sights on any neighbor. The one package we know better than any other is our own soul. Lewis found the need for reform to start with the self, to mock one's own tendencies of vanity and folly. For Lewis, the art of ridiculing oneself enables one to satirize one's neighbors.

Lewis concentrated his satiric talents on bureaucratic officials and modern liberal theologians, as in his depiction of the fat apostate Episcopal Ghost (who wears gaiters) in *The Great Divorce*. (Lewis confessed to being "conscious of a partly pathological hostility to what is *fashionable*."[134]) The unbelieving cleric holds on to his job when he has forsaken his vocation; no longer believing the core doctrines of his church, he asserts the superiority of his own thinking.[135]

What made trendy theologians particularly ludicrous to Lewis were their specious claims for honesty in soul-searching, when they were primarily seeking routes to intellectual success.[136] Lewis mused, "What was at all likely to come of it except what actually came—popularity, sales for your books, invitations, and finally a bishopric?"[137] In *The Pilgrim's Regress*, the modern theologian Mr. Broad aims at making friends with the world; he seeks no truth, only wildflowers. The Anglican clergy ghost in *The Great Divorce* chooses to refuse heaven not only because it lacks "an atmosphere of free inquiry" and requires belief in God as "Fact," but also, most importantly, because he must be "back in hell that Friday to read a paper to a theological society on what Jesus' mature views would have been if his life had not been cut short tragically by the crucifixion."

T clergy who sought to introduce novel doctrines and liturgical experiments, Lewis preached, "I wish they'd remember that the charge to Peter was 'Feed my sheep'; not Try experiments on my rats, or even, Teach my performing Dogs new tricks.'"[138] Through belittlement and exaggeration, Lewis sought to sandpaper the pompous surfaces off posturing clerics.

Lewis copied the satirical masters of the previous centuries. His defense of vulgar jests in satirists like Rabelais is rooted in a basic observation about the dual nature of human beings. He wrote,

> The coarse joke proclaims that we have here an animal which finds its own animality either objectionable or funny. Unless there had been a quarrel between the spirit and the organism I do not see how this could be: it is the very mark of the two not being "at home" together. But it is very difficult to imagine such a state of affairs as original—to suppose a creature which from the very first was half shocked and half tickled to death at the mere fact of being the creature it is. I do not perceive that dogs see anything funny about being dogs. I suppose that angels see nothing funny about being angels.[139]

In *The Four Loves*, Lewis warned against solemnity regarding sex since "every language and literature in the world is full of jokes about sex. Many of them may be dull or disgusting and nearly all of them are old. But we must insist that they embody an attitude to Venus which in the long run endangers the Christian life far less than a reverential gravity."[140] Those who take sex too seriously, opined Chesterton, are those given to phallic worship. Others put it all in perspective, along with the jokes of Rabelais and English cabmen.[141]

Such a notion makes our bodies into satirists, mocking the solemn minds of men and women, as God created our desires in such a way to remind us that they are not our end. Our bodies, as St. Francis discovered, are jokes. And, Lewis observed, "It is a bad thing not to be able to take a joke. Worse, not to take a divine joke; made, I grant you, at our expense, but also (who doubts it?) for our endless benefit."[142]

The tree of Lewis's satire bore fruit he did not expect. One young man identified as Mathews confessed to Lewis in a letter that his satirical *Screwtape Letters* helped transform him from a "simpering little demon" into "a reasoning and fairly loveable Christian." Mathews claimed that by appealing to his sense of humor, the satire enabled him to "literally laugh my way out of the darkness."[143] But it is important to remember that Lewis himself was laughed out of his own darkness by discovering his face in the reflecting glass of satire. He knew the first target of folly requiring reform was his own soul.

Mug Made for Laughter

An editor of *Punch* magazine, erstwhile curmudgeon, and intellectual convert to Christianity, humorist Malcolm Muggeridge (1903–1990) blustered his way onto center stage with gusto. Anyone who titles his autobiography *Chronicles of Wasted Time* has made sympathetic contact with every other writer.

Muggeridge's trek toward Christian orthodoxy began with a vocation as a Communist advocate for the oppressed in this odd world of Christianity.[144] Reading Samuel Butler, he wanted a fight. He wanted to cleanse something. In this, he realized he "had a taste for satire, believing it to be the articulate man's duty to hit what seems wrong to him and to hit it laughingly."[145]He believed that "Bad humor is an evasion of reality; good humor is an acceptance of it." He also conceded "good taste and humor are a contradiction in terms, like a chaste whore."[146] Yet, as one biographer described him, Muggeridge held "a dedication to nonconformity that led him to champion many a lost cause."[147]

Laughter was a sign of godliness, against the worship of power. "I don't attack people," he explained, "I try to point out the absurdities in people." It was a way to remind them of their humanity. He used humor to bring people back to the reality of a mortal existence. When asked if satire effects change or just amuses, Muggeridge answered, "Perhaps both."[148]

As a socialist and leftist, Muggeridge was accused of being a mocker of religion and scorner of sacred things. Muggeridge, however, was an iconoclast. He never disguised his opinions. Yet, like fellow journalist Chesterton, he converted to Roman Catholicism and employed his talents against what he saw as the stupidity of the age. On being asked if he were considering joining the Roman Catholic Church in the 1960s, he quipped, "Have you ever seen a rat joining a sinking ship?" Yet, for Muggeridge, Roman Catholics were saints compared to Anglicans, especially the maundering vicars who sought only approval, pleasure, and status. In his essay, "Backwards Christian Soldiers," Muggeridge attacked what he saw as the spineless, wavering, fashion-conscious, sex-starved ("The orgasm has replaced the cross as the focus of longing and fulfillment") Church of England:

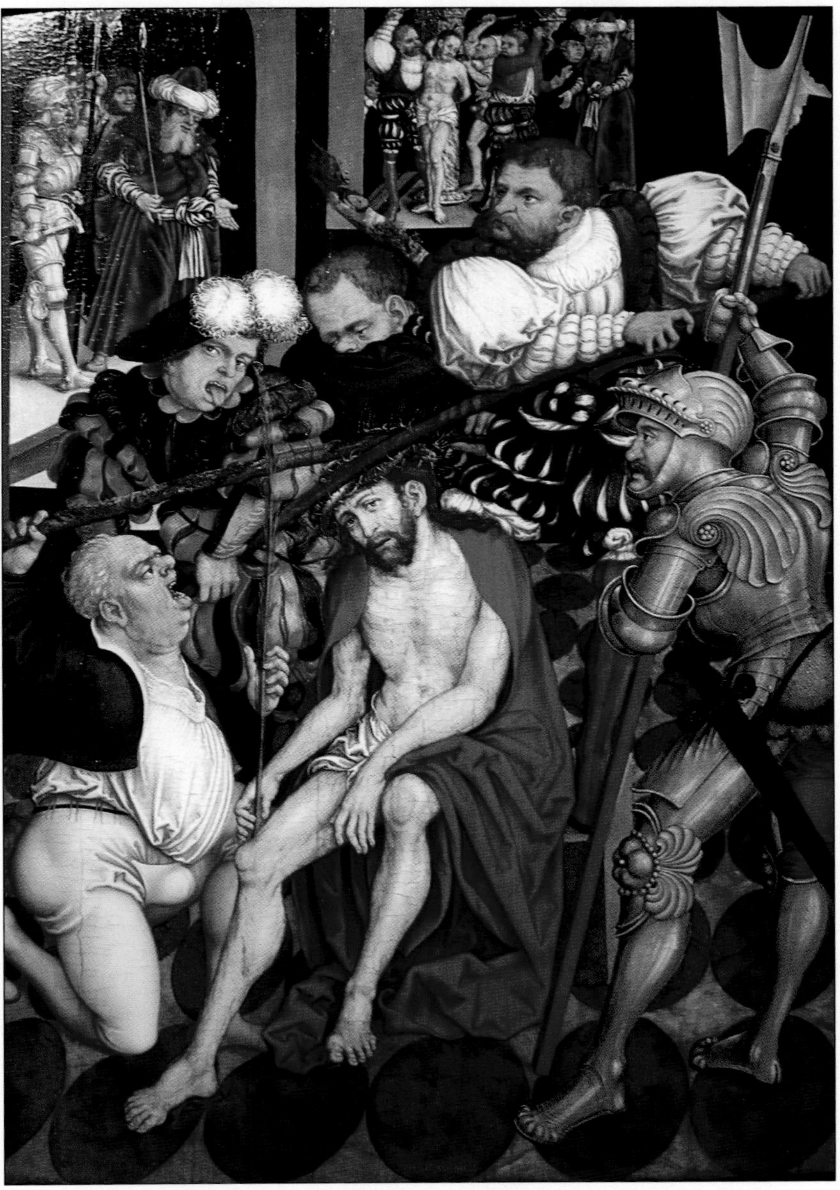

Faces of tormentors exhibit classic expressions of ridicule in "The Mocking of Christ" (Lucas Cranach, 1515). Courtesy of the Lewis Walpole Library, Yale University.

Hans Holbein's religious characters, "The Nun" (1538) and "The Preacher" (1538), are ironically stalked by death as they flirt and pontificate. Courtesy of Peter Huestis, National Gallery of Art.

"Holy Friar" (1807), illustration for Rowlandson the Caricaturist by Joseph Grego (1880). Courtesy of the Lewis Walpole Library, Yale University.

In Sebastian Brandt's classic *Ship of Fools* (c. 1494), Albrecht Dürer gathered various denizens of the religious world practicing their vices. Courtesy of the University of Houston Archives.

With drunkenness, lechery, gluttony, and other vices, Hieronymus Bosch illustrated his "Ship of Fools" (c. 1490–1500) in the late fifteenth century. Courtesy of Art Resource.

RABELAIS dissecting society and writing his book.

Gustave Doré portrayed Rabelais sticking satiric pins in his targets in an illustration from *Gargantua and Pantagruel* (1854). Courtesy of the Houghton Library, Harvard University.

Lucas Cranach the Younger supported the German reformer against the papacy in "Luther Preaching with the Pope in the Jaws of Hell." Calvin, Luther, and Pope pummel and tweak each other. Lucas Cranach the Younger (c. 1600). Courtesy of the Granger Collection.

The Reformers mocked "Where Monks Come From." Courtesy of the Lewis Walpole Library, Yale University. Meanwhile, Johannes Cochlaeus caricatured the German Reformer in his 1529 pamphlet, *Septices Lutherus*, with its cover illustrating the Seven Heads of Martin Luther (Doctor, Martinus, Luther, Clergyman, Enthusiast, Visitor, and Barrabbas) and satirizing him as an Antichrist of the apocalypse in the early sixteenth-century Woodcut Wars. Courtesy of Art Resource.

Puritans were mocked for Sabbath legalism, such as "Hanging a Cat on a Monday for Killing a Mouse on a Sunday" (c. 1616). Courtesy of the Lewis Walpole Library, Yale University.

Engraver William Hogarth's frontispiece illustration to Samuel Butler's satire on the Presbyterian *Hudibras* (1725). Courtesy of the Lewis Walpole Library, Yale University.

Thomas Rowlandson aptly captured "A Sleepy Congregation" (1811). Courtesy of the Lewis Walpole Library, Yale University.

In Jonathan Swift's *Tale of a Tub* (1704), the preacher mounts his pulpit, one of the "oratorical machines" that included the gallows and the stage. Courtesy of the Houghton Library, Harvard University.

Thomas Rowlandson mocked the Anglican Church's exploitation of the poor in "Tithe Pig" (1790), where the cleric with gout surveys his due. Courtesy of the Royal Collection Trust.

In one of his most densely complex satiric engravings, "Credulity, Superstition, and Fanaticism" (1761), Hogarth offers digs on the enthusiasm of Methodists and on elite religious art. Courtesy of the National Gallery of Art.

Hogarth captured the atmosphere of a "Sleeping Congregation" (1736, 1762), with one deacon gazing lustily at a young woman's bodice. Courtesy of the Lewis Walpole Library, Yale University.

An acute Protestant burlesque on "Transubstantiation Satirized" (1794), where one eats the flesh of the Baby Jesus milled through a grinder, possibly by Hogarth (1794). Courtesy of the British Museum.

G. M. Woodward illustrated "A Divine in His Glory" (1799), in which the vicar does the church's business by proxy, loving all doxies, except orthodoxy. Courtesy of the Lewis Walpole Library, Yale University.

In "A Select Vestry" (1806), one of his more decent satires, Rowlandson merrily took on the luxury and gluttony of the wealthier religious class. Courtesy of the Royal Collection Trust.

Rowlandson's "A Man of Feeling" plays off of the Methodist emphasis on enthusiasm, which could be seen as both spiritual and carnal. Courtesy of the Royal Collection Trust and the Lewis Walpole Library, Yale University.

In Richard Newton's comic engraving "Which Way Shall I Turn Me?" (1794), the cleric must choose which of two ways of the flesh he really wants. Courtesy of the Lewis Walpole Library, Yale University.

Richard Newton, who had illustrated Henry Fielding's *Tom Jones*, made a hearty attack on clerical gluttony during a royally proclaimed "Fast Day" (1793). Courtesy of the Lewis Walpole Library, Yale University.

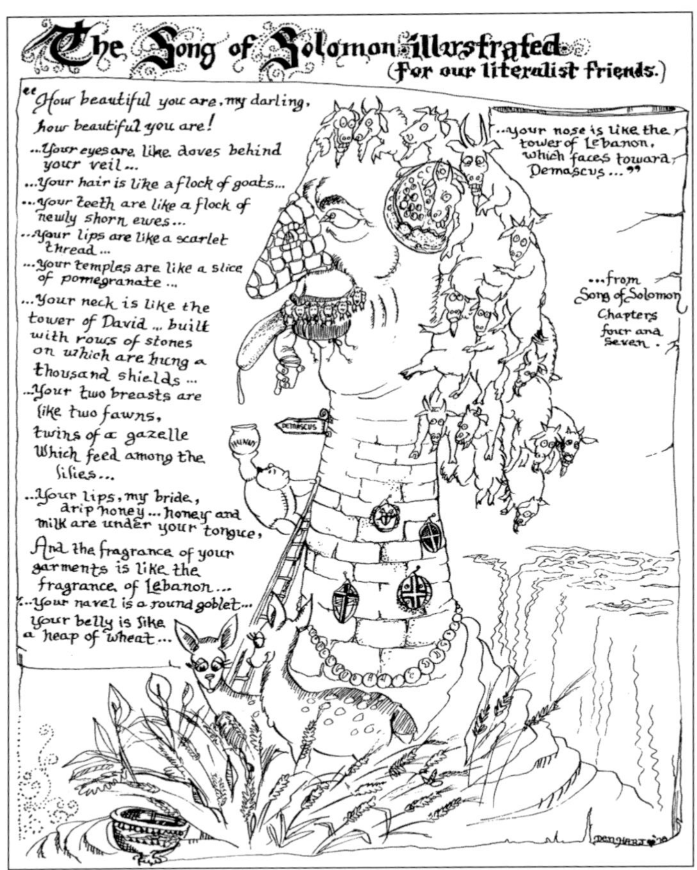

Den Hart's spoofed inerrant interpretations of Scripture in his "The Song of Solomon Literalized" (1978). Courtesy of Robert Darden and the *Wittenburg Door*.

"Folly" (1515) looks in the mirror in Erasmus's *In Praise of Folly*. Courtesy of the Kunstmuseum, Basel.

> Any future historian will certainly want to devote a chapter, if not a volume, to the Christian churches in the mid-twentieth century. Their performance is bound to strike him as hilarious. They were funny enough when with crazy gallantry they tried to defend the Book of Genesis against Darwin's *panzer*; they are even funnier now that, belatedly, they have decided to join the army of progress just when it is in total disarray, if not in headlong retreat. They are like a citadel which resists wave after wave of attack; whose garrison, besieged, starving, decimated, hold desperately on, only when the attackers themselves have lost heart and decided to abandon the struggle, to open the gates and sally forth bearing white flags. Contraceptives and copies of *Lady Chatterley's Lover* have been laid as propitiatory offerings on an expiring altar; the Red Sea opened, but the hosts of Israel, mistaking their direction, took the opportunity to return to Egypt and bondage. [149]

In the political arena, Muggeridge identified himself as a man of the Left, but not diseased like liberals. Appearing on the show *The Firing Line* with conservative William Buckley Jr., he acknowledged his aversion to authority, choosing to identify himself as being on the side of the weaker in a sort of Christian chivalry. He teased that when so many American psychiatrists diagnosed presidential candidate Barry Goldwater as potty, he said that he knew he preferred him to a sane alternative.

In his mildly satirical collection of essays, *Tread Softly for You Tread on My Jokes*, one thought sums up not only his notion of the role of satire, but an underlying theme of this book. "Clearly," he notes, "clearly, the business of a humorous or satirical magazine must be to ridicule the age in which we live, and particularly those set in authority over us. It is the gargoyle grinning beneath the steeple; it is Thersites mocking at pomposity, pretentiousness, self-importance and all the other occupational diseases of the mighty in their seats."[150] It echoes the *Magnificat*, given to Mary, where the proud are scattered and the mighty fall, but delivered with a bit more humor.The modern British invasion of satire revived true satire from traditional and biblical sources. In contrast to the few earlier caustic critics of the religious establishment like Hobbes and Butler, the writers who wedded wit/humor and an appeal for Christians to amend their ways (as well as tweaking the modern mind) fill the Quad. Hogarth, Belloc, Knox, Waugh, Chesterton, Lewis, and Muggeridge stood on foundations of orthodox theology and established morality to yank lethargic, apathetic, and pretentious fellow countrymen to see life and the Catholic faith in new, fresh ways. They tore down only to build up. Key to their strategy was their celebrated identification with their fellow sinners. While Knox wanted satirists to scourge vices like Juvenal and purge consciences like Hogarth, he aimed at straightening a crooked church. Chesterton and Lewis, in particular, set their own fallen nature as the model for satire. One must mock only what one knows in one's heart. The only package that the satirist truly and deeply knows is his own soul. And the confessions and revelation of these British souls became the inspiration for their lively and efficacious satires. But while these British authors were addressing a reflective readership, media would transform satire into the big business of entertainment.

10

Entertainers and Onions

Text! Don't say the Text!
—Monty Python

Monty Python's Flying Circus troupe exploded on the scene in 1969 like a pack of modern goliards, producing BBC sketches like "The Bishop," a faux Church of England production in association with the Sunday Schools Board. The Peter Gunn–type detective series featured the crime-fighting Reverend Nesbitt and his cigarette-smoking clerics. With his crosier, used like Maxwell Smart's shoe phone, the bishop gets emergency calls that vicars are being knocked off at a sermon, baptism, wedding, or funeral. He rushes to the scene and warns the cleric: "Text! Don't say the Text" (Leviticus 3:14), but it is too late, and the vicar explodes, ascending in his pulpit. The bishop laments: "We wuz too late!" While wonderfully silly, the episode captures the futile social and political action of the church in the 1960s. Trying to be trendy and fashionable, the church is too late. Having lost its eternal grounding, it is perennially out of date.

The later twentieth produced a new form of satire, emerging as entertainment business. Through films, television, editorial cartoonists, and Christian magazines like the *Wittenburg Door*, satire took on a professional cast. Yet it also declined as a reforming influence on corruption of religion and culture. While this era invites its own book-length study, several key characters and themes add onions and sauce to the tasty salad.

In their sketch "Crackpot Religions," Monty Python took pot shots at evangelical broadcasting of the 1970s, "barefacedly asking for contributions" in a quid pro quo agreement for salvation. Luther's attack on indulgences has been revived. They expose how the promise of spiritual help is compromised by this business arrangement. Arthur Crackpot, President and God, who inherited the religion from his father, is the official money-grubbing spokesman of the church and offers contests to win a bishopric. The detail of inheriting religion from his father, which is a slighting reference to radio preachers Herbert and Garner Ted Armstrong of the Worldwide Church of God, could be easily applied to a legion of television evangelists.[1] The church, while fun, is only for the wealthy classes.

Archbishop Nudge is the vicar of Naughty Religion, which caters to the "naughty type of person. If you'd like a bit of 'love-your-neighbor'—and who doesn't now and again—then see Vera and Cecily during the hymns." Vicars pilfering from donation boxes, bishops with beer cans, evangelism with sexual license as part of the appeal—all culminate in Terry Gilliam's animated bishop who announces he just wants to be a friend. While he speaks, a devil tries to crawl out of his head, only to be shoved back in, followed by Gilliam's head being nailed shut.[2] Gilliam's Protestant upbringing shape his fantastic satires, and his films reflect the struggle between good and evil, the medieval quest, and a Roman Catholic view of sin.[3]

Probably the most famous episode is "Nobody Expects the Spanish Inquisition," a repetitive play on the inopportune time and ineffectual procedures for inquiring into the lives of modern people. With dramatic musical fanfare, the cardinal inquisitors burst into a tea room, announcing "nobody expects the Spanish Inquisition." Both the timing and the purpose of the church's intervention into the lives of ordinary people seems silly and irrelevant.

While the Python group spouted religious jokes, their crowning achievement in cultural satire began with an idea to produce a naughty movie on Jesus Christ—*Lust for Glory*.[4] Terry Jones explained that as the Monty Python troupe researched the Gospels they found, unexpectedly, that Jesus said great things. They altered their blueprint to deal with how various groups had misinterpreted his words or twisted the message of the Gospel, and thus produced *The Life of Brian* (1979).[5] However, this production of the parodied parallel story of Jesus would become a *cause scandale*. In this satire of misplaced and obsessive faith, Monty Python revived the Rabelaisian spirit of carnival.[6]

The film satirized people's desperate desire for a Messiah, eventually trying to make Brian the Anointed One. Attacks by religious groups followed, with many seeking, without having seen the film, to pressure for censorship, banning, or boycotts. Various misreadings and misinterpretations occurred. Even William Buckley, the articulate Roman Catholic intellectual, opined that "Monty Python himself was crucified at the end of the film, a conclusion that had never occurred to the makers."[7]

In *The Life of Brian*, the meaning of life strikes one as meaningless, even nihilistic. At the culminating crucifixion scene, a chorus line of numerous messiahs hanging on crosses sing: "Life's a laugh and death's the joke, it's true. You'll see it's all a show, keep them laughing as you go. Just remember that the last laugh is on you. Always look on the bright side of life." The lyrics suggest that comedy vainly seeks to fill the void of a God who died for others. When critic Roger Ebert examined *The Life of Brian*, he observed that it did "not mock the life of Christ, but has its fun with the life of one Brian," logically seeking to answer such questions "What would have happened at your typical pre-Christian stoning? How did women find out what was going on when they were allegedly banned from public meetings? What if Pontius Pilate spoke with a lisp?"[8] Rather than being blasphemous, the film, in Ebert's opinion, raised questions about fanatic followers of a religious leader, rather than about Christ himself.

Troupe member Michael Palin revealed a basic assumption of the Python's philosophy when he explained that "if anything can survive the probe of humor it is clearly of value, and conversely all groups who claim immunity from laughter are claiming special privileges which should not be granted."[9] The role of satire in works like *The Life of Brian* is to reveal what is true and good, not just mock it. Their indirect goal, exploiting the title of a book about them, is to "nudge, nudge, think, think."[10]

Lurking Onions

One contemporary source goes for the big laughs and makes its barbed points. *The Onion* is tart and tangy, as exemplified in its classic "Why Are We Skipping Church" survey, presented like a Gallup poll. It lists compelling reasons, such as nobody really listens to sermons, still getting over a big argument with God, Sunday morning being the most convenient time to covet one's neighbor's wife, or Denny's Restaurant had a better pun on its sign out front.[11]

Dispatches from *The Onion* fit our definition of satire, with pungent observations of human religious behavior served with spicy wit in a way that recalls Sydney Smith's recipe in which onions lurk to animate the salad of life. After a startling headline of "God Answers Prayers of Paralyzed Boy," a subheading adds, "'No.', God Says." The mysterious ways of God are reduced to a sardonic commentary in which "no" is a reasonable option.[12] Skewering the superstitious paranoia of some fundamentalists over the wizardry of Rowling's best-selling series, a headline blazons "Harry Potter Books Spark Rise in Satanism among Children," with the article going on to note that some kids now believe that magic is real and the Bible stories are lies. The tendency of some religious groups toward condemnation of nonbelievers found a sly article on Pope John Paul II entitled "Pope Calls for Greater Understanding between Catholics, Hellbound."[13]

Identifying fodder ripe for derision, *The Onion* constructs very funny juxtapositions. Even with no ostensible motive for reform and no heart for engaging its targets, it points to comic incongruities in religion. The claim by televangelists and other religious leaders to have received direct communication from God garners its own spoofing in the report that "Christ 'Categorically Denies' Speaking to Lutheran-College Administrator":

> Jesus Christ insisted to reporters Monday that He has "absolutely never spoken" to Philip Burkett, rejecting the 48-year-old Lutheran-college administrator's claim of having "a close, personal relationship" with the prominent savior. The Lord responded at a press conference called to quell rumors of a Christ-Burkett dialogue: "I categorically deny having had any prior contact whatsoever with Mr. Burkett. At no point have I ever conversed with this man."[14]

Open Doors

Satire from within the church emerged in Christian publications in the late twentieth century when publishers Wayne Rice and Mike Yaconelli, editor Denny Rydberg, and a host of motley writers satirized all that was fit to be skinned.[15] Starting with a four-page mimeographed sheet shared with youth workers in southern California in 1969, they published their first sixteen-page satiric magazine, the *Wittenburg Door*, in June 1971. They accidentally misspelled the title on the masthead and decided not to change it. They pushed for church reform and renewal, such as "exposing a well-known evangelist who shacks up with converts at his crusades" by using a sense of humor. According to his wife, Karla, editor Yaconelli used the "vehicle of the *Door*" for over twenty years to "expose the outrageously fallacious and downright ridiculous things being done in the name of the Jesus he so loved."[16]

The *Door* supplied playfully serious interviews (with, for instance, Tony Campolo and Fred Rogers), "Losers of the Month," and special awards of Green Weenies. The magazine mocked itself: one front cover of an issue entitled "Corruption and the Church" showed a robed and collared assembly of clergy (all staff members), seemingly pious, but on the inside of the cover, seen from behind, they steal from each other, hide pornography in a back pocket, practice graft, and backstab.[17] In another issue on "Merchandizing the Gospel," slickly advertised with a glossy silver cover, a cartoon juxtaposes an old wooden cross with a neon cross. The *Door* mocks real events ("Girl who strips for God—Live! On Stage!" at a local church) and takes on real crises such as divorce, homosexuality, pornography ("You must be Porn again"), and rock and roll. The magazine plays coy with a cartoon of "We Found 'It'" bumper stickers, with various denominations doing "it" in different ways (except the Baptists, who don't do "it"); it also produced an evangelical swimsuit issue.

One sterling cartoon is "The Song of Solomon Illustrated: For Our Literalist Friends," a literal drawing of the description of the beloved from the Hebrew poetic book.[18] When the neck is described as the tower of David, we see its stones; when breasts are compared to two fawns grazing among the lilies, we see the young deer feeding. The one to one correspondence of descriptive detail to image cleverly reveals how holy scriptures should not invite mere literal interpretations.

As "The World's Pretty Much Only Religious Satire Magazine," the *Door* kicked sacred cows, attacked jocks for Jesus, showed the further adventures of the Reverend Oral Fixation, and provided an issue on "The Totaled Woman," a parody of Marabel Morgan's *The Total Woman* (in which Morgan recommended that Christian women welcome their husbands home from work at the front door wearing only transparent saran wrap), complete with a centerfold.[19] The cover showed a slovenly, elderly woman, legs askew, wearing curlers, with Pepto Bismal and dentures beside her, and a foot in a water pail reading Morgan's book recommending that Christian women wear only saran wrap to the front door to meet their husbands.[20]

For Yaconelli, satire was by necessity a risky business. He felt strongly that one cannot satirize with integrity without loving those whom one satirizes. "He who inflicts must feel the pain himself—otherwise he would be just an executioner."[21] But pain is necessary for healing the sickness of the soul.

Contributing Editor Ben Patterson pointed to the need for a "little detachment" in producing humor. Becoming aware of "the disparity between who you think you are and who you really are" enables one to avoid, in part, the danger of committing idolatry and making light of what is sacred; it also enables one to leaven satire with compassion. Humor ceases to follow a Christian ethic, observed Patterson, when it "starts to get destructive, when its basic thrust is to titter, to sneer, to be habitually destructive, rather than be constructive."[22] Underlying such risks is the trap of arrogance, of seeing yourself as the savior satirist.

Novel Approaches

While not usually recognized as a comic Christian, southern gothic author Flannery O'Connor crafted dark and delightfully haunting portraits of the modern condition. In *Mystery and Manners*, she astutely distinguished the Christian novelist from pagan colleagues, noting that the former recognizes "sin as sin. . . . Either one is serious about salvation or one is not. And it is well to realize that the maximum amount of seriousness admits the maximum amount of comedy. Only if we are secure in our beliefs can we see the comical side of the universe."[23]

Comic writers who challenged and simultaneously invigorated faith include O'Connor with her grotesque and violent humor and depictions of peacocks and crow-filled trees, stolen wooden legs, and tattoos of Christ; Walker Percy (*Lost in the Cosmos*; *The Moviegoer*), who slashed satiric targets like pop psychology, which promoted a false sense of health, and who stripped away the fig leaves of self-delusion; and the most Horatian of present communicators, Frederick Buechner (*Telling the Truth: The Gospel as Tragedy, Comedy and Fairy Tale*; *The Book of Bebb*), lays peculiar treasures of the nicked and ragged souls of humanity before his readers.[24] Each, in his or her own way, confronts their readers with their own flawed souls, and yet lifts up the hope and possibility of redemption. They satirize with a vision.[25]

Buechner tells his grandmother's story of a swelteringly hot Sunday morning in which a minister wore nothing under his black robe but what God had given him. Getting excited in the pulpit, he fell over almost into the laps of the congregation and the gown swooped up over his head. He yelled out to his congregation to shut their eyes, saying, "May anyone who looks be struck blind." The whole congregation obeyed except Grandma, who peeked with one eye open, explaining, "I'll risk just one." The experience of reading satire is similar; one doesn't really want to be altered, but there is something tempting, something fun, about exposing yourself to someone exposing even more.[26]

One finds suffering, tragedy, deep sadness, and the presence of evil in Buechner's works; yet in his world, the unexpectedly comic prevails. It is not chirpy optimism, but a grace and gladness that come serendipitously. Buechner's comedy strips the human of pretense. When an atheist debates the perverted but believing Leo Bebb (a sort of Pantagruel), both agree to recognize the "great fecal indictment" of the world, that sin and shit exist. But Buechner affirms even this stink: for him "the shit of the world is productive; if you don't pile it too thick in one place, it makes the seed grow."[27]

Buechner follows Pascal's *Pensées* and Bierce's *Devil's Dictionary* with his little dictionary books, or "mongrel litters" such as *Wishful Thinking* and *Peculiar Treasures*, the latter a Who's Who of the Bible, raising the questions of why God chose the people as mentioned in Exodus 19:5. For example, he introduces Elijah under King Ahab: "If, generally speaking, a prophet to a king was like ants at a picnic, Elijah was a swarm of bees."[28] In *Wishful Thinking*, he defines terms like "anger": "Of the Seven Deadly Sins, anger is possibly the most fun. To lick your wounds, to smack your lips over grievances long past . . . to savor to the last toothsome morsel both the pain you are given and the pain you are giving back—in many ways it is a feast fit for a king. The chief drawback is that what you are wolfing down is yourself. The skeleton at the feast is you."[29] However, Buechner warned, satire moves into irreverence at the point at which "the humor becomes an end in itself, instead of a way of pointing to a truth beyond itself."[30]

Satirical Catechesis

While television satirist Jon Stewart is politically savvy and sharp in deconstructive satire, his former colleague, ersatz conservative Stephen Colbert, has taken on the mantle of Elijah.[31] Columnist Matt Emerson sees in the former Comedy Central host a covert Roman Catholic catechist, sneaking apologetics into hostile territory through his razor-sharp satire.[32] Modeled on the self-congratulatory bombastic character of television news commentators of both political parties, Colbert wears the ironic mask of a classic satirist, like Kierkegaard, on the *Colbert Report*. One just can't tell where he stands on issues, but the issues come into focus in all their complexity and moral cogency. Unlike Jon Stewart's politically driven the *Daily Show*, the *Colbert Report* takes on topics of religion with unmitigated bravado and with cheek, mainly because Colbert knows of which he speaks.[33]

As a practicing Roman Catholic teaching Sunday school, Colbert confessed to a wild "Catholic bender" after a rough weekend. It had started, he said, on Holy Thursday night. Walking past St. Patrick's Cathedral, Colbert "caught a little whiff of incense." Not long after, he was "stumbling through the streets of Manhattan in a chasuble and mitre begging for quarters to buy votive candles." He later "genuflected all over the back of a cab" and eventually passed out near an "abbot illuminating a manuscript." The bacchanal included a concurrent saying of the Hail Mary and the Our Father, or in Colbert's words, "the Catholic speedball. I guess I just have to accept," Colbert concluded, "that I'm a functional Roman Catholic."[34]

Colbert defines satire as "parody with a point."[35] Colbert, who sometimes agrees with his own impertinent character, plays the wise fool with rapid-fire wit. His Roman Catholic roots show forth in supporting the oppressed and needy and in dealing with issues of poverty, suffering, and doubt. When he spoke on Capitol Hill and championed migrant farm workers, he reminded the lawmakers of an old biblical adage: "And, you know, whatsoever you do for the least of my brothers, and these seem like the least of our brothers right now, [you do it to me,]" Colbert said, quoting Jesus. "Migrant workers suffer and have no rights. . . . If this is going to be a Christian nation that doesn't help the poor, either we have to pretend that Jesus was just as selfish as we are, or we've got to acknowledge that He commanded us to love the poor and serve the needy without condition and then admit that we just don't want to do it."[36]

Raised by devout Catholic intellectuals, Colbert the man regularly attends Mass, observes Lent, recites the Nicene Creed, reads the Bible, and teaches Sunday school. "I was raised to believe that you could question the Church and still be a Catholic," he says. "What is worthy of satire is the misuse of religion for destructive or political gains. That's totally different from the Word, the blood, the body and the Christ. His kingdom is not of this earth."[37]

Colbert is probably the only satirist who has sought out his own confessor to oversee that unruly member, his tongue. The Roman Catholic author Friar James Martin (*My Life with the Saints*) serves as unofficial chaplain for the television show, providing insight on salient religious topics like social justice and treatment of the poor. The priest observes that Colbert takes the core doctrines of his faith seriously and actually offers a sort of catechesis for lapsed Catholics; yet in a double mask, his holier than thou persona subverts and reaffirms his orthodoxy. At the end of one interview with Martin, Colbert intoned, "Father, this interview has ended. Go in peace to love and serve the Lord."[38]

Interviewing author Stephen Prothero (*God Is Not One*) on the *Colbert Report*, the host zestfully zeroed in on the question, "Which religion is the best?" Colbert had given up Catholicism for Lent (and ruefully gave up Judaism because it was too fun), so he opened himself up to learn of Islam (the fast growing religion but one with the greatest public relations problems), Quakers (any religion that calls itself "Friends" comes across as "a little too desperate"), and Hinduism (exploring the past lives of Stephen's reincarnated cat).[39]

In the tradition of the holy fool, Colbert throws nuts at any pontificating Pharisee, from the "monkey men" who believe in evolution to those "heathen and excommunicated" Christians who are not Roman Catholic, exuding perverse delight in Pope Benedict XVI's pronouncement that the faith of non-Catholics was "defective." "Catholicism is clearly superior," Colbert crowed beside a picture of the pope. "Don't believe me? Name one Protestant denomination that can afford a $660 million sexual abuse settlement." It wasn't just funny, blogger Diane Houdek said, but "powerful."[40] Here is a man who mocks the powerful and proud, with unbridled liberty.

Colbert's provocative satire dances on a fine line of offensive rhetoric; yet like Chesterton, he dances well. According to Martin, "he shows what is important to the faith and what can genuinely be debated and disparaged." Taking his faith seriously, he takes his own role lightly.[41]

On a channel notorious for coarse humor, here is a satirist chatting up his audience with lectures on saints and sacraments, poking the pope with playful reminders to do his duty, and reminding Christians of their sacred book and traditions. He promotes the moral reform of his own church as much as puncturing the image of Christians as dour and dismal pious people. He shows that intellectual challenges and attached joys are to be found in grappling with and satirizing one's own family of faith. Due to Colbert's indirect satire, he does not easily disclose an agenda. As with the parables of Jesus, one is not quite sure what he is really saying in his monologues, interviews, and skits, but one has a notion that it strikes deeply into the heart, while jogging the lungs with unexpected laughter.

Yet when Colbert introduces his best-selling book, *I Am America*, with a quotation from the Doobie Brothers, "Jesus is just all right with me," he adds his commentary, "but are they all right with Jesus? Drop the reefer, boys, and pick up a Bible!" If we lose our religion, Colbert warns, we would "exist in a state of valueless depravity, like they do in Holland."[42] Like Ambrose Bierce, Colbert identifies key terms and events (along with *sotto voce* inserts), such as the goat path to Protestantism (defined as "a variant form of Christianity, or 'heresy'"). Of the Methodists, he asks, "What, the Church of England wasn't heretical enough for you?" (adding the admonition, "don't be a Meth-head"). While atheism was merely a religion "dedicated to its own sense of smug superiority," agnostics should be viewed as "atheists without balls."[43]

In an interview with Terry Gross of National Public Radio, Colbert explained that he did a segment called "This Week in God" for Jon Stewart's *Daily Show*. He confessed that such a sketch put him on "a tightrope, because I—while I'm, you know, not a particularly religious person, I do go to church, which makes me kind of odd for my profession. You know, most people can't understand why I do, other comedians. And I have to walk that thin line because I don't want to criticize anyone's religion for the fact that it is a religion, and what's funny to me is what people do in the name of religion."[44] Asked how he dealt with the contradictions between his Church's teachings (on, for instance, birth control) and his understanding of the issues, he pointed out that the American Catholic church is not homogenous and does not aim to make zombies or unquestioning people, but values critical loyalty.

Colbert's fascination with religion and comedy led to his thinking about how the "dissonance between the two affects a performer who is actually a believer." He acknowledged that it is more difficult to be comical around a core belief, but that's what makes it all fascinating. On the other hand, Bill Maher can joke about religion because he *hates* it. The challenge is to discern how to satirize what one loves and skip among the landmines. The key criterion for Colbert is whether material disrespects religious belief. However, if someone is using religion as a tool in a destructive or hypocritical way, then all is fair game. He argues that one must retain one's humanity: "If you don't think like a joke is more important than being humane, like not talking about tragedy or not questioning someone's dearly held beliefs religiously, if you can keep in mind a certain level of humanity, then that's a good guide as to what you can and cannot talk about."[45]

Few satirists expose themselves to public challenge with their targets as much as Colbert, who has interviewed belligerent atheists. Guest psychologist Philip Zimbardo interpreted Adam and Eve in a preposterous way, suggesting that God introduced evil into the world by inventing hell. Colbert responded that evil exists due to the disobedience of Satan, who forcibly removed himself from God's love. He then went on to define hell as the absence of God's love and to argue that God doesn't send you to hell, but you send yourself there. Zimbardo feebly tried to counter with a condescending jibe about Colbert's probably learning his lessons in Sunday school, to which Colbert retorted, "I *teach* Sunday school *motherfucker*!" The brash journalistic spirit of Mencken lives on—however, converted to the good side.

This abbreviated sketch of twentieth-century religious satire suggests a tendency of secular satire like that of Monty Python and *The Onion* to follow the Continental emphases of Voltaire, yet without the sneer and with much more hilarity. Their Christian counterparts, such as the

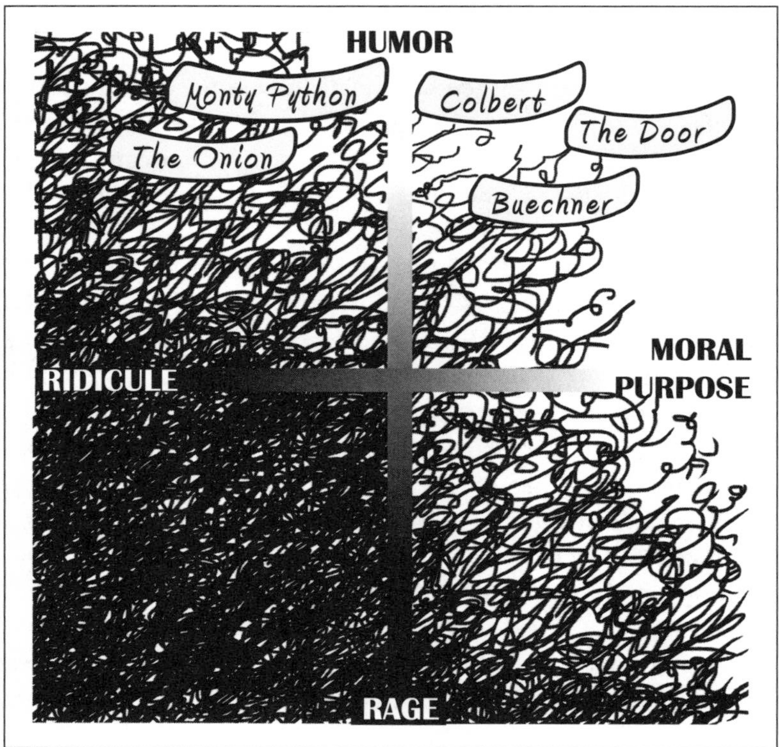

Monty Python, the *Onion*, Colbert, Buechner, and the *Door* on the Quad of Satire.

editors of the *Door* and individual authors like Buechner, poke at fellow saints within the tents of fellowship. Others like syndicated cartoonists Johnny Hart and Wayne Stayskal shoot arrows in the public arena, being saints that mock their culture with piercing quills. However, the apotheosis of true satire stumbles forth in a Kierkegaardian persona of Stephen Colbert. Few pundits take the Christian tradition so soberly yet wear the motley of the fool.

Conclusion

A Fool's Apology and Palinode

If God lived on earth, people would break His windows.
—Yiddish proverb

Satire may sound cruel, like something practiced by mean girls, heartless cynics, or irascible journalists. Yet it appears frequently in the chronicles of the people of God wrestling with each other, and with him, and is also used by their opponents. Saints are mocked, and saints mock others. Satire's central reason for existence is to bring about positive change through humor and wit. It testifies to the ultimate dignity of men and women, even when it laughs at them, or maybe especially when they are the object of the joke.

However, as we have seen, the rhetorical art of religious satire rarely seems to fulfill its purpose of reform with humor. The quadrant presented at the outset of this book may well be a mere façade. In delivering the National Endowment of the Humanities lectures on "Humor and Social Change," scholar Joseph Boskin argued that in spite of its unwelcome intrusion into the many rooms of the American mansions, including those sacred places of religious institutions, humor still invades public squares with serious purposes. But he failed to demonstrate how it actually eventuated into personal or public reform.[1]

So What?

So what might we conclude from all this satire, this scoffing, this dung? In reflecting upon the chronicle of historical practices, we can make seven closing observations concerning the nature and functions of religious satire.

1. True satire requires both wit and moral purpose. Without the first, it is mere condemnation; without the second, it is mere venting of

> the spleen. The employers of the former are the carpers and fault-finders who inhabit any university faculty, sucking laughter out of any fruit. They do not realize that taking something seriously does not mean taking it solemnly. The latter are the sophomores, those who take it all flippantly. They joke but have no purpose beyond cackling laughter.[2]

Alvin Kernan, in *The Cankered Muse*, identifies the two poles around which the definitions of satire revolve: wit and morality. Satire exists to attack fools (and perhaps even improve knaves, although few having teenage sons hold this hope) and correct their folly. With Erasmus, we praise folly ironically in order to discourage folly.

Humor, without a moral purpose, slips into something too comfortable, like spoofing, and unlike satire, as film critic Pauline Kael pointed out, "spoofing has no serious objectives; it doesn't attack anything that anyone could take seriously; it has no cleansing power. It's just a technique of ingratiation: the spoof apologizes for its existence, assures us that it is harmless."[3]

Scholar Conrad Hyers defended satire's use by explaining that "Faith without laughter leads to dogmatism and self-righteousness. Laughter without faith leads to cynicism and despair."[4] Satire must contain both a standard of goodness and a tangy touch of wit, a teeter-totter balancing with equal measures of wit and righteousness. One problem is that satirists are a bit more disposed to castigate wickedness and folly than to exhort virtue and wisdom. This may be why theologian Reinhold Niebuhr confined humor to the "outer sanctuaries" of religious life. Some humor, like satire, tends to have dirty hands, and may need to be cleaned before coming to the wedding feast.

The moral purpose of satire assumes an objective standard that the satirist believes the target will recognize. It would be mere debunking if the satirist wanted only to ruffle some feathers. The true satirist builds his or her case on the idea that the *Tao* exists, that a natural law judges the vice and stupidity of the target.[5] Thus are sinners put into the hands of an angry and funny satirist.

In a letter to his friend Martin Dorp in May 1515, Erasmus defended his folly of trying to do good. He claimed that he didn't merely open a sewer of vice (although facts about bad popes, scandalous bishops, and corrupt priests abound) or splatter anyone with a spot of mud. Quite unlike Plato, St. Jerome and others who did let off steam against specific enemies, Erasmus stayed cool. He preferred to err on the side of charity, arguing that it is "not Christian to repay one insult with another." Leave such behavior to slanging matches between fishwives. Erasmus defends himself by quoting Horace, "telling the truth in a joke, what's wrong with that?"[6] For Erasmus, nothing.

In this wedding of humor and moral reform, the marriage must be built on love. Edward and Lillian Bloom propose that the satirist must "love or at least care for mankind to take the trouble to attack and (hopefully) correct his wickedness."[7] We could say that this is the satirist's practical application of Christ's injunction to love our enemies as found in the Gospels (Matthew 5:44, Luke 6:27–28). Otherwise, we are merely throwing eggs or pies in faces.

2. The history of religious satire shows common threads in subject and style, even as it suggests different emphases during different eras.

Satire must speak truth to power, with wit or coarse humor. It must speak against those principalities and powers of folly that shadow every age.[8] Each era is marked by a particular vice that satire seeks to sting, scald, and correct. In Hebrew wisdom literature, the psalmist celebrates that the "righteous man will laugh" at the mighty man, saying, "Here now is the man who did not make God his stronghold, but trusted in his great wealth and grew strong by destroying others" (Psalm 52:6–7).

One consistent theme across the centuries is an attack on corruption. As cartoonist John Lawing observed, satire demonstrates the doctrine of the Fall. We all know we do not live as we ought. And the effects of the Fall on those with power is even more obvious.

Satirists differ on whether one can attack specific individuals or should instead portray generic types, but all find targets in those who lord over others with arrogance, stupidity, or hypocrisy. The targets endure even as the human endures. There has been no progressive sanctity in the human race; we may have even degenerated. Satire is at its best when it attacks something more powerful than its satirist. The Hebrew proverb warns that those who mock the poor insult their maker and will be punished. Rather, one must find an intimidating and worthwhile enemy. As C. S. Lewis noted, it is "more dangerous to tread on the corns of a live giant, than to cut off the head of a dead one; but it is [also] more useful and better fun."[9]

Differences among satiric frames come from the dominance of a particular contemporary vice. Hebrew prophets took on idolatry, sexual immorality, and social injustices, using carefully crafted digs at those who presumed to be the people of God without responsibility. In contrast to the professional Romans, the Hebrew prophets were amateurs, though highly effective. The early church took on heretics and religious leaders. Medieval satire wildly ran amok against the folly of monks, with Rabelais and Erasmus perfecting the art. In the motley tradition of troubadours and jokesters, preachers were the roosters that woke the world with satire or put them to sleep without it.

A decadent papacy became the target of reformers, even as Luther and his posse became the target of the counter-reformers. The rhetorical artisans of Swift, Pope, and their august company took on fellow poets, whose pride and vanity begged for correction. While rascals like Robert Burns exposed the hypocrisy of his neighbors by confessing his own sins, the Victorian era followed and castigated cant. Early Americans harped on elitist pride, which for the agnostic cynics frequently meant the members of the religious community. Voltaire, Kierkegaard, and the Continentals elevated wit and irony as a means of bringing low those who exalted themselves. Whatever claimed reverences risked ridicule. Finally, while Catholic British authors smuggled Christian orthodoxy back into the conversation, many modern media satirists evolved into entertainers, more eager for a laugh than a change of heart.

3. Religious satire is an effective form of indirect communication, except when it is misunderstood by its audiences. It provides sudden shifts in perspective that surprise and delight and make the target laugh at his or her own self.

In his *Concluding Scientific Postscript*, Kierkegaard's Johannes Climacus recognizes the comic as a necessary means of "indirect communication." It helps to shatter the illusions of the affective poet, the practical businessman, and speculative philosopher. Any thinker who tries to approach the religious question in an inappropriately objective manner is caught in the grip of an illusion that invites the comic, or the satirical, to jolt him or her from stupidity.[10] To those entrenched in the religious illusion of Christendom, Kierkegaard found the indirect means of humor and irony to be the most effective: it forced one to think subjectively and to see oneself from the outside.[11] As gadfly, Kierkegaard prodded his readers to interpret for themselves. The mockery of the jester goes inward, "and we're to recognize ourselves in his fool's mirror."[12] One must awaken rather than lecture. "Christ has not appointed assistant professors," quipped Kierkegaard, "but followers."

If the indirect communication does not work, if the satirist cannot connect with his topic, the result is both tragic and comic. Jonathan Swift was taken to the asylum he had founded in his youth and then he quietly lost his senses there. A story is told that he would often stand before a mirror with an absence of mind and look at himself and mutter, "Poor old man!" The satirist who does not recognize him- or herself, even in direct reflection, will not recognize him- or herself in indirect communication.

But those who do see the comedy of their situation will laugh. In *Either/Or*, a character relates a wonderful experience in which he is taken to heaven and given a wish.

> "Wilt thou," said Mercury, "Have youth or beauty or power or a long life or the most beautiful maiden or any of the other glories we have in the chest? Choose, but only one thing." For a moment I was at a loss. Then I addressed myself to the gods as follows: "Most honorable contemporaries, I choose this one thing, that I may always have the laugh on my side." Not one of the gods said a word; on the contrary, they all began to laugh. From that I concluded that my wish was granted, and found that the gods knew how to express themselves with taste; for it would hardly have been suitable for them to have answered gravely: "Thy wish is granted."[13]

4. Religious satire is necessary and useful, but it may have unintended consequences.

Critic Harry Boonstra proposed that satire constituted an essential aspect of the religious life, a mode that "could be useful and promote health in the body ecclesiastic."[14] His opinion is countered by numerous other critics, who experienced uneasiness and uncertainty with of the presence satire in the vestibules of God, as though an ass had appeared in church. Is one laughing at God? If so, the guardians of the faith need not worry. God can take care of himself.

The sharp prophetic polemics and the gentle graces of humor can be brought together for good purposes, exposing, scourging, and correcting. Theoretically, open democratic governments encourage the use of satire and are able to absorb the barbs. Not so the tyranny of authoritarian organizations, including certain religious establishments.[15]

Satire offends. Satire is meant to disturb the universe, or at least one person. In his work on blasphemy, Brent Plate argues that it is an "art that offends."[16] The power of offensive images to elicit violent reactions occurs in the realm of sacrilege, a mode of discourse given the full protection of free speech. The dire consequences, however, have appeared in the radical Islamic responses to the Danish cartoons of Muhammad (with the ensuing murder of Dutch filmmaker Theo Van Gogh and the fatwa on numerous other cartoonists and publishers). Insulting or cursing God privately is not as dangerous as letting his disciples know that you don't think too highly of their divinity.

Nevertheless, something satirical can be both hilarious and blasphemous or sacrilegious. That is because the nature of humor is rooted in a causal principle (whether incongruity or superiority) that certain forms will elicit laughter. A jest can be both funny and morally bad. The ethic of the joke is secondary to its structure. If it is well made, it will cause laughter. However, once the laugh escapes, one can assess its goodness or evil.

Satire dwells with the vulgar, and even the obscene. Bahktin demonstrated that the highest cannot stand without the lowest. Carnival itself offers a topsy-turvy world—one wherethe lunatics take over the asylum, where humor that is grotesque, ambivalent, and universal is celebrated, and where nonsense reigns so that sense can see its own limits.

College of William and Mary professor John Morreall visited my class on Humor and Theology at the Duke Divinity School and listed a litany of complaints against humor.[17] The very humorous man (he made me laugh out loud) pronounced various judgments that had been levied on religion and laughter, namely, that it was insincere, idle, hedonistic, and prone to foster sexually licentious behaviors. These objections boiled down to the fact that laughter offends the solemn and sanctimonious, those who seek to be more spiritual than God. Morreall also suggested that the Christian must be wholly serious in his or her eternal calling, setting seriousness against comedy. However, comedy's true antonym is triviality; the opposite of the comic is the tragic. Something can therefore be both serious and comic simultaneously.

Religious satire has consequences because it frequently supplies prophetic laughter, a satiric resistance to evil and folly. The pen-wielding satirist is not the most imposing of people (nor the most welcome), but does his or her duty with bravado. Conrad Hyers observed that the comic spirit of this satirist is "iconoclastic, and in that sense has a genuinely prophetic dimension. . . . It topples our various idols, punctures high-flying balloons, and kicks pompous asses."[18] Satire is thus a dangerous sport, as is juggling with knives. In his "Discourse Concerning Satire," Dryden conceded how easy it was to call one's adversary a "rogue and villain and that wittily! But how hard to make a man appear a fool, a blockhead, or a knave without using any of those opprobrious terms!" Yet this pontificating poet called out the Duke of Buckingham, flaying him with names like "fiddler" and "buffoon." However, when the Duke met Dryden in a coffeehouse, he caned him and said, "There, Sir, is for your ill manners." And then gave him a purse of thirty guineas, adding, "And here Sir, is for your wit."[19] Wit may be both reprimanded and rewarded.

The consequences of satirical ideas do not only agitate the targets. Free speech may guarantee the right to speak, but it has not historically protected the jester, nor can it safeguard the soul. The satirist believes, dangerously, that it is his or her calling to ridicule others in the name of God. Satire thus has a corrosive effect even upon its practitioners; it pricks one's own conscience even as one is using it. (One lies awake at night repenting of words uttered during the day, often stuck in a self-accusing mantra of "Stupid! Stupid! Stupid!") The blades of wit shave both ways. It may even compound the anger or frustration of the user, and thus we are more akin to Dorothy Parker, famous wit of the Algonquin Table, who confessed that every time she tried to define humor, "I had to go and lie down with a cold wet cloth on my head."[20] The vocation of the satirist is precarious. He or she is too close to the fool, whose lips bring strife and whose "mouth invites a beating" (Proverbs 18:6).

The consequences of satire are felt not only by society, but by the satirist as well. In 1507, Fra Sarafino, an Italian jester-priest whose mirth ranged from putting pancakes on his head to joking about cardinals and the pope, received one of the worst drubbings of any satirist and had his knuckles sliced.[21] Such dangers sparked Alexander Pope to keep his big dog Bounce with him on his daily walks, as well as two loaded pistols. Ever fearful, Samuel Butler allegedly worried and starved while the king had a copy of *Hudibras* in his pocket. Even King Lear's Fool is warned that if his truths stab too deeply, "take heed, sirrah, the whip!"

For the religious satirist, everything is a fair target, even representations of God. However, while everything is lawful, not everything is edifying. Nothing is safe from the poking of the satirist. However, if God allowed the scoffing of his son on the cross, might he not allow any and every form of mocking? This questions leads to another insight.

5. The history of religious satire is ambivalent with respect to the efficacy of its art. It may not be recognized or understood by its audience.

When the Apostle Paul argued at Mars Hill with the Athenians about the resurrection, some sneered and some believed. Good satirical sermons can lead to confession and change, but more likely, they lead to dismissal. One can laugh and move on. Professor Leonard Feinberg saw satire as peculiarly ineffective as persuasion. It does, he suggested, appeal more to the intellect and can be quite ambiguous and puzzling; as such, it rarely offers the catharsis of tragedy. It often deals with uncomfortable truths and is viewed as negative and even cruel, given that humans need their illusions.[22]

Researchers Charles Gruner and William Lampton explored what would happen with the inclusion of "humorous material in a persuasive *sermon*."[23] The results of their study were inconclusive. They could not determine if the sermon to get people to read their Bibles was more persuasive if it included humor, but the use of humor did make a more positive impact on the "image" of the speaker, whose ethos or credibility was enhanced by the use of humor. Gruner's experiments also pointed to the fact that informed audiences were much more likely to be persuaded than naïve ones. It seems that for a satirical message to be effective, an informed target is required. Stupid people just don't get satire. If the message remains too obscure or ambiguous, if it is not understood or is misunderstood, of course it cannot be effectively communicated. And if one is satirizing the ignorance of a reader, and the reader doesn't get it, can the satire work?

Nevertheless, when one's own folly is recognized in a satire, it can alter behavior. A sudden shift of perspective makes hearers aware of their shortcomings and causes them to erupt in laughter. An old joke by preacher Chuck Swindoll satirizing the creeping indifference of husbands to the plight of wives illustrates such a possibility. A couple went to a counselor. As the husband sat in a chair, bored and resistant, the wife complained and cried and wailed to the psychiatrist. "When we dated he was so interested in me, asking me questions and doing little acts of kindness to me. Now that we are married, he never communicates with me; all he ever does is sit there, watch television, and ignore me."

The counselor got up and walked over to the woman. He picked her up, bent her over and gave her a long passionate kiss. She sat there stunned and breathless.

Turning to the husband, he advised: "She needs *that* at least twice a week."

The husband looked up and said: "Okay, how about I bring her in on Tuesdays and Thursdays?"

Most husbands and wives who have heard this joke, get it. And it may even alter the husband's behavior for the rest of the afternoon, if he remembers it. Kierkegaard pointed out how we all miss the point of satire, even in the inadvertent slips of our own honest tongues. In the magnificent cathedral, the honorable and Right Reverend Geheime-General-Ober-Hof-Pradikant, the darling of the fashionable world, appears before an elect company and preaches with emotion upon the text he himself elected: "God has chosen the base things of this world, and the things that are despised"—and, Kierkegaard notes, nobody laughs.[24]

The enduring question remains: Does satire work? Historical perspectives do not augur well for success. Did the negative, scathing rhetoric of the sixteenth-century accomplish anything good? When English Lord Chancellor Thomas More called Tyndale a "babbler and a devil's ape" and Luther "a pimp, an apostate, a rustic, and a friar," or when Luther launched his attack against the "sludge of the harlot's lies and whoring" of the Roman hierarchy, did good come of it?[25] One thinks not. The great divide between religious adversaries merely grew larger, wider, and more vicious. Such satirists would rather win the battle of wits than win a friend. Back in the early eighteenth century, the publisher of the *Tatler*, Richard Steele, who sought to ridicule the cunning, vanity, and affectation of his age, argued that "the wits of this island, for above fifty years past, instead of correcting the vices of this age, have done all they could to inflame them."[26] Satirists were more like biting beasts of prey or annoying insects than physicians of the soul.

Alexander Pope bid "farewell to satire" in a final footnote in his *Epilogue to the Satires*. He protested the "insuperable corruption and depravity" of humankind; as "bad men had grown so shameless and so powerful, that Ridicule was become as unsafe as it was ineffectual."[27] So, too, the hymnist Cowper lamented,

> What can satire, whether grave or gay?
> What vice has it subdued? Whose heart reclaim'd
> By rigor, or whom laughed into reform?
> Alas! Leviathan is not so tamed.[28]

The Goliath monsters of corruption, vice, and apathy so dominated the targeted audiences that the stones thrown by the Davidic satirist dwindled into the tossing of mere daisies. Satire had been reduced to impotent laughter or mere scoffing. It lost its vision of and power for reform.

Even satirists despair of the minimal effect of their own comic art. Poet Shelley doubted if satire could "wake the slumbering hounds of conscience." Artemus Ward found the art of comedy as useless as an uneven grindstone. For Mark Twain, such humor endured as "only a fragrance, a decoration." He argued out of both sides of his mouth that "humor must not professedly teach and it must not professedly preach, but it must do both if it would live forever. By forever, I mean thirty years. I have always preached. That is the reason that I have lasted thirty years." Lest it be just a "sneeze of humor," laughter must contain some philosophy.[29]

The effects of satire tend to be ephemeral. They tend not to outlive the issues that spawned them and gave them sharp edges. Rarely is satire universal and timeless, and often it is comprehended only by a specific audience. Mocking of holy swindlers in one age may not be understood in a later era.[30] And as British humorist Peter Cook once noted, a high point of European satire took place in the 1930s in Berlin, and look how that thwarted the rise of Nazism.

Cartoonist John Lawing lamented that his target, evangelicals, just didn't get the point of irony. When you are a biblical literalist, you read other texts in the same literal way. Just as when you point to something for a dog, it looks not at the object to which you are pointing, but at your finger. Alas, some audiences see only the satirist giving them the finger. However, the greatest danger falls on the religious satirists themselves, the "irritated missionaries," marked by a "blister on [their] tongue, a crater in [their] tooth. Our nerves are fire; we have been stung by the tarantulas of truth."[31] The old proverb warned that those who play with fire will get burned.

6. Biblical responses to satire include both scathing rejoinders and silence.

In interpreting Hebrew scriptures as prophetic signs for the New Testament event, the psalmist had cried out,

> The smiters whom I did not know gathered together against me,
> They slandered me without ceasing.
> Like godless jesters at a feast,
> They gnashed at me with their teeth. (Psalm 35:15–16)

They gape at him and shout, "Aha! Aha!" which, in the original Hebrew, is much funnier.

To this linguistic assault, the psalmist David does not request from God witty comebacks to counter his adversaries. He simply announces that he will give thanks to God in the midst of this ravaging attack. He focuses on God and pleads that he will not be silent, but arise to his defense and vindicate him. Fearing that his enemies will get just what they wanted—his humiliation—David hopes that God might put them to shame and confusion, clothed with disgrace.

During one of his most humiliating moments, when King David is chased out of his capital by his son Absalom and some treacherous staff, the fleeing king comes upon a very obnoxious character. Shimei, a Benjamite from the former king Saul's family, appears out of nowhere to curse David and pelt him with stones, the physical equivalent of satire.[32] Calling David a man of blood, he mocks him for being ruined because of the violence of his reign. When one of his soldiers asks permission of the king to cut off the head of this cursing dog, David stops him. "If he is cursing because the Lord said to him, 'Curse David,' who can ask, 'Why do you do this?' We must leave him alone." In other words, if the lord has summoned Shimei to curse David, it would be futile to stop him. And, David muses, perhaps the lord may see his distress and repay him with good for the cursing he receives. After such a reasoned response, the angry mocker continues following David and his men, throwing stones and showering them with dirt (2 Samuel 16:5–14).[33]

It was the wisdom of David that he followed that wise proverb, "Do not answer a fool according to his folly, lest you become like him yourself" (Proverbs 26:4).

The closeness of satire to slander is dangerous. St. Peter warned against bold and arrogant men who slander celestial beings. Even powerful angels did not bring slanderous accusation against such depraved brutes. Peter himself cannot resist the application of some ancient Hebrew proverbs to their behavior, as in "a dog returns to its vomit," and "a sow that is washed goes back to her wallowing in the mud" (Proverbs 26:11). Not quite satire, but quite graphic.

The response of Jesus to his scoffers is similar: silence. When he is mocked and held up to ridicule, he is like the lamb that goes before the slaughter and does not bleat. He endures and forgives. It may be that Jesus endured the suffering of ridicule not only to share in the sufferings of others, but also to be a model for dealing with satire. If someone mocked God or the poor in the Hebrew Bible, God would mock back, with the power of *dabar*. But now, in the Passion, Jesus holds his tongue. He does not speak or retort with a divinely inspired quip. There is identification with those who suffer such indignities. As Miguel de Unamuno expressed it in his *Tragic Sense of Life*, one may become a hero in knowing how to face ridicule, but it is "better still, to know how to make oneself ridiculous and not shrink from the ridicule."[34]

7. Religious satire should function as a glass, a *mirror*, not only to society, but more importantly, to its practitioners.

Centuries after the Benedictine monk Nigel had published his *Speculum stultorum* (*A Mirror for/of Fools*), Jonathan Swift penned the preface to his 1704 publication *The Battle of the Books*, in which he defined satire as "a sort of glass, wherein beholders do generally discover everybody's face but their own." For true satirists, the first face they find funny and in need of reform should be their own. The satirist should speak from a vision of his or her own heart. It is by looking in that Swiftian mirror that one sees more than the foibles and vanities of others. We discover with Swift that we do have just "enough religion to make us hate, but not enough to make us love one another." Like the eternal turkey, Michael Doonesbury, who talks to his mirror, which talks back, so satire is talk back to each of us who dabble in satire. Our first target is always our self. (To be above one's own satire is to commit blasphemy in trying to become a god and judging others.)

Lewis's satiric wit flowered in his masterly little book of *The Screwtape Letters*. When asked if he recognized the hypocrisy and evil in the human heart through years of theological study or by reading ethics, he retorted that "some have paid me an undeserved compliment by supposing that my *Letters* were the ripe fruit of many years' study in moral and ascetic theology. They forgot that there is an equally reliable, though less creditable, way of learning how temptation works. 'My heart,'—I need no other's—'showeth me the wickedness of the ungodly.'"[35] The mirror of his own wicked heart prepared him to empathize with the folly of his neighbors and to write a more compelling and authentic satire.

One example will suffice. Lewis satirizes the universal human heart's tendency to possess and claim ownership. The elder devil writes to his charge Wormwood that hell is able to produce a sense of ownership through pride and confusion. "We teach them not to notice the different sense of the possessive pronoun—the finely graded differences that run from 'my boots' though 'my dog,' 'my servant,' 'my wife,' 'my father,' 'my master,' and 'my country,' to 'my God.'" The great joke, Screwtape scoffs, is that in the end, "only Heaven and Hell will be able to say mine" of each thing that exists, and "especially of each man. They will find out in the end, never fear, to whom their time, their souls, and their bodies really belong—certainly not to *them*, whatever happens."[36] It is in and through the mirror of his selfish heart that Lewis first saw his targets.

If the laughter of wit functions primarily, as Freud saw it, as an agent of hostility, it is enlisted to belittle and humble an enemy through scorn or ridicule, seeking the pleasure of this enemy's defeat. The problem is that we construct an adversarial relationship, us-versus-them. Instead of constructing the other as an enemy, the true satirist recreates him or her as a neighbor. The satiric mirror does not allow us the safe vantage point of laughing down. It pulls us down onto a level with our target. It puts us next door. As Chesterton says, when the Gospels tell you to love your enemies and to love your neighbors, it is because they are probably the same persons.

The recurring metaphor of satire as a reflecting glass requires an ethic of love. In his chapter on love, St. Paul pointed out that we only now see through a glass darkly or dimly (1 Corinthians 13:12), but this mirror is quite necessary for reprobates and fools. Seeing the outlines of one's own face distorted in a funhouse mirror is to recognize the image of God, smudged, spoiled, and silly, in desperate need of a satiric tissue to tidy it up. Upbeat reformers might also slip into their own humility and confession, judging not, lest they be judged, but nevertheless, rebuking with wit and humor. They would do unto others as they would have them do unto themselves.

Discussing humor in Hasidic wisdom tales, Ludo Abicht titles his article "Laughing in and at the Mirror," a reference to the merciless self-criticism of much Jewish wit. Two Jews sit in a tavern drinking, when one says, "Life is like a cup of dark tea." "What do you mean life is like dark tea?" asks the second. The first retorts, "What am I, a philosopher?" It is the wisdom and *Witz* of being able to see the other side of a question, that is to warn not only others, but oneself of folly or dogmatism. It is from centuries of wondering, praying, quarreling, thinking, and kvetching, echoing Koheleth, the preacher of Ecclesiastes, and Job that humor can watch over itself, "that is to say, to laugh at its own image in the mirror." Otherwise, as Abicht, concludes, without hope "what are we?" "Certainly not philosophers."[37]

In the twelfth century, the archdeacon of Oxford, Walter Mapes ("If die I must, let me die drinking in an Inn"), capably reconciled divinity with wit in writing his *Mirror of the Church*, a devastating attack upon monastic orders like the Cistercians monks, who did not eat meat but kept pigs for selling. He wrote not merely to amuse, but to reform the avarice of the clergy. In one famous story, he visited a Cistercian abbot who was acutely ill. Mapes recommended he retire from his order and repent of his rapacity. The abbot refused and rebuked Mapes with "get thee behind me Satan!" A short time later, Mapes himself fell ill and the abbot advised him to renounce his "light jesting habits" and join the Cistercian order. Mapes summoned his servants and impressed upon them that if ever in a fit of sickness he should speak of becoming a monk, they were to "consider it a sign that he had lost his senses and keep him in close confinement."[38]

Satire lifts up and casts down its citizens through its reflecting glass. To return to Sebastian Brandt's prologue to his *Ship of Fools*, the trope of the mirror stands as an exemplary and revelatory lesson:

> For fools a mirror shall it be,
> Where each his counterfeit may see.
> The glass of fools the truth may show.[39]

The best satire reveals the truth of self-recognition. If one does not first satirize oneself, one will either be a blasphemer or a bully. The best satirist writes satire out of his or her follies and vices. What is shared with one's targets is more important than what perturbs. Part of the habitual furniture of our minds should be the vanity we see in the mirror, the selfishness we practice in the office, the ignorance we display in our prejudices. Satirists should meet their targets as equals, like a spouse, loved and mocked at the same time, and knowing when to wink and when to be quiet. We should not patronize others, nor coddle them, but treat them as we would treat ourselves under such ridiculous circumstances.

In Albert Camus' novella, *La Chute* (*The Fall*), the lawyer-narrator, Clarence, a "judge-penitent," ironically reflects on the failure of his life and suspects that people are laughing at him behind his back, or looking at him with a hidden smile, and then imagines with the whole universe beginning to spitefully laugh at him. He comforts himself with Jesus's words "Woe to you when all men speak well of you!" as no one speaks well of lawyers. He decides to hurl himself into "the general derision," to put "the laughers on his side, or at least to put myself on their side" by jostling the blind on the street and slapping infants on the subway. He would go where the professional humanitarian free thinkers and café atheists gathered, and let fly a forbidden expression: "Thank God!" All was to be covered with a cloak of ridicule. The satirical pessimism of *The Fall* yet yearns for salvation and meaning. The narrator satirizes religions that moralize, noting that "God is not needed to create guilt to punish. Our fellow men suffice, aided by ourselves."[40]

Even the Last Judgment pales in comparison to the meanness of men, as evidenced in Camus's description of the spitting-cell, where others spit into the walled-up faces of prisoners, and of the dungeon cells of little-ease, not high enough to stand up in nor yet wide enough to lie down in. All of this reduces the human to "living hunch-backedness." People are all dunces, who spit on one another and sentence each other to the little-ease. For Camus, even Jesus suffered melancholia and guilt from the Slaughter of the Innocents, the children massacred because of him. Through his self-centered narrator, Camus paints the ironic portrait of those atheist novelists who pray every night, but who cannot hail the name of God because they "love themselves" and loathe themselves.[41]

At the end of his self-aggrandizing confession, the judge-penitent proposes to make a carnival mask that all will recognize, because it is also a mirror. And, as he confesses, "I was the lowest of the low," he manages an imperceptible trick in which the "I" becomes a "we." All are in the soup together. Here is the great triumph of the satirist, when the victim and the perpetrator become one, and the latter joins the former in the confession of a need for moral reform, all the while laughing. Ironically, *The Fall* may be Camus's most autobiographical work. It is his mirror. Like his narrator who hears that a young woman has committed suicide into the canal and does not respond, so Camus was haunted by personal guilt. The satire works as well, as the mask fits all, beginning with the satirist, who sees too clearly his own soul in the mirror.

Unfortunately, as Swift recognized, most of us are like the man who looks at his "natural face in a mirror; for once he has looked at himself and gone away, he has immediately forgotten what kind of person he was." As Swift realized the chief reason that so few people are offended by satire is that they do not recognize their own face (James 1:23–24).

Hans Holbein the Younger included the fool's self-image in Erasmus's *In Praise of Folly* as a marginal illustration known as "self-love." In the engraving, the fool (and author) peers into a looking glass and sees his image mocking his own face, tongue protruding. The fool looking at his own reflection had occurred in Brandt's *Ship of Fools*. But now, it is Erasmus who confesses "et sum ipse mihi ostensus in speculo," namely "I too have been revealed to myself in the mirror."[42] An annotation suggests that "it is the act of a wise man—even decorous—to look for his own ass's ears."[43] The best satirist satirizes him- or herself best and most of all. As Chesterton observed, "for if a man really cannot make a fool of himself, we may be quite certain that the effort is superfluous."[44]

Satire, we hope, might be instructive and witty. It might correct and improve human institutions and humanity itself, inspiring either a remodeling or renewal. We might complain of the toxicity of contemporary satire, pointing back to what seems like superannuated practices where one satirized what one loved. There was affection in Chaucer for the characters he lampooned. He traveled and drank and laughed with his fellow pilgrims. This is very different from throwing verbal spears in hatred. Yet Swift noticed such a bite among his contemporaries as well: "Among the rest," says he, "there is a serpent that wants teeth, and consequently cannot bite, but if its vomit (to which it is much addicted) happens to fall upon anything, a certain rottenness or corruption ensues." These serpents "frequently emit a poisonous juice, whereof whoever drinks, that person's brain flies out of his nostrils."[45] The practice of satire throughout history can be summed up in the proverb, where a man deceives his neighbor and excuses himself by asking, "Was I not joking?" He is, says the proverb, like a madman who shoots flaming arrows (Proverbs 26:18–19).

In his work on the use of humor during the Holocaust, *Laughter in Hell*, Steve Lipman tells the story of how storm troopers barged their way into an Evangelical church. In the name of racial purity, they demanded that anyone with a Jewish grandparent leave immediately. A dozen departed quickly. Then they ordered out anyone whose father was a Jew. Another score left quietly. Finally, the SS commander shouted that anyone whose mother was a Jew had to leave. At this point, the pastor took hold of a crucifix, looked at Jesus, and said: "Brother, now is time for you and me to get out."[46]

Jacqueline Bussie's *The Laughter of the Oppressed* echoes Lipman in finding the laughter through the tears of the oppressed to be a liberating rebellion against "the banality of evil."[47] Satire can enable one to resist despair and envision hope. In the life of Dietrich Bonhoeffer or the novels of Shusaku Endo, one finds Christian martyrs laughing, but revealing a hidden transcript of theological hope in an age of abandonment. At some level, laughter empowers one to defy suffering and evil. Perhaps satirists do hear God mocking those who scorn the poor.

In older writings, an author, either unsure of his or her own ideas or fearful of official retribution might add a palinode, essentially a retraction of all that has gone before. So, reflecting upon Paul's admonition in Galatians (6:7), "Do not be deceived; God is not mocked. Whatever a man sows, this he will also reap," I humbly acknowledge my own transgressions.

We can look at this writing and hear Socrates responding to Hermogenes in Plato's dialogue with *Cratylus*. The Greek sage said, "Son of Hipponicus, you ask a solemn question; there is a serious and also a facetious explanation of both these names; the serious explanation is not to be had from me, but there is no objection to your hearing the facetious one; for the Gods too love a joke. Dionusos is simply *didous oinon* [giver of wine], as he might be called in fun, and *oinos* is properly *oionous*, because wine makes those who drink, think [*oiesthai*] that they have a mind [*nous*] when they have none."[48] Even as we are intoxicated with laughter, the wine of satire may have made us think we have minds; our patient readers, we hope, will forgive the illusion.

But what, after all, shall we conclude of the Quad of Satire? Perhaps the most appropriate ending for this work is to remember that, according to Dante, when Pope Gregory arrived in paradise, he discovered that his Decretals on the celestial hierarchy, over which he labored diligently, were completely wrong. "We are told how the redeemed soul behaved: 'di se medesmo rise.' It was the funniest thing he'd ever heard."[49] Perhaps he realized not only were they a joke, but so was he, and the most appropriate and healthiest response was to join in the laughter of his own folly. He saw in the radiant light of the Lord of heaven his own fractured image, and it was good and it was funny.

NOTES

INTRODUCTION

1 Sebastian Brandt, *The Ship of Fools* (Dover, 2011).

2 Ibid., x.

3 Ibid.

4 Jacques Ellul, *Subversion of Christianity* (Eerdmans, 1986).

5 For the comic perspective, there exists a discrepancy between the nature of the cosmos and the myopic way we often see it. It takes a jolt to help us see, even if that jolt is laughter. And humor, for the great philosopher Ludwig Wittgenstein, is "not a mood but a way of looking at the world." *Culture and Value* (University of Chicago Press, 1984), 83.

6 Surah 2:104, 4:46, accessible at http://www.muslimaccess.com/quraan/arabic/002.asp. The chapter accuses the Jews of distorting words and twisting their tongues, saying "we hear and disobey" so that their religion is dishonored. For example, Samson devises a clever couplet about how he piled his enemies in a mass (*hamar*) with the jawbone of an ass (*hamor*).

7 Very close to what Germans call *Schadenfreude*, or delighting in the misfortune of others.

8 Northrup Frye, *Anatomy of Criticism* (Atheneum, 1968), 224.

9 Mikhail Bakhtin, *Rabelais and His World*, trans. Helen Iswolsky (MIT Press, 1968), 59.

10 Ibid., 69n; Bakhtin cites an ancient Egyptian papyrus that attributes the creation of the world to God's laughter: "when God burst out laughing, there was light."

11 Robert Alter not only recognizes the danger of sitting in the "session of scoffers," but sees puns throughout the psalter, even on idols as being *'al* (no) *'el* (god). Alter, *The Book of Psalms* (Norton, 2007), 3.

12 Chesterton's offered an apt apology: "If we in any sense propose for discussion the subject of Laughter, we shall normally notice that our neighbors receive it in one of two ways. Either they laugh, which is perhaps the best thing they could do with a proposal for the analysis of laughter; since practice is better than precept; and anyone sitting down, as I do here, to write a whole article on this subject is a very proper object for the derision of mankind. But if they have sense enough to laugh, they will also probably have sense enough to go away; the colloquy will be cut short and exhibit only the kind of wit which is identified with brevity. If, on the other hand, we mention Laughter to them and they do not laugh, what they always do is this; they twist their silly faces into expressions of ferocious gravity and gloom and begin to talk" about everything Chesterton has missed, such as how "laughter is, after all, founded on some form of the instinct of cruelty" and all mirth born of malignity." But such criticism will reflect the critic. Chesterton, "The Frivolous Man," in *The Common Man* (Sheed and Ward, 1951). When my wife, Karen, challenged me about my delving into this precarious topic of satire, reminding me that I should try to be more like God before I handled these sharp tongues, I responded that I really was trying to be more like God. For God sat in his heavens and mocked those below. So, I told her, I am trying to imitate him. But, my wife responded, you can only do that when you are as good as him.

13 "It is the heart that is not sure of its God," wrote Scottish author George MacDonald, "that is afraid to laugh in His presence." C. S. Lewis, *George MacDonald: An Anthology* (Geoffrey Bles, 1946), 132.

14 Antonia Szabari, *Less Rightly Said: Scandals and Readers in Sixteenth-Century France* (Stanford University Press, 2010), 5.

15 Edward Bloom and Lillian Bloom, *Satire's Persuasive Voice*, 17. In *Satire: Spirit and Art*, Test fiddles through a host of conceptual tunes on satire to catch readers' attention when he employs metaphors, like Lady Montagu's "polished razor keen" or Ben Jonson's "whip of steel" (15–16).

16 In *The Golden Bough*, Frazer suggests a close link between magical incantations and the power of the word as a weapon of verbal abuse. "Unable to discriminate clearly between words and things, the savage commonly fancies a link" (216).

17 Frye, *Anatomy of Criticism*, 223; and Berger, *Redeeming Laughter*, 157. Frye also noted that two of the greatest masters of invective, Rabelais and Swift, had been "recruited from the clergy." "The Nature of Satire," *University of Toronto Quarterly* 14 (1944–1945): 80.

18 Augustine, *On Christian Doctrine*, trans. D. W. Robertson, Jr. (Bobbs-Merrill, 1958), 75.

19 However, one of the important themes that I have not developed throughout these pages, although it permeates the entire range of satiric material, is that of Jewish and anti-Semitic satire, a topic that deserves its own fuller treatment, such as that of Avner Ziv and Anat Zajdman's *Semites and Stereotypes: Characteristics of Jewish Humor*. (Greenwood Press, 1993).

20 Ralph Wood, *The Comedy of Redemption* (University of Notre Dame Press, 1988)

21 Lewis, *Screwtape Letters*, 49–52; Feibleman, *In Praise of Comedy*, 205.

22 Søren Kierkegaard cited in Michael Strawser, *Both/And: Reading Kierkegaard from Irony to Edification* (Fordham University Press, 1996), 131. For Kierkegaard, people starved by having too much knowledge in their mouths so that they couldn't chew, swallow, or digest it all.

23 C. S. Lewis, *God in the Dock* (Eerdmans, 1970), 259.

24 G. K. Chesterton, *Orthodoxy* (Doubleday, 1959), 11–12.

25 G. K. Chesterton, "Humour," in *Encyclopedia Britannica*, 14th edition (New York, 1929), 883

26 Morreall, *Comedy, Tragedy, and Religion*, 154.

CHAPTER 1. CIRCUMCISED SATIRISTS

1 In *Sudden Glory*, a history of laughter as a subversive phenomenon, Barry Sanders, likewise, chronicles the cross-fertilization of religion with humor.

2 Eugene Fisher makes this point by shedding light on the puns of the Hebrew Bible, such as the name Adam meaning "earth" or "clay," with disobedience leading to the curse upon the "earth." Fisher calls for a Semitic hermeneutic in translating the scriptures so that one might fully understand the wisdom and wit of the sacred texts. "The Divine Comedy: Humor in the Bible" *Religious Education* 72 (November–December, 1977): 571–79. The biblical view of human nature sets up a comic juxtaposition quite conveniently. In the creation story of Genesis, incongruity appears twice before the fall of man. In the first instance, God creates the human using two distinct elements, his breath and dust. Both spirit and earth combine to form that amazing oxymoron, a spiritual animal, related on one side to the transcendent, the angelic, the Amish, and on the other side to weasels, toads, and lawyers. These two elements provide ontological fodder for the comedy of the human being. The physical and sexual aspects of human nature contrast directly with the mind and soul of the individual. Thus, when Ezekiel uses obscene and pornographic imagery to discuss the infidelity of God's people, he juxtaposes their calling with their carnality. The second source of incongruity in the creation account occurs when God splits his image into two, into male and female. The roots of much comedy reside in there being these two genders, so divinely alike and so frustratingly different

3 Satire was rescued from its alleged beginnings among the Romans by Thomas Jemielity who found early traces of satire in the Hebrew Prophets. See Jemielity, *Satire and the Hebrew Prophets.*

4 Elliott, *The Power of Satire*, argues that satire evolves from the habit of cursing, associated with the primitive belief that satire can kill. Kernan, *The Cankered Muse*, also interprets satire's relation to magic as a cankered muse appraising the ills of the world.

5 Elliott sees in this ridicule the dark magical power of a curse. See Elliott's *The Power of Satire*, 3; Words have consequences. For this tale I am indebted to my colleague, classics scholar Ben Haller.

6 Jeffrey Scott Anderson, "The Nature and Function of Curses in the Narrative Literature of the Hebrew Bible" (Ph.D. diss., Vanderbilt University, 1992), argues that the curses were speech "acts of power designed to derogate, exclude, and marginalize their victims." Elliot notes that the satirist-magician figures were warriors, with "lethal verses their weapons" (259).

7 If satire is like throwing stones, one must remember George Herriman's classic Krazy Kat comic strips, where Ignatz the mouse throws bricks at the love-obsessed cat.

8 Yahuda Radday, *On Humor and the Comic in the Hebrew Bible* (Sheffield Academic Press, 1991).

9 The story reminds me of the wheeze about the Swedish farmer and his wife who were driving their mule to town. When the donkey refused to budge before a hill, the farmer took out his whip and struck him and said, "That's one." When the donkey turned aside to eat some thistle, the farmer struck him again and said, "That's two." Finally, when the donkey sat down in the road, the farmer said, "That's three," got out his gun and shot him. His wife yelled at him, "That's the stupidest thing you could do! Why are you such an idiot?" The farmer looked at her and said, "That's one."

10 The Talmud records the advice that "if one man says to thee, 'Thou art a donkey,' do not mind; if two speak thus, purchase a saddle for thyself" (Bereshit Rabbah 74:2), cited in H. Freedman and Maurice Simon, *Midrash Rabbah* (Soncino Press, 1983). Perhaps the best contemporary female satirist is Becky Garrison. In *Jesus Died for This? A Satirist's Search for the Risen Christ* (Zondervan, 2010), she reminds readers of the four best biblical moments for donkeys (89).

11 Biblical satire smacks of prophetic fire. It shames its subjects with mocking directness, even when those subjects are themselves prophets of God. In fact, biblical satire most often confronts those in religious authority who misuse their power. Centuries after Isaiah, Martin Luther would find in the donkey one of his strongest tropes to attack the Roman papacy as an institution of the devil, while his friend, artist Lucas Cranach, would mischievously craft the woodcut of "The Donkey-Pope of Rome." As Luther wrote, "a donkey knows it is a donkey and not a cow. A stone knows it is a stone; water is water, and so on through all the creatures. But you mad asses do not know you are asses." Martin Luther, *Against the Roman Papacy*, in *Works of Martin Luther*, trans. A. Steimle (FQ Books, 2010), 41, 360.

12 The verb *hitnabbe*, meaning "to act like a prophet," is also translated "to act crazy."

13 Against the wicked and snarling dogs who would tear him apart, the psalmist cries out to God to "break the teeth in their mouths" and "tear out the fangs of the lion" so that "when they draw the bow, let their arrows be blunted. Like a slug melting away as it moves along, like a stillborn child, may they not see the sun." Those who scoff are to be held accountable for "the sins of their mouths and words of their lips." Psalm 58:6–8; 59:6–7, 12.

14 Bloom and Bloom, *Satire's Persuasive Voice*, 18.

15 Ibid., 29.

16 Abraham J. Hershel, *The Prophet* (Harper and Row, 1962), x, 10. For Hershel, the prophet's word is like "a scream in the night. While the world is at ease and asleep, the prophet feels the blast from heaven" (16).

CHAPTER 2. CAESAR SALAD SATIRISTS

1 C. S. Lewis, *A Grief Observed* (Seabury, 1961), 57.

2 Aristotle found little connection between laughter (*gelos*, a word that may have had an etymological connection with ideas of light or shimmering brightness) and the divine realm. Homer, however, portrayed Olympian gods laughing, mostly at each other.

3 Jesse Bier, *The Rise and Fall of American Humor* (Holt, Rinehardt, and Winston, 1968).

4 According to the jingoistic Quntilian's claim, "satura quidem tota nostra est," satire was invented by Romans. *Institutio oratoria*, trans. H. E. Butler (Harvard University Press, 1966) 10: 1, 93

5 Ruben Quintero, ed., *A Companion to Satire: Ancient and Modern* (Blackwell, 2007), 4.

6 Cited in Bloom and Bloom, *Satire's Persuasive Voice*, 128.

7 Horace, *Satires and Epistles*, trans. John Davie (Oxford University Press, 2011), 25.

CHAPTER 3. SATIRE MADE FLESH

1 Harry Boonstra, "Satire in Matthew," *Christianity and Literature* 29, no. 4 (1980): 32–45; see also William Phipps, *The Wisdom and Wit of Rabbi Jesus* (John Knox Press, 1993)

2 Wolfgang Zucker, "The Clown as the Lord of Disorder," in Hyers, *Holy Laughter*, 84. A medieval Chester nativity play expands the comic irony of Mary's song: when Herod hears of "the newborn king," he ejaculates, "What the Devill shold this be! / A Boy, a groome of Low Degree, / shold raigne above my Soialtie / and make me but a goose!" Cited in Conrad Hyers, *The Comic Vision* (Pilgrim Press, 1981), 139. Herod's frustration previews Nathanael's sly question: "What good thing can come out of Nazareth?"

3 Thomas Aquinas, *The Summa Theologica* II-II q. 168 a. 2, trans. Fathers of English Dominican Province (Catholic Way Publishing, 2011) . See also Hugh Rahner's "*Eutrapelia*: A Forgotten Virtue," in Hyers, *Holy Laughter*, 185–97.

4 Thomas Fuller, the seventeenth-century cheery-tempered and boyish wit (said to be as full of mirth as the grasshopper is of chirping), mocked those of such a dismal "Holy State" by noting that "Christ reproved the Pharisees for disfiguring their faces with a sad countenance. Fools! Who to persuade men that angels lodged in their hearts, hung out the devil for a sign in their faces." Cited in Shaw, *Our Religious Humorists*, 67.

5 Elton Trueblood, *The Humor of Christ*; See also Terry Lindvall, "A Mark of Humor: Laughter in the Gospel of Mark," *Agora* 4, no. 4 (1980): 12–16.

6 In his poem "Redemption," George Herbert follows a man seeking his landlord up to heaven, but finds that he resides amid the "noise and mirth" of "theeves and murderers" and pays the price for his residence.

7 Dudley Zuver, *Salvation by Laughter* (Harper and Brothers, 1933), 250–51.

8 John Chrysostom, "Easter Sermon," http://anglicansonline.org/special/Easter/chrysostom_easter.html.

9 Martha Bayless, *Parody in the Middle Ages* (University of Michigan, 1977), 179. In Eugene O'Neill's play *Lazarus Laughs*, the resurrected dead man summons the community to join him in contagious laughing: "Laugh with me! Death is dead! Fear is no more! There is only life! There is only laughter!" *Nine Plays* (Garden City Publishing, 1940), 418.

10 Anonymous, "Biblical Humor and Translation," *Tic Talk* 18 (Winter 1992): 1. See also Ruth Zakovich, *Introduction and Commentary* (Am Oved, 1990), 76.

11 See M. A. Screech, *Laughter at the Foot of the Cross* (Westview Press, 1997). How apt that such would be the words and acts directed against God himself on the cross, an attempt to tear apart God and flesh, more inseparable than the seamless cloak they could not divide.

12 Ibid., 79.

13 The sign "IJRN," for Jesus Christ, King of the Jews, was written in mockery yet ironically spoke the truth of the Gospels.

14 Paul Schulten, "Humour on Religion in the Greco-Roman World," in Geybels and Van Herek, *Humor and Religion*, 72.

15 Arthur Koestler, *The Act of Creation* (Hutchinson, 1964), 52–53; Screech, *Laughter at the Foot of the Cross*, 79.

16 Karl-Josef Kuschel, *Laughter: A Theological Reflection*, trans. John Bowden (SCM Press, 1994), 90.

17 See David Heim, "And Jesus Laughed: A Joking Matter," *Christian Century*, August 9, 2003, 2730.

18 Hans Geybels, "The Redemptive Power of Humour in Religion," in Geybels and Van Herck, *Humour and Religion*, 11. Yet after such gallows humor, particularly in the case of Esther and Mordecai, the laughter is all celebration in the Feast of Purim.

19 Simon Foulkes and Gary Jenkins see the cross as a satire on supposed human wisdom in their *Laughing at Unbelief* (Grove Books, 2004), 13.

20 See Umberto Eco's *The Name of the Rose*, in which Franciscan monk William of Baskerville debates the Benedictine Jorge over biblical (and Aristotelian) views of laughter (147–53). Eco also includes what is known as *The Supper of Cyprianus*, an allegorical parody of allegorical interpretations, irreverently treating biblical characters, in which God invites a group to a banquet at Cana. Bayless, *Parody in the Middle Ages*, 215; Timmerman, John "Umberto Eco and Aristotle: A Dialogue on the Lost Treatise: *Comedy*," *Christian Scholars' Review* 17, no. 1 (1987): 9–24.

21 Halliwell, *Greek Laughter*, 18.

22 Bayless, *Parody in the Middle Ages*, 201.

23 Tertullilan, *Tertullian: Apology and De Spectaculis*, trans. T. R. Glover (Loeb Classical Library, 1931), 183.

24 Jaroslav Pelikan, *The Christian Tradition: A History of the Development of Doctrine. Volume One: The Emergence of the Catholic Tradition (100–600)* (University of Chicago Press, 1971), 75.

25 An aside must be made to the Gnostic Jesus in the ancient fourth-century Coptic texts. In the Second Treatise of the Great Seth, the Secret Book of John, the Gospel of Judas, and The Apocalypse of Peter, the docetic (purely spiritual) Jesus laughs not only at his disciples and their stupid questions but also at his physical counterpart being crucified on the cross. The laughter echoes the Gnostic's rejection of ignorance of the blind who do not grasp illusion of the physical world. There is a cosmic cruelty, a mocking meanness toward the spiritually blind. Ingvild Saelid Gilhus, "Why Did Jesus Laugh? Laughing in Biblical-Demiurgical Texts," in Geybels and Van Herck, *Humour and Religion*, 123.

26 Tertullian, *Apology*, 16:12.

27 Ibid., 299. On the murder of Domitian, Juvenal also seems to gloat with unnecessary malice. See William S. Anderson's *Anger in Juvenal and Seneca* (University of California Press, 1964).

28 Stephen Halliwell, *Greek Laughter: A Study of Cultural Psychology from Homer to Early Christianity* (Cambridge University Press, 2008), 471.

29 St. Clement "Chapter Five: On Laughter," in *The Paedagogus (The Instructor)*, trans. Alexander Roberts (Amazon Digital Services, 2014). Clement did find it a farce "and a thing to make one laugh outright" at men and women bringing in silver urinals and gold receptacles for excrement to ease themselves richly. For Clement, man is a "rational laughing animal" (8.6.21).

30 Maria Plaza, *The Function of Humour in Roman Verse Satire* (Oxford University Press, 2006), 318.

31 Sari Kivisto, "Laughter, Jubilation and Religion," in *Sour Faces, Happy Lives?: On Laughter, Joy, and Happiness of the Agelists*, http://www.helsinki.fi/collegium/e-series/volumes/volume_3/07_Kivisto_2008_3.pdf, 15.

32 Clement of Alexandria, "Chapter V: On Laughter," in *Ante-Nicene Fathers*, ed. Cleveland Coxe (Hendrickson, 2004), 2:249–50.

33 Ibid., 250.

34 Ibid.

35 *Arguments of Celsus, Porphyry, and the Emperor Julian against the Christians*, trans. Nathaniel Lardner and Thomas Taylor (London, 1830), np.

36 Ibid.

37 Archibald Robertson, "Prolegomena," in *Select Writings and Letters of Athanasius, Bishop of Alexandria*, ed. Archibald Robinson (Parker and Co., 1891), xxxix.

38 John Cassian, *The Conferences*, trans. Boniface Ramsey (Newman Press, 1997), 842.

39 Augustine and Henry Chadwick, *Confessions* (Oxford University Press, 1998), 33.

40 Ibid., 57.

41 Ibid., 97, 99.

42 Ibid., 46–47, 229.

43 Augustine *Confessions* (Create Space, 2009), 44–47. Note passages on mocking and on his mother's dream of the laughing messenger, as well as the contrast between a fakir's walking on coals and Jesus's walking on water. John Horton also points to the salty and sublime satire of Augustine's *City of God* where the Romans distributed power among their many pagan gods, but to no avail. Attacking the notion that Rome fell because it had abandoned its original deities, Augustine teased that even geese were better guardians than the sleeping gods against Alaric's invading Goths. John Horton, "The *De Civitate Dei* as Religious Satire," *The Classical Journal* 60, no.5 (February 1965): 193–203.

44 Church fathers like St. John Chrysostom argued that laughter was neither fitting nor convenient. "The present is no season for loose merriment, but of mourning, of tribulation, and lamentation: and dost thou play the jester?" His key concern was that the time was not ripe for laughter, as Christ had been crucified. He warned, "To laugh, to speak jocosely, does not seem an acknowledged sin, but it leads to acknowledged sin. Thus, laughter often gives birth to foul discourse, and foul discourse to actions still more foul. Often from words and laughter proceed railing and insult; and from railing and insult, blows and wounds; and from blows and wounds, slaughter and murder. If, then, you would take good counsel for yourself, avoid not merely foul words and foul deeds, or blows and wounds and murders, but unseasonable laughter itself." John Chrysostom, *On the Priesthood; Ascetic Treatises; Select Homilies and Letter*, in *A Select Library of the Nicene and Post-Nicene Fathers of the Christian Church*, ed. Philip Schaff (Christian Literature Co., 1889), 9:442.

45 Gregory of Nyssa, *Homilies on Ecclessiastes* 2 (44.645), trans. Richard MaCambly, ed. John Litteral (CreateSpace, 2014), 29–34.

46 Ibid.

47 Paul Carroll, trans., *Satirical Letters of St. Jerome* (Regnery Gateway Edition, 1956); Jerome did accuse Crassus of being an extreme case of antigelastic, who laughed only once at the maxim of "thistles are like lettuce to the lips of a donkey," referring to the idea of a donkey chewing something unexpected. See M. Griffith, "Horsepower and Donkeywork: Equids and the Ancient Greek Imagination," *Classical Philology* 101 (2006): 185–246, 307–58.

48 Conversation with William Griffin, Divine Comedies Conference, Baylor University, 2005; See Robert Kantra, *All Things Vain*, (Pennsylvania State University Press, 1984), 44.

49 Cited in Beard, *Laughter in Ancient Rome*, 266, n.98.

50 Screech, *Laughter at the Foot of the Cross*, 70.

51 Ibid., 217. One must remember that in the earlier monastic tradition of the Essenes, anyone who "guffawed foolishly" in council was disciplined with a penance of thirty days. In contrast, Jerome was quite a maverick. Geza Vermes, *The Complete Dead Sea Scrolls in English* (Penguin, 1990), 31, 107.

52 Cicero also advised that if you want to make your audience laugh at the end, make them cry at the beginning. He also recognized that "old men are garrulous," and "there is nothing so ridiculous but some philosopher has said it." For Cicero, merriment "relieves dullness and tones down austerity, and, by a jest or a laugh, often dispels distasteful suggestions not easily weakened by reasonings."*De Oratore*, trans. E. W. Sutton and H. Rackham, (Harvard University Press, 1967), 1:viii, 236. A fellow rhetorician noted that Cicero, the prince of orators, was "unduly addicted to jests, not merely outside the courts, but in his actual speeches as well." *Instituto Oratoria*, trans. Harry Caplan (Loeb, 1922), 6:3. Three books of Cicero's jests were even published, such as the one in which a man tells his friend that his wife hung herself on a fig tree; to which the friend asks if he can have "some cuttings from that tree of yours to plant" (ibid.).

53 Screech, *Laughter at the Foot of the Cross*, 217.

54 Jerome, "An Ideal for Lukewarm Christians," in *The Satirical Letters of St. Jerome*, trans. Paul Carroll (Gateway, 1956), 68.

55 Ibid..

56 Jerome, "An Ideal for Lukewarm Christians," 69.

57 See David Hugh Farmer, *Oxford Dictionary of Saints* (Oxford University Press, 2011), 180.

58 Przemyslaw Marciniak, "Laughing against All the Odds: Some Observations on Humour, Laughter and Religion in Byzantium," in Geybels and Van Herck, *Humour and Religion*, 144.

59 Guy Halsall, ed., *Humor, History and Politics in Late Antiquity and the Early Middle Ages* (Cambridge University Press, 2004), 69.

CHAPTER 4. MEDIEVAL JESTERS AND ROOSTERS

1 Lewis Grizzard, *I Haven't Understood Anything Since 1962 and Other Nekkid Truths* (Wheeler Publishers, 1993).

2 See James Feibleman, *In Praise of Comedy* (Horizon Press, 1970), 39.

3 Bayless, *Parody in the Middle Ages*.

4 Bakhtin, *Rabelais and His World*, 11, 12, 25.

5 E. K. Chambers, *The Medieval Stage* (Oxford University Press, 1903), 1:32.

6 The author must confess that during long Sunday evenings in church, he and some roguish conspirators would insert the phrase "under the sheets" after hymn titles (e.g., "Joy to the World" under the sheets; "Abide with Me . . ."; "Rise up O Men of God . . . ," and worse) just for the purpose of provoking suppressed laughter.

7 G. R. Owst, *Literature and Pulpit in Medieval England* (Barnes and Noble, 1961), 214.

8 Nathan Schachner, *The Mediaeval Universities* (London, 1938), 368.

9 John Addington Symonds, ed., *Wine, Women and Song: Mediaeval Latin Students Songs*, (Kessinger, 2007), 366.

10 "Goliard," http://goliard.co.tv/.

11 Liam Ethan Felsen, "Medieval Monks: Funnier than You Thought," in *Medieval Misconceptions*, ed. Stephen Harris and Bryon Lee Grigsby (Routledge, 2008), 73; Bayless, *Parody in the Middle Ages*, 349, 352–53. A contemporary variation of the AA prayer reads, "Lord, grant me coffee to change the things I can, and wine the things I can't."

12 Bayless, *Parody in the Middle Ages*, 57.

13 Marcia L. Colish, *Medieval Foundations of the Western Intellectual Tradition, 400–1400* (Yale University Press, 1997), 202

14 Or the Trinity in Charlottesville, Virginia.

15 Parton, *Caricature and Other Comic Art*, 68.

16 Laura Kendrick, *Chaucerian Play: Comedy and Control in the Canterbury Tales* (University of California Press, 1988), 62.

17 Screech, *Laughter at the Foot of the Cross*, 219.

18 Kendrick, *Chaucerian Play*, 257.

19 Thomas Wright, *A Selection of Latin Stories from Manuscripts of the Thirteenth and Fourteenth Centuries* (Astor Library, 1842), http://books.google.com/books?id=40UNAAAAYAAJ&pg=PR1&source=gbs_selected_pages&cad=3#v=onepage&q&f=false.

20 Kendrick, *Chaucerian Play*, 238, 274.

21 **Disraeli,** *Curiosities of Literature*, 91.

22 Dante Alighieri, *Inferno*, trans. Charles Eliot Norton (Encyclopedia Britannica, 1952), 86.

23 Disraeli, *Curiosities of Literature*, 91. St. Francis believed that preachers should be *joculatores Domini*, or "God's jesters." Beatrice K. Otto, *Fools Are Everywhere: The Court Jester around the World* (University of Chicago Press, 2001), 169.

24 John Steadman, "'Teeth Will Be Provided': Satire and Religious and Ecclesiastical Humor," *Thalia: Studies in Literary Humor* 6, no. 1 (Spring–Summer 1983): 23–31.

25 According to Peter Bayle's *Historical and Critical Dictionary* (Royal Society of London, 1734), Barletta distinguished himself "in a manner of preaching much more becoming a Buffoon, than a minister of the Gospel," cavalierly mixing the sublime and the ridiculous (651). On Barletta's fondness for jesting in the pulpit, see Jacques de Vitry and Thomas Frederick Crane, *The Exempla or Illustrative Stories from the Vulgares of Jacques de Vitry* (Kessenger, 2004), lxv.

26 Jolanta Rzegocka, "Being Serious About Laughter: The Case of Early Modern Biblical Plays" in Geybels and Van Herck, *Humour and Religion*, 158–61.

27 Nancy Regalado, *Poetic Patterns in Rutebeuf* (Yale University Press, 1970), 180.

28 Eco, *The Name of the Rose*, 137.

29 See "Ecumenical Council of Florence," http://www.ewtn.com/library/councils/florence.htm. Max Harris corrects the image of the Feast of Fools as an unruly, transgressive event by grounding it in a celebration of the Incarnation, in which God puts down the mighty and elevates the humble. Max Harris, *Sacred Folly: A New History of the Feast of Fools* (Cornell University Press, 2011).

30 Parton, *Caricature and Other Comic Art*, 67.

31 Buckley, *The Morality of Laughter*, 35.

32 Ibid., 48.

33 Agnes Repplier, *In Pursuit of Laughter* (Houghton Mifflin, 1936), 10.

34 Actually, this category endured. Peter the Great (1672–1725) created a parody of the Russian church and court in the *Drunken Synod of Fools & Jesters* (also known as the *All-Mad, All-Jesting, All-Drunken Assembly*). Ernest Zitser, *The Transfigured Kingdom: Sacred Parody and Charismatic Authority at the Court of Peter the Great* (Columbia University Press, 2004).

35 Illuminated manuscripts held their own sly comedy, giggling at the vulgar, scatological, and erotic marginalia slipped into holy texts. A key figure was the trickster figure known as Marcolf, who engaged in witty dialogues with King Solomon. Marcolf mischievously turns the king's "turgid truths into turds." For example, when Solomon intones, "Give the wise an opportunity, and wisdom will be added unto him," Marcolf responds, "Let the belly be stuffed, and shit will be added unto you." Michael Camille, *The Image on the Edge: The Margins of Medieval Art* (Reaktion, 2004).

36 Parton, *Caricature and Other Comic Art*, 61.

37 Saward, *Perfect Fools*, 27.

38 Belden Lane, "Spirituality and Politics of Holy Folly," *Christian Century*, December 15, 1982, 1281–86.

39 Vittore Branca, *Boccaccio*, trans. Richard Monges (New York University Press, 1976), 75.

40 Ibid., 206.

41 Frances Gray, *Women and Laughter* (University Press of Virginia, 1994), 6.

42 Nineteenth century author George Shaw argued that Langland's religious teaching prepared the soil for the Reformation, as he tore "the coat from ignorant vicious Churchman of his day." Shaw, *Our Religious Humorists*, 29.

43 George Economou, *William Langland's Piers Plowman*, 112.

44 Ibid., 85.

45 Ibid., 24.

46 Ibid., 28.

47 One other medieval mystic, the fourteenth-century scholastic Meister Eckhart, affirmed that God laughed out of an abundance of energy, joy, love, and divine life. Spirituality, he argued, must not be divorced from humor, even as the Trinity displays such playfulness. "When the Father laughs to the Son, and the Son laughs back to the Father, the laughter gives pleasure, that pleasure gives joy, that joy gives love, and love gives the persons of which the Holy Spirit is one." See Raymond Blakney, *Meister Eckhart* (Harper/Torchbooks, 1941), 245.

48 Chaucer, *Canterbury Tales*, 163.

49 Ibid., 170.

50 "Many seditious and ignorant people had abused the liberty granted them for reading the Bible" and caused mischief. Parliament, Great Britain, "Act for the Advancement of True Religion," in *The Parliamentary History of England from the Earliest Period to the Year 1803* (T. C. Hansard, 1806), 558.

51 Barbara C. Bowen, "The 'Honorable Art of Farting' in Continental Renaissance Literature," in *Fecal Matters in Early Modern Literature and Art*, ed. Jeff Persels and Russell Ganim (Ashgate Publishing, 2004), 1–13.

52 Ibid., 3.

53 An update is Gary Larson's Car of Idiots.

54 Brandt, *The Ship of Fools*, 42.

55 Ibid., 193.

56 Parton, *Caricature and Other Comic Art*, 61.

57 James Kinsley, *The Poems of William Dunbar* (Oxford University Press, 1979), 284.

58 W. H. Auden, "Notes on the Comic," in *Comedy: Meaning and Form*, ed. Robert Corrigan (Chandler Publishing, 1965), 71.

59 Kinsley, *The Poems of William Dunbar*, 469. The medieval reformer Odo of Cluny categorized his own potential corpse as a "sack of shit." This "coprophilia," or dwelling on excrement, produced a view of human nature not as "*homo cogitans*, but as *homo cacans, homo eructans, homo futuens*, the shitting, farting, fucking human." "Satire trawls in the trash can of the human" (Quintero, *Companion to Satire*, 427).

60 William Dunbar, *William Dunbar: Selected Poems*, ed. Harriet Harvey-Wood (Routledge, 2003), 45.

61 William Smeaton, *English Satires* (BiblioBazaar, 2008), xxiv, 14–18.

62 C. S. Lewis, *English Literature in the Sixteenth Century, Excluding Drama* (Oxford University Press, 1973), 94, 98.

63 "Sinners, be glad and penance do, / And thank your Maker heartily; / For He that you might not come to, / To you comes most humbly." See Alister McGrath, *Christian Literature* (Blackwell, 2001), 272.

64 Arthur F. Kinney, *John Skelton: Priest as Poet* (University of North Carolina Press, 1987). See also A. R. Heiserman, *Skelton and Satire* (University of Chicago Press, 1961).

65 Michael Schmidt, Lives of the Poets (Knopf, 1999), 114.

66 Ibid., 116.

67 Wolsey was also the target of the great court fool to King Henry VIII, Will Somers, even as Archbishop Laud would later be stung by the royal jester Archy Armstrong, whose famous punning jibe was "All praise be to God, and little Laud to the Devil!" Otto, *Fools Are Everywhere*, 159–61.

68 John Skelton, "Colin Cloute," in *John Skelton: Everyman's Poetry*, ed. J. M. Dent (Everyman, 1977), 74.

69 Ibid., 75.

70 Schmidt, *Lives of the Poets*.

71 Skelton, "Colin Cloute," 75.

72 Anonymous, *Till Eulenspiegel*, ed. and trans. Paul Oppenheimer (Routledge, 2001).

73 Kenneth Mackenzie, trans., *The Marvelous Adventures and Rare Conceits of Master Tyll Owlglass* (Trubner, 1860), 140–42.

74 Dom Jean Leclercq offers insights into the "monastic humor" of the medieval Benedictines, particularly in averring that humor characterizes the truly spiritual man, in *The Love of Learning and the Desire for God* (Fordham University Press, 1982)

75 Rabelais uses an anagram of his own name, Alcofrybas Nasier, as the author of a little chapbook of tales. I did the same in a counseling class at Fuller Seminary, where I quoted the nonexistent Swedish sociologist Yret Lavdnil's nonexistent book, *Death of the One Way Street*, as part of a prank in my class presentation. Unfortunately, the psychology professor presumed to know the work, which put me in a comic bind.

76 Rabelais, *Gargantua and Pantagruel*, 185–86.

77 In one Christmas reading of the begats of the Matthew genealogy, I stunned some saints and woke up the kids by explaining that the begats were all about sex. Rabbits begat other rabbits; asses begat other asses; everything begats, except lawyers and the elders of that church, because they were all men. I have not to this day been asked to read Scripture in that church again.

78 Terry Gilliam and Terry Jones, dir., *Monty Python and the Holy Grail* (Python Pictures, 1975).

79 Rabelais, *Gargantua and Pantagruel*, 36.

80 As Screech notes in *Laughter at the Foot of the Cross*, "huge eating leads to huge stools; copious drinking means overflowing chamber pots" (248).

81 Ibid., 235. Screech argues that this juggling of holy texts in grotesque contexts works as an homage to the holy word of God, revealing God's glory even in the most trivial and common of bits. In *Gargantua*, faith is not gullible credibility in swallowing tall tales or even intellectual assent to truths about God; faith "means trust in God" (241).

82 Rabelais, *Gargantua and Pantagruel*, 188.

83 Ibid., 33.

84 Ibid.

85 Screech, *Laughter at the Foot of the Cross*, 283; Rabelais, *Gargantua and Pantagruel*, 16–24.

86 Sara Beam, *Laughing Matters* (Cornell University Press, 2007), 102.

87 Rabelais, *Gargantua and Pantagruel*, 47.

88 Bakhtin, *Rabelais and His World*, 198.

CHAPTER 5. REFORMERS AND FOOLS

1 Thomas More, *Utopia*, trans. Clarence Miller (Yale University Press, 2001), 6–7.

2 Ibid., 84..

3 Shaw, *Our Religious Humorists*, 34.

4 More, *Utopia*, 73.

5 Lewis, *English Literature*, 167.

6 Warren Wooden, "Anti-Scholastic Satire in Sir Thomas More's *Utopia*," *Sixteenth-Century Journal* 8, no. 2 (July 2, 1977): 30.

7 Elizabeth McCutcheon, *My Dear Peter: The "Ars Poetica" and Hermeneutics for More's "Utopia"* (Angers, 1983), 683.

8 Edward Hall, *Chronicle*, ed. H. Ellis (Johnson, 1809), 761, 818.

9 Constance Furey, "Invective and Discernment in Martin Luther, Erasmus, and Thomas More," *Harvard Theological Review* 98, no. 4 (October 2005): 435, 471.

10 Lewis, *English Literature*, 167.

11 Walter M. Gordon, "Thomas More's *Utopia*: Preface to Reformation," *Renaissance and Reformation* 33, no. 3 (1997): 25. More's "merry tales" were amusing, but piercing homiletic counterparts to Luther's table talks. See Anne Lake Prescott's "Thomas More's Merry Tales," *Criticism* 45, no. 4 (2003): 417–33, who notes that for More to "joke when facing juries, political opponents, courtly competitors, angry heretics, worrisome rules, or even shrewish wives is to signal a smiling urbanity—*eutrapelia*" (417).

12 Lewis, *English Literature*, 167.

13 Desiderius Erasmus, *The Praise of Folly and Other Writings*, trans. Robert M. Adams (Norton, 1980), 25.

14 Ibid., 62.

15 Ibid., 81.

16 Ibid., 87.

17 In his *Adages*, Erasmus calls Christ a sort of Silenus, the old drunken man who accompanies Bacchus in his revelry. His explanation is that little statues of this obese sot often contained precious ointments, and so in His earthen vessel, Jesus too contained salvation for all men. Cited in Erasmus, *The Praise of Folly and Other Writings*, 241fn2.

18 Desiderius Erasmus, "Letter to Martin Dorp," in *In Praise of Folly*, trans. Clarence H. Miller (Yale University Press, 2003), 143. Erasmus's essay "*Lingua*: On the Tongue" (1525) extends the advice of taming this wild member by St. James in his epistle warning against calumny and the dangers of sick and accusatory speech (3:1–18).

19 Ibid., 242.

20 Erasmus, "Convivium fabulosum," in *Colloquies*, 266.

21 John Huizinga, "Erasmus's Mind," in *The Praise of Folly*., 298. Comedian Jon Stewart continues in this tradition, donning a "clown nose on, clown nose off" routine when he puts forward a passionate opinion to be taken seriously, and if challenged, he excuses himself as a mere comedian.

22 Erasmus, "Letter to François Dubois" (March 13, 1526), in *The Correspondence of Erasmus: Letters 1658 to 1801, January 1526–March 1527*, ed. Charles Garfield Nauert and Alexander Dalzell, (University of Toronto Press, 2003), 79.

23 Arthur Lionel Smith, *Erasmus: Humorist, Scholar, Divine* (Oxford University Press, 1874), 55

24 Zuver, *Salvation by Laughter*, 226.

25 Lewis, *The Screwtape Letters*, 5.

26 Martin Luther, "Against Hanswurst," in *Luther's Works* (Fortress Press/Concordia, 1957), 41: 185.

27 Steven Ozment, *The Serpent and the Lamb: Cranach, Luther, and the Making of the Reformation* (Yale University Press, 2011), 108–9.

28 Ibid., 150–51

29 Cited in Harry Gerald Haile, *Luther: An Experiment in Biography* (Princeton University Press, 1980), 116. Later, American Ambrose Bierce would pick up on Luther's levity and define a "reliquary" as "a receptacle for such sacred objects as pieces of the true cross, short-ribs of the saints, the ears of Balaam's ass, the lung of the cock that called Peter to repentance and so forth. A feather from the wing of the Angel of the Annunciation once escaped during a sermon in St. Peter's and so tickled the noses of the congregation that they woke and sneezed with great vehemence three times each." Ambrose Bierce, *The Devil's Dictionary*, in *The Collected Works of Ambrose Bierce* (Neale Publishing, 1911), 283.

30 Cited in Eric W. Gritsch, *The Wit of Martin Luther* (Fortress Press, 2006), 120. Luther's oldest child, Little Hans, solemnly imagined "what fun it must be in heaven to eat and jump and play. There is a river of milk there and nice breakfast rolls grow of themselves." So, his father observed, "A child's life is the happiest for he has no political cares, nor ecclesiastical abuses to contend with, nor does he fear death, nor future infirmity, but sees only the good." Martin Luther, *Conversations with Luther*, ed. Preserved Smith (Pilgrim Press, 1915), 41.

31 Ibid., 118.

32 Ibid., 119.

33 See John Jackson and William Andrew Chatto, *A Treatise on Wood-Engraving* (Charles Knight and Co., 1839).

34 Josef Schmidt and Mary Simon, "Holy and Unholy Shit: The Pragmatic Context of Scatological Curses in Early German Reformation Satire," in *Fecal Matters in Early Modern Literature and Art*, ed. Jeff Persels and Russell Ganim, 109–17. Luther proposed that "out of a desperate ass never comes a cheerful fart" (quoted in Gritsch, *Wit of Martin Luther*, 114).

35 Gloria Klein, *A Metaphysical and Anecdotal Consideration of the Fart* (Alphabeta Press, 1995), 32.

36 Quoted in Gritsch, *Wit of Martin Luther*, 74.

37 Lewis, *The Screwtape Letters*, 5

38 Luther cited in Eric Gritsch, "Luther's Humor: Instrument of Witness," *Dialog* 22 (Summer 1983): 177–80.

39 Roland H. Bainton, *Here I Stand: A Life of Martin Luther* (Pierce and Smith, 1950), 308.

40 Martin H. Manser, *Westminster Collection of Christian Quotations* (John Knox Press, 2001), 225.

41 Hugh Young Reyburn, *John Calvin: His Life, Letters and Work* (Hodder and Stoughton, 1914), 329.

42 John Calvin, *John Calvin's Commentaries on the Psalms 93-119*, ed. William Barry (Jazzybee, 2012), 104:15.

43 Calvin is more apt to use "mocking and derisory rhetoric," pointing out his adversaries "with the finger" of scorn. In his *Disputations* (1544), he endorses ridicule as a "joyous and pleasant manner of teaching," which subverts foolish superstitions. He censures those irreverent, Epicurean writers like Rabelais who had tasted the Gospels, but now were "struck with blindness" for their "ribald mockery," and whom he considers, in his *De scandalis*, to be "atheist." Antonia Szabari, *Less Rightly Said* (Stanford University Press, 2010), 127 See also Serene Jones, *Calvin and the Rhetoric of Piety* (Westminster John Knox, 1995), 126; Rabelais returns the attack on the former lawyer by accusing him of propagating "monstrous children of Anti-nature, who have heads entirely round like a ball and roll upside down, with bulging eyes glued to their heads as "heels glued to shoes," with legs in the air and "ears pricked up large like donkeys." (95)

44 Schmidt-Clausing, *The Humor of Huldrych Zwingli*, 11.

45 Ibid., vii, 11, 45.

46 Ibid., 19.

47 Ibid., 25.

48 Ibid.

49 Pierre Viret, *Metamorphose chretienne* (1561), 2:454.

50 Szabari, *Less Rightly Said*, 161, 164. Szabari points out that during the great era of discovery of the New World with all its fresh cosmographic models, this was the largest satirical image published in the sixteenth century, and it portrayed the pope's summer palace as hell, even as the map was placed in the drooling and salivating mouth of the devil. Even as it caricatures reformers attacking Dame Transubstantiation and destroying idols, the papists build the Rotunda and rape Dame Truth. The Ferryman Charon transports a boatload of prelates to hell, with a running inventory of insults. He confesses he was about to "split and die from laughing at these beasts" (172).

51 Robert Linder, "Forgotten Reformer," *Christian History*, July 1, 2001, 36.

52 *Satyres chrestiennes de la cuisine papale*, ed. Charles Antoine Chamay (Librairie Droz, 2005).

53 Lewis once described purgatory as a kitchen where everything was going wrong, with cauldrons of milk boiling over, animals running wildly, and the burning of toast. What made it purgatory was that the women had to learn to sit still and mind their own business while the men had to learn to jump up and do something about it. William Griffin, *Clive Staples Lewis* (Harper and Row, 1986), 430.

54 Szabari, *Less Rightly Said*, 102.

55 Ibid., 105, 112.

56 Ibid., 118.

57 Screech, *Laughter at the Foot of the Cross*, 46.

58 Merle D'Aubigne, *History of the Reformation in Europe* (Sprinkle Publications, 2000), 223.

59 Marguerite of Navarre, *Selected Writings*, trans. Rouben Cholakian and Mary Skemp (University of Chicago Press, 2008), 2.

60 Davis, *Storytellers in Marguerite de Navarre's Heptameron*, 17.

61 Marguerite of Navarre, *The Heptameron*, 5:41, 377–79.

62 Ibid., 5:46, 406–7.

63 By the end of the century, Gallic wit reached another pinnacle with the publication of the free-wheeling *Satyre Menippee* (1593), a collaborative medley of cheerful intellectual texts that attacked the leaders of the fundamentalist Catholic League. As the English translation suggested, it sought to wisely rebuke vice without regard to persons, revealing how ridiculous the speeches of the League of the Estates-General were. In the preface, a Spanish charlatan and his League compatriot try to sell Catholicon, their version of the Catholic faith, a mind-numbing drug and panacea promising forgiveness of all sins and freedom to do whatever one wishes. As satire, it worked, helping moderates to usher in the reign of Henry of Navarre. The dislike of the King of Spain is expressed with grotesque imagery. He has so much wealth and power that "when he exudes sweat: it is diadems; when he blows his nose: it is crowns; when he belches: it is scepters; when he goes to the toilet: it is counties and duchies that come out of his body." Szabari *Less Rightly Said*, 177.

64 Stephen Gosson, *Schoole of Abuse* (1579), https://scholarsbank.uoregon.edu/xmlui/bitstream/handle/1794/738/gosson.pdf?sequence=1.

65 See Matthew Milner, *The Senses and the English Reformation* (Ashgate Publishing, 2011), 323.

66 Anselment, *"Betwixt Jest and Earnest,"* 41.

67 Thomas Wilson, *The Art of Rhetoric* (Benediction Books, 2010), np.

68 Horace, *Satires of Horace and Persius, trans. Niall Rudd (Penguin Classics, 2005),* 4. For a fuller treatment, see Jennifer L. Ferriss-Hill, *Roman Satire and the Old Comic Tradition* (Cambridge University Press, 2015), 27.

69 Anselment, *"Betwixt Jest and Earnest,"* 64.

70 Ibid.

71 Francis Bacon, *The Philosophical Works of Francis Bacon*, ed. Peter Shaw (J. J. and P. Knapton, 1733), 2: 293

72 John Milton, "An Apology for Smectymnuus," in *A Complete Collection of the Historical, Political, and Miscellaneous Works of John Milton*, ed. Thomas Birch (A. Millar, 1738), 116

73 Anselment, *"Betwixt Jest and Earnest,"* 63–66.

74 James Doelman, "Religious Epigram in Early Stuart England," *Christianity and Literature* 54, no. 4 (2005): 497–520.

75 Nashe has been called the English Aretino, attacking self-promoting intellectuals, inventing neologisms, and being a bit of a naughty boy.

76 Donne cited in Wells, *The Devil and Doctor Dwight*, 18–19.

77 He is no Gnostic, though, as he celebrates "full nakedness! / All joys are due to thee, / As souls unbodied, bodied unclothed must be, / To taste whole joys." Elegy XIX, "To His Mistress Going to Bed" 1:33.

78 John Donne, *The Complete Poems of John Donne* (Routledge, 2010), 391.

79 John Peter, *Complaint and Satire in Early English Literature* (Clarendon Press, 1956), 134.

80 Donne, *Complete Poems*, 188.

81 Ibid., 387.

82 James Cleugh, *The Divine Aretino Pietro of Arezzo* (Blond, 1965). Pietro Aretine/ Aretino was infamous for his obscene illustrations and scurrilous poetry and being the most erotic writer in Christendom, becoming the bane of religious leaders in the corrupt sixteenth century. Using racy and ribald wit, he attacked bishops and wannabe popes. When Hanno, the pet white elephant of Pope Leo X died, Aretino rushed off a pamphlet on "The Last Will and Testament of the Elephant Hanno," even bequeathing the pachyderm's genitals to one of the lusty cardinals. Patronized by Cardinal de Medici, Aretino was known for his gusto and audacity in attacking everything and blackmailing many, seeking to earn the sobriquet he gave himself, *flagello dei principi*, "scourge of princes." Credited and blamed for inventing modern literate pornography, he allegedly died of suffocation from "laughing too much." When Pope Leo X died, one final pasquinade popped up: "If you desire to hear why at his last hour, Leo could not the sacraments take, know he had sold them." Parton, *Caricature and Other Comic Art*, 258.

83 Isaac Barrow, "Against Foolish Talking and Jesting," in *Theological Works of Isaac Barrows*, ed. Alexander Napier (Cambridge University Press, 1999), 16.

84 Ibid.,18.

85 Ibid., 21.

86 Ibid., 37.

87 Ibid., 38.

88 Isaac Barrow, "Sermons on Evil Speaking," http://www.shdbbs.com/book/1584932/Sermons-on-Evil-Speaking/num_1.html.

89 By 1900, Reverend Anselm Kroll recommended "Eutrapelia: Hints for Jovial Priests" in *American Ecclesiastical Review* 22 (1900): 163–77.

90 Agnes Repplier, *In Pursuit of Laughter* (Houghton Mifflin, 1936), 68.

91 Tim Harris, *Restoration: Charles II and His Kingdoms, 1660–1685* (Allen Lane, 2005), 52–53.

92 Wasserman, *Samuel "Hudibras" Butler*.

93 Samuel Butler, *Hudibras* (Oxford University Press, 1967) 9.

94 Ibid., 14. The internal militancy of the church was caricatured wherein the fissure between Roman Catholics and Reformed Protestants provoked one Dutch artist, Adriaen Pietersz van de Venne, to paint *Fishing for Souls* (1614), a political/religious allegory reconstituting spiritual battles for conversion between the Dutch Republic and Spain as a mere parable of jealousy over capturing the most "fish" for their side.

95 Ibid., 15.

96 Ibid., 262.

97 Wasserman, *Samuel "Hudibras" Butler*, 91.

98 Richard Zoglin, *Comedy at the Edge* (Bloomsbury, 2008), 7.

99 Butler, *Hudibras*, 107. A skimmington was a common way to morally express criticism of a husband or wife with inversions of the sexual hierarchy.

100 Ibid.

101 Isaace D'Israeli, "On the Hero of *Hudibras*: Butler Vindicated," in *Curiosities of Literature*, 359–60.

102 Joke Spaans, *Graphic Satire and Religious Change: The Dutch Republic, 1676–1707* (Brill, 2011), 27.

103 Frederick Turner, "On Satire in the Arts," *American Arts Quarterly* (Fall 2012): 29.

CHAPTER 6. AUGUSTAN POETS AND PUNDITS

1 In fact, one may detect a bit of egoism when he scripted his wife's epitaph: "Here lies my wife; here let her lie! Now she's at rest, and so am I."

2 C. N. Manlove, *Literature and Reality, 1600–1800* (St. Martin's Press, 1978), 57.

3 John Dryden, *John Dryden: The Major Works*, ed. Keith Walker (Oxford University Press, 1987), 228

4 John Dryden, *Discourse Concerning the Original and Progress of Satire* (Nabu Press, 2012), 65. See Stephen Zwicker, *The Cambridge Companion to John Dryden* (Cambridge University Press, 2004).

5 John Dryden, *The Works of John Dryden*, ed. H. T. Swedenberg, Jr., and Vinton A. Dearing (University of California Press, 1974), 4:71

6 Hilary, *Verses of the Poet Laureate*, 17.

7 Ironically enough, laughter for Shaftesbury belonged with the lower classes of porters, clowns, jailbirds, and all the inhabitants of Bedlam; thus, to be laughed at was especially galling. Vic Gatrell, *City of Laughter: Sex and Satire in Eighteenth-Century London* (Walker and Company, 2006), 163.

8 Hippolyte A. Taine, *History of English Literature* (Frederick Ungar, 1965), 3:52–53.

9 John Dryden, "Absalom and Architophel," in *The Poems of John Dryden*, ed. Paul Hammond Routledge, 1995), 1:469.

10 Taine, *History of English Literature*, 158.

11 Wells, *The Devil and Dr. Dwight*. Shaftesbury was described as a "philosophical bumblebee" whose key works offered a great deal of "idle buzzing" (ibid., 8).

12 Shaftesbury offered three propositions as religious bases of laughter: First "that wit and humour are corroborative of religion and promotive of true faith"; second, "that they are used as proper means of this kind by the holy founders of religion"; and last, "that notwithstanding the dark complexion and sour humours of some religious teachers, we may be justly said to have in the main a witty and good-humoured religion." Martin, *The Triumph of Wit*, 13.

13 See W. K. Thomas, *The Crafting of Absalom and Achitophel* (Wilfrid Laurier University Press, 1978), 7.

14 Ibid., 29–30. Dryden defined the art of "True Satire" as consisting of "fine Raillery," a natural, inborn gift of Genius, in which one knew "How easy is it to call Rogue and Villain, and that wittily! But how hard to make a Man appear a Fool, a Blockhead, or a Knave, without using any of those opprobrious terms! To spare the grossness of the Names, and to do the thing yet more severely, is to draw a full Face, and to make the Nose and Cheeks stand out, and yet not to employ any depth of Shadowing. This is the Mystery of that Noble Trade." John Dryden, "A Discourse on Satire," in *Poetical Works*, ed. John Wharton (George Routledge and Sons, 1873), 380.

15 Dryden "Absalom," 103–4.

16 Ibid., 20–21.

17 It is the nature of religion and politics to overlap, as Edward and Lillian Bloom point out, bleeding into each other especially when the institution of the church becomes Christendom and nominal Christianity is supplanted by the secular priest craft. Bloom and Bloom, *Satire's Persuasive Voice*, 78.

18 Murray Roston, *The Comic Mode in English Literature* (Continuum, 2011), 11. The sexual improprieties of Charles II were notorious, leading to Dryden's salacious in-joke.

19 John Dryden, "Preface to the Fables," in *John Dryden: The Major Works*, 552.

20 Bloom and Bloom, *Satire's Persuasive Voice*, 83.

21 Ibid.

22 Dryden was not so kind to Jonathan Swift, writing "Cousin Swift you will never be a poet." Cited in Henry Craik, *The Life of Jonathan Swift* (McMillan and Co., 1894), 277–88.

23 Chris Boswell, "The Culture and Rhetoric of the Answer Poem, 1485–1626" (Ph.D. diss., University of Leeds, 2003); Arnold Davenport, "The Quarrel of the Satirists," *Modern Language Review* 37 (1942): 123–30. Boswell calls these "provocative

RSVPs," citing Cicero's clever dictum, "to retort is human" (http://www.cultureandrhetoric.net/).

24 English physician Thomas Lodge's classical *A Fig for Momus* (1579) identified Momus, the god of satire, as etymologically connected to the Greek "blame or censure." Leering out from behind a mask, he was exiled from Olympus for excessive mocking of the gods.

25 Joseph Hall, "Satire III," in *The Works of the Right Reverend Father in God, Joseph Hall X*, ed. Josiah Pratt (C. Whittingham, 1808), 366.

26 Bloom and Bloom, *Satire's Persuasive Voice*, 17.

27 Hall, "Satire III," 283.

28 Ibid., 352.

29 Elliott, *The Power of Satire*, 70.

30 Congreve believed it the business "of a comic poet to paint the vices and follies of human kind." His wit circled around gender relations, regarding which he observed in *The Way of the World* that marriage "makes man and wife one flesh, it leaves 'em two fools." But "Marry'd in haste, we may repent in leisure." *The Works of Mr. Congreve* (W. Lowndes, 1788), 78, 63.

31 According to Swift, this burlesque of Tom Thumb made him laugh for the second time in his life. Henry Fielding, *Joseph Andrews and Shamela*, ed. Thomas Keymer (Oxford University Press, 2008), viii.

32 Ibid., vi. Fielding added several barbs at old Walpole, portraying him as a character called Jonathan Wild, a highwayman who ends up getting hanged, and the poet laureate of England, Colley Cibber.

33 Ibid., 337.

34 Thomas Lockwood, "*Shamela*," in *The Cambridge Companion to Henry Fielding* (Cambridge University Press, 2007), 44.

35 Henry Fielding, *Joseph Andrews* (Houghton Mifflin, 1961), xx.

36 Roston, *The Comic Mode*, 10. See George Meredith, "Essay on Comedy," in *Comedy*, ed. Wylie Sypher. (Doubleday Anchor, 1956). In seeking to preserve the status quo, Meredith reminds one of the old uppity Episcopal woman who complained that while "it takes all kinds of people to make a world, I thank God I am not one of them."

37 See George Meredith, *George Meredith's Essay on Comedy*, ed. Maura C. Ives (Associated University Press, 1998), 140. In his *Serious Call to a Devout and Holy Life* (CreateSpace, 2010), the father of evangelicalism, William Law, defended the use of humor in exposing such vanity and lambasting sanctimonious posturing. His character of Flavia, who paid her milliner more than she gave in charity, "once commended a sermon that was against the pride and vanity of dress, and thought it very just against Lucinda, whom she takes to be a great deal finer than she needs to be" (62–68).

38 Fielding, *Shamela*, 318.

39 Fielding, *Joseph Andrews*, 270; See James Evans, "The World According to Paul: Comedy and Theology in 'Joseph Andrews,'" *Review of International English Literature* (1984), in which the novel is interpreted through the biblical passage of Paul's first letter to the Corinthians 3:18–19. Fielding praised the apostle's facility in combining humor and seriousness: "Not to mention the Instance of St. Paul, whose writings do in my Opinion contain more true Wit, than is to be found in the Works of the unjustly celebrated Petronius." Fielding and Paul's holy fools, like Don Quixote and St. Thomas a Kempis, are praiseworthy fools, because they "refused to accept what was universally accepted by the world" (Evans, 46).

40 Paul Baines, "*Joseph Andrews*," in *The Cambridge Companion to Henry Fielding*, 96.

41 Ibid., 44–45.

42 Cited in ibid., 89.

43 Fielding satirized "not men, but manners, not an individual, but a species," of which the Methodists were ripe for correcting. Cited in Gatrell, *City of Laughter*, 173.

44 Henry Fielding, *The History of Tom Jones* (Digireads, 2009), 407.

45 Ibid., 14

46 Henry Fielding, *The Works of Henry Fielding* (Smith, Elder and Co., 1882), 5:388.

47 Fielding, "Apology for the Clergy," *The Champion* (1740), np.

48 Raymond J. S. Grant, *Laughter of Love: Study of Robert Burns* (Detselig, 1986), 5.

49 One very old, well-concocted, and repeated Scottish joke tells of Burns' only visit to a Roman Catholic confessional: "Forgive me faither, for I have sinned; I hae committed Adam's sin o' the flesh." "With whom did ye dae this?" asked the priest. "Oh faither, I canna tell ye the girlie's name." "Well, was it Mary McEwen? Maggie MacLeod? Peggy MacLaren?' "I'm sorry faither, but it wad nae be richt tae tell ye the quine's name." "Oh well," sighed the priest, "say ten Aves and ten paters every night for a week." Coming out of the church, his friend asked if it did any good for his soul. "Na, na, but I got us the names o' three certainties."

50 Satirist John Cleveland described Scotland as "A land where one may pray with cursed intent, / Oh, may they never suffer banishment! / Had Cain been Scot, God would have chang'd his doom— / Not forc'd him wander, but confin'd him home." Cited in Wells, *The Devil and Doctor Dwight*, 32.

51 Robert Burns, *Burns in English: Select Poems of Robert Burns*, ed. Alexander Corbett(Corbett, 1892), 69.

52 Grant, *Laughter of Love*, 17.

53 Cited in ibid., 24.

54 Robert Burns, *Complete Poetical Works of Robert Burns*, ed. Nathan Haskell Dole (Nabu Press, 2010), 52.

55 Having just squashed the Scottish farmer's rooster, the English tourist apologizes: "I say old chap, I'm frightfully sorry but I seem to have run over your rooster. I'd like to replace him." To which the Scottish farmer replies: "Suit yerself—-the hens is roun' back."

56 Burns, *Complete Poetical Works*, 15.

57 Cited in Grant, *Laughter of Love*, 83.

58 John Gibson Lockhart and James Currie, *The Works of Robert Burns* (William Pearson, 1835), iv.

59 George Gordon Byron, *The Works of Lord Byron* (A. and W. Galignani, 1831), 589.

60 Ibid., 724.

61 One hellish torment given by this grim, mischief-making chap of hell appears in Burns's "Address to the Toothache," in Burns, *Complete Poetical Works*, 155

62 Ibid., 171–73.

63 Ibid., 79

64 Ibid.

65 Ibid.

66 Thomas Crawford, ed., *Burns: A Study of the Poems and Songs* (Stanford University Press, 1960), 74.

67 Burns, *Complete Poetical Works*, 219; Grant, *Laughter of Love*, 123.

68 Grant, *Laughter of Love*, 118 (my emphasis).

69 Alexander Pope, *An Essay on Man*, in *Works of Alexander Pope* (William Durrell, 1808), 2:55.

70 Alexander Pope, *The Poetical Works of Alexander Pope*, ed. John Wilson Croker (John Murray, 1886), 9:104.

71 In *An Essay on Criticism*, Pope challenged would-be critics and writers to imitate classic authors like Virgil while warning that "fools rush in where angels fear to tread." He recommended that one imbibe the inspiration from the Muses at the Macedonian site of the Pierian springs, admonishing that "A little learning is a dangerous thing: Drink deep, or taste not the Pierian spring." Of course, he also includes here the blessing that "to err is human, to forgive divine."

72 Prime Minister Robert Walpole was chief magician for George II and well known for his Great Glistening Belly, *Gaster Argos*, celebrated in the Festival of the Golden Rump, in which his large rump of solid gold directed toward his worshippers. Such an image alluded to both the sycophants who sought to curry the king's favor and the king's coarse habit of turning his ample backside on any who displeased him.

73 Pope, *The Poetical Works*, 3:507

74 Alexander Pope, "Epistle IV," in *The Works of Alexander Pope*, ed. William Warburton (Willis P. Hazard, 1856), 250.

75 Alexander Pope, *The Works of Alexander Pope: Satires* (Ulan Press, 2012), 316.

76 Alexander Pope, *One Thousand Seven Hundred and Thirty Eight: Dialogue II*, 2:145–46.

77 Pope, *The Poetical Works*, 5:363.

78 Pope, *Essay on Man*, 622–25.

79 Queenan, *The Malcontents*, 710, 713.

80 Pope, *The Works of Alexander Pope*, ed. Warburton, 245.

81 Ibid., 245–46

82 Ibid., 246–47.

83 Mack, *Alexander Pope*, i, 184, 225.

84 Cited in ibid., 277. See Dustin H. Griffin, *Alexander Pope: The Poet in Poems* (Princeton University Press, 1978), 50, and Robert H. Bell, "Homer's Humor: Laughter in the Iliad" *Humanitas* 10, nos. 1–2 (2007): 99–100. Of all his friends, Pope was the sickly one, the "only wit of the day who wasn't fat. Swift was fat; Addison was fat; Gay was preposterously fat—all that fuddling and punch-drinking, that club and coffee-house boozing, shortened the lives and enlarged the waistcoats of the men of that age." Thackeray, *The English Humorists*, 216.

85 Pope, *The Poetical Works*, 10:554.

86 Walpole was himself caricatured in religious terms as vomiting, in an allusion to Job 20:15: "He hath Swallowed down Riches and he shall Vomit them up again." God shall cast them out of his belly. Mack, *Alexander Pope*, 192.

87 Ibid., 636.

88 Ibid., 300.

89 Martin Blocksidge, *The Sacred Weapon: Introduction to Pope's Satire* (Book Guild Publishing, 1993), 22.

90 Edward Bensly, "Pope," in *The Cambridge History of English Literature: IX, From Steele and Addison to Pope and Swift*, ed. A. W. Ward and A. R. Waller (Cambridge University Press, 1962), 66–90.

91 Lady Mary Wortley Montagu. *The Poetical Works* (J. Williams, 1768), 170.

92 Joseph Addison, quoted in Thackeray, *English Humorists*, 88, n2.

93 Alexander Pope, *Memoirs of the Extraordinary Life, Works, and Discoveries of Martinus Scriblerus*, ed. Charles Kerby-Miller (Russell & Russell, 1966).

94 Alexander Pope, "Epilogue to the Satires," in *Imitations of Horace*, ed. John Butt (Metheun, 1961), 1:53.

95 Mack, *Alexander Pope*, 337. Pope established the "Club of Little Men," who kept their annual founders' day feast on the shortest day of the year over a dish of shrimps, and were sworn to uphold "the Dignity of littleness under the Noses of those Enormous Engrossers of manhood, those Hyperbolical Monsters of the Species, the tall Fellows that overlook us" (ibid., 213). A group in Virginia Beach still meets each year on December 21 at Bubba's Restaurant to commemorate a "Club of Little Men and Women" by reading couplets, haiku, clerihews, and other short verse and consuming shrimp, shortening bread, and half-pints.

96 Cited in Wallace Jackson, *Vision and Re-Vision in Alexander Pope* (Wayne State University Press, 1983), 170.

97 Pat Rogers, *An Introduction to Pope* (Routledge Revivials, 2014), 103.

98 Alexander Pope, *The Dunciad*, ed. Valerie Rumbold (Routledge, 2009), 109.

99 Aubrey Williams, *Pope's Dunciad* (Archon,1968), 132.

100 Robert Griffin, "Pope, the Prophets, and *The Dunciad*," in Harold Bloom, ed., *Alexander Pope: Modern Critical Views* (Chelsea House, 1986), 133.

101 Ibid., 134.

102 Bloom, ed., *Alexander Pope*, 140

103 Alexander Pope, "Satires of Horace," in *Works of Alexander Pope* (C. Bathhurst, 1770), 4:125.

104 Griffin, "Pope, the Prophets, and *The Dunciad*," 139, 143.

105 Maynard Mack, *The Garden and the City*, (University of Toronto Press, 1969), 232

106 Pope, *The Poetical Works*, 286.

107 Alexander Pope, *The Works of Alexander Pope*, ed. John Wilson Croker (John Murray, 1881) 3:368.

108 Ibid., 9:214.

109 Ibid., 508

110 Jonathan Swift, *The Works of Jonathan Swift, D. D.*, ed. Thomas Roscoe (Derby Jackson, 1859), 1:254.

111 Pope, *Dunciad*, 1:19–20. Like Pope, Swift was incapacitated by disease—in his case, Meniere's disease, which struck him with fits of vertigo or giddiness from excess water in his ears. "I have the noise of seven watermills in my ears." Cited in Reg Wright, *Satirists and Humorists* (Marshall Cavendish, 1989), 10.

112 Jonathan Swift, *Gulliver's Travels*, (Penguin, 2003), 178. However, as Edward and Lillian Bloom caution, "don't confuse an author with his excremental obsessions" (Bloom and Bloom, *Satire's Persuasive Voice*, 30). Swift saw the positive; he still wanted to shock his readers.

113 Todd C. Parker, *Swift as Priest and Satirist* (University of Delaware Press, 2009). As Parker notes, "Swift's sermons suggest that the true Christian engages society actively with an aim of reforming vice and promoting virtue" (100).

114 Walter Scott, ed., *Memoirs of Jonathan Swift* (I. A. & W. Galignani, 1826), 179.

115 Martin Banham, ed., *The Cambridge Guide to Theatre* (Cambridge University Press, 1998), 414.

116 John Gay, *The Beggars' Opera and Polly*, ed. Hal Gladfelder, (Oxford University Press, 2013), 5.

117 Christopher Fox, "Swift and the Rabble Reformation: A Tale of the Tub and the State of the Church in the 1690s," cited in in Parker, *Swift as Priest and Satirist*, 102.

118 Swift, *The Works*, 1:289.

119 Ibid., 322.

120 Fox, "Swift and the Rabble Reformation," cited in in Parker, *Swift as Priest and Satirist*, 101.

121 Sarah Ellensweig, *The Fringes of Belief* (Stanford University Press, 2008).

122 Swift, *The Works*, 1:331.

123 Peter Leithart, *Against Christianity* (Canon Press, 2003), 12; Peter Leithart, *Miniatures and Morals: The Christian Novels of Jane Austen* (Canon, 2004), 74.

124 Anselment, *"Betwixt Jest and Earnest,"* 127.

125 Ibid., 132

126 Bloom and Bloom, *Satire's Persuasive Voice*, 29.

127 Ibid., 131.

128 Jonathan Swift, "Author's Preface," in *A Modest Proposal and Other Satires* (Digiread, 2007), 68.

129 Swift, *The Works*, 1:82.

130 Anselment, *"Betwixt Jest and Earnest,"* 134.

131 Ibid., 135. See Ronald Paulson's *Don Quixote in England: The Aesthetics of Laughter* (John Hopkins University Press, 1998).

132 Swift quoted in Dustin Griffin, *Swift and Pope: Satirists in Dialogue* (Cambridge University Press, 2010), 78.

133 After it was published, Swift told his friend Pope about the credulity of a "Bishop here [who] said that Book was full of improbable lies, and for his part, he hardly believed a word of it." Swift, *The Works*, 1: 166.

134 Ibid., 196.

135 Edward and Lillian Bloom suggest that the Brobdingnagian king who looks upon Gulliver and muses that he "cannot but conclude the bulk of your natives to be the most pernicious race of little odious vermin that nature ever suffered to crawl upon the surface of the earth" might even be a stand-in for Swift (*Satire's Persuasive Voice*). In *The Screwtape Letters*, Lewis echoes this ridicule with his devil expressing his disgust at this "human vermin" (85).

136 Vickers, *The World of Jonathan Swift*, 16.

137 G. A. Aitken, "Swift," in Ward and Waller, *Cambridge History*, 91–128.

138 Swift, quoted in Thackeray, *English Humorists*, 202.

139 Basil Hall, "'An Inverted Hypocrite': Swift the Churchman," in Vickers, *The World of Jonathan Swift* (Blackwell, 1968), 38–68; David Nokes, *Jonathan Swift, A Hypocrite Reversed* (Oxford University Press, 1986).

140 Swift quoted in Aitken, "Swift," 112.

141 H. Dooley, "Satire and Satirists," *The Scottish Review* (January 1856): 22.

142 Henry Miller, "Some Relationships between Humor and Religion in Eighteenth-Century England," *Thalia: Studies in Literary Humor* 6, no. 1 (Spring/Summer 1983): 48–59.

143 Bloom and Bloom, *Satire's Persuasive Voice*, 115.

144 Jonathan Swift, *Works of the Rev. Dr. Jonathan Swift*, ed. Thomas Sheridan (Bathurst, Strahan, and Collins, 1784), 476.

145 Louis Bredvold, "The Gloom of the Tory Satirists," in *Pope and His Contemporaries*, ed. James Clifford and Louis Landa (Clarendon Press, 1949), 1–19.

146 Swift quoted in ibid., 111.

147 Pope, *The Works of Alexander Pope*, 266

148 Zuver, *Salvation by Laughter*, 22.

149 Swift, *The Works* 7:24; see Vickers, *The World of Jonathan Swift*, 17.

150 Swift, *The Works*, 7:171.

151 Swift, "An Argument for the Abolishing of Christianity," in *Works*, ed. Sheridan, 4:7.

152 Ibid., lxiii.

153 Ibid., 235.

154 Ibid., 227.

155 Sir Walter Scott defended the "Argument" as "one of the most felicitous efforts in our language to engage wit and humor on the side of religion." Cited in *The Works of Jonathan Swift*, ed. Walter Scott (Edinburgh, 1814), 8:183.

156 See Irvin Ehrenpreis, *Swift: The Man, the Works, and His Age* (Harvard University Press, 1962), 1: 210–11.

157 Shaw, *Our Religious Humorists*, 110.

158 Ibid., 108.

159 Swift, *The Works*, 8: 586.

160 Samuel Johnson, ed., *The Works of the Poets: Volume VI Alexander Pope* (Andrew Miller, 1800), 399. In 1713, Roman Catholic poet Pope drolly expressed concern over his Anglican friend Swift's salvation, since Swift "must certainly be damned to all eternity" for having "composed more libels than sermons." Cited in Milburn, *The Age of Wit*, 270–71; In contrast, Swift playfully shows jealousy over Pope's verses (he could do more in one couplet that I can do in six) and prays that the Pox takes him and his wit. He notes that when he dies, Pope may grieve a month, Gay a week, and Arbuthnot a Day. And as soon as a year is past, there will be no further mention of the Dean whose Kind of Wit is now out of Date; as his moral view to cure the Vices of Mankind, exposing fools and lashing knaves, suffers as he may have had too "much Satyr in his Vein." His Satyr points at no Defect, But what all Mortals may correct. . . . Those, who their Ignorance confess'd, He ne'er offended with a Jest." Swift, *The Works*, 367. His satire here also previews biographer and critic Samuel Johnson critical reaction over Swift's means and limits of satire. For a fascinating treatment, see Jordan Hall Richman's *Johnson's Quarrel with Swift* (ArthurHouse, 1968), 34-55.

161 Søren Kierkegaard, *Søren Kierkegaard's Journals and Papers*, trans. Howard Hong and Edna Hong (Indiana University Press, 1970), 2:264.

162 James Boswell, *The Life of Johnson*, ed. William Wallace (William P. Nimmo, 1873), 478. Boswell countered Samuel Johnson's pronouncement with the observation that he must have been "a bold laugher who would have ventured tell Dr. Johnson of any of his particularities."

163 Ibid., 258. See C. Colton, *Hypocrisy: A Satire* (Taylor and Hessey, 1812), 6n.

164 Samuel Johnson, *Samuel Johnson's Prologue Spoken at the Opening of the Theatre in Drury Lane in 1747* (Nabu Press, 2012).

165 Samuel Johnson, *London: A Poem in Imitation of the Third Satire of Juvenal* (Gale ECCO, 2010), 1:166.

166 Conrad Brunstrom, *William Cowper: Religion, Satire, Society* (Bucknell University Press, 2004), 43.

167 Cowper, William "The Task," in *The Works of William Cowper*, ed. Robert Southey, H. G. Bohn, 1854), 2:57; See also *William Cowper: Selected Poetry and Prose*, ed. David Lyle Jeffrey (Regent College, 2007).

168 Brunstrom, *William Cowper*, 76.

169 Ibid., 72. This work was followed by Cowper's "Moral Satires."

170 Cited in Brunstrom, *William Cowper*, 70.

171 Cowper, "The Flatting Mill," in ibid., 230.

172 Cowper, "The Task," 36.

173 Burns, *Complete Poetical Works*, 52.

CHAPTER 7. CONTINENTAL WITS, RAKES, AND IRONISTS

1 Louis Clark Keating, *Joachim du Bellay* (Twayne Publishers, 1971), 72.

2 Joachim du Bellay, *Les regrets / The Regrets*, ed. and trans. Richard Helgerson (University of Pennsylvania Press, 2006), 131. The sonnets are reproduced as translated by Helgerson.

3 . Federico Fellini, dir., *La Dolce vita* (Pathe Consortium Films, 1960).

4 Du Bellay, *Regrets*, 81.

5 Ibid., 156.

6 Ibid.

7 Ibid., 159, 160.

8 Ibid., 187.

9 Ibid., 128.

10 Conversation with David Kornegay, New York City, April 8, 2011.

11 Lord Byron, *Don Juan*, ed. Jerome J. McGann (Oxford University Press, 1986), 768.

12 Miquel de Unamuno, *Tragic Sense of Life*, trans. Crawford Flitch (Dover, 1954) 315. "Those who put reason above faith die comically, while those die tragically who put faith above reason. For the mockers are those who die comically, and God laughs at their comic ending, while the nobler part, the part of tragedy, is theirs who endured the mockery" (316). With classic understatement, Unamuno once noted that among the people of his country, the admirable reply to the customary interrogation, "How are you?" was "Living" (303).

13 Coleridge quoted in Bloom and Bloom, *Satire's Persuasive Voice*, 26.

14 The author is indebted to Gabrielle Linnell for this translation and insight.

15 Francisco de Quevedo, *Dreams and Discourses*, trans. R. K. Britton (Aris & Phillips, 1989), 12.

16 Ibid., 65.

17 Ibid., 67.

18 Ibid. (my emphasis).

19 Ibid., 69.

20 Ibid., 290

21 Ibid., 291. I am indebted to Barry Ulanov for this insight.

22 Molière, *Tartuffe*, trans. Richard Wilbur (Harcourt Brace, 1963), 83 (my emphasis).

23 Ibid., 126–27.

24 H. G. Hall, "Molière, Satirist of Seventeenth-Century French Medicine: Fact and Fantasy," *Proceedings of the Royal Society of Medicine* 70 (June 1977): 428.

25 Molière quoted in "Molière," *Encyclopedia Britannica* online, 2007, http://www.britannica.com/EBchecked/topic/388302/Moliere.

26 Andrew Calderand David Bradby, *The Cambridge Companion to Molière* (Cambridge University Press, 2006), 224,n1.

27 F. H. Buckley, *The Morality of Laughter*, 93.

28 Blaise Pascal, *The Provincial Letters and Pensées*, ed. William Benton (University of Chicago, 1952), 81. He jabbed them further by asking if they didn't realize that "in blaming me for laughing at your absurdities, you may only afford me fresh subject of merriment." Indeed, Pascal argues, "there is a vast difference between laughing at religion and laughing at those who profane it by their extravagant opinions" (81).

29 Ibid., 83.

30 Ibid., 196.

31 Ibid., 265.

32 Olga Wester Russell, *Humor in Pascal* (Christopher Publishing, 1977), 123.

33 Pascal, *Pensées*, 347.

34 Blaise Pascal, *Pensées*, trans. Roger Ariew (Hackett, 2005), 38.

35 Pascal quoted in Buckley, *The Morality of Laughter*, 94. See Marc Escholier, *Port Royal: The Drama of the Jansenists* (Hawthorne, 1968), 102.

36 Francois Fénelon, *Dialogues on Eloquence*, trans. William Samuel Howell (Princeton University Press, 1951).

37 Edward Eggleston, *The Schoolmaster in Comedy and Satire* (American Book Company, 1894), 73–75.

38 François de Salignac de la Mothe Fénelon, *The Adventures of Telemachus, the Son of Ulysses*, trans. Tobias Smollett (University of Georgia Press, 1997).

39 Fénelon, *Fénelon's Finest Works* (Insight, 2009), 38

40 Voltaire would argue that Fénelon's *folie*, or madness, was heroic. See Karen Pagani, "Forgiveness and the Age of Reason," Ph.D. diss., University of Chicago, 2008), 279.

41 "As Horace did before me, so will I." Cited in Howard D. Weinbrot, *Alexander Pope and the Traditions of Formal Verse Satire* (Princeton University Press, 1982), 82. His *Lutrin* would provide a model for Pope's *The Rape of the Lock*.

42 Nicolas Boileau, "Sixth Satire," in *The Satires of Nicolas Boileau Despreaux and "His Address to the King,"* trans. Hayward Porter, (Glasgow University Press, 1904), 44.

43 Julian White, *Nicolas Boileau* (Twayne, 1969), 48.

44 Boileau, "Sixth Satire," 30.

45 Cited in A. F. B. Clark, *Boileau and the French Classical Critics in England* (E. Champion, 1925), 475.

46 Ibid., 468.

47 Boileau, "Le Lutrin: Canto II," http://en.wikisource.org/wiki/Le_Lutrin/Canto_II.

48 Gregory Carlson, "Four Revealing Moments in the Visual Intersection of Religion and Fables," *Journal of Religion & Society* 8 (2012): 77.

49 Ibid., 78.

50 Voltaire saw Pope as one of the most elegant and harmonious poets of England, reducing the "harsh blare of the English trumpet to the sweet sound of the flute." Quoted in Judson Milburn, *The Age of Wit: 1650-1750* (Macmillan, 1966), 178.

51 Voltaire, *Candide* (Dover, 1991), 86.

52 Voltaire, *God and Human Beings* (Prometheus, 2010), 11. Voltaire ridiculed the kinds of deities which people might invent, including "dea Rumilia" (god of nipples), "deus Stercutius" (god of the water closet), or "deus Crepitus" (god of flatulence). Voltaire, *The Works of Voltaire*, trans. John Morley (E. R. DuMont, 1901), 12:240.

53 Kent Wright Johnson, "*Candide*, Voltaire and the Enlightenment," in *Candide*, trans. Burton Raffel (Yale University Press, 2006), xvi; Theodore Besterman, *Voltaire* (University of Chicago Press, 1977).

54 Voltaire, *Candide*, trans. Roger Pearson (Oxford University Press, 2008), 10.

55 Voltaire, *Works*, 3:14.

56 Ibid.

57 Ibid.

58 Voltaire, "The Ecclesiastical Ministry," in *The Portable Voltaire*, trans. Ben Ray Redman (Penguin, 1977), np.

59 Voltaire, "Lent," in *Works*, 9:112.

60 Ibid., 9:43.

61 Hippolyte Taine, *History of English Literature* (Frederick Ungar, 1965), 3:92.

62 Susan Ratcliffe, Letter to Étienne Noël Damilaville (May 16, 1767), in *Oxford's Essential Quotations* (Oxford University Press, 2014).

63 Søren Kierkegaard, *Provocations: Spiritual Writings of Kierkegaard*, ed. Charles E. Moore (Plough, 2014), ix.

64 As Socrates was a supreme master of irony, he pretended to be ignorant by asking questions. His indirect communication prompted his learner to see the incongruity of his position and arrive at the truth.

65 Oscar Parcero Oubinha, "Comic/Comedy," in *Kierkegaard's Concepts*, ed. Steven M. Emmanuel (Ashgate, 2014), 6.

66 Søren Kierkegaard, "The Journals," *A Kierkegaard Anthology*, ed. Robert Bretall (Princeton University Press, 1946), 7.

67 Howard Johnson, "Kierkegaard and the Church," in *Philosophical Fragments*, trans. Walter Lowrie (Princeton University Press, 1991), xxii. See also Malcolm Muggeridge, *A Third Testament* (Collins, 1997).

68 Søren Kierkegaard, *The Gospel of Sufferings* (Lutterworth, 1987), 141–42. Many of these Christian satirists (such as Muggeridge and Lewis) confess to being reluctant and stubborn converts, looking for ways to escape the compelling truth of the Gospel.

69 Kierkegaard, Søren *The Prayers of Kierkegaard*, trans. Perry LeFevre (University of Chicago Press, 1956), 132.

70 Cited in Walter Lowrie, *A Short Life of Kierkegaard* (Princeton University Press, 1970), 235–36. One of my favorite palindromes (other than "Dennis sinned" or "Dennis and Edna sinned") is "do geese see God," a truly Kierkegaardian aphorism.

71 Kierkegaard, *Provocations*, 412–13.

72 Søren Kierkegaard, *The Journals of Søren Kierkegaard*, trans. Alexander Dru (Harper and Row, 1959), 50.

73 Ibid., 471.

74 Kierkegaard, *Provocations*, 16.

75 Søren Kierkegaard, *The Humor of Kierkegaard*, ed. Thomas C. Oden (Princeton University Press, 2004), 10.

76 Stephen Evans, "Kierkegaard's View of Humor: Must Christians Always Be Solemn?" *Faith and Philosophy* 4, no. 2 (April 1987): 177.

77 Søren Kierkegaard, *Stages on Life's Way*, trans. Howard V. Hong and Edna H. Hong) (Princeton University Press, 1988), 47.

78 John Lippitt, *Humor and Irony in Kierkegaard's Thought* (Macmillan, 2000).

79 Steven Emmanuel, ed., *Kierkegaard's Concepts* (Ashgate, 2014), 2:9.

80 Cited in Morreall, *Comedy, Tragedy, and Religion*, 2.

81 Kierkegaard, *Either/Or*, 272.

82 Søren Kierkegaard, *Parables of Kierkegaard*, ed. Thomas C. Oden (Princeton University Press, 1989), 3.

83 Georg Friedrich Meier, *Thoughts on Jesting*, trans. Joseph Jones (University of Texas Press, 1947), 55.

84 Barry Ulvanov, "Most Lamentable Comedy . . . Most Cruel Death: Rhetoric of Christian Comedy," *Literature as Christian Comedy*, McAuley Lectures, St. Joseph College, 1961, 69.

85 See C. S. Lewis, "Sad," in *Studies in Words* (Cambridge University Press, 1967), 75–85.

86 Knox, *Essays in Satire*, 25.

87 Allegedly, in 1790, he confessed in his Venetian Epigram 67 that he hated "tobacco smoke, bugs, garlic, and +" (presumably referring to the Christian cross), but still described himself as not anti-Christian. Cited in James Thompson and Bertram Dobell, *The City of Dreadful Night* (General Books, 2010), 1:229.

88 Johann Wolfgang Von Goethe, *Faust, Parts One and Two*, trans. George Madison Priest (Encyclopedia Britannica, 1952), 7.

89 Ibid., 9.

90 Ibid. 245–46; His later countryman Hermann Hesse warned readers (albeit in a novel): "You take the old Goethe much too seriously, my young friend. You should not take old people who are already dead seriously. It does them injustice. We immortals do not like things to be taken seriously. We like joking. Seriousness, young man, is an accident of time. It consists . . . in putting too high a value on time. Eternity is a mere moment, just long enough for a joke." *Steppenwolf* (Holt, 1990), 108.

91 François Boespflug, "Laughing at God," in Geybels and Van Herck, *Humour and Religion*, 210.

92 Ibid.

93 Robert Solomon and Kathleen Higgins, *What Nietzsche Really Said* (Schocken, 2001), 233.

94 Friedrich Nietzsche, *Beyond Good and Evil*, trans. Marion Faber (Oxford University Press, 1998), 175.

95 Solomon and Higgins, *What Nietzsche Really Said*, 86.

96 Cited in George Bataille, *On Nietzsche* (Paragon, 1998), 59.

97 Frederich Nietzsche, *Ecce Homo*, trans. Anthony Ludovici. (George Allen and Unwin, 1927), 88.

98 Friedrich Nietzsche, *Ecce Homo: How One Becomes What One Is*, trans. Dugan Large (Oxford University Press, 2007), 88.

99 Solomon and Higgins, *What Nietzsche Really Said*, 4. In a letter to a professor friend in Basel that resulted in his institutionalization in a mental ward, Nietzsche began: "In the end I would much rather be a Basel professor than God."

100 Nietzsche, *Beyond Good and Evil*, 65.

101 Ibid., 63.

102 Friedrich Nietzsche, "On Reading and Writing," in *Thus Spake Zarathustra*, trans. Robert Pippin (Cambridge University Press, 2006), 28.

103 Ibid., 226.

104 Brander Matthews, "The Wit and Humor of Continental Europe," in *The World's Wit and Humor Encyclopedia*, ed. Lionel Strachey (Review of Reviews Company, 1906).

105 Karl Barth, *Church Dogmatics: The Doctrine of the Word of God*, trans. G. W. Bromiley (T & T Clark, 1978), 1:§2:469.

106 Karl Barth, *A Late Friendship: Letters of Karl Barth and Carl Zuckmayer*, ed. Carl Zuckmayer (Eerdmans, 1982).

107 Daniel L. Migliore, "Reappraising Barth's Theology," *Theology Today* 41, no. 3 (April 1986): 309.

108 Barth, *Church Dogmatics: The Doctrine of Creation*, 3:§4:665.

109 Karl Barth, *Ethics*, trans. Geoffrey Bromiley (Seabury Press, 1981), 511.

110 See Karl Barth and Eberhard Busch, *Insights: Karl Barth Reflections on the Life of Faith* (Westminster, 2009), 6.

111 Migliore, "Reappraising Barth's Theology." See Karl Barth, *Church Dogmatics: The Doctrine of God*, 2:§1:665.

112 Karl Barth, *The Humanity of God*, trans. Thomas Wieser (Westminster John Knox Press, 1996), 61.

113 Giovanni Guareschi, *The Little World of Don Camillo*, trans. Una Vincenzo Troubridge (Pelligrini and Cudahy, 1950), 19–20.

114 Alan R. Perry, *Don Camillo Stories of Giovannion Guareschi: A Humorist Portrays the Sacred*, (University of Toronto Press, 2008), 186.

115 Ibid., 30.

116 Ibid., 31, 32.

117 Lipman, *Laughter in Hell*, 14–15. In Alexander Solzhenitsyn's *Gulag Archipelago* (Harper and Row, 1973), a man is arrested for merely smiling at something in *Pravda*: "the fact of smiling at the central organ of the party was in itself sacrilege" (283).

118 Guareschi quoted in Perry, *Don Camillo Stories*, 38, 39.

119 Guareschi quoted in ibid., 167.

120 Guareschi quoted in ibid., 189.

CHAPTER 8. AMERICAN NAIFS AND AGNOSTICS

1 Peter Briggs remarks on the "simultaneous newness and oldness of early American humor," as evidenced in Yale's John Trumbull. "English Satire and American Wit," in *American Humor*, ed. Arthur Power Dutton (Oxford University Press, 1989), 5.

2 Huston Diehl, "Disciplining Puritans and Players: Early Modern English Comedy and the Culture of Reform," *Religion and Literature* 32, no. 2 (2000): 81–104.

3 W. Howland Kenney, *Laughter in the Wilderness* (Kent State University Press, 1976), 8–9.

4 Laughter, for Chesterfield, was "easily restrained by a little reflection." Cited in Samuel Shellabarger, *Lord Chesterfield and His World* (Biblo and Tannen, 1951), 79. See also Covici, *Humor and Revelation in American Literature*.

5 Holden, *Anti-Puritan Satire.*

6 Cited in Samuel Eliot Morison, ed., *Of Plymouth Plantation, 1620–1647* (Knopf, 1963), 206.

7 Thomas Morton, *New English Canaan*, ed. John Dempsey (Applewood Books, 1999), 137.

8 Nathaniel Hawthorne, *The Scarlet Letter* (Continental Books, 1944), 276.

9 Blair and Hill, *America's Humor*, 74.

10 Cited in Moses Coit Tyler, *A History of American Literature* (G. P. Putnam, 1890), 1:49. . As neither death nor religion could awe Green into gravity, his epitaph contained the words that his "life was whim; his soul was pun, / And if you go too near his hearse, / He'll joke you, both in prose and verse."

11 Blair and Hill, *America's Humor*, 74.

12 Franklin quoted in Kenneth Lynn, ed., *The Comic Tradition in America* (Norton, 1968), xiii. See also Paul M. Zall's *Benjamin Franklin's Humor* (University of Kentucky Press, 2005).

13 Franklin quoted in Carl Japikse, ed., *Fart Proudly: Writings of Benjamin Franklin You Never Read in School* (Enthea Press, 2002).

14 Franklin quoted in Richard Amacher, ed., *Franklin's Wit and Folly* (Rutgers University Press, 1953).

15 Walter Blair, *Horse Sense in American Humor* (University of Chicago Press, 1942); Labaree, *Papers of Benjamin Franklin*, 1, 331.

16 Cited in Parton, *Caricature and Other Comic Art*, 301.

17 Cartoonist Wilhelm Busch, the grandfather of the comics, drew his *Pictures of the Jobsiade*, imaging such incidents as when Job must undergo an examination in theology from twelve clergymen in white wigs. His answers are so stupid that the examiners shake their heads in unison. Eva Weissweiler, *Wilhelm Busch: The Laughing Pessimist* (Kiepenheuer and Witsch, 2007).

18 Franklin quoted in Richard Amacher, "Humor in Franklin's Hoaxes and Satires," *Studies in American Humor* 1 (1974): 4, http://www.compedit.com/franklin's_hoaxes.htm.

19 Ibid.

20 Parton, *Caricature and Other Comic Art*, 303.

21 Ibid., 201.

22 Covici, *Humor and Revelation in American Literature*, 125.

23 Blair, *Horse Sense*, 53–57.

24 Franklin quoted in Theodore Hornberger, *Benjamin Franklin* (University of Minnesota Press, 1962), 45.

25 Ibid.

26 Cited in J. A. Leo Lemay, *The Life of Benjamin Franklin* (University of Pennsylvania Press, 2006), 1:321.

27 Blair, *Horse Sense*, 43.

28 Wells, *The Devil and Doctor Dwight*.

29 Ibid., 30.

30 Ibid., 188.

31 Ibid., 203.

32 David LaRocca, *Estimating Emerson* (Bloomsbury Academic, 2013), 342.

33 Johnson Jones Hooper, *Adventures of Captain Simon Suggs*, ed. M. E. Bradford (J. S. Sanders, 1993).

34 Ibid., 120–23

35 William Stanley Hoole, *Alias Simon Suggs* (University of Alabama Press, 2008).

36 Blair, *Horse Sense*, 213.

37 George Washington Harris, "Parson John Bullen's Lizards," in *Sut Lovingood: Yarns Spun* (Dick and Fitzgerald, 1867), 54.

38 When Bullen tries to preach again the following week, no women appear in the congregation, even though parsons "generally have a pow-ful strong holt on women, but there ain't many of 'em kin run stark nakid over an' thru a crowd of three hundred women an' not injure their character *some*."

39 Blair and Hill, *America's Humor*, 214–15.

40 Covici, *Humor and Revelation in American Literature.*

41 Ibid., 27.

42 See Kenneth Lynn, *Mark Twain and Southwestern Humor* (Little, Brown, and Co., 1959).

43 Cited in Douglas Wilson, ed., *The Genteel Tradition in American Philosophy* (Harvard University Press, 1967).

44 Artemus Ward, *Artemus Ward: Complete* (Chatto and Windus, 1890), 514

45 Blair and Hill, *America's Humor*, 379. Mark Twain favorably compared the effects of reading it with "a three-day drunk."

46 Oliver Wendell Holmes, *The Works of Oliver Wendell Holmes* (Houghton Mifflin, 1892), 12:206.

47 Ibid., 207.

48 Blair and Hill, *America's Humor*, 43.

49 Josh Billings, *Everybody's Friend, or Josh Billings' Encyclopedia and Proverbial Philosophy of Wit and Humor* (American Publishing, 1874), 75.

50 Ibid., 442.

51 Ibid., 591.

52 Herman Melville, *Moby-Dick* (Modern Library, 1950), 302; see a similar metaphor in Graham Greene's *The Comedians*, in which a narrator imagines his ship is "driven by an authoritative practical joke towards the extreme point of comedy" (Penguin, 1967), 32.

53 Anonymous, "Feminine Humour," *Saturday Review* 32 (July 15, 1871): 75.

54 Stephen Crane, *The Poetry of Stephen Crane*, ed. Daniel Hoffman (Columbia University Press, 1956), 53

55 Crane quoted in Harold Bloom, *Stephen Crane* (Infobase, 2009), 26.

56 Gerald McDonald, ed., *Poems of Stephen Crane* (Thomas Crowell, 1964).

57 Ingersoll, "Heretics and Heresies," in *On the Gods and Other Lectures*, 14.

58 Tim Page, ed., *What's God Got to Do with It?: Robert Ingersoll on Free Thought* (Random House, 2005).

59 Susan Jacoby, *The Great Agnostic: Robert Ingersoll and American Freethought* (Yale University Press, 2013), 69.

60 Ibid., 12–13.

61 Ingersoll, "Heretics and Heresies," 36.

62 Ibid., 36–37.

63 Ibid., 111–14. He continues: "The Catholic burned the Lutheran, the Lutheran burned the Catholic, the Episcopalian tortured the Presbyterian, the Presbyterian tortured the Episcopalian. Every denomination killed all it could of every other; and each Christian felt duty bound to exterminate every other Christian who denied the smallest fraction of his creed."

64 David D. Anderson, *Robert Ingersoll* (Twayne, 1972), 22–23.

65 Mark Twain, "A Humorist's Confession," *New York Times*, November 26, 1905.

66 Mark Twain, *Huckleberry Finn*, (Dover, 1994), 58.

67 Ibid.,128.

68 Ibid., 133.

69 Blythe McGarvie, "Humor and Rapprochement," *Huffington Post*, December 5, 2010, http://www.ibrarian.net/navon/blogReaderTop.jsp?id=302463333&URL=http://www.huffingtonpost.com/blythe-mcgarvie/humor-and-rapprochement_b_791641.html.

70 "Ah, well, I am a great & sublime fool. But then I am God's fool, & all His works must be contemplated with respect." Lewis Hill, *Mark Twain, God's Fool*, (Harper and Row, 1973), xiii.

71 Gladys Carmen Bellamy, *Mark Twain as a Literary Artist* (University of Oklahoma Press, 1950), 136.

72 After so many travels abroad, Twain concluded that "the humorous story is American, the comic story is English, the witty story is French." McGarvie, "Humor and Rapprochement."

73 One of the funniest twists on the Calvinist doctrine was Katherine Ken Child Walker's article in the September 1864 issue of the *Atlantic*, entitled "The Total Depravity of Inanimate Things" including pins, needles, coins, vegetables, and disembodied words.

74 Twain quoted in Joe B. Fulton, *The Reverend Mark Twain* (Ohio State University Press, 2006), 82.

75 Twain, *Autobiography*.

76 Will Willimon, *And the Laugh Shall Be First* (Abingdon Press, 1986) and *William Willimon's Last Laugh* (Abingdon Press, 1991). Youth Specialties, ed., *Door* 104–14 (1989): 152. On dogs and religion, Stephen Colbert opined that "*All dogs go to heaven*? Sorry, kids. It's only the dogs who've accepted Christ." *I Am America* (Grand Central Publishing, 2007), 34.

77 Tuffy, "The Confessions of St. Tuffy" *Onion*, September 18, 2002, http://www.theonion.com/articles/im-not-proud-of-some-of-the-things-ive-done,10689/.

78 C. S. Lewis compared dogs and cats to publicans and Pharisees respectively, the canine humbly acknowledging his sin and the feline feeling superior to all other creatures, "thanking God that he is not as these dogs, or these humans, or even as these other cats." *Letters to an American Lady* (Eerdmans, 1986), 40.

79 Blair and Hill, *America's Humor*, xviii.

80 Twain quoted in Harold H. Kolb Jr., *Mark Twain: The Gift of Humor* (University Press of America, 2015), 301

81 Albert Paine, *Mark Twain* (Harper, 1912), 1:84; Paine notes that Twain did celebrate humor as one of God's most blessed characteristics.

82 Mark Twain, *Letters from the Earth* (EMP Press, 2013), 7. Not only that, Twain continued, "more men go to church than want to."

83 Ibid. 11. In *The Screwtape Letters*, Satan again writes of music in the context of laughter; herein he also finds it wholly disgusting, for it expresses a divine laughter of joy.

84 John Betjeman wrote light satiric verse "In Westminster Abbey" where his character prays, "Gracious Lord, oh bomb the Germans, spare their women for thy Sake, And if that is not too easy, We will pardon Thy Mistake. But, gracious Lord, whate'er shall be, Don't let anyone bomb me." His sunshine patriot leaves the service in Westminster a bit early, "and now, dear Lord, I cannot wait; because I have a luncheon date."

85 Mark Twain, "The War Prayer," *Mark Twain on Religion* (Forgotten Books, 2007), 341–45.

86 Mark Twain, *Mark Twain's Library of Humor*, ed. Steve Martin (Modern Library, 2000), xiv.

87 Mark Twain, *The Writings of Mark Twain: Following the Equator* (P. F. Collier and Sons, 1899), 273.

88 Twain quoted in William E. Phipps, *Mark Twain's Religion* (Mercer University Press, 2003), 308. Arguing with some Baconians (who believed that Francis Bacon wrote Shakespeare's plays), Twain indicated that when he got to heaven he would ask Shakespeare who did write his plays. To which his host countered, somewhat snootily, "I don't think, Mr. Clemens, you will find Shakespeare in heaven." Twain replied, "Then you ask him." Cited in Alex Ayers, ed., *The Wit and Wisdom of Mark Twain*, (Harper and Row, 1987), 211.

89 Twain quoted in Zuver, *Salvation by Laughter*, 185.

90 Mark Twain, "Letter to Brother" (1865), quoted in Stanley Brodwin "Mark Twain's Theology" in *The Cambridge Companion to Mark Twain, ed.* Forrest G. Robinson (Cambridge University Press, 1995), 222.

91 Samuel Langhorne Clemens, *Mark Twain's Notebooks* (Cooper Square, 1972); Bible quotation cited in John R. W. Stott, *Christ the Liberator* (InterVarsity Press, 1971), 214. According to Harold Bush, Twain constructed a particularly American Adam, who is self-reliant and self-propelled, and more psychological and less theological in his pioneering spirit. "Mark Twain's American Adam: Humor as Hope and Apocalypse," *Christianity and Literature* 53, no. 3 (2004): 291–314.

92 O'Connor, *Ambrose Bierce*, 9.

93 Ambrose Bierce, *The Devil's Dictionary* (Bloomsbury, 2003), 51.

94 Ambrose Bierce, "The Timorous Reporter," in *Collected Works* (Forgotten Books, 2011), 10:283.

95 William Keough, *Punchlines: The Violence of American Humor* (Paragon House, 1990) 67. See Bierce, "Wit and Humor," in *Collected Works*, 10:98–102.

96 Cited in Keough, *Punchlines*, 63.

97 M. E. Grenander, ed., *Poems of Ambrose Bierce* (University of Nebraska Press, 1995), xxxii.

98 Bierce, *Devil's Dictionary*, 216.

99 Ibid., 149.

100 Ibid., 186

101 See Lawrence Berkove, *A Prescription for Adversity: The Moral Art of Ambrose Bierce* (Ohio State University Press, 2002).

102 Ibid., 36.

103 Ibid., 29; Twain chipped in "If Christ were here now there is one thing he would not be—a Christian." Cited in James Melville Cox, *Mark Twain: The Fate of Humor* (University of Missouri Press, 2002), vii.

104 Bierce, *Devil's Dictionary*, 209.

105 Ibid., 166.

106 S. Joshi and David Schultz, eds., *A Much Misunderstood Man: Selected Letters of Ambrose Bierce* (Ohio State University Press, 2003).

107 Cited in Fitzpatrick Vincent, *H. L. Mencken* (Mercer University Press, 2004), 37.

108 Mencken cited in Walter D. Wagoner, *Bittersweet Grace* (World Publishing, 1967), 13.

109 Feinberg, *The Satirist*, 17.

110 H. L. Mencken, ed., "The Iconoclast," in *A Mencken Chrestomathy* (Vintage, 1982), 17. People remember a "jocosity much longer than they remember a syllogism" (ibid., 115).

111 H. L. Mencken, "Holy Clerks," in *Prejudices: Fourth Series* (Knopf, 1924).

112 Hobson, *Mencken*, 478.

113 Nicholas von Hoffman, "Celebrating Mencken," *Saturday Review*, September 1980, 29.

114 Mencken, "The Hills of Zion," in *A Mencken Chrestomathy*, 392–98.

115 Bierce, *Devil's Dictionary*, 26.

116 Mencken, "Hills of Zion," 395.

117 Ibid., 398.

118 Hobson, Fred *A Serpent in Eden: H. L. Mencken and the South* (University of North Carolina Press, 1974), 3

119 Raymond McCall, "Mencken and the Glass of Satire," *College English* 23, no. 8 (May 1962).

CHAPTER 9. BRITISH CATHOLICS AND CURMUDGEONS

1 Charles Caleb Colton, *Hypocrisy: A Satire* (Taylor and Hessey, 1812), 1, 58.

2 Ibid., 27.

3 John Miller, *Religion in the Popular Prints 1600–1832* (Chadwyck-Healy, 1986), 15.

4 Bloom and Bloom, *Satire's Persuasive Voice*, 117.

5 Daniel Defoe, *Jure Divino: A Satyr in Twelve Books* (London, 1706), xxvi.

6 Daniel Defoe, *The Works of Daniel Defoe*, ed. G. H. Maynadier (Jensen Society, 1904): 11:235

7 Thomas Hobbes, *The Treatise on Human Nature*, ed. Philip Mallet (J. Johnson and Co., 1812), 65.

8 Thomas Hobbes, *Leviathan*, ed. Richard Tuck (Cambridge University Press, 1991), 75.

9 Ibid., 42.

10 Ibid., 481

11 Elizabeth Telfer, "Hutcheson's Reflections upon Laughter," *Journal of Aesthetics and Art Criticism* 53, no. 4 (Autumn 1995): 363; Walter Van Herck, "Humour, Religion, and Vulnerability," in Geybels and Van Herck, *Humour and Religion*, 191–203.

12 Francis Hutcheson, *Reflections upon Laughter*. (Nord Press, 2011), 61.

13 Ibid., 35.

14 G. K. Chesterton, "Humour" *Encyclopedia Britannica*, 14th ed. (New York, 1929), 2:884.

15 Max Eastman, *The Enjoyment of Laughter* (Simon and Schuster, 1936). See James Beattie, "An Essay on Laughter and Ludicrous Composition," in *Essays* (London, 1779), 310.

16 G. K. Chesterton, "Humour," 884.

17 Horton Davies, "A Spur for the Somnolent: Wit in the English Pulpit, 1588–1645," *Thalia: Studies in Literary Humor* 6, no. 1 (Spring/Summer 1983): 32–47.

18 Ronald Paulson, *Don Quixote in England: The Aesthetics of Laughter* (John Hopkins University Press, 1997).

19 Hogarth satirized Dutch painting with an affectionate parody in *Paul before Felix Burlesqued* (1751), which is populated by Jews and common Dutch folk, with the realism of Rembrandt exaggerated to the point that the apostle is so short he has to stand on a stool, wherein a sooty little devil maliciously saws away at the stool.

20 William Hogarth, *Anecdotes of William Hogarth* (BiblioBazaar, 2008), 62.

21 Parton, *Caricature and Other Comic Arts*, 145.

22 Cunningham cited in Hogarth, *Anecdotes*, 195.

23 Anthony Trollope, *Barchester Towers* (Oxford University Press, 1996), 52.

24 Hogarth, "Credulity, Superstition and Fanaticism: A Medley," in *Anecdotes*, 262. An early version of this engraving was "Enthusiasm Delineated," dedicated to the Archbishop of Canterbury, in which he burlesques "religion run mad." A vociferous preacher "treats his congregation with a bull roar." He may be considered a "Methodistical Papist" or a "Popish Methodist," as Hogarth hits the two extremes between the *via media* of the Anglican Church. The cleric's shaven crown suggests his Jesuit leanings, while his Harlequin undergarment denotes other religious professions. In her holy fervor, the female in the pew, seduced by the touch of the nobleman, lets her religious icon fall to the ground. All the while, there is the "sighing, weeping, groaning" worship of the Dissenters. The pigeon on the brain of the Methodist is a parody of the Holy Spirit dove. In the subsequent engraving, much is altered, with the artist including Wesley's sermons and Glanvil's book on witches as the two inspirations for the Methodist brain. Again, Hogarth warned: "believe not every spirit." The work sublimely attacks both the "idolatrous emblems of popery with the mummery of modern enthusiasts." Ibid., 259–64.

25 In this engraving, Hogarth declared that he sought to give a "Lineal representation of the strange Effects of literal and low conceptions of Sacred Beings and also of the Idolotrous Tendency of Pictures in churches and prints in Religious Books." See Misty Anderson, *Sacred Satire: Lampooning Religious Belief in Eighteenth-Century Britain* (Yale University Press, 2011), 10

26 In his *Masquerade Ticket* (1727), Hogarth includes a lechometer, with an altar to Priapus, in the bacchanalian debauch. Fielding would later write about how "cardinals, quakers, and judges dance" at *The Masquerade*, and "grave churchmen here at hazard play." It is Satan who coordinates the ball where "Fortune sends the gamesters luck, / Venus her votary a—[fuck]." Gatrell, *City of Laughter*, 205.

27 Bernd Krysmanski, "We See a Ghost: Hogarth's Satire on Methodists and Connoisseurs," *Art Bulletin* 80, no.2 (June 1998): 1–2.

28 Albert M. Lyles, *Methodism Mocked: The Satiric Reaction to Methodism in the Eighteenth Century* (Wipf & Stock, 2015), 15.

29 Donald Spaeth, *The Church in an Age of Danger: Parsons and Parishioners, 1660–1740* (Cambridge University Press, 2000).

30 Hogarth, *Anecdotes*, 72

31 In dealing with "Comic History Painting," Douglas Fordham demonstrated a definitive generic connection between William Hogarth and Henry Fielding in their respective practices of painting and writing, in which they champion a new type of visual and written description, called "comic history." "William Hogarth's *The March to Finchley* and the Fate of Comic History Painting," *Art History* 27, no. 1 (2004): 95–128; Glasgow, *Madness, Masks, and Laughter*; Paulson, *Don Quixote in England*; and Tessa Watt, *Cheap Print and Popular Piety, 1550–1640* (Cambridge University Press, 1991).

32 Hogarth, *Anecdotes*, 248.

33 Carretta, *The Snarling Muse*.

34 Psalms 35:15; 16:10; 17:6.

35 Misty Anderson and Cynthia Roman, "Sacred Satire: Lampooning Religious Belief in EighteenthCentury Britain," Exhibition Brochure (Lewis Walpole Library, Yale University, September 22, 2011–March 2, 2012), 10.

36 Rabelais, *Gargantua and Pantagruel*, 122.

37 John Dunton, *The Hazard of a Death-Bed Repentance* (London, 1708), 12, 62; see also William Thom's cleverly titled *The Happiness of Dead Clergymen, Provided They Die in the Lord* (Glasgow, 1769).

38 Miller, *Religion in Popular Prints*, 104–5.

39 Gatrell, *City of Laughter*, 94.

40 Colton, *Hypocrisy*, 45

41 Anonymous, *The Gentleman's Bottle Companion: A Collection of Eighteenth-Century Bawdy Ballads* (P. Harris Publishing, 1979), 38.

42 Richard Savage, *The Progress of a Divine: A Satire* (London, 1735), 54, http://www.poemhunter.com/poem/the-progress-of-a-divine-satire/.

43 Ibid.

44 Ibid. Others, like Dr. Cringe Croucher, expressed a similar hostility to the ministers, but not the church itself: "But think not, with sceptical malice and pride / The church, or the clergy, I mean to deride." Cringe Croucher, *Modern Manners* (1781), cited in Penelope J. Corfield, *Power and the Professions in Britain, 1700–1850* (Routledge, 1995), 52.

45 Johnson, *Lives of the Poets*, 53–125.

46 Ibid. In a parody of Pope's "Essay on Man," Wilkes forgets moral standards in his "Essay on Woman" and scandalizes readers with his use of taboo words (e.g., "since life can little more supply / Than just a few good fucks, and then we die"). 445; See John Sainsbury, *John Wilkes: The Lives of a Libertine* (Ashgate, 2006), 249.

47 Gatrell, *City of Laughter*, 179

48 Robert Horton, *John Howe* (Kessinger Publishing, 2006), 113.

49 Professor Porson, (a.k.a. Samuel Coleridge and Robert Southey) *The Devil's Walk: A Poem* (Marsh and Miller, 1830), 14.

50 Wells, *The Devil*, 95, 96.

51 Johnson defined irony as a "mode of speech in which the meaning is clearly contrary to the words." His immediate example was "Bolingbroke is a holy man," indicating quite the obverse. See John Winokur, *The Big Book of Irony* (St. Martin's Press, 2007). Johnson also distinguished between satire and lampoon, the latter equivalent to censure written "not to reform but to vex." Lyles, *Methodism Mocked*, 19.

52 Gatrell, *City of Laughter*, 482.

53 Ibid., 542.

54 What is funny about such a large, three-hundred-pound cleric is that he once challenged a young man about to marry a widow twice his age and three times his size. "Going to marry her? Going to marry her! Impossible! You mean, a part of her; he could not marry her all himself. . . . There is enough of her to furnish wives for a whole parish." Nancy McPhee, *The Second Book of Insults* (St. Martin's Press, 1981), 90.

55 Pearson, *The Smith of Smiths*, 11. Chesterton described Smith as "wilder than a humorist," and the originator of nonsense.

56 S. H. Romilly, ed., *Letters to "Ivy" from the first Earl of Dudley* (Longman, Green, and Co., 1905), 111.

57 Feinberg, *The Satirist*, 99.

58 McPhee, *Second Book of Insults*, 96.

59 Lady Holland, ed., *Memoir of the Rev. Sydney Smith* (1855), 158.

60 Ibid., 43.

61 Smith quoted in Shaw, *Our Religious Humorist*, 1:13.

62 Pearson, *The Smiths of Smith*, 12.

63 Sydney Smith, "Recipe for Salad," cited in *A Memoir of the Reverend Sydney Smith by His Daughter Lady Holland* (Scholarly Publishing, 2005), 1:366. "What you don't know," wrote Smith smiling, "would make a great book" (380).

64 Martin, *Triumph of Wit*, 75.

65 Leigh Hunt, "On the Combination of Grave and Gay," in *Leigh Hunt's Literary Criticism* (Oxford University Press, 1956), 559.

66 Richard Le Galliene, *The Romantic 90's* (Putnam and Co, 1925).

67 Merlin Holland, ed., *Complete Works of Oscar Wilde* (Harper Collins, 1994).

68 Ibid., 120.

69 Ibid., 227. Of course, they might just satirize you, as Gilbert and Sullivan did to Wilde in their light opera *Patience*: "Though the Philistines may jostle, you will rank as an apostle in the high aesthetic band, If you walk down Piccadilly with a poppy or a lily in your medieval hand. And everyone will say, As you walk your flowery way, 'If he's content with a vegetable love which would certainly not suit me, Why what a most particularly pure young man this pure young man must be!'"

70 G. K. Chesterton, "George Bernard Shaw," in *Collected Works of Chesterton*, ed. Dennis J. Conolon (Ignatius Press, 1989), 11:40.

71 Quoted in Jan Jedrzejewski, *Thomas Hardy and the Church* (Macmillan, 1996).

72 In the rough transcript of *Shaw v. Chesterton, A Debate* (Third Way Movement, 1928/2000), the topic of "Do We Agree?" was the focus. Shaw began the evening by noting that the audience probably did not care what issue they debated, provided "we entertain you by talking" (5).

73 Darl Larsen, *Monty Python's Flying Circus* (Scarecrow, 2008), 22.

74 Eugene O'Neil, *Satire in the Prose Writings of Hilaire Belloc: A Weapon of Truth in His Defense of the Catholic Church* (Boston College, 1939), http://www.worldcat.org/title/satire-in-the-prose-writings-of-hilaire-belloc-a-weapon-of-truth-in-his-defense-of-the-catholic-church/oclc/37439387. Belloc could be blunt in challenging the church as well. In James Andrew Froude's "Philosophy of Christianity," in *Essays in Literature and History*, ed. Ernst Rhys (J. M. Dent, 1906), Belloc introduces a gentle parable of the Christian faith, in which "A Moss rose-bud hiding her face among the leaves one hot summer morning, for fear the sun should injure her complexion, happened to let fall a glance towards her roots, and to see the bed in which she was growing. 'What a filthy place!' she cried. 'What a home they have chosen for me! I, the most beautiful of flowers, fastened down into so detestable a neighborhood!' She threw her face into the air; thrust herself into the hands of the first passer-by who stopped to look at her, and escaped in triumph, as she thought, into the centre of a nosegay. But her triumph was short-lived: in a few hours she withered and died" (184).

75 Joyce Kilmer, "Introduction" in Hilaire Belloc's *Verses* (Laurence J. Gomme, 1916), xviii.

76 Ibid., xx.

77 Hilaire Belloc, *Cautionary Tales for Children* (Knopf, 1922), 66.

78 Hilaire Belloc, *Cautionary Tales for Children* (Duckworth, 1974), 67.

79 Max Beerbohm, *Seven Men and Two Others* (London, 2001). In Beerbohm's book *Enoch Soames*, a third-rate, miserable poet makes a Faustian pact with the devil to see what his fame will be one hundred years in the future, only to find himself in an obscure academic footnote, with his name misspelled.

80 Ian Turnbull Ker, *The Catholic Revival in English Literature, 1845–1961* (University of Notre Dame Press, 2003), 69.

81 Jay P. Corrin, *G. K. Chesterton & Hilaire Belloc: The Battle Against Modernity* (Ohio State University Press, 1991); Joseph Pearce, *Old Thunder: A Life of Hilaire Belloc* (Ignatius Press, 2002).

82 Ker, *Catholic Revival in English Literature*, 68.

83 Ibid., 85.

84 G. K. Chesterton, "Introduction to Pickwick Papers," in *Collected Works of G. K. Chesterton*, ed. Alzina Stone Dale) (Ignatius Press, 1989), 253.). "We speak of 'seeing' a joke just like we 'speak' of seeing a ghost or a vision. If we have seen it, it is futile to argue with it."

85 G. K. Chesterton, *All Things Considered* (John Lane, 1913), 12. A character in the incomparable Max Beerbohm's *Seven Men and Two Others* (William Heinemann, 1950) did recognize that one "can't really understand what one doesn't love, and one can't make good fun without real understanding" (88). Beerbohm was, self-admittedly, born to "juggle golden balls."

86 G. K. Chesterton, *All Things Considered* (CreateSpace, 2015), 78. I suspect, but cannot prove, that Chesterton influenced Theodor Geisel, Dr. Seuss. Compare the line "From there to here, from here to there, funny things are everywhere" from Dr. Seuss's *One Fish, Two Fish* (Random House, 1960).

87 G. K. Chesterton, "The Frivolous Man" in *The Common Man* (Sheed and Ward, 1951).

88 Chesterton, *Heretics* (Serenity, 2009), 160–61, 89.

89 G. K. Chesterton, *Orthodoxy* (Doubleday, 1959), 42.

90 G. K. Chesterton, *Heretics*, 121.

91 Ibid.

92 G. K. Chesterton, *The Man Who Was Thursday* (Ignatius Press, 1908); *Where All Roads Lead* (Ignatius Press,1922); "Humour," 883–85.

93 G. K. Chesterton, Column, *Illustrated London News*, July 16, 1910.

94 Ibid., August 13, 1932.

95 Chesterton, "Humour," 883–84.

96 Ibid., 885.

97 Frederick Buechner, *Telling the Truth* (Harper, 1977).

98 Zuver, *Salvation by Laughter*, 64.

99 Ibid., 79.

100 Knox, *Essays in Satire* (Sheed and Ward, 1928), 37, 29.

101 Milton Walsh, *Ronald Knox as Apologist* (Ignatius Press, 2007); Milton Walsh, *Second Friends: C. S. Lewis and Ronald Knox in Conversation* (Ignatius Press, 2008).

102 Knox quoted in Ronald Paulson, ed., *Satire: Modern Essays in Criticism* (Prentice-Hall, 1971), 61.

103 Knox, *Essays*, 42; herein Knox presciently noted that "no country, I suppose, has a greater need of a satirist today than the United States of America."

104 Knox quoted in Walsh, *Ronald Knox as Apologist*, 29.

105 Knox, *Essays*, 36.

106 Ibid., 127, 140; Waugh, *Life of Ronald Knox*.

107 Knox, *Essays*, 62.

108 Anonymous, "Don's Delight," *Time Magazine*, March 27, 1939.

109 Robert Speaight, *Ronald Knox the Writer* (Sheed and Ward, 1965).

110 Knox, *Essays*, 21.

111 Carens, *Satiric Art of Evelyn Waugh*, 65.

112 Ibid., 93. His comic techniques included a booby trap device, which would set "off a silly and inconsequential chain of events."

113 Waugh quoted in Joseph Pearce's *Catholic Literary Giants* (Ignatius Press, 2005), 25.

114 Evelyn Waugh, "Converted to Rome: Why It Has Happened to Me." Waugh echoed Pope by titling the first volume of an unfinished autobiography "A Little Learning."

115 Waugh cited in Joseph Pearce, *Literary Converts* (Harper Collins, 1999), 236.

116 Waugh, "Converted to Rome," 172.

117 Waugh quoted in George McCartney, *Evelyn Waugh and the Modernist Tradition* (Indiana University Press, 1987), 30.

118 Dana Greene, *The Living of Maisie Ward* (University of Notre Dame Press, 1997), 91.

119 Wilfrid Sheed, *Frand and Maisie: A Memoir with Parents* (Simon and Schuster, 1985), 123.

120 Frank Sheed, *The Church and I* (Doubleday, 1974), 228.

121 Ibid., 237.

122 Wilfrid Sheed, "My Life on the Street Corner," *Saturday Review*, May 10, 1968, 23.

123 Sheed, *The Church*, 56.

124 Ibid., 134.

125 George McDonald, *Sir Gibbie* (Hurst and Blackett, 1905).

126 See Chesterton, *Tremendous Trifles*, 98–99.

127 C. S. Lewis, *Mere Christianity* (Macmillan, 1952), 56 . . .

128 G. K. Chesterton, *Everlasting Man* (Doubleday, 1955), 68. Robert Kantra, "Undenominational Satire: Chesterton and Lewis Revisited," *Religion and Literature* 24, no. 1 (Spring 1992): 33- .See also Kantra, *All Things Vain*, and Peter Schakel, "The Satiric Imagination of C. S. Lewis," *Studies in the Literary Imagination* 22:2 (Fall 1989), 129-48.

129 Milton Walsh, *Second Friends* (Ignatius Press, 2008), 13.

130 Lewis, *Screwtape Letters*. In the preface to his book, Lewis quoted both Martin Luther and Sir Thomas More as laughing fellow Christian satirists.

131 One of the best examples of this *via negativa* occurs in Joseph Heller's satirical novel, *Catch-22* (1961). The protagonist Yossarian's discusses theology with Scheisskopf's (whose name means "shit head") atheist and adulterous wife. One Thanksgiving, Yossarian and Mrs. Scheisskopf lie in bed arguing about a good, just God who would create tooth decay and phlegm. However, the woman who adamantly denies the existence of God is so deeply disturbed by Yossarian's devilish accusation of God's bumbling ineptness or intentional sadism that she breaks into tears and retorts: "I don't believe in God, but the God I don't believe in is a good God."

132 Lewis, *Screwtape Letters, 50.*

133 Ibid., 16.

134 Walter Hooper, ed., *Letters of C. S. Lewis* (Harcourt, Brace and World, 1966), 179.

135 Schakel, "The Satiric Imagination of C. S. Lewis," 129–48.

136 Lewis, "Cross-Examination," in *God in the Dock*, ed. Walter Hooper (Eerdmans, 1970).

137 C. S. Lewis, *The Great Divorce* (Macmillan, 1946), 37.

138 C. S. Lewis, *Letters to Malcolm* (Fontana, 1966), 6.

139 C. S. Lewis, *Miracles* (Macmillan, 1947), 132.

140 C. S. Lewis, *The Four Loves* (Harcourt Brace Jovanovich, 1960), 140–41.

141 See G. K. Chesterton, *The Common Man* (Sheed and Ward, 1950).

142 Lewis, *The Four Loves*, 142.

143 William Griffin, *C. S. Lewis* (Harper and Row, 1986), 298.

144 Richard Geoffrey and George Price, "Back in the Main Stream: Malcolm Muggeridge's Editorship," in *A History of Punch* (Collins, 1957), 317.

145 Ibid., 324.

146 Muggeridge cited in Rappoport, *Punchlines*, 45.

147 Gregory Wolfe, *Malcolm Muggeridge, a Biography* (Hodder & Stoughton, 1995)

148 "Door Interview: Malcolm Muggeridge," *Door* 87 (October/November 1985): 20.

149 Malcolm Muggeridge, "Backwards Christian Soldiers," in *Tread Softly for You Tread on My Jokes* (Collins, 1972), http://www.malcolmmuggeridge.org/gargoyle/gargoyle-12-200610.pdf.

150 Malcolm Muggeridge, *The Most of Malcolm Muggeridge*, (Simon and Schuster, 1966), 318. Chesterton's character Adam (in *Notting Hill*) connects the blasphemous grotesques of medieval cathedrals with the laughter and love of God's people. In his satire *The Flying Inn*, Chesterton's saint fights like a rascal against the "lukewarm gospel of international toleration," offering hope with a floating pub that serves the spiritual needs of persecuted Englishmen, with the punning sign: "All roads lead to Rum." See Kantra, 123.

CHAPTER 10. ENTERTAINERS AND ONIONS

1 Luke Dempsey,ed., *Monty Python's Flying Circus: Complete and Annotated . . . All the Bits* (Black Dog, 2012), 452–53.

2 Ibid., 454.

3 Christopher McKittrick, "Blasphemy in the Name of Fantasy: The Films of Terry Gilliam in a Catholic Context," in *Roman Catholicism in Fantastic Film: Belief, Spectacle, Ritual and Imagery*, ed. Regina Hansen (McFarland, 2011), 29–30.

4 Robert Hewison, *Monty Python: The Case Against* (Eyre Methuen, 1981). See also Humphrey Carpenter's *That Was Satire that Was* (Victor Gollancz, 2000) and his *A Great Silly Grin: The British Satire Boom of the 1960s* (Da Capo Press, 2003).

5 Paul Provenza, *iSatiristas!: Comedians, Contrarians, Raconteurs, and Vulgarians* (It Books, 2010), 193.

6 Ellen Bishop, "Bakhtin, Carnival and Comedy: The New Grotesque in *Monty Python and the Holy Grail*," *Film Criticism* 15, no. 1(Fall 1990): 49–64.

7 Perry George, *Life of Python* (Pavilion, 2007), 170.

8 Ebert, Roger "*The Life of Brian*," *Chicago Tribune*, December 1, 1979.

9 Palin quoted in Turner, "On Satire in the Arts," 29.

10 Gary Hardcastle, et al., *Monty Python and Philosophy: Nudge, Nudge, Think, Think*. (Open Court, 2006).

11 "Why Are We Skipping Church?," *Onion*, April 13, 2007, http://www.theonion.com/articles/why-are-we-skipping-church,21084/.

12 Simon Warren, "Finding a Religion that Doesn't Disrupt your Current Life Style," *Onion*, April 13, 2007, 17. Robert Siegel, ed., *Dispatches: Best of The Onion* (Three Rivers Press, 2001), 11, http://www.theonion.com/articles/finding-a-religion-that-doesnt-disrupt-your-curren,10334/.

13 Siegel, *Dispatches*, 36.

14 Ibid., 43.

15 Denny Rydberg, "The Subtle Prophet in Christian Humor," *Spectrum* 9 (Fall 1978): 12–15.

16 Michael Yaconelli, *Messy Spirituality: God's Annoying Love for Imperfect People* (Zondervan, 2002), 11.

17 "Corruption and the Church," *Wittenburg Door* 17 (February/March 1974), cover.

18 Den Hart, "The Song of Solomon Illustrated," *Wittenburg Door* (February/March 1978).

19 Murray Stiller, *Nailin' It to the Church: Religious Satire and the Gospel According to the Wittenburg Door* (Film documentary, 2008).

20 "The Totaled Woman," *Wittenburg Door* 26 (August/September 1975), cover.

21 Michael Yaconelli, "Satire Is Risky Business," *Wittenburg Door* 88 (December 1985/January 1986): 31.

22 Annie McWilliams, "The Pain of Laughter: Reflections on the Nature of Christian Humor by Five Suffering, Chuckling Writers," *Focus Magazine* 4, no. 1 (Winter 1981): 12.

23 Flannery O'Connor, *Mystery and Manners* (Farrar, Straus & Giroux, 1961), 167.

24 Ralph Wood, *The Comedy of Redemption* (University of Notre Dame Press, 1988).

25 The tradition of homiletic humor leading to Buechner is chronicled in Horton Davies treatment of witty poetic preachers in *Like Angels from a Cloud: English*

Metaphysical Preachers 1588–1645 (Wipf and Stock, 2004) and *Mirror of the Ministry in Modern Novels* (Oxford University Press, 1959).

26 Frederick Buechner, *The Sacred Journey* (Harper, 1982), 28–29.

27 Frederick Buechner, *Love Feast*, in *The Book of Bebb* (Atheneum, 1979), 352; for a fuller treatment of Buechner's humor, see Marie-Helene Davies, *Laughter in a Genevan Gown: The Works of Frederick Buechner* (Eerdmans, 1983), 151.

28 Frederick Buechner, *Peculiar Treasures* (Harper and Row, 1979), 9.

29 Frederick Buechner, *Wishful Thinking: A Theological ABC* (Harper and Row, 1973), 2.

30 Tina Bruton, "A Peculiar Treasure: Frederick Buechner," *Focus Magazine* (Winter 1981): 17.

31 However, Brian Kaylor has capably written on "Modern Hebrew Prophets? *The Daily Show* and Religious Satire," in *The Daily Show and Rhetoric: Arguments, Issues, and Strategies*, ed. Tishcha Goodnow Knapp (Lexington Books, 2011).

32 Matt Emerson, "Colbert's Cloak and Dagger Catechesis," *Patheos*, May 27, 2011; Paul Farhi of the *Washington Post* (July 11, 2012) investigated the attention given to Colbert from the solemn Academy. See also Paul Farhi, "Funny Study," *Virginian-Pilot*, July 28, 2012, 1, 3, noting Villanova University's 2010 publication of *Concepts*, showcasing "The Word Made Fresh: A Theological Exploration of Stephen Colbert."

33 Julia Fox, "Wise Fools: Jon Stewart and Stephen Colbert as Modern-Day Jesters in the American Court" in *The Stewart/Colbert Effect: Essays on the Impacts of Fake News*, ed. Amarnath Amarasingam and Robert McChesney (McFarland, 2011), 149–63; Kaylor, "Modern Hebrew Prophets?" Horton cites *Sojourners*' editor Jim Wallis's praise of Stewart as a modern Hebrew prophet, chasing the moneychangers out of the temples; Neil Strauss, "The Subversive Joy of Steve Colbert: Stephen Colbert on Deconstructing the News, Religion and the Colbert Nation," *Rolling Stone*, September 2, 2009, emphasizing how "a God-loving square became TV's most dangerous man," cover, http://www.rollingstone.com/culture/news/stephen-colbert-on-deconstructing-the-news-religion-and-the-colbert-nation-20090902; and Don J. Waisanen, "A Citizen's Guides to Democracy Inaction: Jon Stewart and Stephen Colbert's Comic Rhetorical Criticism," *Southern Communication Journal* 74, no. 2 (2009), 119–40.

34 Matt Emerson, "Stephen Colbert: Catholicism's Best Pitch Man" *OnFaith*, June 2, 2011, http://www.faithstreet.com/onfaith/2011/06/02/stephen-colbert-catholicisms-best-pitch-man/10756.

35 Ibid., 28.

36 Colbert quoted in Matt Pittman and Terry Lindvall, "The Colbert Report Is All Folly" *Reel Spirituality*, May 8, 2013, http://www.brehmcenter.com/initiatives/reelspirituality/film/articles/the-colbert-report-is-all-folly-part-2-well-intentioned-and-poorly-informed. See also Kimberly Wilson, "Stephen Colbert May Play Religion for Laughs, but His Thoughtful Catholicism Still Shows Through," *Washington Post*, October 15, 2010.

37 Colbert quoted in Strauss, "The Subversive Joy of Steve Colbert."

38 Quoted in Emerson, "Stepehn Colbert."

39 "Stephen Colbert Talks Religion with Steve Prothero," March 30, 2011, http://www.huffingtonpost.com/2011/03/30/whats-the-best-religion-c_n_842353.html.

40 Houdek cited in Winston "Stephen Colbert May Play Religion for Laughs."

41 Ibid.

42 Stephen Colbert, *I Am America: (And So Can You)* (Grand Central, 2007), 45.

43 Ibid., 45–62. Colbert names St. Sebastian (pierced with arrows) the "worst Beanie baby ever" (59).

44 Colbert quoted in Terry Gross "A Fake Newsman's Fake Newsman: Stephen Colbert," January 24, 2005, http://www.npr.org/templates/story/story.php?storyId=4464017.

45 Colbert quoted in Ann Althouse, "Colbert and the Dissonance between Religion and Comedy," NPR Interview with Terry Gross, (January 28, 2006), http://althouse.blogspot.com/2006/01/colbert-and-dissonance-between.html (Accessed April 1, 2015)

CONCLUSION

1 Joseph Boskin, *Humor and Social Change in Twentieth-Century America* (Trustees of the Public Library of the City of Boston, 1979). Unfortunately the lectures do not demonstrate any direct correlation between humor and moral or social change. For example, while discussing the "God is dead" jokes of the 1960s, Boskin does not connect such laughter to any changes in religious consciousness or church policy. Humor remains merely ejaculatory; it does not fertilize the social milieu (112).

2 Christie Davies, *Jokes and Targets* (Indiana University Press, 2011) deals with jokes targeted at stupid people, Jews, lawyers, blondes, and sex. "What's a Jewish American Princess's idea of kinky sex? She moves" (115). However, little is done on religion or satire. For Davies, "jokes have no consequences for society as a whole" (266), which suggests that wit without a motive to reform falls flat. Even when the joke deals with religion, it works on comic stereotypes and does not suggest positive change. Davies mentions the joke where a minister, a priest, and a rabbi playing golf are frustrated by a slow group in front of them. When they find the foursome is blind, the minister marvels at such courage in the face of adversity and decides to preach on it next Sunday; the priest is likewise impressed that such a miracle could occur and finds inspiration; finally, the rabbi complains: "Why can't the schmucks play at night?" Christie Davies, *The Mirth of Nations* (Transaction Publishers, 2002), 57.

3 Cited in Richard Kercher, *Revel with a Cause: Liberal Satire in Postwar America* (University of Chicago Press, 2006), 446.

4 Hyers, *The Comic Vision*, 51; Hugo Rahner, "Eutrapelia: A Forgotten Virtue," in *Holy Laughter*, ed. Conrad Hyers (Seabury Press, 1969), 185–97.

5 C. S. Lewis, *The Abolition of Man* (HarperSanFrancisco, 1974).

6 Erasmus, "Letters: To Martin Dorp," in *In Praise of Folly* , 230.

7 Edward and Lillian Bloom, "The Satiric Mode of Feeling," *Criticism* 11 (1969): 115–37.

8 Martin Peretz, "Brief Review," *New Republic*, October 24, 1977, 39.

9 C. S. Lewis, *Studies in Words* (Cambridge University Press, 1967), 305.

10 See John Lippitt, "Illusion and Satire in Kierkegaard's Postscript," *Continental Philosophy Review* 32, no. 4 (1999): 451–66.

11 See Søren Kierkegaard, *Practice of Christianity*, trans. Howard Hong and Edna Hong (Princeton University Press, 1991), where Kierkegaard tries to "introduce Christianity into Christendom" (36).

12 Edward Mooney, *On Søren Kierkegaard* (Ashgate, 2007), 217, 221.

13 Kierkegaard quoted in Thomas Oden, ed., *Parables of Kierkegaard* (Princeton University Press, 1978), 125.

14 Harry Boonstra, "Uneasy Smile for Satire," *Christianity Today*, June 23, 1978, 28–29.

15 Paul Krassner's *Realist* magazine mocked the Roman Catholic Church in the early 1960s as an unyielding monolith. Leonard Freedman, *The Offensive Art: Political Satire and Its Censorship around the World from Beerbohm to Borat* (Praeger, 2008), 51.

16 Brent Plate, *Blasphemy: Art that Offends* (Black Dog, 2006).

17 John Morreall, "Comic Vices, Comic Virtues," *Humor: International Journal of Humor Research* 23, no. 1 (February 1, 2010).

18 Conrad Hyers, "The Comic Vision in a Tragic World," *Christian Century*, April 20, 1983, 366.

19 Cited in Judson Milburn's *The Age of Wit: 1650–1750* (Macmillan, 1966), 17.

20 Dorothy Parker quoted in Liza Donnelly's *Funny Ladies* (Prometheus, 2005), 20.

21 Otto, *Fools Are Everywhere*, 176.

22 Feinberg, *Introduction to Satire*, 255.

23 Charles Gruner, *Understanding Laughter* (Nelson Hall, 1978), 143.

24 Kierkegaard, *Provocations*, 356.

25 Constance Furey, "Invective and Discernment in Martin Luther, Erasmus, and Thomas More," *Harvard Theological Review* 98, no. 4 (October, 2005), 469–88.

26 Richard Steele, *Tatler*, no. 159, cited in Milburn, *The Age of Wit*, 198.

27 Pope, *Epilogues to the Satires*, 703.

28 William Cowper, "The Task," in *The Poems of William Cowper*, ed. John Baird and Charles Ryskamp (Oxford University Press, 1980), 2:147

29 Twain quoted in Phipps' *Mark Twain's Religion*, 366. Quoting William Makepeace Thackeray, Twain quipped, "The humorous writer professes to awaken and direct your love, your pity, your kindness—your scorn for untruth, pretension, imposture. . . . He takes upon himself to be the week-day preacher. "Notes on Thackeray's Essay on Swift," cited in Harold K. Bush, Jr., *Mark Twain and the Spiritual Crisis of His Age* (University of Alabama Press, 2007), 221.

30 Leland Peterson, "Swift's Project: A Religious and Political Satire," *Modern Language Association* 82, no. 1 (March 1967): 54.

31 Roy Campell quoted in Walter Wagoner, *Bittersweet Grace*, 3. Cf. Donald Davidson, "Expectancy of Doom," *Virginia Quarterly Review* 7, no. 3 (July 1931): 438.

32 2 Samuel 16:5–13. The tongue may only be a small part of the body, says the apostle James, but it makes great boasts. Like a small spark that sets a great forest on fire, it can corrupt the whole person, setting one's soul on fire, even as it is set on fire by hell. (Proverbs 3:5–6)

33 Of course, as David lay on his deathbed, he did charge his son Solomon to remember Shimei "who called down bitter curses on me." And while David vowed not to put him to death, he explained to Solomon that the accuser was not innocent, and as "you are a man of wisdom you will know what to do to him. Bring his gray head down to the grave in blood" (1 Kings 2:8–9). So endeth the last words of King David, a man after God's own heart and one who knew how to handle mockers.

34 Unamuno, *Tragic Sense of Life*, 315.

35 Lewis, *Screwtape Letters*, xiii.

36 Ibid., 98.

37 Ludo Abicht, "Laughing in and at the Mirror," in Geybels and Van Herck, *Humour and Religion*, 121.

38 Alfred Guy Kingan L'Estrange, *History of English Humour* (Repressed Publishing, 2015), 1:189. Allegedly, Mapes also compiled the *Apocalypse of Golias* for the seven churches of England, castigating the gluttony and lust of the monks and attributing animal characteristics to various church offices. Serving as a clerk in the court of Henry II, he also slipped in some goliard poetry, folktales, gossip, and trifling anecdotes about marriage (possibly cited by the Wife of Bath's late husband) in *Of Courtiers' Trifles* (*De Nugis curialium*). He probably also produced the seeds of the Lancelot legend and the famous opening line of the bacchanalian lyric (of a drinking song) beginning "It is my proposal to die in the tavern. / Let wine be set at the mouth of the dying one, / so that the choirs of angels may say, when they come, / May God be propitious to this drinker!" Even in their light and playful vein, his courtly jests had "a grave moral purpose." *Henry Morley, English Writers* (Chapman and Hall, 1866), *1*:587–90.

39 Brandt, *Ship of Fools*, 58.

40 Albert Camus, *The Fall* (Knopf, 1991), 110

41 Albert Camus, *La Chute/The Fall*, in *Sixteen Short Novels: An Anthology*, ed. Wilfrid Sheed (Dutton, 1966), 533, 538, 545. One of the narrator's friends in the story had been a model husband as an atheist, but when he got converted, he became an adulterer.

42 F. Saxl, "Holbein's Illustrations to the 'Praise of Folly' by Erasmus," *Burlington Magazine for Connoisseurs* 83, no. 488 (November 1943): 276.

43 Jessica Milner Davis, "The Fool and the Path to Spiritual Insight," in Geybels and Van Herck, *Humour and Religion*, 229.

44 For Chesterton, the secret of life lay in humility and laughter. Citing the old Calvinist Thomas Carlyle, Chesterton quipped, "Carlyle said that men were mostly fools. Christianity, with a surer and more reverent realism, says that they are all fools. This doctrine is sometimes called the doctrine of original sin." *Heretics*, 129.

45 Jonathan Swift "A Tale of a Tub," in *Works of Jonathan Swift* (George Bell and Sons, 1880), 102

46 Lipman, *Laughter in Hell*, 85–86.

47 Jacqueline Bussie, *The Laughter of the Oppressed: Ethical and Theological Resistance in Wiesel, Morrison, and Endo* (T&T Clark, 2007).

48 Plato, *Cratylus, in The Dialogues of Plato*, ed. Benjamin Jowett (CreateSpace, 2014), 2:97.

49 Lewis, *Christian Reflections*, 11.

BIBLIOGRAPHY

Adams, Doug. *Humor in the American Pulpit*. Sharing Co., 1975.

Amacher, Richard, ed. *Franklin's Wit and Folly*. Rutgers University Press, 1953.

Anderson, David, *Robert Ingersoll*. Twayne Publishers, 1972.

Anonymous. *Till Eulenspiegel*. Routledge, 2001.

Anselment, Raymond A. *"Betwixt Jest and Earnest": Marprelate, Milton, Marvel, Swift and the Decorum of Religious Ridicule*. University of Toronto Press, 1979.

Arbuckle, G. A. *Laughing with God*. Liturgical Press, 2008.

Baetzhold, Howard, and Joseph McCullough, eds. *The Bible According to Mark Twain*. University of Georgia Press, 1995.

Bakhtin, Mikhail. *Rabelais and His World*. Translated by Helen Iswolsky. MIT Press, 1968.

Bataille, Georges. *On Nietzsche*. Paragon, 1998.

Baudelaire, Charles. *The Essence of Laughter*. Edited by Peter Quennell, Meridan, 1956.

Bayless, Martha. *Parody in the Middle Ages*. University of Michigan Press, 1997.

Beard, Mary. *Laughter in Ancient Rome*. University of California Press, 2014.

Berger, Peter. *A Rumor of Angels*. Doubleday, 1969.

———. *Redeeming Laughter*. Walter deGruyter, 1997.

Bier, Jesse. *The Rise and Fall of American Humor*. Holt, Rinehard and Winston, 1968.

Bierce, Ambrose. *Collected Works of Ambrose Bierce I*. IndyPublish, 2005.

———.*The Devil's Dictionary*. Peter Pauper Press, 1958.

Billings, Josh. *Everybody's Friend, or Josh Billings' Encyclopedia and Proverbial Philosophy of Wit and Humor*. American Publishing, 1874.

Bindman, David. *Hogarth and His Times*. University of California Press, 1997.

Black, Joseph L. *The Martin Marprelate Tracts*. Cambridge University Press, 2011.

Blair, Walter, and Hamlin Hill. *America's Humor*. Oxford University Press, 1978.

Blocksidge, Martin. *The Sacred Weapon: Introduction to Pope's Satire*. Book Guild, 1993.

Bloom, Edward, and Lillian Bloom. *Satire's Persuasive Voice*. Cornell University Press, 1979.

Bloom, Harold, ed. *Alexander Pope: Modern Critical Views*. Chelsea, 1986.

Brandt, Sebastian. *Ship of Fools*. Translated by Alexander Barkley. Project Gutenberg, 2006.

Brunstrom, Conrad. *William Cowper*. Bucknell University Press, 2004.

Buckley, F. H. *The Morality of Laughter*. University of Michigan Press, 2003.

Butler, Samuel. *Hudibras*. Edited by John Wilders. Clarendon Press, 1967.

Calder, Andrew. *Molière: The Theory and Practice of Comedy*. Athlone Press, 1993.
Carens, James. *Satiric Art of Evelyn Waugh*. University of Washington Press, 1966.
Carretta, Vincent. *The Snarling Muse*. University of Pennsylvania, 1983.
Carroll, Paul, trans. *Satirical Letters of St. Jerome*. Henry Regnery, 1956.
Cervantes, Miguel de. *Don Quixote*. Translated by J. M. Cohen. Penguin, 2003.
Chambers, E. K. *The Medieval Stage*. Oxford Press, 1903.
Chaucer, Geoffrey. *Canterbury Tales*. Edited by David Wright. Oxford University Press, 2008.
Chesterton, G. K. *All Things Considered*. Dufour, 1969.
———. *Heretics*. In *Collected Works*. Ignatius Press, 1986.
———. *Tremendous Trifles*. Metheun, 1927.
Colbert, Stephen. *I Am America*. Grand Central, 2007.
Covici, Pascal, Jr. *Humor and Revelation in American Literature*. University of Missouri Press, 1997.
Cowper, William. *Poems of William Cowper*. Edited by John Baird and Charles Ryskamp. Oxford University Press, 1980.
Cox, Harvey. *Feast of Fools*. Harper and Row, 1972.
Davis, Betty. *Storytellers in Marguerite de Navarre's Heptameron*. French Forum Publishers, 1978.
Disraeli, Isaac. *Curiosities of Literature*. Edited by Bolton Corney. Nabu Press, 2010.
Dixon, Peter, ed. *Alexander Pope*. Ohio University Press, 1972.
Donald, Diana. *The Age of Caricature*. Yale University Press, 1996.
Eastman, Max. *Enjoyment of Laughter*. Simon and Schuster, 1936.
Eco, Umberto. *The Name of the Rose*. Warner Books, 1984.
Economou, George. *William Langland's Piers Plowman*. University of Pennsylvania Press, 1996.
Elliott, Robert. *The Power of Satire: Magic, Ritual, Art*. Princeton University Press, 1960.
Ellul, Jacques. *Subversion of Christianity*. Eerdmans, 1986.
Erasmus, Desiderius. *Colloquies*. London, 1878.
———. *In Praise of Folly*. Translated by Clarence Miller. Yale University Press 2003.
Feibleman, James. *In Praise of Comedy*. Horizon Press, 1970.
Feinberg, Leonard. *Introduction to Satire*. Iowa State University Press, 1967.
———. *The Satirist: His Temperament, Motivation, and Influence*. Iowa State University Press, 1963.
Fielding, Henry. *The History of Tom Jones*. Vintage, 2007.
———. *Joseph Andrews: A Satire of Modern Times*. Twayne Publishers, 1990.
Franklin, Benjamin. *Autobiography and Other Writings*. Edited by Ormand Seavey. Oxford University Press, 2009.
Frazer, James. *The Golden Bough: A Study of Magic and Religion*. Palgrave, 1990.
Fry, William. *Sweet Madness: A Study of Humor*. Pacific Books, 1968.
Gatrell, Vic. *City of Laughter: Sex and Satire in Eighteenth-Century London*. Walker and Company, 2006.

Gaunt, William. *The World of William Hogarth*. Anchor Press, 1978.
Geybels, Hans, and Walter van Herek. *Humour and Religion*. Continuum Press, 2011.
Gilhus, Ingvild. *Laughing Gods, Weeping Virgins: Laughter in the History of Religion*. Routledge, 1997.
Glasgow, R. D. *Madness, Masks, and Laughter: An Essay on Comedy*. Farleigh Dickinson University Press, 1995.
Grant, Raymond. *The Laughter of Love: A Study of Robert Burns*. University of Alberta Press, 1986.
Gritsch, Eric. *Wit of Martin Luther*. Fortress, 2006.
Guareschi, Fiovanni. *The Little World of Don Camillo*. Translated by Una Vincenzo Troubridge. Pelligrini & Cudahy, 1950.
Halliwell, Stephen. *Greek Laughter*. Cambridge University Press, 2008.
Hammond, Gerald, ed. *John Skelton, Selected Poems*. Routledge, 2003.
Harris, Max. *Sacred Folly: A New History of the Feast of Fools*. Cornell University Press, 2011.
Headly, John, ed. *Companion Works of St. Thomas More*. Yale University Press, 1969.
Heiserman, Arthur. *Skelton and Satire*. University of Chicago Press, 1961.
Hill, Hamlin. *Mark Twain, God's Fool*. University of Chicago Press, 2010.
Hobbes, Thomas. *Leviathan*. Edited by Nelle Fuller. University of Chicago, Great Books, 1952.
———. *Treatise on Human Nature*. Nabu Press, 2010.
Hobson, Fred. *Mencken: A Life*. Random House, 1994.
———. *A Serpent in Eden: H. L. Mencken and the South*. University of North Carolina Press, 1974.
Holden, William. *Anti-Puritan Satire*. Archon Books, 1968.
Holland, Merlin. *Complete Works of Oscar Wilde*. Harper/Collins, 1994.
Hoole, Stanley. *Alias Simon Suggs: The Life and Times of Johnson Jones Hooper*. University of Alabama Press, 1952.
Hooper, Johnson Jones. *Adventures of Captain Simon Suggs*. Carey and Hart, 1845.
Horace. *The Satires, Epistles, and Art of Poetry*. Translated by John Conington. Dodo Press, 2008.
Hornberger, Theodore. *Benjamin Franklin*. University of Minnesota Press, 1962.
Hunt, Leigh. *Wit and Humor Selected from the English Poets*. Wiley and Putnam, 1846.
Hutcheson, Francis. *Reflections upon Laughter*. Nord Press, 2011.
Hyers, Conrad. *Holy Laughter*. Seabury Press, 1969.
Ingersoll, Robert. *The Gods and Other Lectures*. Liberal and Scientific Publishing, 1876.
———. *On the Gods and Other Essays*. Edited by Paul Kurtz. Prometheus Books, 1990.
Jemielity, Thomas. *Satire and the Hebrew Prophets*. Westminster/John Knox Press, 1992.
Johnson, Samuel. *Lives of the Poets: Addison, Savage and Swift*. Hardpress, 2010.
Kantra, Robert. *All Things Vain: Religious Satirists and Their Art*. Pennsylvania State University Press, 1984.
Kenney, Howland, ed. *Laughter in the Wilderness*. Kent State University Press, 1976.

Kernan, Alvin. *The Cankered Muse: Satire of the English Renaissance*. Archon Books, 1976.

Kierkegaard, Søren. *Concluding Unscientific Postscript*. Translated by David Swenson Princeton University Press, 1941.

———*The Humor of Kierkegaard: An Anthology*. Edited by Thomas Oden. Princeton University Press, 2004.

———. *Stages on Life's Way*. Translated by Howard and Edna Hong. Princeton University Press, 1988.

———. *Either/Or*. Edited and translated by Howard and Edna Hong. Princeton University Press, 1987.

Kinney, Arthur. *John Skelton: Priest as Poet*. University of North Carolina Press, 1987.

Knox, Ronald. *Essays in Satire*. Sheed and Ward, 1928.

Kupersmith, William. *English Versions of Roman Satires*. University of Delaware Press, 2007.

Kuschel, Karl-Josef. *Laughter: A Theological Reflection*. Translated by John Bowden. SCM Press, 1994.

Labaree, Leonard, ed. *The Papers of Benjamin Franklin*. Yale University Press, 1959.

Larsen, Darl. *Monty Python's Flying Circus*. Scarecrow Press, 2008.

Laurie, Hilary. *Verses of the Poet Laureate*. Orion Press, 1999.

Lewis, C. S. *English Literature in the Sixteenth-Century*. Oxford University Press, 1973.

———. *The Four Loves*. Harcourt Brace Jovanovich, 1960.

———. *The Screwtape Letters*. Macmillan, 1968.

Lindvall, Terry. *Surprised by Laughter: The Comic World of C. S. Lewis*. Thomas Nelson, 2012.

Lipman, Steve. *Laughter in Hell: Humor during the Holocaust*. Jason Aronson, 1991.

Lippitt, John. *Humor and Irony in Kierkegaard's Thought*. Macmillan, 2000.

Love, Harold. *English Clandestine Satire*. Oxford University Press, 2004.

Luther, Martin. *Table Talk*. Edited by Thomas S. Kepler. CreateSpace, 2011.

Lynn, Kenneth. *Mark Twain and Southwestern Humor*. Greenwood Press, 1972.

Mack, Maynard. *Alexander Pope: A Life*. Yale University Press, 1985.

———. *The Garden and the City*. University of Toronto Press, 1969.

Marguerite of Navarre. *The Heptameron*. Translated by P. A. Chilton. Penguin Books, 1984.

———. *Selected Writings*. Edited by Mary Skemp. University of Chicago Press, 2008.

Martin, James. *Between Heaven and Mirth*. HarperOne, 2011.

Martin, Robert. *The Triumph of Wit*. Clarendon Press, 1974.

Mencken, H. L. *The Vintage Mencken*. Edited by Alistair Cooke. Vintage Books, 1956.

Molière. *Tartuffe*. Translated by Richard Wilbur. Harcourt Brace, 1963.

More, Sir Thomas. *Utopia*. Edited by Paul Turner. Penguin, 2003.

Morreall, John. *Taking Laughter Seriously*. State University of New York Press, 1983.

Muggeridge, Malcolm. *Tread Softly for You Tread on my Jokes*. Collins, 1966.

Nietzsche, Friedrich. *Beyond Good and Evil*. Translated by Judith Norman. Cambridge University Press, 2002.

———. *Ecce Homo*. Translated by Anthony Ludovici. George Allen and Unwin, 1927.
Nokes, David. *Jonathan Swift, A Hypocrite Reversed*. Oxford University Press, 1985.
Nurse, Peter. *Molière and the Comic Spirit*. Droz, 1991.
O'Connor, Richard. *Ambrose Bierce: A Biography*. Little, Brown, 1967.
Owst, G. R. *Literature and Pulpit in Medieval England*. Barnes and Noble, 1961.
Parker, Todd, ed. *Swift as Priest and Satirist*. University of Delaware Press, 2009.
Parton, James. *Caricature and Other Comic Art in All Times and Many Lands*. Harper and Bros., 1887.
Pascal, Blaise. *Pensées*. Translated by A. J. Krailsheimer. E. P. Dutton, 1958.
Paulson, Ronald. *Don Quixote in England: The Aesthetics of Laughter*. Johns Hopkins University Press, 1998.
Pearce, Joseph. *Old Thunder: A Life of Hilaire Belloc*. Ignatius Press, 2002.
Pearson, Hesketh. *The Smith of Smiths: Being the Life, Wit, and Humour of Sydney Smith*. Faber and Faber, 2009.
Perry, Alan. *Don Camillo Stories of Giovannion Guareschi: Humorist Portrays the Sacred*. University of Toronto Press, 2007.
Plaza, Maria. *The Function of Humour in Roman Verse Satire: Laughing and Lying*. Oxford University Press, 2006.
Polhemus, Robert. *Comic Faith: The Great Comic Tradition from Austen to Joyce*. University of Chicago Press, 1981.
Pope, Alexander. *Epilogues to the Satires*. In *Poems of Alexander Pope*. Edited by John Butt. Yale University Press, 1963.
———. *An Essay on Man*. In *Poetical Works of Alexander Pope I*. Edited by H. F. Cary. Amazon Digital Services, 2011.
Queenan, Joe. *The Malcontents*. Running Press, 2002.
Quevedo, Francisco de. *Dreams and Discourses* trans. R. K. Britton Aris & Phillips, 1989
Quintero, Ruben. *A Companion to Satire: Ancient and Modern*. Cambridge University Press, 2007.
Rabelais, François. *Gargantua and Pantagruel*. Translated by M. A. Screech. Penguin, 2006.
Radday, Yahuda. *On Humor and the Comic in the Hebrew Bible*. Sheffield Academic Press, 1991.
Rummel, Erika. *Scheming Papists and Lutheran Fools*. Fordham University Press, 2003.
Russell, Olga. *Humor in Pascal*. Christopher Publishing House, 1967.
Sanders, Barry. *Sudden Glory: Laughter as Subversive History*. Beacon Press, 1995.
Saward, John. *Perfect Fools: Folly for Christ's Sake in Catholic and Orthodox Spirituality*. Oxford University Press, 1980.
Schmidt-Clausing, Fritz. *The Humor of Huldrych Zwingli*. Edwin Mellen Press, 2007.
Screech, M. A. *Laughter at the Foot of the Cross*. Westview Press, 1997.
Seidel, Michael. *Satiric Inheritance*. Princeton University Press, 1979.
Shaw, George. *Our Religious Humorists*. Simpkin, Marshall, and Co, 1880.
Shelden, Michael. *Mark Twain: The Man in White*. Random, 2010.

Shutter, Marion. *Wit and Humor of the Bible*. Arena Publishing, 1893.

Smith, Sydney. *The Works of Rev. Sydney Smith*. Edward Taylor, 1846.

Swift, Jonathan. *Gulliver's Travels*. Edited by Robert Hutchins. Encyclopedia Britannica, 1952.

———. *Works*. Edited by Herbert Davis. Oxford University Press, 1965.

Sypher, Wylie. *Comedy*. Doubleday Anchor, 1956.

Test, George. *Satire: Spirit and Art*. University Press of Florida, 1986.

Thackeray, William. *English Humorists of the Eighteenth Century*. Smith, Elder, and Co. 1858.

Trueblood, Elton. *The Humor of Christ*. Harper & Row, 1975.

Twain, Mark. *The Autobiography of Mark Twain*. Edited by Charles Neider, Harper Perennial Classics, 2000.

———. *Mark Twain's Notebooks and Journals*. Edited by Frederick Anderson, University of California Press, 1976.

Unamuno, Miquel de. *Tragic Sense of Life*. Translated by Crawford Flitch. Dover, 1954.

Voltaire. *The Portable Voltaire*. Edited by Ben Redman. Penguin Books, 1977.

Walsh, Milton. *Ronald Knox as Apologist*. Ignatius Press, 2007.

Wasserman, George. *Samuel "Hudibras" Butler*. Twayne Publishers, 1989.

Waugh, Evelyn. *The Essays, Articles, and Reviews of Evelyn Waugh*. Methuen, 1983.

———. *The Life of Ronald Knox*. Chapman & Hall, 1959.

Wells, Colin. *The Devil and Doctor Dwight: Satire and Theology in the Early American Republic*. University of North Carolina Press, 2001.

White, Julian Eugene, Jr., *Nicolas Boileau*. Twayne Publishers, Inc., 1969.

Willimon, William. *And the Laugh Shall Be First*. Abingdon Press, 1986.

Wilson, Doug. *A Serrated Edge*. Canon Press, 2003.

Wolfe, Gregory. *Malcolm Muggeridge*. Hodder & Stoughton, 1995.

Zuver, Dudley. *Salvation by Laughter*. Harper & Brothers, 1933.

INDEX

ABOUT THE AUTHOR

Terry Lindvall occupies the endowed C. S. Lewis Chair of Communication and Christian Thought at Virginia Wesleyan College and is the author of seven books, including *Surprised by Laughter: The Comic World of C. S. Lewis*. A Fulbright Scholar, he has produced over forty award-winning films and taught at Duke University, College of William and Mary, Fuller Theological Seminary, Regent University, and other institutions. He is married to Karen, with whom he has two children, Chris and Caroline.